Get Shown the Light

Get Shown the Light

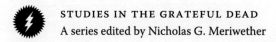

STUDIES IN THE GRATEFUL DEAD
A series edited by Nicholas G. Meriwether

IMPROVISATION *and*
TRANSCENDENCE *in the*
MUSIC *of the* GRATEFUL DEAD

Michael Kaler

DUKE UNIVERSITY PRESS
Durham & London   2023

Project Editor: Lisa Lawley
Designed by Courtney Leigh Richardson
Typeset in Warnock and Queens Compressed
by Westchester Publishing Services

Library of Congress Cataloging-in-Publication Data
Names: Kaler, Michael, author.
Title: Get shown the light : improvisation and transcendence in
the music of the Grateful Dead / Michael Kaler.
Other titles: Studies in the Grateful Dead (Duke University
Press)
Description: Durham : Duke University Press, 2023. | Series:
Studies in the Grateful Dead | Includes bibliographical
references and index.
Identifiers: LCCN 2023008309 (print)
LCCN 2023008310 (ebook)
ISBN 9781478024972 (paperback)
ISBN 9781478020349 (hardcover)
ISBN 9781478027324 (ebook)
Subjects: LCSH: Grateful Dead (Musical group) | Improvisation
(Music)—Social aspects. | Rock music—Social aspects—
History—20th century. | Rock music—United States—
History—20th century. | BISAC: MUSIC / Genres & Styles /
Rock | RELIGION / General
Classification: LCC ML421.G72 K354 2023 (print) |
LCC ML421.G72 (ebook) | DDC 782.42166092/2—
dc23/eng/20230818
LC record available at https://lccn.loc.gov/2023008309
LC ebook record available at https://lccn.loc.gov/2023008310

Cover art: The Grateful Dead (Jerry Garcia, Donna Godchaux,
Phil Lesh, and Bob Weir) in Copenhagen, April 1972. Courtesy
Getty Images/Jan Persson/Redferns.

publication supported by a grant from

The Community Foundation for Greater New Haven

as part of the **Urban Haven Project**

Contents

Acknowledgments

This book began as an idea that I discussed with Rob Bowman, of York University, when I was thinking about studying there. As I had a wealth of practical experience and a doctorate in religious studies, but little formal musical training, I was hoping to get admitted as an upper-year undergraduate student; I was more than a little surprised when Rob suggested I might be a candidate for the doctoral program in ethnomusicology. The idea that we discussed I probably would not have developed without Rob's ongoing encouragement, smart feedback, and really deep knowledge of all things relating to popular music. Thanks, Rob!

My Deadological investigations have benefited enormously from Nicholas Meriwether's enthusiasm and erudition, and his tireless and multifaceted efforts to advance the study of the Grateful Dead. I was impressed by his writing before I ever met him; over the past decade that we've worked together on various projects, I've been even more impressed by—and have benefited from—his skills as editor, archivist, and community builder. Thanks, Nick!

I've worked on these ideas in a variety of contexts, sometimes publicly, and I am very grateful for permission to make use of adapted versions of earlier work in some chapters. Thanks to the *Journal of Religion and Popular Culture, Studies in Religion/Sciences Religieuses, Critical Studies in Improvisation,* and to *Grateful Dead Studies,* and thanks again to Nicholas Meriwether for permission to use material published in the book *Reading the Grateful Dead: A Critical Survey.*

I have been extremely fortunate to have worked with a wide range of talented, dedicated, and welcoming musicians. I have learned (and explored) a lot about how to do this whole improvisational rock thing in my work with two bands in particular, the Starfires and Alaniaris, and my association with the Toronto improvising scene through such organizations as the Association of Improvising Musicians Toronto and the dearly missed club Somewhere There. So I owe thanks to a whole lot of people, including (but not limited to) Jonny Bakan, Chris Cawthray, Mike Daley, Scott Good, Michelangelo Iaffaldano, Pete Johnston, Arnd Jurgensen, Germaine Liu, Martin Loomer, Geoff Marshall, Dan Monich, Conny Nowe, Paul Newman (the Toronto sax player, not the actor), Karen Ng, Alexei Orechin, Nicole Rampersaud, Michael Rosenthal, Erik Ross, Mark Segger, Joshua Skye Engel, Joe Sorbara, Andrew Staniland, Jason Steidman, Scott Thomson, Jack Vorvis, Ben Walker, Andy Yue, and Mark Zurawinski. Thanks, everyone!

This book is dedicated to two musicians in particular, both guitarists, and both of whom have now left the planet. It was Alaniaris' guitarist, Ken Aldcroft, who more than anyone taught me about how improvisation could be approached as a rigorous, challenging, and fulfilling art form; it was the Starfires' guitarist, Braz King, who more than anyone showed me how grandeur and joy—pure rock magnificence—could emerge out of any jam. Neither of them will have the chance to read this book, but I wouldn't have been able to write it without their friendship and our mutual explorations of improvisational music-making. I hope you both are having interesting times, wherever you are!

And, as always, this book wouldn't be what it is—and I wouldn't be who I am—without the love and support of my partner, Wendy Banks (along with the cats, whose love is somewhat more transactional but no less real). Love to you (and the cats—not that they care).

An Autobiographical Introduction

In this book, I discuss how a group of people got together, realized that their music had the potential to be magic, and created a way to help it realize that potential. In this introduction, I will be talking about how and why this book came to be, so you can know its origin story.

The book came out of my time in the Toronto improvising or creative music scene, which I was involved in from roughly 2005 to 2015. I had spent the 1990s mostly playing rock music, with a side order of dishwashing, before making a fairly radical shift to studying ancient gnosticism full time, starting in 2000. Heavily influenced by Greil Marcus's *Lipstick Traces*, I had come to see ancient gnosticism as the spiritual origin of many of the currents in modern culture that most interested me. I'm talking about things like situationism, Discordianism, Jung, the Church of the SubGenius, the psychedelic anarchy of thinkers such as Robert Anton Wilson, and, of course, punk rock and hardcore music. In fact, I still think that the myth structures and critiques created by these mostly anonymous early Christian writers are the best, smartest, and most visionary challenges to institutional power and hierarchy that anyone has ever come up with, and they set the stage for a lot of what came after. If you want to develop your ability to see through bullshit, you could do a lot worse than spending some time with some of the gnostic writings, like the Gospel of Truth, the Gospel of Thomas, or the Gospel of Philip. I'll never regret the years I spent doing just that.

But—and this is a big but—the gnostic authors don't seem to me to be nearly as strong when it comes to talking about what you see once you've seen through the bullshit. They speak of liberation, but it's never clear (at least, it was never clear to me) how that liberation felt, or what it meant in the lived experience of the authors and readers of these texts. This was at least partly deliberate: for one thing, gnostic authors emerged out of a milieu that highly valued esoteric, coded communication, and, even when they were being more or less direct, their discussions were deeply influenced by language and approaches indebted to contemporary intellectual movements like Neoplatonic philosophy. Neoplatonic philosophy is great for many things, but clarity is not one of them. Consequently, it seemed and seems to me that gnosticism provides the smartest, trickiest, and most detailed "no" that I have ever encountered, but it's kind of weak on the "yes" side of things—"big no, little yes," you might say.

The "yes" is essential, though, if we don't want to spend our whole lives in a state of cranky disillusionment. And, for me, that "yes" has always come through music—mainly rock music, with a few exceptions (some free and spiritual jazz, some free improv, some ambient music, some minimalism, some dub). After several years of just focusing on gnosticism, I got reminded of how "yes" could really feel when I was exposed to the Toronto improvised music scene, which at the time—around 2005—was going through a creative renaissance. If you knew where to look, you could find a plethora of tiny shows in deserted back rooms and dingy clubs, with utterly dedicated musicians playing some of the most powerful music I'd ever heard, much of it completely improvised. This music promised (and sometimes even delivered, for seconds on end!) an escape from history, happening in real time right in front of me. I got obsessed.

I also got unemployed; 2008 was not a good time to be launching a career in the study of weird, esoteric early Christianity. After my wife, Wendy, sensibly pointed out, "You're good at music, and you're good at academia. Why not combine them?," I enrolled in York University to study ethnomusicology. My focus was on rock-based improvisation. Most of the musicians I was seeing and, by this point, playing with were coming from a jazz background, or an avant-garde classical one, or from non-European traditions that valued improvisation. However, as someone whose first favorite band had been the British psychedelic space rockers Hawkwind, and who had been a pretty serious Deadhead in the 1980s, I knew full well that rock also had an improvisational tradition, and I wanted to explore it, as a way of defining myself in the scene as something other than the rock barbarian. Also, I had rediscovered my love of the Grateful Dead's music, after about fifteen years of not feeling it or feeling ashamed of it (there are few bands less cool than the Grateful Dead). Since they were the rock improvisational band par excellence, it made sense to me to go back to their earliest preserved performances in order to figure out how they came up with an authentic rock approach to improvisation. I spent many hours listening to hissy, muffled, and often wonderful tapes of the band from the mid-to-late 1960s, ultimately deriving the "framework" that I describe in this book.

Understanding how the band did what it did was only half the battle; the other half was to understand—at least a little bit—why they did it. The idea that there was some kind of transcendent, spiritual, or religious significance to the Grateful Dead's music was not foreign to me: remember, I had been a Deadhead, and, anyway, the topic was impossible to escape in writing about the band. However, discussion of the Grateful Dead's music and its relation to transcendent experience focused on the reception of the music—in other words, whether it was carried out by condescending popular media people or by worshipful Deadheads, it tended to be about how the band's fans felt about the music.

What I found when I started digging into interviews with the band—and especially into bassist Phil Lesh's autobiography—was that the band themselves not only agreed that their music had the potential to manifest transcendent experiences but also that they seemed to have worked deliberately to develop an approach to playing that would make such experiences more likely. The framework wasn't just a vehicle for artistic expression; it was an approach to playing that could, once in a while and "in the strangest of places," serve to bridge heaven and earth. These thoughts never left me; for a number of years following, I kept chewing over them and developing them, in papers and conference presentations as well as more informal discussions. This book is the result of that thinking and development.

I've tried to write this book in such a way that it can be appreciated regardless of your own views on the Grateful Dead. Like I said, I'm a Deadhead, which is to say that I believe that they were right, and that this musical machine that they built really did have the potential to pay off with a "big yes" that could balance out and fulfill the "big no" that I found in gnosticism. You don't have to believe that to enjoy this book, though: the Grateful Dead's innovations and justifications are fascinating whatever your perspective, and they occupy a tremendously important place in the modern Western rediscovery of improvisational art. But I think it's important to let you know that I am not speaking as an outside observer here.

The Grateful Dead

A SPIRITUALLY MOTIVATED,
IMPROVISING ROCK BAND

Thirty years ago it was as if rock had tapped into a wellspring where Being gushed forth in a play of light and sound that was free and unnamed and not yet frozen into the forms that history and culture demand . . . as if [fans] had stepped through a waterfall to behold nothing that could be named, nothing that one could carry back, but just a promise, a possibility, a mystery . . . Rock insisted that meaning emerges only when we have dispensed with the narrative of coherence. —NICK BROMELL, *Tomorrow Never Knows: Rock and Psychedelics in the 1960s*, 2000

Successful rock bands tend to be unique, idiosyncratic entities, and the Grateful Dead were no exception. Some of the distinctive aspects of their career have been well covered—the tie-dyes, the rampant drug use, the eternal touring, the devotion of their fans, the jovial and enigmatic twinkle in Jerry Garcia's eye. But, in this book, my focus will be on a less frequently appreciated aspect of the group—namely, the fact that they were one of the first rock bands to incorporate the extensive use of improvisation into their musical practice. I say "appreciated," because, of course, the group's penchant for instrumental improvisation ("jamming" to fans; "noodling" or "going on endlessly" to others) is frequently *acknowledged*. But it is very rare that anyone stops to think about the real weirdness of a group playing improvisationally to the point where tonality, rhythm, and even pulse were optional and spontaneously negotiable—and then taking this approach to playing to audiences of thousands at every show. When the Grateful Dead formed, the touch of feedback at the start of the Beatles' "I Feel Fine" was a radical gesture; bands wore suits; and a four-minute song was considered daring. Within a year of forming, the Grateful Dead were stretching numbers to ten minutes; within two years, entire sets could be made up of snippets of composed material interspersed with extended improvisational sections, including long passages of amplifier feedback. Even in a jazz or avant-garde context, this would be odd; for the rock world, it's beyond odd.

It is also important. A number of very interesting things happened in the mid-1960s to turn "rock and roll" into "rock," to open up the possibilities for this urban and electrified form of folk music. One of those things was the development of approaches for extended improvisational playing. Along with several other groups that formed in 1965 and 1966—including the Velvet Underground, Pink Floyd, the Jefferson Airplane, and Cream—the Grateful Dead extended the range of rock's improvisational possibilities, creating a distinct approach to playing rock music that emphasized ensemble-based, collaborative spontaneity. If I was pressed, I might be tempted to argue that the development of a distinctive approach to improvisation is one of the signs that a distinct musical genre has come fully into being, because the act of defining its improvisational parameters necessarily involves defining what musical gestures are identified with the genre (see chapter 4). So we can see the development of an improvisational approach to rock as corresponding to and complementing the increasingly sophisticated and innovative approach to composition in the mid-1960s—both of them crucial moves in terms of defining what rock music really was, or could be.

In this book, I will not be looking at the Grateful Dead's pioneering improvisational work solely as a musical practice. What I am most interested in is linking this musical development to something altogether more radical. What I hope to show is that the band developed a whole new way of playing rock music in the course of pursuing transcendent spiritual experience. Their distinctive musical approach was both a means, to creating this transcendent experience in themselves and others, and an end, to manifesting (as they believed) superhuman forces. Just as trumpets allegedly broke down the walls of Jericho, the Grateful Dead—and many of their fans—seem to have believed that their music could dissolve the walls separating the ordinary life from realms of transcendent strangeness.

When I state it so baldly, it looks like a ridiculous idea—the sort of scheme a bunch of deranged acidheads might have dreamed up. And maybe it was. If we know anything at all about the Grateful Dead, we know that they and many of their fans were deeply familiar with LSD, sometimes to the point of reverence. But, as I will also demonstrate, the band's understanding of and hopes for their music are not really so unique after all: there are plenty of musical traditions in which improvisation is seen as the gateway to miraculous occurrences and realizations. What the Grateful Dead were doing, then, can be seen as a youthful, vigorous, unbelievably naive, and, in the eyes of their fans, unbelievably successful attempt to create their own tradition, their own way of accessing transcendent states from a starting point of the Western—specifically North American—rock tradition. Whether or not this goal is ridiculous, it is at the very least extremely interesting.

And, if it is ridiculous, at the very least it is in good company. The past half-century has seen a wide variety of attempts to "reenchant" the Western modern world, to bring access to transcendence back into our more or less secularized popular culture.[1] Popular music has been one of the main fields within which this reenchantment has been attempted, and there is a truly stunning range of ways in which it has manifested, including the spiritual impulses of rave culture, the Krishnacore movement in hardcore, and the "amplifier worship" of drone metal, and the low-end reverence of dub.[2]

In the first part of this book, I will focus on *how* the Grateful Dead developed their unique approach to improvisation, detailing their performance model for rendering its practice possible. This is important because "improvisation" does not have a fixed definition: it takes on different meanings in different traditions, and it works according to various parameters. Think of the difference between the *alaap*, the extended, rhythmically open introduction to a raga, in which the sitar is given an enormous amount of space and freedom to introduce that raga's unique characteristics, and a blues solo by B. B. King, which takes place over a set arrangement of chords and a fixed groove. Both of these are improvisations, and both are appropriate to their traditions, but they are very different from each other. The Grateful Dead had to develop an approach to improvising, a guiding model, that would work for rock the way that B. B. King's solos worked for the blues. In addition to looking at the creation of this model, I will discuss its development and put it into context with the work of several of the Grateful Dead's improvising contemporaries.

The second part of the book will focus on discussing *why* the band chose to develop this unique approach to playing rock music. I will argue that their practice was at least partly inspired by, and was designed to be coherent with, the transcendent spiritual experiences that several band members underwent in 1965 and 1966—and here, just so you know, is where the LSD kicks in. The Grateful Dead, I will argue, cannot be understood simply as a rock band, but as a group that was motivated by spiritual imperatives. They weren't just trying to crack the charts; they also wanted to crack open the Pearly Gates. To bring out its distinctiveness, I will compare and contrast their spiritual-musical approach with that of several contemporaries who combined spiritual inspiration with extensively improvisational practice—namely, Sun Ra, John Coltrane, and Albert Ayler.

As I mentioned earlier, although it is extremely common to talk about the Grateful Dead as an improvising band, to my knowledge no one has ever laid out precisely how and why they became one. It may seem contradictory, but improvisation as a musical practice doesn't just spring into being: it needs to be developed and cultivated and refined. Showing how the band did this—and, in the process, uncovered the secretly religious inspiration that led them to play this way—will illuminate the earliest period of the Grateful Dead, who were one of rock's most popular bands over their thirty-year career. More generally, I hope to contribute to the exposition of the nature and development of rock-based improvisation: a hidden stream of tradition whose importance is only beginning to be realized.

Finally, and perhaps most intriguingly, I hope that this discussion will extend our understanding of the ways in which art and religious revelation can be combined. It is all too easy to forget the astonishing variety of human reactions to the experience of the transcendent. The story I am about to tell, which began at the Acid Tests under the influence of LSD that kept millions of people dancing in thousands of concerts over thirty years, and that changed our understanding of what rock was and what it could do, is one of the more fascinating tales in the hidden history of popular culture's pursuit of transcendence.

A Rock Band

The Grateful Dead were a San Francisco–based rock band whose career lasted thirty years, from their formation in 1965 to their breakup in 1995 following the death of lead guitarist and vocalist Jerry Garcia (1942–1995). They briefly reformed in 2015, and band members have performed, recorded, and toured together in various permutations since 1995.

The band's origins can be traced to two complementary sources, both tremendously important for the myriad cultural revolutions that would come to define "the Sixties." The infectious exuberance of the rock explosion led by the Beatles, especially in the movie *A Hard Day's Night* (released in August 1964), seems to have been the trigger that led the band away from folk music and blues to playing electric rock. As Garcia put it, "And all of a sudden there were the Beatles, you know. *Hard Day's Night*, the movie and everything. Hey great, that really looks like fun."[3] The Grateful Dead wanted their music to be about energy, fun, excitement—in short, they wanted joy, and rock was the means of accessing that joy.

The second foundational context for the band was created at the Acid Tests, beginning in the fall of 1965: all-night parties hosted by author Ken Kesey and his group of Merry Pranksters (see chapters 8 and 9). These events drew on the Happenings and other forms of spontaneous art creation that were becoming popular in the mid-1960s, but added on surrealistic exuberance, popular (as opposed to "artistic") appeal, and lots and lots of LSD, moving the Pranksters far away from the pure art realm and turning them into the predecessors of such cultural phenomena as rave culture and Burning Man. The Grateful Dead performed at most of the Acid Tests, which they prioritized over other gigs: in fact, judging from the band's accounts, the Acid Tests were where the band began to perceive just how powerful their music could be, and how capable it was of generating truly odd experiences that seemed to tap into some normally unattainable level of cosmic synchronicity. "The Acid Test," Garcia would recall, "was the prototype for our whole basic trip . . . stuff happening spontaneously and everyone being prepared to accept any kind of a thing that was happening and to add to it."[4]

The utter strangeness of the scene at the Acid Tests, especially its spontaneous and unplannable nature, mixed with the pure joy of the Beatles-led rock explosion, can be seen as a template for the Grateful Dead's entire approach to music. This mixture is clearly audible in their first single, "The Golden Road (To Unlimited Devotion)," a song in which the band invites their listeners to "try on your wings" at a party that would end up lasting for thirty years.[5]

Over the next nine years, from 1965 to 1974, the band's commitment to weird, spontaneous joy led them through a myriad of changes and varied experiences. They quickly became the representative band for the Haight-Ashbury scene (buttons advertising the "good ole Grateful Dead" were being sold less than two years after their formation), playing the ballrooms and working with scene luminaries such as Chet Helms and Bill Graham as their songs got longer, louder, and stranger, and as they learned both how to play their instruments and how to play them together as a group.[6] They had many opportunities to do so, as they toured relentlessly, playing ever-longer concerts with a mixture of discrete songs and extended material emphasizing jamming. As I will discuss in chapter 5, the Grateful Dead can be seen as moving through four periods in their first decade, from what could be described as a garage rock band approach (1965–67) to a more frenetic, hard-edged, expansive psychedelic direction (1967–70), then bringing in more folk and roots music elements and emphasizing a rapprochement with American music traditions (1970–72) before adding in components strongly reminiscent of contemporary electric jazz and avant-garde music (1972–74). Deeply concerned with live sound quality, they devoted enormous amounts of time and money to developing their sound system, culminating in the iconic "Wall of Sound" setup (1973–74).

In terms of recordings, the band signed to Warner Brothers in 1967 and released a string of albums, moving from the hard-rocking garage folk sound of their eponymous first album to the all-out exploratory psychedelia of 1968's *Anthem of the Sun*. In 1969, they integrated their psychedelic extremes with their folky origins on *Aoxomoxoa* as well as recorded *Live/Dead*, perhaps the purest expression of their improvisational side. In 1970, they released a pair of studio albums—*Workingman's Dead* and *American Beauty*—that fully integrated their distinctive approach and worldview into the tradition of what we would now call "Americana," an integration also demonstrated in a live context on 1971's *Grateful Dead*.

In 1972, the band released the triple live album *Europe '72*, covering as well as any album could all the aspects of their musical development to date; many (myself included) would argue that this album is the band's definitive statement. Unfortunately, it was followed by the uninspired *History of the Grateful Dead, Volume 1 (Bear's Choice)*, a selection of live recordings that has not been regarded favorably and that ended the band's relationship with Warner Brothers. Following this, they released the pastoral *Wake of the Flood* and the charming but relatively mainstream *From the Mars Hotel* on their own label.

In this book I will be discussing only the first decade of the band's existence, from 1965 to 1974—a choice of boundaries that needs a little explanation. 1974 is a good stopping point for me, because it was one for the band as well. After having spent nine years continuously developing their music and expanding their organization and popularity, the Grateful Dead took most of 1975 off, only returning to live performing in 1976. There are a variety of reasons why they took this hiatus, ranging from the practical (their approach to performance had gotten so complex and labor intensive that they needed time for a rethink) to the economic (their infrastructure had grown unsustainably large), to the simply human (weariness after nine years of composing and performing music that consistently pushed the boundaries of the band and their audience).

When the band returned to full activity in 1976, they deemphasized the open improvisation that had been a characteristic of their earlier years. This is not to say that they ceased to improvise—only that improvisation in some other parts of their shows tended to be more controlled, less extreme, than it had been before. Ironically, part of the way that they accomplished this was to create and isolate two sections of the show, "Drums" and "Space," in which the drummers (in "Drums") and the rest of the band (in "Space") could explore sounds, create musical collages, and generally go "outside."

In one way, this can be seen as valorizing extensive improvisation, by creating designated space for it in the second set, but, in another, as ghettoizing it, by confining the most daring experimentation to a more or less consistent area of the second set and by removing its integral link to songs. Although "Drums" and "Space" would arise out of songs, they were not linked to them in the same way that earlier jams would be, and certainly there was little surprise about them: everyone knew what was going to happen in the second half of the second set, even if the exact specifics of the music were negotiated in the moment. The band was to continue for another twenty years, playing many fine shows, writing a solid body of songs, and giving a great deal of pleasure and community to their audience; nonetheless, their most groundbreaking achievements in terms of integrating open improvisation into a rock context were all made before the break.

In fact, there are intriguing suggestions that the band was exploring new improvisational possibilities in 1975. Speaking of their earlier improvised music, Garcia noted in an interview that "we used to rehearse a lot to get that effect. It sounded like chaos, but was in reality hard rehearsal. So the thing is, we need the stuff that lets us play at that edge of chaos, but doesn't require rehearsal, dig? . . . The next level of development was when we went to *Blues for Allah*. There, we came up with some very interesting, *other* alternate ways to invent openness that would be developmental as well."[7] In the same interview, he goes on to discuss one other way of "inventing openness"—used in their song "Blues for Allah"—which involved holding chords and freely and incrementally changing them so as to cause them to transform into different chords and melodies. This approach, however, was not one that the band pursued, and indeed it would have worked against the band's professed desire (and the economic necessity) to provide music for ecstatic dancers.

With regard to the band's members, Garcia, the lead guitarist, main vocalist, and unofficial leader of the band, has become an iconic figure and was a member of the band for its entire career—in fact, it was Garcia's death that led the group to break up in 1995. Drummer Bill Kreutzmann, rhythm guitarist/vocalist Bob Weir, and bassist/vocalist Phil Lesh, who were also founding members, stayed with the band through its career, while second drummer Mickey Hart joined in 1967, left the band in 1971, and then rejoined in 1974. The Grateful Dead had a number of different keyboard players: in the period that I will be discussing, their keyboardists were Ron "Pigpen" McKernan, who played, sang, and played percussion from their founding until 1972; Tom Constanten, who played with the band from 1968 to 1970; and Keith Godchaux, who played with them from 1971 to 1979. Donna Godchaux sang with the band from 1972 to 1979.

The Grateful Dead were influenced by many styles of North American popular music, including folk, rock and roll, rhythm and blues, and jug band music. In addition to drawing from various traditions of popular music, the Grateful Dead helped to shape them: their music of the mid-to-late 1960s can, in some regards, be seen as prefiguring heavy metal and hard rock, due to its volume and use of distortion. From 1969 to 1971, especially, they participated in the development of "roots rock," or "country rock," breaking country approaches into the rock mainstream, and their early 1970s music takes part in the development of jazz-rock such as that being produced at the time by Miles Davis or John McLaughlin.

The Grateful Dead were known for being one of the pioneering "psychedelic" bands, whose music was intended to express and induce altered states of consciousness. They were inextricably associated with both the hippie movement of the mid-to-late 1960s and the drug LSD. They rose to prominence as members of the San Francisco music scene of the time that included such bands as Quicksilver Messenger Service, Big Brother and the Holding Company, and the Jefferson Airplane, but they surpassed these bands in terms of longevity, eventual popularity, and commitment to improvisation, thus making them the founding fathers of the "jam band" scene that arose in the late 1980s and 1990s with such groups as Phish and Blues Traveler.

The Grateful Dead's approach to improvisation involved live performance, which was their main focus and the source of their income and popularity. While their records sold respectably, they did not have a real hit until 1987's "Touch of Grey." Rather, their reputation was built around their shows, which were known for extended improvisations, or "jamming." Interestingly enough, this meant that it was perfectly possible for someone to be a die-hard fan, spending much of their leisure time and disposable income on the band, but not own all of their officially released albums—in fact, that was my situation exactly. Listening to, thinking about, and playing their music have been among the most profound experiences of my life over the past thirty years, and yet, to this day, there are several of their studio albums that I have never heard (*Shakedown Street, Go to Heaven*), and several more that I have heard and would not recommend to anyone. As far as I know, this sort of situation is unique to this band.

Over the past thirty years, the Grateful Dead have released many more live recordings from that period on their own record label, including a three-volume *From the Vault* series; a *Dick's Picks* series (named for band tape archivist Dick Latvala) that ran to thirty-six volumes; a *Digital Download* series; a *Road Trips* series that summarized tours rather than focusing on individual shows; numerous special collections, such as *Winterland 1973: The Complete Recordings* (presenting the shows played on November 9–11, 1973 at the Winterland Arena in San Francisco), or the seventy-two-disc collection of the band's tour of Europe in 1972; and a *Dave's Picks* series (named for David Lemieux, who succeeded Latvala as band tape archivist) that took over where the *Dick's Picks* series left off.

Many of the band's fans were committed to making and circulating tapes of their performances; consequently, in addition to these official releases, the vast majority of Grateful Dead performances are accessible, in recordings of greatly varying fidelity. These recordings, which originally circulated through "tapers'" networks, can be accessed at the archive.org site. In this book, I will deal almost exclusively with live recordings, which I will identify both through references to the collection at archive.org and to the release that they appeared on, if they have been officially released. My reason for preferring to discuss live material is simple: I am interested in understanding how the band worked as a group of musicians who were dedicated to real-time, improvisational practice in a rock idiom. Reference to the archive.org collection will enable readers to quickly access the material that I discuss; details about each of the shows that I mention are given in the appendix at the end of this book.

An Improvising Rock Band

In musical contexts, "improvisation" can mean a great many things. In a general sense, it is often used to refer to music that is marked by the "suddenness of the creative impulse" and often contrasted with "composition."[8] However, the "suddenness" of improvisation does not mean that it is entirely uncontrolled or ungoverned, for "improvised music is not produced without some kind of preconception or point of departure. There is always a model which determines the scope within which a musician acts," and the "improvised" aspect of the performance represents the musician's spontaneous negotiation of this model, just as the "composed" aspect represents the negotiation of the model that was carried out prior to the performance.[9] Thus, in his canonical article on the topic, ethnomusicologist Bruno Nettl concludes that "perhaps we must abandon the idea of improvisation as a process separate from composition and adopt the view that all performers improvise to some extent."[10]

That last phrase ("to some extent") is extremely important. The precise nature of that extent—in other words, the limits and characteristics of the improvisation—is determined through the interaction of the performer and the models within which they work.[11] Hence, improvisation is defined by Nettl as "the creation of a musical work, or the final form of a musical work, as it is being performed. It may involve the work's immediate composition by its performers, or the elaboration or adjustment of an existing framework, or anything in between." This makes improvisation a universal activity, since "to some extent every performance involves elements of improvisation, although its degree varies according to period and place," and it is always guided by "a series of conventions or implicit rules."[12] We discussed the differences between B. B. King and the playing of an Indian classical musician such as Ravi Shankar: it is easy to imagine what would happen if one of these great artists subbed in for the other's gig. It would probably not end well.

Because the parameters of improvisation vary so much, there is a strong tendency for those who study such music to leave "improvisation" as a general concept along the lines of Nettl's definition and to allow its meaning in a specific setting to arise through the examination of the musical practice in that context—in other words, rather than studying improvisation generally, they would study how improvisation works in *qawwali* music, or in free jazz. This is the approach taken in really interesting works by, for example, Qureshi (qawwali), Berliner (jazz), Jost (free jazz), Bailey (various styles), Porter (John Coltrane), Heffley (European free jazz), Borgo (free improvisation), and

Malvinni (the Grateful Dead); this will be my approach as well.[13] So, when I speak of the Grateful Dead or other groups as "improvising" bands, what I mean to say is that they pursued an approach in which aspects of their music were open to in-concert negotiation to a greater and more explicit degree than was the case with the music of most of their peers. I will spend a considerable amount of time delineating the precise nature and parameters of this negotiation in the case of the Grateful Dead.

I do not mean to imply, however, that the Grateful Dead were the only band that explored improvisational approaches to rock music. They were an improvising rock band whose origins are to be found in the earliest years of rock's "modern" period, which can be conveniently, if roughly, considered to have begun with the emergence of Beatlemania in 1963 in England, spreading to North America in 1964. While we can never know exactly what may have been transpiring, unrecorded and unpreserved, in the British and North American garages and basements in the first half of the 1960s, it is in late 1965—the period of the Grateful Dead's formation—that experiments with extended improvisation by rock-associated bands started to make its way into the public arena. This period saw the emergence of a number of groups who were well known for their improvisational approach to some or most of their music-making.

The New York–based band the Velvet Underground, formed in 1965, became known for their distinctive fusion of pop, pop art, raga-influenced avant-garde sonic aesthetics, and the willingness of their members to improvisationally stretch the boundaries of popular music, particularly with regard to timbre and dissonance. Although the band would, later in its career, come a good deal closer to the rock mainstream (in terms of its music, if not its popularity), one thing that never altered was the use of extended, often drone-based improvisation.[14]

In London, meanwhile, Pink Floyd, which formed in 1964, discovered the potential of improvisational playing in 1965 during their residency at the Countdown Club.[15] By 1966 the band was playing enormously extended songs for the very first wave of the psychedelic generation of rock fans, although they would replace the Velvet Underground's love of Brill Building–style pop and minimalism with an appreciation for instrumental rock music such as that made by the Shadows, and surrealistic whimsy and science fiction would take the place of pop art in their underlying conception.[16]

Also in the early-to-mid-1960s, the London-based Yardbirds—at that time known as a rhythm and blues band—had become famous for their "rave-ups": instrumental sections of their songs that had the potential for some quite prescient leaps into improvisational freedom. Michael Hicks writes that "the rave-up was a pseudo-double time section with a corresponding intensification of dynamics . . . the rave-up made a small narrative curve that introduced a basic conflict (backbeats versus offbeats), drove that conflict to a climax (by getting more and more raucous), then resolved it (by returning to a normal beat)."[17] The break in the song "Here 'Tis" from their *Five Live Yardbirds* album displays the proto-improvisational tendencies of the rave-up quite well and is well worth a listen;[18] Chris Cutler, an eyewitness to the early British R&B and psychedelic scenes, affirms that the band's live sets were considerably more improvisational and experimental than the band's recorded legacy suggests, a point seconded by Clayson.[19]

Eric Clapton was the first of the Yardbirds' three influential lead guitarists, the other two being Jeff Beck and Jimmy Page. After leaving the band, Clapton formed Cream, the first rock "supergroup," in 1966. Cream brought an unprecedented degree of instrumental virtuosity to their blues-rock, which they expressed through lengthy improvisations, which were often more "soloistic" and more clearly linked to earlier blues or jazz understandings of improvisation than was the case with the Velvet Underground or Pink Floyd. Cream's enormous popularity and the individual reputations of their members did a great deal to legitimate heavily improvisational playing in rock; however, their improvisational work stayed within tight conceptual parameters, and they certainly never explored the potential for distinctively rock, egalitarian group improvisation to the same degree as the other bands mentioned here.

Another significant early improvising band—based, like the Grateful Dead, in San Francisco—was the Jefferson Airplane, formed in 1965. The Airplane had a musical approach that featured a driving and aggressive take on folk rock; improvisation soon came to play a significant role in their music as well, both in specific pieces (as, for example, their early showpiece "The Thing") and in their general instrumental approach, particularly for bassist Jack Casady and guitarist Jorma Kaukonen.

In short, it is clear that, in this period, extended rock-based improvisation was in the air, and, as we will see, the Grateful Dead were one of the major bands to participate in its development. The importance of the band was increased by their longevity. Cream and the Velvet Underground broke up after fairly short careers, while Pink Floyd and the Jefferson Airplane went through dramatic changes in aesthetics and musical approach (in the case of the Jefferson Airplane's change to the Jefferson Starship and then Starship), effectively becoming different bands. The Grateful Dead certainly did change musically, but their changes were more gradual, more developmental, than those of the other bands that I have mentioned and were furthermore supported by and integrated smoothly into the group's overall evolution through their dedication to ongoing live performance.

Since its birth in 1965, the rock improvisational tradition has proven remarkably sturdy as well as adaptable; streams of it are to be found in many of the significant rock scenes or movements. For instance:

1   The high-energy Detroit rock tradition relied on such heavily improvisational bands as the MC5 and the Stooges.
2   Early German "kosmische music," more colloquially known as "krautrock," was based on improvisational jamming.
3   Hawkwind and later bands such as Ozric Tentacles showed improvisation's applicability to space rock.
4   In the early punk rock scene, Television demonstrated the joys of extended improvisation, while such bands as Black Flag, Hüsker Dü, and Toronto's Nomind did the same in the later hardcore scene.
5   Sonic Youth demonstrated its importance for the noise rock that started in the late 1970s (presaged by such improvisationally minded noise bands as the Red Krayola in the 1960s or the Taj Mahal Travelers in the 1970s).
6   The importance of the tradition for the "jam band" scenes of the 1990s and 2000s (e.g., Phish, Blues Traveler) goes without saying.
7   Many of the bands in the "free" or "freak" folk movement of the 1990s and 2000s, such as Animal Collective, Sunburned Hand of the Man, and Espers, drew on it.
8   The past several decades have seen a new wave of what one might call "heavy psychedelic music" played by such groups as Black Mountain and Wooden Shjips [sic], featuring extended improvisation. Bands of this style tend to draw heavily on the influence of Neil Young's ongoing work with Crazy Horse—lots of barre chord–based riffing.

The Grateful Dead stand at the head of that tradition. While they were not the first rock band to open up their songs to improvisational exploration, they were in the first wave of such bands to do so, and they were the most consistent in terms of sticking to their original vision. Ultimately, they were among the most popular rock bands ever, period. They are, then, an extremely important band for any understanding of rock's development and, particularly, its use of improvisation.

They are also an intrinsically *fascinating* band. At their peak, the Grateful Dead were able to play sets that included largely improvised, fifteen-to-thirty-minute pieces before thousands—on occasion hundreds of thousands—of wildly appreciative dancing people. And they did this largely without sex appeal, without flashy stage moves, and without being hip or cool. By and large, they just *played*—and in the playing created magic times for millions who recreated, were inspired by, and passed on their own revelatory religious experiences. How odd—how distinctively, modernly odd—is that?

A Spiritually Motivated, Improvising Rock Band

As mentioned, I have two main jobs to do in this book. The first job is to trace the parameters and development of the Grateful Dead's improvisational practice in their first decade—and we have just seen how important this task is, both for understanding the Grateful Dead specifically, and for understanding the rock improvisational tradition more generally. Because it is not possible to understand a musical practice without understanding its context of origin, my second job will involve discussing the transcendent spiritual experiences that seem to have motivated the Grateful Dead, especially in their formative period, but, to a lesser degree, throughout their career.

Improvisation, as I have defined, is a universal musical phenomenon, and music and spirituality have often overlapped or been associated (to be discussed in chapter 7). Therefore, we should not be surprised to find that more or less improvisatory playing is often found in spiritual or religious contexts and made to do spiritual or religious work. To take a few examples, we find abundant use of improvisation in such contexts as north Indian and Pakistani qawwali performances, Near and Middle Eastern Sufi ceremonies, African American gospel events, and free and "spiritual" jazz performances.

This is not to say that improvisational playing must have a spiritual underpinning—to the best of my knowledge, the pioneering guitarist and improviser Derek Bailey, for instance, never associated his work with any metaphysical aspects, and the same could be said of his contemporaries and musical fellow travelers, such as Paul Rutherford. But improvisation certainly can have motivation of this kind—Steve Lacy, another of Bailey's contemporaries, was open about the influence of Confucianism, Buddhism, and other religious traditions on his work, likewise the experimental and free jazz musician Alice Coltrane with regard to Hindu thought, and we will discuss the spiritual understandings of John Coltrane, Albert Ayler, and Sun Ra (see chapter 9).[20] There is considerable evidence—most prominently, the statements of band members themselves (which we will discuss at length in chapters 7–9) to indicate that the Grateful Dead's motivation was also spiritual in nature.

For now, we can say that extant testimony indicates that the Grateful Dead developed their improvisational approach to rock at least partly in response to, or through the inspiration of, their spiritual experiences in the mid-to-late 1960s while under the influence of LSD. I will address the issue of the interaction of spirituality and drugs at length later; for the moment, it is important for me to make clear my own position in this context. I will be speaking in this book from an ethnomusicological or historical point of view (as opposed to, say, a theological or religiously committed one); from that position, I see no reason why the use of LSD or other drugs in provoking an experience should rule out the possibility that such an experience might be legitimately considered real, at least or if only from the point of view of the experiencer or the standards at play within their context.

In fact, many people have claimed to have had real experiences of transcendence or contact with divine powers while under the influence of such substances, including LSD (like the Grateful Dead and just about every acidhead ever—see, e.g., the testimonies collected in *Tripping*), marijuana or hashish (such as the Rastafarians and some Tantric and Sufi teachers), ayahuasca, and psilocybin.[21] Many other people have claimed to have touched on transcendence following serious modifications of their physiological state, such as by fasting, prolonged repetitive activity, extreme emotion, and so on. All of these people are implicitly or explicitly saying, "I do weird stuff to my body or my mind—and Something shows up."

Some of these people, certainly, are untrustworthy, or simply deluded, and it is good to have a healthy dose of skepticism in these matters. But that healthy dose should also extend to skepticism of debunkers who would argue that the very claim that one's life has been profoundly affected by transcendent experience is a sign of gullibility or dishonesty. It is far more reasonable—far more skeptical, really—to conclude that many of those who do "weird stuff" and find that it has led them to God are, at the least, not wrong, if only as far as they are concerned.

The next question is this: Beyond being not wrong, are they right? Are they right in an objective sense—that is, is "God" really there? I do not know. Are they subjectively right? In other words, do many people genuinely believe that, after they did the weird stuff, something unique and transcendent took place and perhaps changed their lives? In many cases, it seems clear that they are right in that sense—that they did perceive something as happening.

It is that perception that I am dealing with here. I am not making claims about the objective "reality" of whatever the Grateful Dead touched on when they were on LSD, or—for that matter—what Jesus touched on after starving himself in the desert; or what Bob Marley touched on in Rasta ceremonies involving hours of chanting, "reasoning," and smoking marijuana; or what Charles Manson touched on while tripping; or what neurologist Jill Bolte Taylor touched on during and after her stroke.[22] I am simply noting that whatever happened to these people, it led them to utterly change their lives: it was real to them, and it had real effects on them and, through them, the world.

In the case of the Grateful Dead—as with Bob Marley—those effects were spread through their music.[23] So, my second job in this book is to look at how this spiritual aspect of the Grateful Dead's collective experience was manifested through their music, how it influenced the music, and how it influenced the band's understanding of itself and its mission—to the point that the music was structured so as to permit the weird stuff to happen, thus completing a circle. The conjunction of this discussion with the strictly musical discussion will, I hope, result in a more complete presentation of the Grateful Dead as a musical-spiritual phenomenon than has previously been possible.

Now, discussion of the spiritual aspects of the Grateful Dead involves choosing the personal narratives and interpretations to deal with. As I will show, the tendency in Grateful Dead scholarship has been to look at things from the outside. To put it simply, there has been a lot of discussion of how the Deadheads, the Grateful Dead's devoted followers, look similar to a cult or a new religious movement (NRM). Whether at the popular level or in the work of people such as sociologist Rebecca Adams, we find many references to intriguingly "religious" aspects of the social phenomenon that grew up around the Grateful Dead.[24] To take just one example, in an article about the band's brief reunion in 2015, fan Bob Pisani looked back on his experience with the Grateful Dead and noted that "the Cult of the Dead had all the hallmarks of that mystery religion: sacred rites, sacred drugs, ecstatic dancing, and a mystical union with some vague Other, all representing a release, a liberation from civilization's stifling rules."[25] While that fan-based perspective is valid—and has been much discussed—it is not my focus here. In order to link the spiritual aspects of the band members' experiences to their practice, we need insider discussion, coming from the band members themselves.

I know of no discussions of spiritual issues by drummer Bill Kreutzmann or vocalist/keyboardist Pigpen, and, although guitarist/vocalist Bob Weir does mention it occasionally in published interviews, he does not provide much information, being more concerned to downplay the messianic roles that some fans have ascribed to the members of the band. As he has noted, "It's not that one doesn't appreciate the adulation, but some of the importance that people ascribe to what we're doing may be undue."[26] More bluntly, he says, "I know the guys in the band pretty well, I think. By and large they are some philosophically adept individuals. But I wouldn't go so far as to call any of them spiritual masters."[27] In his published comments, drummer Mickey Hart talks about it more than Weir, but, nonetheless, guitarist/vocalist Jerry Garcia and bassist Phil Lesh are by far the most outspoken on the matter, with Lesh tending to be much more detailed and clear about his interpretation.

Lesh's autobiography, which I will be drawing on heavily, provides a more considered and reflective view of the matter than we get from Garcia, whose interviews, as we will see, indicate that he is very invested in not clarifying whatever spiritual conceptions he may have had. Consequently, while Lesh cannot be taken as the sole authoritative voice on the spiritual significance of the Grateful Dead's music and their development of their music, I will be using him, to a greater degree than the other members, as a representative voice, due both to the volume and the clarity of his testimony.

To sum up: it is my hope that this book will shed light on the Grateful Dead's improvisational practice; anchor its development in its spiritual and musical context; help to make rock music more visible in the modern scholarly interest in improvised music; expand our knowledge of the ways in which religious experience translates into this-worldly practice, especially in artistic realms; and increase our understanding of one of the many NRMs that arose in the 1960s.

But, above and beyond those aims, what I really hope is that you as a reader will come away from this book with an expanded appreciation for how interesting, subtle, and strange human interactions with the divine—or transcendence—can be. As the Grateful Dead themselves put it, "Once in a while, you can get shown the light / In the strangest of places if you look at it right."[28] And maybe my hopes go further than that: maybe I am also hoping, just a little bit, that seeing how these dedicated and determined people built a transcendence machine might inspire you to devise means of bringing your own weird and interesting experiences to life.

Setting the Scene

WHERE THEY CAME FROM

Well everybody's dancin' in a ring around the sun
Nobody's finished, we ain't even begun.
So take off your shoes, child, and take off your hat.
Try on your wings and find out where it's at.
—"The Golden Road (To Unlimited Devotion)"

Art does not come from a vacuum. Works of art, like the motivations of their creators, are best understood when we know the contexts from which they arose. The members of the Grateful Dead are no exceptions, and their embrace of improvisation was not without support from the contexts in which they lived and worked. As I will discuss, it seems to have been their experiences under the influence of LSD that definitively moved them in an improvisational direction, but the groundwork was laid by the valorization and expansion of the possibilities of this technique in their immediate environment. In other words, improvisation was available to them as a hip approach to try.

This has not always been the case in mainstream Western culture. Nowadays, improvisation, especially musical improvisation, gets respect from all quarters—you hear improvised jazz performances such as Miles Davis's *Kind of Blue* album in every Starbucks;[1] music therapists and educators alike emphasize its benefits;[2] and almost every musician, young or old, has spent at least one evening (or maybe an entire career) jamming out to and over their favorite tunes.[3] But improvisation was not always so positively regarded in popular music of the West.

Broadly speaking, artistic improvisation enjoyed a rise in its fortunes in the period following the Depression, as Daniel Belgrad has ably charted.[4] In all spheres of art, appreciation increased for the use of spontaneous techniques as generators or structuring agents as the world fought World War II and then roared into the new conditions that arose from it. We should note as well that the use of improvisation always makes a statement of some kind. As Nettl puts it,

> In musical cultures that distinguish between improvised and precomposed music, the improvisor—or groups of improvisors—is inevitably making a statement: it may be that by following the freedom of improvisation, we are fighting for personal and political freedom; it may be . . . that in improvising you share your personality in ways that the composed genres don't permit; it may be that group improvisors relate to each other differently and more closely than musicians in other ensembles. Or it may be that a subculture shows its individuality by specializing in improvised music. . . . In any event, improvisers are—as Ingrid Monson notes . . . saying something simply by engaging in the act of improvisation.[5]

In his book, Belgrad emphasizes the different and successive justifications that North American artists brought to their use of such approaches, including the Jungian pursuit of access to the unconscious through invocations of "primitive" myths and symbols and the Gestalt-therapy-related "celebration of spontaneous art."[6] The justifications as laid out by Belgrad have a central theme: they all cluster around a concept of gaining access to an otherwise hidden realm of authenticity, which is thought to reside either in the recesses of one's own psyche; in the alleged and Orientalized "purity" of Eastern cultures; in the reverence for the alleged profound meaningfulness of life in primitive cultures; or in the transient freedom and enlightenment to be found in the fleeting moment. However it was presented, improvisation in its rebirth in the West has been understood as being about accessing a deeper, more authentic, level of reality than we can get to by deliberate planning. This broadly shared understanding is clearly compatible with religious or spiritual understandings of improvisation, which are shared by many modern improvisers—as Jason Bivins writes in his wonderful *Spirits Rejoice!*, "The notion of spirits being present in the music is widespread, often attributed to the peak experiences so many players chase. . . . These things beyond us, within us, seem made really present in notes, pulses, timbres and lines, their sounds like gateways into . . . hidden realms."[7]

Improvisation gained currency throughout the art world, and various members of the Grateful Dead were influenced by other art forms than music, particularly the writing of Beat authors such as Jack Kerouac, who strongly valued improvisation: Kerouac wrote about producing "spontaneous prose", and Ginsberg's motto of "first thought, best thought" is appropriate here as well.[8] But the Grateful Dead were musicians first and foremost, so it is important to understand how their musical influences would have supported their interest in improvisation.

Jazz

Musically speaking, in the early-to-mid-1960s, jazz enjoyed a special cachet among progressive listeners. It was, or was capable of being, "serious" music that made significant aesthetic statements, while not being as conservative and culturally rehabilitated as mainstream "serious" music. Furthermore, (some) jazz at that time was in the process of moving into previously unimagined realms, improvisational and otherwise.

Modal jazz, which became prominent in the latter half of the 1950s (and is canonically represented on Miles Davis's album *Kind of Blue*) stripped away a great deal of the harmonic complexity of earlier forms such as bebop, in favor of an approach to playing that focused on exploring modes or scale patterns rather than chord changes. In this context, solos would not be locked into preset and unchanging chord patterns, giving soloists—at least in theory— much more freedom in terms of how they conceived of and built their solos. Rhythm sections were less likely to base their parts around guiding the listener through the harmonic changes; rather, a focus on setting up durable and repeating grooves kept the music moving forward without unduly restricting the soloist.

Although there are examples of jazz musicians playing "free" from as early as the late 1940s, when Lennie Tristano recorded "Intuition" and "Digression," it was not until the late 1950s and 1960s that "free jazz" became a movement.[9] This approach to playing, led by such musicians as Ornette Coleman, Albert Ayler, and Cecil Taylor, went beyond modal jazz, often discarding the rhythm section groove as well as any sense of conventional Western harmony. Furthermore, musicians would often make use of "extended techniques"— that is, extremely unorthodox or unusual sounds. Although there were some quiet free jazz groups (e.g., Jimmy Giuffre's band in the early 1960s), there was a strong tendency for this music to be aggressively dissonant and abrasive by conventional musical standards, in keeping with the revolutionary political or social views with which the genre was often associated.

For those working in or listening to these styles of jazz, extended improvisation was often regarded both as a liberatory gesture, freeing its practitioners from genre-based and ethnicity-related restrictions, and as a means of extending musical parameters, opening new realms of possibility to discover and explore.[10] Song and album titles, as well as comments in interviews, by musicians working through either or both of these approaches often show a pursuit of new possibilities and a sense of universalism, which was enhanced by the tendency of newer forms of jazz to move away from many of the musical tropes of the bebop and "cool" jazz period.[11] The lack or diminished importance of these tropes, such as the use of the standard thirty-two-bar form, the hitherto obligatory "walking" bass line, and show-tune-style cadence patterns, simultaneously made the new jazz seem less limited by or tied to history than older forms might have been and may also have rendered it more accessible to listeners and players who were not steeped in or interested in the mainstream jazz tradition—while, of course, making it less accessible for traditionally minded people. (There are always tradeoffs.)

For the first wave of improvising rock musicians generally, and for San Francisco musicians specifically, John Coltrane's work with his classic quartet was particularly important, as testimonies from Spencer Dryden, David Crosby, Jerry Garcia, and Phil Lesh show.[12] Frank Kofsky wrote at the time that "while Coltrane enjoys a comparatively small but nonetheless dedicated following among rock listeners, his reputation among working rock *musicians* could hardly be higher."[13]

Coltrane was a leading figure in both modal jazz (he played on *Kind of Blue*) and free jazz (on such enormously influential albums as *Ascension*, *Om*, and *Live in Japan*).[14] Moreover, his universally acknowledged virtuosity did a great deal to legitimate free jazz, whose practitioners were often dismissed as musicians who were unskilled or did not understand the jazz tradition. No one could say these things about Coltrane, who not only demonstrated the range of potential in improvisation that was moving away from bebop idioms but also showed that such potential could be actualized without the elaborate harmonic frameworks characteristic of earlier jazz. As Grateful Dead bassist Phil Lesh writes, "I urged the other band members to listen closely to the music of John Coltrane, especially his classic quartet, in which the band would take fairly simple structures . . . and extend them . . . with fantastical variations, frequently based on only one chord."[15] Evidently Lesh was successful at getting his bandmates to listen.

Although it is important to note the influence of Coltrane and other jazz musicians on the Grateful Dead, this is not to say that the band (or their contemporaries) simply aspired to play jazz. As Thomas Allbright points out, for the hippies, "collective . . . expression was emphasized. Jazz, always chiefly a soloists' art, gave way to rock music, which was built on a more integrated concept, emphasizing textures that rose in vertical blocks of sound."[16] This might help to explain the appeal of the Coltrane Quartet and modal jazz, as well as much free jazz: these forms were more amenable to this aesthetic than bebop or hard bop, because of the emphasis on the band and collective creation of musical contexts, rather than simply running through cycles of changes over which the soloist could play. Free jazz in particular was more liable to create the sorts of "blocks of sound" that would have paralleled rock developments. Other aspects of free and modal jazz appealed to rock musicians: simplified or absent harmonic structures lessened the degree of harmonic knowledge required to play over them, for instance, and the use of repeated ostinato riffs in both styles would have been accessible, as well as being similar to rock and blues practice (think of the main riff to the Rolling Stones' "[I Can't Get No] Satisfaction").

Classical Music: India

In addition to these jazz-related approaches to improvisation, two classical music traditions impinged on the Grateful Dead's musical scene that put a high value on improvisation. The Indian classical music tradition, which places an extremely strong emphasis on improvisation, guided by traditions of rigorous and subtle guidelines, was becoming more and more present in North American musical circles during the period of the band's formation. Thanks in no small part to the enthusiastic support of Yehudi Menuhin, in 1955 Ali Akbar Khan's *Music of India: Morning and Evening Ragas* was released on Angel Records, a classical label based in New York, while Ravi Shankar released *The Sounds of India* in 1957 on Columbia, with introductions to the pieces by Menuhin.[17]

These records, along with live work in the West by both Shankar and Khan, helped to bring Indian classical music to a new level of prominence in North America. In this context, George Harrison's use of sitar on the Beatles' "Norwegian Wood" (December 1965) was both a sign of the times and a powerful intensifier of the interest. Even before this, in 1961, Ali Akbar Khan had begun teaching at McGill University in Montreal and, in 1965, at the American Society for Eastern Arts (its very name another sign of the times) in Berkeley, California.[18]

As Peter Lavezzoli has exhaustively demonstrated, Indian classical music was in the air. In addition to the music becoming more culturally accepted—and surely contributing to that acceptance—is the demographic fact that "there were more Indians in America at just the time when Americans were becoming more open to the East. In 1965, for example, the Hart-Celler Act established an immigration system based mainly on family ties to those already living in the United States and those with preferential skills," allowing "qualified people from Asian countries to migrate to the United States, and many thousands did."[19] Indian classical music seemed to offer a legitimizing way into improvisational playing for popular musicians who might be intimidated (especially harmonically) by mainstream jazz. As Mickey Hart notes, "Raga is a virtuosic form. But when you first hear it, you say 'I can do that.' . . . Jam bands came from raga, as far as I'm concerned. It gave us a license to jam, made it legal. It was different from jazz because jazz . . . was harder to understand."[20]

Indian classical music is certainly no simpler a system than jazz, but, to the uninformed Western listener, it can seem to be, which made it inviting for relatively novice rock improvisers. As Charles Perry puts it, "When it came time for the [typical San Franciscan] guitarist to take a lead break, he often noodled up and down the notes of the scale in a way that might owe as much to inexperience in improvisation as to the influence of Indian ragas. The musicians were also stoned a lot of the time, another reason to stick to simple [sic] raga-like improvisations."[21]

For the Western listener, coming to Indian classical music with a point of view informed by Orientalizing, exoticizing or esotericizing tendencies, and without an understanding of the structuring principles of the underlying melodic and rhythmic patterns or the importance of tradition in guiding the soloist, Indian classical music can seem to be entirely improvised, a simple and "natural" manifestation of pure music. This misunderstanding seems to have helped to both inspire and legitimate some white rock musicians' own improvisational explorations, making them "legal," as Hart put it.

At this time, Indian music would also have been heard by many white or Black North Americans as an exotic, "other" tradition. It was beginning to be invoked in rock music (e.g., in "Norwegian Wood" or the Kinks' "See My Friends"); as early as December 1966, Sandy Pearlman published in the pioneering rock journal *Crawdaddy* a detailed and insightful essay on such invocations and their function in rock.[22] As should go without saying, these invocations were Orientalist, but it is worth quoting at length Brian Ireland and Sharif Gemie's nuanced discussion of the situation:

> These virtual and actual journeys represented a "neo-orientalist" position which resembles the older, imperialist orientalism in its tendency to simplify and romanticize the East, but is different from it in the passionate sincerity of its appreciation for certain Eastern forms. Of course "orientalisms," whether past or present, often feature admiration for the "other," so this appreciation does not by itself indicate anything new about the turn eastwards in the 1960s. What, however, is distinct about the neo-orientalism of the 1960s is that . . . it was . . . rooted in a belief that embracing the music, culture and religions of the "East" could help achieve a deeper knowledge of the human experience.[23]

It is important to remember that even when the evaluation is overwhelmingly positive, we are still dealing with appropriation and othering, just as we are with the way that the Grateful Dead, and many other white groups and listeners, appropriated African American musical traditions such as blues or soul, presenting them as inherently more pure or authentic than mainstream pop.

In sum, Indian classical music would have functioned as an improvisational genre that was both an exotic other and a living presence in the Grateful Dead's musical milieu. I use the word "exotic" deliberately: it is important to note that this word, for all its quite appropriately negative and problematic connotations, also has a positive aspect in a psychedelic context. As Patrick Lundborg points out, there is a smooth fit between psychedelia and the search for "exotic" and different presentations of reality that accompanied the increasing presence of "world music" in the North American musical environment, in that "exotica," like the psychedelic experience itself, presents "an alternate reality that is *almost real*" and that is easily accessible.[24] Lundborg argues that the defining characteristic of psychedelia is the idea that reality is both multiple and mutable; exposure to traditions considered exotic, such as Indian classical music, was attractive to psychedelicists precisely for the way that it helped to destabilize consensus reality and reveal the potential for more.

Classical Music: The Western Avant Garde

Hart was introduced to Indian classical music by Phil Lesh.[25] Lesh himself might well have encountered it in his work in the new music scene, because it was present in the Bay Area avant-garde classical music tradition that I will briefly discuss here, from which (or as a reaction against which) the aspect of the Western classical music tradition known as minimalism arose. While the definition of *minimalism* is disputed, and the term itself was not universally popular among composers associated with it, its links both to improvisation (especially in its early days) and San Francisco, and even to one member of the Grateful Dead, are clear.[26] Like free jazz, it began in the 1950s, but bloomed in the 1960s.

In his autobiography, Lesh unambiguously presents avant-garde art music as the foundation for his work with the Grateful Dead. In 1961, Lesh enrolled at the University of California, Berkeley, where he studied music, with a particular interest in such innovative and challenging artists as Stockhausen and Boulez. He volunteered at the radio station KPFA, which featured extremely diverse programming, and used the opportunity to listen to and make his own recordings of European avant-garde music.[27] After dropping out of Berkeley, Lesh audited a graduate composition class at Mills College led by Luciano Berio, an Italian experimental composer closely associated with the development of electronic music. Lesh had arrived at Berkeley just a few years after the departure of pioneering minimalists La Monte Young and Terry Riley. Young, who left San Francisco in 1960, spent the rest of his career in New York, but Riley returned to San Francisco in the spring of 1964 and premiered his piece *In C* at the Tape Music Center, one of the hubs of the San Francisco experimental music community.[28]

In C, one of the pioneering minimalist pieces, does not have a preset form, nor is it simply repetitive; rather, it has a number of modules that instrumentalists move through at their own pace—albeit with a pulse set by a pianist hammering away at a single note. I have not come across any references by Grateful Dead members to this piece, and there is no indication that Lesh was present at the premiere but the way that *In C* moves gradually and somewhat raggedly through its fifty-three different modules, changed at will by the instrumentalists (admittedly within a prescribed order and meter) to create an overall band feel that is never precisely defined bears significant similarities with practices that the Grateful Dead would adopt.[29] Whether or not it had a direct influence on the Grateful Dead, it definitely shows a similar spirit and understanding of music at work.

It was also in 1964 that Lesh first took LSD. He writes that "with my first psychedelic experience I had broken through my depression and was now ready to seek out less solitary forms of creative pursuit. . . . First I ran into my Mills composition classmate Steve Reich," who was the musical director for the Mime Troupe, a San Francisco–based anarchist artists' collective, and who was also working with Riley. Lesh notes that he and Reich, who was "heavily into improvised music," were looking for "a chance to do some improvised music making."[30] As Lesh describes the resulting piece, which involved music, dance, and lights and music: "We just wanted to throw all these elements together . . . and see what happened. . . . This event, the manifestation of a collective *unconscious*, served as the prototype for what became the Acid Test (at that time, of course, lacking the Main Ingredient [LSD]), a manifestation of collective *consciousness*."[31]

Lesh's point is clear: he sees this event, firmly rooted in the avant-garde art music scene, as providing an avant la lettre demonstration of the technical aspects of what would arise at the Acid Tests. But this precursor event lacked LSD and hence the directed ("conscious") purpose that LSD provided Lesh and his bandmates.

In short, there was a thriving avant-garde musical scene in San Francisco in which Lesh and future Grateful Dead keyboardist Tom Constanten were involved. The music being produced and consumed in this scene featured electronic experimentation and manipulation of sound (as in the work of Reich and European composers such as Berio and Stockhausen); minimalistic music that emphasized repetition with small, incremental variations (as in Riley's *In C*); an appreciation for the spontaneous artistic event that presaged future Happenings and the Acid Test; and, just as importantly, a feeling of belonging to an advance guard, a revolutionary community. As David W. Bernstein notes, "Adopting an artistic and social agenda shared by avant-garde artists and musicians, the Grateful Dead saw themselves as members of an independent musical subculture."[32]

Stewart Brand was one of the organizers of the 1966 Trips Festival, which was intended to carry on the multimedia agenda of the Acid Tests, but with a wider representation of San Francisco's bohemian underground. In Brand's view, the Grateful Dead appropriated many of the innovations developed in the city's avant-garde underground: "The Trips Festival was like a changing of the guard in the Bay Area [arts scene]. The Pranksters [Ken Kesey's associates] and the Grateful Dead pretty much stole the show. Bill Graham . . . grabbed that and ran with it. . . . *It was the beginning of the Grateful Dead and the end of everyone else.*"[33] Although their perspectives are different, both Brand and Lesh agree that significant elements of the Grateful Dead's practice and artistic approach were borrowed from or influenced by contemporary developments in the avant-garde music scene.

One aspect of minimalism that may well have influenced the Grateful Dead's practice is its rethinking of the teleological or goal-related imperatives of much of Western art music. Much of Western harmonic music over the past five hundred years creates a process that is organized through its pursuit of goals. When we listen to most classical music, we are looking forward to our arrival at a "home" that was forecast at the beginning of the piece of music. Maybe we will get "home" after just a few minutes; maybe we are listening to Wagner, and it will take us hours to get there (but with plenty of preliminary and partial homecomings to keep us interested). Either way, the vast majority of Western classical music can be seen as similar to orgasm-focused sex: it's that single, definitive, *climactic* moment that is the goal.

If we want to keep the analogy going, we can say that the sort of improvised music that the Grateful Dead create, along with forms of minimalism that are based around pulses, might be better compared to the kind of love-making that often gets sloppily described as "tantric," in which orgasm might not occur and, in any case, isn't the whole story. For this approach to music, the climactic moment(s) is (are) seen as part of the whole trip, not the point of the trip. Robert Fink argues that "there are some truly nonteleological musical styles (John Cage, La Monte Young, Brian Eno), but any music with a regular pulse, a clear tonal center, and some degree of process [all of which applies to the Grateful Dead's music] is more likely to be an example of *recombinant teleology*."[34] Recombinant teleology refers to musical approaches that do not abandon teleological gestures, but rather utilize them as a means instead of an end. Thus, motion toward climax, and climax itself, can be integrated into their surrounding musical contexts instead of defining or completing those contexts.

In modern repetitive musical styles such as minimalism, such integration often involves using extended time scales or "splitting off the tension-release mechanism from the 'rest' of the musical fabric . . . marking a . . . break with classical teleology."[35] Fink writes that "the actual experience of repetitive music is often a series of fragmented tensionings and releases with (let's be honest) periods of directionless ecstasy—or wool-gathering—in between. The shape of the piece no longer coincides with the shape of the teleological mechanism as we experience it."[36] What arises out of such experimentation, he contends, is an array of structural possibilities: "Detach teleology from form and an entire panoply of new arrangements opens up: One might create tension-release arcs that organize only some of the musical space . . . or a composer could present incomplete tension-release cycles . . . or, more interestingly, long build-ups with no clear moment of release."[37]

The structurally bounded but teleologically open space that Fink describes is startlingly similar to the musical space created in Grateful Dead jams, with the difference that the Grateful Dead access such space through improvisation rather than compositional preplanning. Nonetheless, the boundaries between these two approaches are porous, particularly so in the present instance, as minimalist composers often incorporate space for improvisation (e.g., with regard to how long one plays a given melodic cell in *In C*), and improvisers often build structures in the course of focused rehearsals and live performance. In their early days, the Grateful Dead spent a great deal of time rehearsing, developing improvisational possibilities and (after Mickey Hart joined the band) learning how to work in different time signatures than rock's standard 4/4, including 11/4 ("The Eleven"), 10/4 ("Playing in the Band"), and, later, the really odd 7/4 reggae feel of "Estimated Prophet."[38]

It is possible that the Grateful Dead picked up ideas about "recombinant teleology" through their association with specifically minimalist new music circles in San Francisco and incorporated these ideas into their playing, specifically into the way that they emphasized ongoing movement between peaks and swells and changes of direction all contained within the broader outlines of the piece as a whole. The approach that Fink describes certainly coheres more closely with the Grateful Dead's improvisational practice than most jazz practice (with its conversational, soloistic emphases) and is somewhat more appropriate than the emphases on raga exposition and development found in Indian art music—which is natural when we consider that Fink's work deals with music arising from a primarily North American, twentieth-century context, rather than from a millennia-old Indian tradition.

We could even go further and argue that the Grateful Dead's open improvisational approach to playing music is comparable to the minimalist emphasis on "audible structure," in which "part of early minimalism's mystique was to have no secrets, to hold the music's structure right in the audience's face, and have that be listened to."[39] The Grateful Dead's spontaneous movement through sections allows the audience to hear the music's process as it happens.

I have focused here on the potential influence of minimalism on the Grateful Dead's music specifically; more generally, many characteristics of avant-garde music in the 1960s are comparable to the Grateful Dead's practice. Michael Nyman's classic description of experimental music makes the overlap clear: he writes that "experimental composers are by and large not concerned with prescribing a defined *time-object* whose materials, structuring and relationships are calculated and arranged in advance, but are more excited by the prospect of outlining a *situation* in which sounds may occur, a *process* of generating action . . . , a *field* delineated by certain compositional rules."[40] As we will see in our discussion of the Grateful Dead's development of a paradigm for their improvisational playing, this is precisely the approach that they took.

Rock Grows Up

There is one last development that I want to mention, one that is less easy to pinpoint or underline but is nonetheless significant: the increased sense of self-confidence and artistic autonomy and status that many rock musicians seem to have enjoyed during this period. In its earliest years, rock (or rock and roll) tended to be marked as disreputable juvenilia, or as the younger and less respectable sibling of more established musical genres, especially blues, R&B, or country. It took time—and technological innovations—for rock to develop a sense of its own aesthetic identity, on all levels.

I have worked as a rock bassist for many years, so let me take my own instrument as an example. Rock bass playing of the 1950s tends to be not only unaccomplished technically but also, and much more importantly, usually indistinguishable from uninspired examples of country or, especially, blues acoustic bass playing. Admittedly, this is a general statement, and there are isolated exceptions, such as Elvis Presley's powerful and defiantly electric bass introduction to "You're So Square (Baby I Don't Care)."[41] I also want to be clear that when I speak of "uninspired" blues or country bass playing, I certainly do not mean to imply that all blues or country bass playing is uninspired; my point, rather, is that early rock basslines tend more in that direction than they do in the way of, for instance, Willie Dixon's majesty.

In listening to rock bass from the 1950s, it's rare to hear much that is distinctively "rock" about it yet, in the way that Link Wray or Chuck Berry are clearly already rock guitarists. This has to do much more with feel and approach than it does with musicality: for example, you certainly couldn't call Peter Lucas of the Troggs an "accomplished" musician based on his playing on such caveman stomps as "Wild Thing," but you can't deny that he's a *rock* player, for better or worse.[42] This changeover might have something to do with the instruments themselves. It is not until the rise of instrumental and surf music in the very early 1960s, forms in which the specifically *electric* bass is fundamental, that we see a distinctively rock and distinctively electric approach to bass playing emerge that could only have come from electric instruments being played in a rock context.

I know that this probably sounds like just another version of the story where a bassist desperately tries to claim that he's cool, but it matters. In fact, Jim Roberts argues that the electric bass was the fundamental innovation required for rock to truly become itself. Specifically, he critiques the idea that it was the electric guitar that led in the rock era. "The notion of rock as an important musical and social force is directly linked to the acceptance of the electric bass," he writes. "The other crucial rock instruments—the electric guitar and the drum kit—had been around for decades, but the 'new bass,' which changed the way rhythm sections worked and altered the dynamic contours of popular music, was the last piece of the puzzle."[43]

The upright bass is what was typically used in early rock and roll music, but "there was still a need for an instrument that could assert a well-defined bass sound and enable the music to get louder (and therefore more powerful)," and so "it was really the Fender bass that made possible the forward progress of this new genre," with the early 1960s surf/instrumental music period as the period when electric bass became absolutely essential to rock.[44] According to Roberts, "The Fender bass gave bass players a new, assertive identity. . . . They could take a more prominent role in the music and use different bass patterns," especially when given the extra boost in both volume and clarity of the new bass amplifiers that were developed in the early 1960s.[45]

Rock approaches to electric guitar, as well, developed along with the guitars and amplifiers that the musicians played. Again, many of these innovations came out of surf music, including an incorporation of a wider variety of melodic and harmonic structures than had been commonly used before, the enormous weight placed on guitar sound and effects, and the heightened emphasis on the lead guitar as the band's main instrument.[46] Speaking generally, the overall level of virtuosity in rock also increased, although this is less important for rock's development than is the production of a distinct variation in aesthetics.

This discussion of instrumental developments brings up the issue of the way technology interacts with art, and it is significant to note as well the developments in terms of amplifiers and sound systems that took place during this period. As Theodore Gracyk notes, the achievements of such bands as Cream, the Grateful Dead, and other San Francisco bands "depended on superior sound systems; improvisational rock was hardly possible when musicians had no stage monitors and the cheap amplification system distorted the music into a dull roar."[47] Throughout their career, the Grateful Dead emphasized the importance of quality live sound; in the period under discussion in this book, their sonic innovations culminated in an enormous array of speakers, the Wall of Sound, that allowed both musicians and audience to hear the music with unparalleled clarity.[48]

By the mid-1960s, then, rock had roots: it had been around long enough to constitute a tradition in which many of its practitioners had grown up, rather than being a novelty style. In addition to roots, it had a distinctive sound that owed a great deal to—but was clearly distinguishable from—blues, country, and folk. Furthermore, spearheaded by the Beatles and their astonishing commercial, cultural, and aesthetic success, rock was in the process of acquiring significant amounts of cultural capital and, thanks to the economic good fortune of the first wave of baby boomers, financial power.[49] Finally, it had developed a supportive technology that enabled musicians to work at their peaks.

All of these elements led to an increased sense of self-confidence for rock musicians. They were coming to regard themselves as artists and—with the influence of folk-related tropes regarding the status of the musician as community spokesperson—even potentially as representatives of their generation, as in some ways prophetic figures, who have the potential to speak authoritatively in order to reveal the true spiritual nature of their time. This is a role that musicians have played in many cultures, but it was not characteristic of 1950s rock musicians: for instance, Elvis or Jerry Lee Lewis might have been seen as forces of nature, but few would have granted them the intellectual and spiritual authority that Bob Dylan or John Lennon were given in the 1960s.

This increase in musicians' social, artistic, and intellectual capital in turn increased their willingness and ability to reach out into new musical realms, particularly those that combined high status with a somewhat daring reputation. Improvisation was one such realm. And, as we have seen, for the musicians of the San Francisco scene, it would have been especially accessible, thus laying the essential conceptual groundwork for the Grateful Dead's own innovations.

One further aspect of rock's maturity should be mentioned in this context. As Mike Heffley points out, improvisational activity often arises from knowledge of and comfort in a given tradition: "Improvisation qua improvisation, then, is not a universal way for musicians from various situations to collaborate, any more than mastery of one language equals mastery of another."

Rather, "the master improvisers/composers of Western art music [such as Bach, Mozart, or Beethoven] were so because they were comfortable and proficient in [their] court tradition."[50] This applies to our current discussion as well: the first generation of rock improvisers were the first generation of people to have grown up with rock and roll, which became rock. They were the first people for whom the music had been a presence since at least their adolescence, if not their childhood. They lived in rock, they felt comfortable in it, in a way that their older siblings or parents could not, no matter how much they might have loved it; this music was *home* to the musicians who came of age in the early 1960s, a form that they understood well enough and intuitively enough to be able to play authoritatively and to improvise over.

The San Francisco Scene

The musical developments that we have discussed established the potential for the Grateful Dead's musical breakthroughs. Potential, however, needs to be actualized in a specific context. The San Francisco rock music scene in the mid-1960s, just before its emergence as one of rock's major centers (both in commercial terms, and in terms of its reputation for innovation), was particularly conducive to such actualization. As I see it, three main elements made the scene such a hospitable environment for the improvisational breakthroughs of the Grateful Dead and other groups. The first is its "end of history" celebratory aspect, privileging experimentalism, eclecticism, and diversity; the second, its communal focus; and the third, its emphasis on dancing.

A CARNIVAL AT THE END OF HISTORY

The great jazz bandleader Sun Ra had a song called "It's After the End of the World," with the lyrics: "It's after the end of the world / Don't you know that yet?"[51] Many in the San Francisco scene seem to have shared that sense—except that, rather than lament their perceived situation, they preferred to celebrate it. Speaking with Phil Lesh of the origins and significance of the name "Grateful Dead," interviewer David Gans noted that it could be taken as "a rationale for hedonism—'we're already dead, let's party!,'" a suggestion that Lesh supports and extends: "Sure. Hey, what do you think the Acid Test was, partly? You're dead when you're born."[52] At the dances that anchored the scene, "there was a sense of confronting ultimate reality, moving toward a breakthrough";[53] there seems to have been a feeling in the air that, by joining the San Francisco hip scene, one was committing to "living in the new world."[54]

Part of this feeling was definitely drug induced. Nick Bromell presents a very compelling and insightful discussion of the ramifications of this feeling of living outside of—or after—history that often arises with the use of psychedelic drugs. He argues that the use of psychedelics gave "insight into the world's instability," bringing trippers to an awareness of the world's "radical pluralism" and a feeling that they were "submerged in the pluralism of the fluid world, no longer presuming to stand above it and no longer troubled by the seeming 'unreality' of the social construction that has fixed this world in place."[55] The combination of psychedelic drugs and rock music, Bromell contends, created the feeling that "meaning emerges only when we have dispensed with the narrative of coherence."[56]

Consciously or not, the San Francisco scenesters absorbed the contemporary countercultural trope of the "plastic" or artificial nature of the modern world. Such a critique was common to a number of vanguardist political and artistic movements, but was perhaps most cogently expressed by Guy Debord and the Lettrist International, which became the Situationist International.[57] As Debord put it in the first aphorism in *The Society of the Spectacle*, "the whole life of those societies in which modern conditions of production prevail presents itself as an immense accumulation of spectacles. All that was once directly lived has become mere representation."[58] This critique harmonized with the views of many in the various art scenes at the time that fundamental breakthroughs were in the process of being made, which Ken Kesey has described as a "Neon Renaissance": "It's a need to find a new way to look at the world, an attempt to locate a better reality."[59] Even just within the music world, this is the period of the birth of minimalism, conceptual art, and the first wave of free jazz, to say nothing of rock's transformations, with the exploration of new possibilities in terms of timbre, harmony, rhythm, and melody. The members of the San Francisco scene took this period of creativity and the inauthenticity of modern society as an invitation to pillage with manic energy what had come before: "Costumes. Dressing up. Playing a part. It was all a glorious game, everyone feeding off each other's fantasies."[60]

As Mike Pritchard, a member of the then enormously influential but now almost forgotten band the Charlatans, put it: "Bohemians have a tradition of what bohemia means. It was centuries old, really, and it meant being sensitive, being willing to suffer for what you believed in. We were more eclectic. We had no real roots. We attached ourselves to whatever was available, picked up on whatever caught our attention—blues, art nouveau, comic books."[61] Thus, for instance, Charlatans member George Hunter could move smoothly from an interest in John Cage and electronic music to founding the Charlatans, who were perhaps the pioneering San Francisco group, whose look and sound appropriated the atmosphere of the 1890s, psychedelically augmented.[62] Similarly, in their multipart composition "That's It For the Other One", the Grateful Dead could move unproblematically between biblically themed folk music, multiply overdubbed and cross-faded recordings of live aggressive rock and roll, snatches of musique concrète, and off-kilter pop melodies with surrealistic lyrics.[63]

In multiple ways beyond this one composition, the Grateful Dead drew from this openness. Indeed, the extremely varied backgrounds of its members (Lesh: avant-garde art music; Garcia: folk and bluegrass; Kreutzmann: rock and roll; Pigpen: blues; Weir: folk and rock) are typical of the San Francisco approach, as was their rejection of the purism often associated with several of those backgrounds. As Ralph Gleason puts it, "In the hands of the Grateful Dead, rock was the soundtrack for a scene agog at the unfolding spectacle of psychedelia. Mystical eastern arcana, Indian headtrips, sci-fi fantasy flights, the secret teachings of the delta blues fathers, motorcycle fetishism, the Beat cosmos, the Wild West and the next frontier—somehow the Dead personified it all."[64]

In all of this diversity, the one common denominator seems to have been the ludic atmosphere, the refusal to take anything too seriously, especially in terms of status. Whereas Happenings in New York could be quite serious affairs, presenting themselves as Artistic Statements, the San Francisco scene was more lighthearted and playful.[65] This comes across clearly in Gleason's review of a performance by New York's Exploding Plastic Inevitable, featuring the Velvet Underground: "Warhol's films are a triumph of monotony into boredom. The Plastic Inevitable is the same principle applied to a rock 'n' roll dance."[66] Perry notes that "what was unique to the hippies was their attitude—an expansive, theatrical attitude of being cool enough to have fun."[67] Speaking of the impact of the Beatles on the Grateful Dead's scene, Garcia chooses not to emphasize their music; instead he notes that "they were making people happy. That happy thing—that's the stuff that counts—something that we could see right away."[68] Margaret Gaskin, wife of hippie spiritual teacher Stephen Gaskin, speaks eloquently of her conversion from a beatnik to a hippie: "I was secure in the cavelike corner you crawl into when you're a beatnik. It took a lot for me to stop being down all the time. . . . The hippie thing was a complete change . . . to consciously making an effort to be good, kind, and cheerful. . . . Like the bright clothes are very much part of it. . . . To be bright and shiny for everybody else. To have a pretty world to look at."[69]

What this meant for the Grateful Dead is that they were part of a scene in which experimentation was encouraged, with an overall atmosphere of exuberance and enthusiastic amateurism. The "after the end of the world" feeling diminished concerns about "authenticity" or about how one could fit one's artistic activities into a preexisting artistic hierarchy, thus encouraging the sort of invention and experimentation engaged in by the Grateful Dead engaged. Furthermore, the scene's openness to all sorts of stimuli made it easier for a band to have faith in its inspirations, when those inspirations (which, I will argue, involved having transcendent religious experiences while playing rock music on LSD) might easily have seemed laughable in other contexts.

COMMUNITY FEELING

The San Francisco scene was known for its strong community feeling, particularly with regard to the Grateful Dead, who were an iconic band almost from the start of their career. Speaking of Thanksgiving 1966, McNally writes that "the band had achieved a particular kind of status within their world. They'd been a band for less than two years, yet there was an apartment . . . in the Haight whose tenants sold buttons that read 'Good Ol' Grateful Dead.'"[70]

This feeling that the band was a beloved institution is to be expected, given how the Grateful Dead's activities overlapped with many of the characteristic features of, and main players in, the San Francisco scene. They were integrally associated with the iconic Acid Tests at the start of their career; they worked with all of the major promoters, most notably Bill Graham; they helped to pioneer the tradition of free public performances; they were known for their friendship with the Hell's Angels—wherever the San Francisco hip community looked, it would see the Grateful Dead reflected there.

Psychedelic drug use also played a significant role in establishing the identity of this scene and linking it to rock music, dancing, and the promise of a new age. As Perry writes, "Throughout the spring and summer of 1966 there were at least two rock dance concerts each weekend night, all marked by the same accepting spirit that presumed that anyone who came was hip to psychedelics and probably stoned. The mere fact of being immersed in a sea of like-minded heads produced an intoxication of its own. San Francisco's LSD users developed a special confidence about what they were doing. . . . They were publicly outrageous."[71]

The hip community was theoretically open to all: it merely required its members to recognize themselves as members—that is, as not belonging to the "square" world, or to prior and now-outmoded bohemias of the past, although such bohemias could be drawn upon for influence or revered as forerunners, as was the case with the Beats, two of whose icons (Neal Cassady and Allen Ginsberg) crossed over to the new scene. As Garcia puts it, in discussing his first LSD experiences and decision to drop out of mainstream culture and join the counterculture, "It made me immensely happy because like suddenly I knew that what I thought I knew all along I really did know and it was really, it really was the way I hoped it might be."[72]

The community did not completely reject hierarchical power arrangements, but an effort was made to keep the hierarchies within the community. As Ralph Gleason notes, for instance, the new promoters "were unlike any that I had ever seen. . . . They entered into the occasion as participants, not organizers."[73] Some musicians, too, paid at least lip service to egalitarian ideals; according to Garcia, "the leader thing don't work because you don't need it. Maybe it used to, but I don't think you need it anymore because everyone is the leader."[74] Others took these ideals much further, including the activists united under the name of the Diggers, a guerilla theater group active in distributing food and anarchist ideology in San Francisco in the mid-to-late 1960s.[75]

In addition to often seeing (or at least presenting) themselves as part of the community, musicians represented the community, in that many of their songs emerged from or sought to articulate the drug experiences that were defining for so many members of the scene, whether they were musicians or not. The musicians "were speaking of the Great Unspeakable of being stoned, like prophets emerging from the community to address its deepest concerns. . . . They themselves had faced the situations described in the lyrics in all the vulnerability of being stoned on psychedelics."[76]

The San Francisco hip community seems to have been open enough that the various experimental or marginal groups or scenes could overlap in this larger scene, with Kesey and the Merry Pranksters collaborating with avant-garde theater group the Mime Troupe and the experimental musicians from the Tape Music Center to set up events, attended by Hell's Angels, among others, at which the music would be provided by the new generation of rock and folk-rock bands. There were, however, a few landmark events that brought the scene together, and one of them seems to have been a Rolling Stones gig.[77] Several sources present the show in San Francisco on May 14, 1965, as an important harbinger of the new scene, noting that among "a smattering of prescient adolescents, the mildly curious, and the simply misplaced," there were also "a handful of people with nothing better to do than to take all the seething, unfocused energy of the time and manhandle it into a scene."[78]

Another landmark event was the opening in August 1965 of the Matrix Club, which established a hip, artist-run, foothold in the San Francisco music scene, as it was founded and comanaged by Marty Balin of the Jefferson Airplane.[79] That winter, two significant scene-building events took place: first, the Rolling Stones returned to California, playing in San Jose on December 5; on the same day, the second of Ken Kesey and the Merry Pranksters' Acid Tests took place, also in San Jose, and was the first Acid Test at which the Grateful Dead performed.[80]

Several more Acid Tests followed over the next month, culminating in the Trips Festival (January 21–23, 1966), the event at which the scene self-consciously came into being. Many of the people who were important in the hip scene were present at this festival, which drew a very large and flamboyant audience. The feeling that a new community had emerged was palpable; as Sculatti and Seay put it, "the idea was to gather up all the separate but equally groovy elements of the local scene, toss 'em into one big pot, and invite the whole town to supper," even if, for some—such as Stewart Brand, quoted earlier—the Trips Festival was an ending rather than a beginning.[81]

In addition to this more generalized community, the Grateful Dead's scene itself (frequently—and significantly—referred to as a "family") was strongly linked, with musical, romantic, or social ties between many of the participants, going back for years.[82] This communal aspect was important to the band members, who made efforts to maintain the tribal feeling: as Garcia put it in 1972, "our whole scene had been completely cooperative and entirely shared. We never structured our situation where anybody was getting any money. What we were doing was buying food, paying rent, stuff like that."[83]

DANCING

The San Francisco scene was a dancing scene. Indeed, one of the reasons that rock-based improvisation became so firmly identified with it is precisely because long jams over rock beats was what the dancers wanted. People went to the San Francisco ballrooms to dance, and bands obliged them with dramatically extended songs.[84] As Davin Seay and Mary Neely write, "The improvisation and stylistic blends that came to characterize the . . . San Francisco sound weren't the result of sophisticated musical savants stepping boldly into the unknown. . . . The Avalon and Fillmore faithfuls weren't interested in skill. All they required was bands that could play long and loud. . . . Suddenly, people wanted to dance . . . and their stamina was daunting."[85]

As we have seen, the range of influences that the bands could draw from to support such extensions was vast, but, in order for a band to survive commercially, they had to be adept at bringing those influences into a danceable, rock context. Consequently, "the Dead, along with all the other successful psychedelic aggregates in the city, was first, foremost and finally a dance band."[86]

The San Francisco scene did later become notorious for overindulgence—not every band, and certainly not every lead guitarist, could sustain interest over extended lengths of blues-derived soloing. But, at least in the beginning, the emphasis on danceability served to give the bands focus. Whatever else they might have intended to do, they needed first of all to make sure that the dancers kept dancing. As long as they could do that, they could play "In The Midnight Hour" for over half an hour without complaints, as the Grateful Dead did, or incorporate hitherto unheard of amounts of dissonance into their music. We have noted that every musical tradition has its own parameters for how its musicians will improvise; for the San Francisco scene, the need to produce danceable music was one of the more important of them.

This emphasis was not lost on the bands. When an interviewer pointed out that "the music that the Dead, Quicksilver and the Airplane performed at concerts beginning in 1966 included long instrumental pieces," manager Rock Scully responded: "That's because those early concerts were dance concerts, and the dancers didn't want the songs to end. Dancing was a real important part of it, and the band wasn't always the focus of attention."[87] Taking up the same point from a different angle, when discussing the Grateful Dead's efforts to imply rhythm rather than explicitly state it, Garcia notes that at the same time they are concerned to "keep it groovy and yet make it so people can still move to it. . . . We still feel that our function is as a dance band . . . and that's what we like to do. We like to play with dancers. . . . Nothing improves your time like having somebody dance. Just pulls the whole thing together. And it's also a nice little feedback thing."[88]

The importance of the dances might have been partly due to the fact that, for many attendees, they were more than just opportunities to dance. Aidan Kelly, one of the founders of the New Reformed Orthodox Order of the Golden Dawn and thus one of the architects of the neopagan revival, notes that "few people remember now that the rock dances in San Francisco began as quasi-religious events. . . . These dances immediately became the center of the social life of all the people in their 20s who had been converted to Hippiedom by the Beatles' first film, *A Hard Day's Night*.[89] The whole purpose of the dances—the reason for every one of their details—was to get stoned on grass or acid or some other mild psychedelic and to trip out on the lights, the music, and the scantily clad bodies gyrating wildly in the dimly lit auditorium. . . . We were primed to create our Order because we hoped the Sabbats could again create the magick we had felt at the dances."[90]

The emphasis on dancing is important to note because, as Melvin Backstrom observes, one could easily have expected that "rock music's newfound artistic seriousness" could have been defined "in opposition to its functional accompaniment for dancing, as had occurred in the transition from swing to bebop jazz in the 1940s." Instead, he writes,

> in the Bay Area of the mid-to-late 1960s such an accompanying role was instead a defining component of its avant-garde character as a manifestation of the interaction between musicians and their audiences, and thus of bridging the divide between them. Although such an accompaniment role of rock bands in relation to dancers has an obvious lineage to earlier rock & roll dances, the difference here is the explicit role that improvisation plays in the performance, both in terms of how what the bands perform is understood to be informed by their engagement with their audience, as well as the individualistic, free-form kind of dancing practiced by audience members.[91]

So it wasn't just that dancing audiences provided a receptive environment for improvisational experimentation; in fact, the dancers and the band together formed the environment within which improvised and "wildly gyrating" magic could take place.

Conclusion

The Grateful Dead were fortunate enough to begin their career in a context in which a variety of new or different musical approaches that privileged improvisation and experimentation were available to be drawn on as resources. The environment in which these resources could be deployed was one that emphasized celebration and eclecticism, thus encouraging musicians to take chances and expand their approaches. It had a strong communal element as well, with the community made up of friends and fellow musicians of long standing, along with people brought together and feeling themselves to be unified simply by virtue of enthusiasm to develop and parade their individualist approach to life. This sense of community provided a nurturing environment for development in all sorts of activities, music among them.

This development was grounded, on the one hand, by the commercial need to ensure that music, no matter how experimental it might get, would be (mostly) danceable; on the other hand, it was furthered by the enthusiasm of the dancers for extended pieces—unlike, for example, the late 1970s and early 1980s hardcore punk scenes, which were also predominantly dancing scenes, but in which the musical requirements were extremely tight and hence limiting. "Although the [hardcore] philosophy implied 'no rules,'" writes Steven Blush, "the music wasn't avant-garde, experimental, nor did it have unlimited possibilities. It was about playing as fast as possible."[92] The San Francisco dancers of the mid-1960s were more tolerant than this: as long as "it's got a good beat and you can dance to it," they were willing to accept a great deal of sonic and structural experimentation. This openness provided a fertile environment for rock musicians, such as the Grateful Dead, to figure out how exactly they were going to stretch their songs to satisfy their audience's desires.

How the Grateful Dead Learned to Jam

BUILDING A FRAMEWORK
FOR IMPROVISATION

An ideal thing would be to go onstage with absolutely nothing in your head, and everybody get together and pick up his instrument and play and improvise the whole thing. . . . And perhaps that's a place where we can all get. But it's in the experimental stage. It's kind of like an alchemical experiment that you have to repeat. Again and again and again, the same experiment, exactly the same . . . We don't repeat the music—the details of the music—over and over again. *There's a framework for that too.* But it's like the same effort. The effort is to get higher.—JERRY GARCIA (1970)

We play cues to each other, and depending upon whether or not anybody's listening, or whether anybody cares to second the motion, we'll go that way. If you can get two on a trip, you generally go there. It can be something we all know or a completely new idea introduced within the context of what we're doing. If the movement gets adopted, then we can go to a completely new place. Or if somebody introduces a familiar line from an old place—it may be a song or a passage that we're more or less familiar with—we can go that way. . . . Sometimes we know what we're doing. Sometimes we're completely lost in what we're doing, and maybe it just grabs us and takes us there too. It seems to fall into place a lot to me also. It's a tenuous art of trying to make format out of chaos, of course. As we get better practiced at it, we can get looser and freer in our associations, and let the music more or less move us in a given direction. Sometimes, if what we're doing just really wants to go somewhere and the air is just pregnant with it, it's undeniable, we'll just go there. On a really good night, it'll happen a succession of times. No one will even play a cue, yet bang we're just off. —BOB WEIR (1972)

The Dead don't "jam" in the sense of complete improvisation. Although the riffs may be spontaneous, the structure of their instrumentals is not. —JOHN KOKOT (1973)

The challenging part is coming up with structures that have the element of loose-ness to them, which means they can expand in any direction, go anywhere from any-where—or come from anywhere—but also have enough form that we can lock into something. —JERRY GARCIA (1968)

Now that we have an idea of the social and musical context in which the Grateful Dead were working when they developed their unique approach to improvisation, it is time to discuss their own brand of improvisation. Bor-rowing from the approach taken by Ekkehard Jost, which he developed for the study of the radically new improvisational strategies of the Free Jazz pio-neers, I will focus on establishing the idiosyncratic and paradigmatic model that guided the musicians' practice; this model is what I call the "Frame-work." In this chapter, I want to take a closer look at what the band produced out of their context—in other words, to explore the Grateful Dead's transfor-mation from a fairly conventional folk/blues/rock band into the exponents of a unique, improvisational way of playing rock music, and to present the Framework as the means they used to make that transformation.

I should warn you that, in doing this, we will be heading into somewhat unknown territory: the earliest phase of the band's development is often minimized in critical work on their musical practice—for instance, David Malvinni presents this time as preliminary, leading up to the period when he considers that the "programmatic, transcendental turn of Deadness became apparent," which he illustrates through a discussion of their covers of Otis Redding's "Hard to Handle" (which they began playing in 1969), and, of course, their epic "Dark Star," for which he focuses on versions performed in the early 1970s. Similarly, in Dennis McNally's canonical history of the band, *Long Strange Trip*, it is only with the composition of "Dark Star" in 1968 that he begins looking at the specifics of the band's music.[1] And when Jason Winfree, in an article in *The Grateful Dead in Concert*, invites us to look back over the band's career, we are to do so "from 1968, when the Grateful Dead acquired a sound all their own. . . . Today, 40 years separate the '68 sound and the present."[2]

Nicholas Meriwether, by contrast, takes a more nuanced approach: in *The Deadhead's Taping Compendium*, he presents 1965–66 as the beginnings of "what [the Grateful Dead] began to do more formally in 1967," thus both integrating the band's earliest years with their later career and, very significantly, pointing out that they developed a process for their practice.[3] But Meriwether is an exception in this regard. Reading much of the writing on the Grateful Dead, it would be easy to get the impression that 1965, 1966, and 1967 were nothing more than warm-up years, time spent waiting for the full glory that would be revealed at the Fillmore West in 1969, or at the Fillmore East in 1970, or at Veneta, Oregon, in 1972, or at Barton College in 1977—or whenever your own favorite show happens to be, because very few people (myself included) would choose a show from 1966 or 1967, or even early 1968, as their favorite. And while it is completely true that the music that the band made starting in fall 1968 has a sophistication and depth that surpasses their earlier efforts, the thing is that, when we listen to the music that they made at the end of the 1960s or later, we are hearing the fruits of the labor that they put in from 1965 on, as they worked doggedly to develop an authentic, rock-based approach to improvisation that they could use.

The creation of this approach didn't just happen. The chapter epigraphs from Garcia and Weir suggest that there were coherent organizational principles behind the Grateful Dead's musical development, a suggestion that is backed up by analysis: close examination shows that the band's performance practice for the period that I am discussing can be broadly fitted into a conceptual model that I call the Framework. The Framework developed in the first half of 1966, reached its full expression in 1967, and was partially superseded by the band's further artistic and professional developments—but it never disappeared completely.

The Framework represents a way of understanding the Grateful Dead's early solution to the problem of designing a means through which live rock music could be transformed into a flexible, improvisational art form. Interviews with the band members and insider accounts, which will be detailed in the second half of this book, suggest that the impetus to create and develop their improvisational approach to rock music derived from what can be described as the revelation of a new mode of consciousness for the band.

As I will argue, the Grateful Dead's experiences with LSD, particularly at the Merry Pranksters' Acid Tests, led them to believe that in the right circumstances their music could have the power to create extraordinary experiences for its players and listeners. What this means for us is that the Grateful Dead's early career can only be fully understood when it is seen—at least in part—as the attempt to recreate and represent these extraordinary experiences and to speak and play from this new mode of consciousness. It is in that conceptual environment that the Framework's true usefulness becomes apparent. It was a means of creating musical contexts in which such experiences could be made more accessible. To put it very simply: *they built the Framework in order to give themselves a way to make weird shit happen.*

It is tempting to ask, "Who needs a Framework? If they want to jam, why don't they just jam?" I hope that part of the answer to that will be clear at this point: we previously discussed how all improvisational practice is based on paradigmatic models, whether those models have been explicitly conceptualized (sometimes, as in the case of raga traditions, in forms that have been developed over millennia) or whether they are implicit. It seems that, actually, nobody "just jams": musicians are always working within parameters and paradigms, whether they are set by a revered tradition, audience expectations, or the musicians' own needs or aspirations.

We also need to remember that the Grateful Dead were a working rock band long before they were established rock stars. What this means is that they were young men performing and rehearsing hundreds of times a year, often under challenging or deeply strange circumstances, and often without a lot of the material comforts that most of us require to consistently do our best work. Inspiration is a wonderful thing, but it does not always come through: if musicians want to be able to reliably deliver explorations into new musical directions, night after night, no matter how stoned or tired or homesick they might be, no matter how long the day's drive took or how exhausting soundcheck was, they need a structure that can guide them when pure inspiration is no longer doing the job.

Furthermore, we know from the band's testimony that the goal of improvisation in this case was not just self-expression, but the creation of an environment in which a certain type of extraordinary events could take place, meaning that the approach to playing had to be conducive to these sorts of outcomes, and not to others.[4] The testimony of the recordings, along with Garcia's straightforward declaration, makes it clear that the Framework was there as an explicit or implicit guiding paradigm to help them make the magic happen, night after night after night.

More or Less in Line

Overall, the Grateful Dead's approach to improvisation can be described as the group's spontaneous creation of, manipulation of, and progression between musical structures. It is very, very rare for them to even approach "free" or unstructured improvisation such as free jazz and free improvisation players often do; there is almost always a pulse in their music, there is usually a rhythm, and the tonal center is rarely in question—in other words, you can usually dance or at least shuffle to it, and, even if you can't exactly sing along, you know roughly what notes are "home."[5] Furthermore, while many shows in the band's first decade (1965–75) did feature periods of "outside" or improvised music that was not necessarily attached to song structures, the vast majority of the Grateful Dead's improvisation took place within relatively tightly structured songs, especially in their earliest period. They did not "just play," at least in live contexts: the playing usually arose from songs.

What we find in the Grateful Dead's music, then, is not the rejection of preexisting structure, such as we might see in a performance by a contemporary free improviser like Derek Bailey, where the musician simply starts making sounds without a predetermined form.[6] The Grateful Dead's approach involves taking up the freedom to work with and to work within structure, to move from form to form either directly or with periods of liminal formlessness in between. This motion through forms is not soloistic or individualistic; instead, it is guided and cued by the spontaneous interplay between band members and the commitment to group solidarity. The Grateful Dead do not abandon structure—or, rather, they do so only very briefly, and not at all in the period that we are discussing. Instead, we can say that they take an outsider's view of structure, seeing it as unfixed and impermanent. At any given moment the group will be more or less invested in a given form or matrix, but they will not be identified with it, because it could (and will) change. While playing within a form, they also play *around with* it; throughout, they retain their collective autonomy—and also their home in otherness.

The Grateful Dead's approach was influenced by jazz practice, particularly (to judge by their interviews) the more open, modal jazz of the late 1950s and early 1960s, rather than the free jazz that was developing contemporaneously with them. Although Jerry Garcia did appear on an Ornette Coleman album, *Virgin Beauty*, this was not until many years later, when Coleman's approach had considerably mellowed—and, not coincidentally, in a period when Coleman was drawing very heavily on rock- and funk-influenced grooves, played mainly on electric instruments.[7] This was a much more natural environment for a rock-rooted player such as Garcia.

As we have discussed, interviews with Grateful Dead band members throughout their career show them to be unstinting in their praise for the work of John Coltrane: for instance, Lesh writes that "I urged the other band members to listen closely to [the Coltrane quartet]" for the way that "the band would take fairly simple structures . . . and extend them far beyond their original length with fantastical variations, frequently based on only one chord."[8] But you will search in vain for references to more radical, noisy, purely "out" players such as Albert Ayler or Cecil Taylor, and even the reverence for Coltrane seems to be for his early 1960s work, rather than the completely "out" material that he did in the year or two before his death. So the influence of jazz upon their musical concept is clear, and guitarist Bob Weir went so far as to say, "Our basic premise is rock and roll . . . We just approach it from a jazz point of view."[9] But we need to nuance this a bit more: as the reverence for Coltrane and the references to Miles Davis's band reveal, the jazz that seems to have most impacted the Grateful Dead is the modal and rock-influenced jazz that was developing in the 1960s and that shares with rock a harmonic simplicity and attachment to a groove (as opposed to, say, bebop, with its fiendishly complex harmonic elaborations and often deliberately jarring melodies)—note Lesh's reference to the Coltrane band jamming on just one chord.

However, the Grateful Dead's concept is significantly different from that typical of jazz groups, especially in terms of the status of the interrelationships between the musicians—that is, whether those interrelationships are seen as means or end. Jazz improvisation has frequently been likened to a conversation between separate voices individually responding to and commenting on their situation; hence the very title of Ingrid Monson's *Saying Something: Jazz Improvisation and Interaction.*

Although the conversational element is certainly present in the Grateful Dead's playing, here it is the means to the end rather than the end itself. The Grateful Dead functions very much as a group—one whose musical directions arise from the interaction of its component members, true, but nonetheless the focus throughout is on the organization as one thing composed of several independent but aligned voices, unified if raggedly so. As they put it in their song "Truckin'": "Together, more or less in line." Garcia brings this out in a 1967 interview with Ralph Gleason, noting that "what we're thinking about is, we're thinking, we're trying to think away from solo lines. From the standard routine of *this* member comps, *this* member leads. We're trying to think of ensemble stuff, you know."[10]

The importance of a ragged-but-right, laid-back approach to ensemble playing for the Grateful Dead is made clear when we consider "Cleo's Back," an instrumental twelve-bar blues song that was released by Junior Walker and the All-Stars as the B side to "Shake and Fingerpop."[11] "Cleo's Back" came out at the same time that the Grateful Dead were forming, and Garcia singled out the song as being especially important for the band as they were developing their aesthetic; he notes that it "was also real influential on . . . our whole style of playing. There was something about the way the instruments entered into it in a kind of free-for-all way, and there were little holes and these neat details in it—we studied that motherfucker! We might have even played it for a while, but that wasn't the point—it was the conversational approach, the way the band worked, that really influenced us."[12] His phrasing is significant—there is a "conversational" approach, but that conversation is subsumed in "the way the band worked" as a whole. In other words, he values it for the musical dialogue that underpins the band sound.

Keeping in mind the approach that the Grateful Dead developed, we can hear why the song was so influential: the various instruments interact in a ramshackle way as the song ambles along, occasionally to the point of seeming to stumble over one another (1:50). Moreover, while each instrument (sax, guitar, keyboards, bass, and drums) plays a conventional role, no one of them is overwhelmingly in the forefront. The song's identity is provided not by a lead melody, but by a catchy two-note guitar riff; however, this riff simply disappears for the last two choruses of the song. Despite this surface-level incoherence, however, "Cleo's Back" has a very distinct identity, created through the sensitive, apparently spur-of-the-moment, and more or less egalitarian interaction of its various musicians. It is very much a group creation. As we will see, all of these characteristics were present in the approach that the Grateful Dead would develop. If you cue up "Cleo's Back" on YouTube, you can imagine that you are listening to the launch pad of the Grateful Dead's sound.[13]

Playing in the Band

As we will see in chapter 5, the modern discussion of improvisation in Western popular music has been heavily influenced by jazz practices and aesthetics. This is reasonable, given the emphasis that jazz places on improvisation, and the role of jazz as the conduit through which the West rediscovered improvisation after centuries during which it was minimized or overlooked; that said, the emphasis on jazz in discussion of improvisation does have its consequences. One of those consequences is that those who work in the jazz world—and, hence, those who work in the improvising scenes that come from the jazz world or draw heavily on it—have a strong tendency to favor the extreme ends of a continuum that stretches from individuals to the overarching tradition when they conceptualize the social organizations at play in the music.

What I mean by this is that the presentation and discussion of jazz music and the jazz scene often focuses on the scene, or, more widely, the tradition, as the conceptual container within which individuals work and interact. When we speak in jazz terms, then, we tend to talk about specific musicians, who emerge out of musical-historical contexts and are either representative of (or perhaps not representative of) those contexts—and this has been the context of much discussion of improvising musicians. Books on the development of improvisation tend to deal with musical scenes or regions, or individuals rather than groups.[14] For instance, there are books on Miles Davis's career as a whole, and on segments of it, but there are no books that I know of dedicated specifically to any of the bands that he led, although in the latter half of his career his contribution as a bandleader was arguably as significant as his contribution as an instrumentalist.[15] There are a few, rare exceptions, such as Paul Steinbeck's *Message to Our Folks: The Art Ensemble of Chicago*, but, even there, it is significant that the group's self-description as an "art ensemble" indicates a claim for validation as a high-art institution rather than a mere group.

In other words, the discourse about jazz and improvised music often presents the individual as being fitted within the context of his or her scene or tradition, and the *band* as being less important. It acquires its significance insofar as it provides the vehicle for the realization of a given musician's musical goals, or the space within which the dialogues between individual musicians can take place. We might talk about Musician X, whose sound is characteristic of mid-1950s Detroit tenor players, with some influence from what was going on in St. Louis, and who was influenced by Musicians Y and Z. Musician X certainly played in bands, but those bands will probably not be the focus of our discussion (except insofar as the bands are presented as the manifestation of a given musician's compositional or conceptual development)—instead, we will focus on Musician X, Musician X's branch of the tradition, and the other musicians Musician X worked with.

Consequently, a good deal of the writing on jazz and jazz-derived improvisation has had a strongly dialogic focus, in two ways. Jazz music-making is often presented as an activity whose goal is to produce a space—defined conceptually by the tradition or scene—that structures the sorts of dialogues that the individual players can have with each other, Ingrid Monson's *Saying Something: Jazz Improvisation and Interaction* and Paul Berliner's *Thinking in Jazz* being the classic examples. Sometimes the conceptual space is felt to be too constricting, and then liberatory impulses arise, seeking to loosen the rules, as we see throughout the history of jazz, perhaps most strongly— certainly archetypally—in the creation of free jazz. At other times, or with other people, there will be the perception that the dialogues need tighter structures in order to be meaningful, and then there comes a call for more fixed forms or greater respect for tradition.

Alternately, the musician's tradition can be presented as a dialogue partner, when the musician's musical choices are analyzed as responses to the traditions within which he or she is working, and the other musicians present assume the role of assistants or bystanders in these interactions with the tradition. For a very clear example, see Hall Crook's discussion of tradition in the introduction to his instructional book, *Ready, Aim, Improvise: Exploring the Basics of Jazz Improvisation*: "Of course, a certain degree of originality . . . is important when improvising in the jazz idiom. But here, especially during the early stages of learning how to improvise, a soloist's search for originality must be balanced and tempered with authenticity and tradition. . . . Knowing traditional jazz vocabulary influences the shapes and sounds of a player's more modern and creative improvised ideas."[16] Or, as Paul Berliner puts it, you "learn to speak jazz" by "acquiring a complex vocabulary of conventional phrases and phrase components."[17]

This approach to the analysis of music, however, is not the only way to go about things. In between the extremes of the individual and the scene or tradition there lies the middle ground of the band, and there are musical traditions in which the band, not the individual musician, is the privileged vehicle of musical identity—rock being one of them.

Of course, when dealing with a continuum, there are no hard and fast divisions. For example, the classic Coltrane Quartet, made up of John Coltrane, McCoy Tyner, Elvin Jones, and Jimmy Garrison, is one of modern jazz's greatest icons, and it is iconic not just because of the musicianship of the individuals—and this despite the virtual deification of John Coltrane— but also because of the group feeling that has been attached to it. Thus Eric Nisenson speaks of Jimmy Garrison joining the group by saying that he was "the last piece to [Coltrane's] classic group" and goes on to say that the group became "a whole greater than the sum of its parts but absolutely dependent on each of the four parts."[18] Bill Cole, too, takes Garrison's arrival as creating something sui generis: "These weren't just four individuals in Trane's band, but a unit led by a matured spirit. . . . The fruits of the quartet's relationship began to manifest themselves from the moment that Garrison stepped into the band."[19]

Such an appreciation for the band as a musical grouping is not entirely alien to jazz, then, but it is not foregrounded the way that it is in some other traditions. Jazz bands, for all their distinctness, are often closely identified with the leader, as with Miles Davis's classic quintet and subsequent electric bands, or with the orchestras of Count Basie or Duke Ellington; from the late 1960s on, the presentation of a jazz group as a group is often accompanied by an association with a rock or pop context, as in the case of Weather Report or Return to Forever.

While this group feeling is not unknown in jazz contexts, it is fundamental in the rock world(s): rock musicians tend to be strongly associated with bands, and even many of the apparent exceptions such as Neil Young or Bruce Springsteen have strong ties to their previous or ongoing bands. Indeed, when artists who are regarded both as solo performers and group members rejoin their original bands, it often reads as a move back to rock from folk, pop, or whatever genre the solo artist is associated with. When Neil Young works with Crazy Horse, or Springsteen with the E Street Band, or Elvis Costello with some version of the Attractions, or Belinda Carlisle with the Go-Gos, the choice connotes a desire to "rock out" again.[20]

Rock musicians are individuals just as jazz musicians are, of course, and they live and work in a scene, but the core of the rock scene, conceptually and practically, is the band, which coalesces out of the individuals in the scene. Bands are units, more or less stable, whose artistic role is to create a unique group approach to music. In their richest and most successful manifestations, such group approaches create a whole symbolic or mythological universe, a cosmos with distinctive approaches to symbolism, iconography, and, for lack of a better word, headspace, as well as music. Think of the archetypal rock bands, whether the Beatles, Led Zeppelin, the Ramones, or REM: the individual members are deeply important, but that importance comes out in terms of how they all, together, make up the group.

Thus, for rock players, the band becomes the fundamental location of identity, and the creation of the band and development of its unique approach is the musician's basic task. We can illustrate the difference this way: jazz musicians (and, by and large, most other improvisers, in my experience) establish their backgrounds and social status by talking about which people they've played with; rockers talk about the bands they have been in.

The band is a social context that can not only produce extremely interesting music-related art; it also provides a wonderful example of one way in which we can steer our artistic practice past the Scylla of facile individualism and the Charybdis of sterile and anonymous social process; thus it can provide a model for our nonart practice as well. Thinking in terms of bands valorizes the creation of unique, nuanced, and collaborative works of art that have organic extension through time. Working in a group places great demands—artistic and social—on musicians and listeners (it can be difficult for listeners or players raised on or in more dialogic art forms to fully appreciate or even perceive the subtle artistic worlds that bands create, as anyone who has defended rock to a jazz snob will appreciate), but, when the band is successful, these demands are more than repaid by the quality of music produced, and by just how uniquely interesting it can become.

For those of us who grew up in the rock tradition, bands are a marvelous example of how a small group of people can come together and do more than just create marvelous works of art: in fact, what bands do is to create themselves both as works of art, and as the contexts in which further works of art can arise. Bands are magic, and we might even go so far as to say that rock itself starts getting truly and distinctively magical when the 1950s leader or leader-and-sideman approach (e.g., Chuck Berry, Buddy Holly and the Crickets) gives way to the 1960s band approach (e.g., the Beatles, the Beach Boys, the Rolling Stones). Bands are like a person created through the fusion of four or more other people, each with their own unique role to play in this larger being—which is very reminiscent of science fiction author Theodore Sturgeon's book *More than Human*, in which a small group of mutants come together to create a gestalt groupmind. (Not at all coincidentally, *More than Human* was a big influence on the Grateful Dead, as we will discuss.)

By defining themselves clearly as a *band*, the Grateful Dead fit into the mainstream of the rock and popular music tradition; as an *improvising band*, though, they stand out. Given that we are thinking in terms of bands, and keeping the Grateful Dead's focus on dancing in mind, it might seem logical here to draw a comparison with a funk band. Here, as is the case with the Grateful Dead, the soloist is not ignored, but is even accorded the foreground; nonetheless, the emphasis remains on the group as a cohesive unit whose purpose is to induce dancing. However, funk music is often static in a way that the Grateful Dead never are (it sets up grooves and maintains them, where the Grateful Dead move through grooves), and is also precisely and polyrhythmically organized (we will discuss rhythmic congresence in African American music in chapter 4), whereas the Grateful Dead's modus operandi allows for—even requires—a great deal of creative disorganization. For good or bad, the Grateful Dead are messy in ways that no self-respecting funk band would want to be.

Maybe a better comparison would be with an African dance band—say, a Nigerian juju or highlife band: in listening to the music of such artists as I. K. Dairo, the Oriental Brothers, or Sunny Adé, we find the same focus on the group as a gathering of individuals and the soloist as an element within that group, the same extended songs, the same openness to changing parts and lines to suit new developments in the music or its surrounding context, the same willingness to accept and even revel in a certain degree of looseness, or openness: see, for instance, John Miller Chernoff's *African Rhythm and African Sensibility*, or simply listen to I. K. Dairo.[21]

There certainly are musical precedents for the Grateful Dead's approach to music; however, nonmusical influences also play a role. As I have noted, my argument in this book is that, during this period, the band members were on what can be understood at least in part as a religious or spiritual quest. Their goal, to judge from extant testimony, was to create a group consciousness that would enhance or fulfill rather than suppress the individuality of the various band members, and that would be able to create in spontaneous yet unified ways, with its members being intuitively in sync. As Lesh puts it, they were seeking "to learn, above all, how to play together, to entrain, to become, as we described it then, 'fingers on a hand.' . . . The unique organicity of our playing reflects the fact that each of us consciously personalized his playing; to fit with what the others were playing, and to fit with who each man was as an individual, allowing us to meld our consciousnesses together in the unity of a group mind."[22]

This sort of perception of experiences of group consciousness could well be attributed to the band's use of LSD (with the exception of Pigpen) and their willingness to be influenced by experiences and insights received while tripping. But the band's drive to create this group consciousness could also be framed in terms of contemporary American popular culture, specifically contemporary science fiction. Lesh says that, "for us, the philosophical basis of this concept was articulated" in *More than Human*, and in his autobiography Lesh uses Sturgeon's neologism "blesh" ("blend" and "mesh") to describe the state of group consciousness.[23] Related descriptions of small but advanced groups being linked mentally can be found in many other classic works of science fiction popular at the time, including Robert Heinlein's *Stranger in a Strange Land* and "Lost Legacy," Olaf Stapledon's *Odd John*, Frederick Pohl and C. M. Kornbluth's *Wolfbane*, and Henry Kuttner's *Mutant*, to name just a few.

In fact, the hopes and aspirations for radical transformation (whether on a personal, social, cosmic, or species level) that are found in speculative fiction, in the form of books, stories, and comics, played an underappreciated role in the various intellectual and cultural revolutions of the 1960s. Ken Kesey and his guerilla art group, the Merry Pranksters, treated several science fiction books as "precognitive myths," including *More than Human, Stranger in a Strange Land*, and Arthur C. Clarke's *Childhood's End*.[24] Thomas Wolfe brings out the importance of comic books for Kesey, and their importance is also noted by hippie religious leader Stephen Gaskin—his friends would "use metaphors from comic books in their trips."[25] For any contemporary reader of speculative fiction, the group consciousness theme would have been difficult to avoid, especially after having been sensitized to it through shared psychedelic experience, and as Daniel Merkur has really clearly demonstrated, this idea of group consciousness was fundamental to both the experience and the aspirations of the spiritual seekers in San Francisco as they transitioned from beatniks to hippies.[26] With the unitive experiences of LSD use supported by their social environment and echoed in contemporary popular literature, it is no surprise that the band incorporated such aspirations into their art.

The flexible group consciousness that was the Grateful Dead's raison d'être is manifested in several interesting ways. First of all, it is noteworthy that traditional instrumental roles are rarely challenged in the band. It is rare indeed, especially in the early days, for Weir or Lesh to play a solo—Weir plays chords or rhythm fills; beginning in mid-1966, Lesh takes on a frontline role that was uncommon for contemporary rock bass playing, but he is a very active member of the rhythm section, rather than a soloist per se. Conversely, Garcia's guitar is almost always the lead instrument.

But, although Garcia is the lead voice, he is not always the leader. As we will see, the impetus to move the band into new musical spaces can and does come from any of the members; any one of them can become the momentary center of musical attention, the group's leader, and the others will adapt their parts accordingly.[27] In other words, the traditional rock division of roles within the group (lead guitar playing lead lines and melodies; bass playing lines that establish the rhythm and harmony; rhythm guitar playing midrange lines and chords; drums playing the rhythm and giving signaling structural changes; keyboards playing chords and ostinatos) is largely retained; what changes is where the emphasis is placed at any given point, the source of that moment's guiding inspiration. The vision of the band as being a whole, and each of the musicians as playing a given and predetermined role within that whole, based on their instrument, is firmly maintained. To put it simply, the Grateful Dead's improvisational procedure does not challenge our expectations of a rock band's division of labor; it merely *extends* them.

Practically speaking, this choice lessens the "shock of the new" for the band's audience, enabling the band to continue to function as the dance ensemble that at heart they were. On a more abstract level, to return to the realms of science fiction, it brings to mind Sturgeon's group mind in *More than Human*, whose members have interlocking but separate and defined roles. Moving from the literary back alleys of science fiction to the thoroughfares of organized religion, this is also and crucially reminiscent of the Christian tradition of seeing the community of believers as one body with each of the parts having its separate roles, a tradition that stretches back to the ecstatic Christian community addressed in Paul's Corinthian correspondence (1 Cor. 12:4–31). Such a comparison might seem far-fetched, but there is evidence behind it; Phil Lesh, for one, has invoked traditional Christian sacramental terminology to describe the effect of the Grateful Dead's music, referring to improvising as "praying" and saying that their approach to musical transcendence is to play and then "hope" that "the dove descends."[28] In the epilogue to his autobiography, he strikes the messianic note very strongly: "It felt as if we were an integral part of some cosmic plan to help transform human consciousness."[29]

As the traditional instrumental roles are more or less unchallenged, so, too, do song forms retain their integrity. Some aspects of these forms are treated as being mutable, in the sense that there might be a variable amount of time spent grooving before a song starts, or instrumental breaks might extend for an extra few bars.[30] But, by and large, songs are played the same way every time, with the improvisational section occupying a precise and unchanging (save for its length) slot in the tune. While the amount of time that the band spends jamming between verses in "China Cat Sunflower" may vary, the order of verses in the song is fixed, as is the modulation from G to E for the second major instrumental break. The essential structure of the songs, like the traditional roles of the players, is respected, if elastic.

And as with the song, so with the playing. The Grateful Dead's music almost always has, if not a precise rhythm, then at least a strong pulse. Although energetic, it is rarely chaotic. While the band frequently abandons specific chord changes, their music usually has a clear tonal center, and extremes of strong dissonance are generally avoided, at most being treated as special effects. At its heart, the Grateful Dead's music remains traditional and easily comprehensible in ways that do not apply, for instance, to the music of more "out" contemporaries such as Albert Ayler, Cecil Taylor, or AMM.

In other words, the music that the band produces is experimental in a distinctly modernist way: it plays *through* forms, more than playing *within* forms, but it does so without a postmodern flaunting of disturbance or abnormality. The band is not showing off how radical they are: they are just playing. The Grateful Dead's real innovation, their distinctive approach, lies in their determination to show the potentialities that lie hidden within the structures and codes that make up normal lived experience. What the Grateful Dead do is not so much change these codes and structures—the song remains a song, the band remains a band—but, rather, crack them open and show the freedom at their heart.

I referred earlier to Nicholas Meriwether's relatively unusual validation of the band's early work. I want to return to his comment in *The Deadhead's Taping Compendium*, this time with a bit more context. He writes that, "from their first definite if inchoate stirrings in 1966 through their last shows, there was usually an element in the Dead's jams that approached what they began to do more formally beginning in 1967 . . . a free-form group improvisation."[31] As Meriwether points out, this "element" took time to develop, which is understandable given its novelty—and not only time, but a mechanism by which, or a conceptual playing context within which, it could be nurtured. This context, which for the sake of simplicity I call the Framework, can be discerned through the analysis of the band's earliest forays into improvisational rock.

The Framework

The Framework, the conceptual model that underlies the band's first explorations into improvisation, can be summarized as follows:

- Extended improvised sections *may* occur in some songs (such as "You Don't Have To Ask"); invariably *do* occur in other songs (such as "Viola Lee Blues"); and *do not* occur in yet other songs (such as "Cold Rain and Snow").
- When they happen, these extended improvisational sections occur at the end of the song, after the form has been played through, although shorter, more restricted improvisational sections may occur at the very start of the song or between verses.

- The extended improvisational sections emerge from the main groove of the song, as defined by a combination of rhythm, characteristic riffs, and harmonic movement, and return to it when they are finished.
- The improvisational sections are made up of a variable number of smaller sections, each lasting from fifteen to sixty seconds.
- Movement between these sections will be initiated by band members making musical statements that are either joined by other band members or used by them in constructing new musical contexts.
- Any member can make such statements.
- Although traditional instrumental roles are not challenged, any of the band members can opt to move into the foreground; thus leadership both in terms of direction between contexts, and within a given context, is potentially available to any member.
- Jamming sections tend to conclude with a climax, a high point (if not necessarily the highest point) in terms of dynamics, volume, or frenzy.
- Following this climax, the band will frequently either reintroduce the main groove of the song, with or without a sung coda, or play the song's characteristic riff.

In the period discussed here (1965–67), extended improvisational activity takes place in a number of songs, the most notable of which are listed in TABLE 3.1. The amount of improvisation in the band's sets steadily increases as time goes on. Thus, for example, while there is only one extended number, "Caution," in the set from February 25, 1966, by October 22, 1967, the entire set is made up of pieces that feature extended improvisation. From 1966 to 1969 there is a gradual increase in the amount of improvisational activity in the band's sets, both in terms of the number of songs with such activity and in terms of the length of the improvisations. (In the appendix of personnel and performances, you'll find archive.org links to all the shows that I discuss.)

Of the various styles of songs in the Grateful Dead's repertoire, the least represented in this list are the driving rock or folk-rock tunes such as "Going down the Road Feeling Bad" (which only later became an extended vehicle), "Cold Rain and Snow," or "You Don't Have to Ask," with the Love-inspired "Cream Puff War" being an exception to this general rule.

I should also note here that the improvisations found in Pigpen-sung R&B or blues rave-ups with extended vocal exhortations (especially "In the

TABLE 3.1. Improvisational Activity of the Grateful Dead (1965–67)

Song	Significant Improvisational Activity
"Alligator"	Always
"Caution (Do Not Stop on Tracks)"	Always
"Cream Puff War"	Sometimes
"Dancing in the Streets"	Always
"Death Don't Have No Mercy"	Sometimes
"Good Morning, Little Schoolgirl"	Sometimes
"In the Midnight Hour"	Always
"Morning Dew"	Sometimes
"New Potato Caboose"	Always
"The Other One"	Always
"The Same Thing"	Sometimes
"(Turn On Your) Love Light"	Always
"Viola Lee Blues"	Always

Midnight Hour," "Good Morning Little Schoolgirl," and "[Turn on Your] Love Light") are structured differently from that found in the other material, and I will discuss them later on. In fact, even from the band's early period there are two streams of improvisational practice at work. One stream led the band into fairly open improvisation, in which potentially all aspects of a song, including its rhythm and harmony, could be spontaneously renegotiated. The approach to jamming that the band adopted for the material led by Pigpen, by contrast, is less open (albeit frequently more danceable), especially in terms of the basic rhythm and the harmony, which do not vary. The Pigpen songs represent a less radical form of improvisation: it is not so very different from what one could hear other rock, blues, and R&B bands do when they "stretched out" in concert.

With regard specifically to the Framework material (i.e., the non-Pigpen songs), in the period currently under discussion improvisation takes place in up to three sections in a song:

1 in the introduction, in which case it is relatively restrained;
2 in brief instrumental statements between verses, again with restrained improvisation; and
3 in full-on jamming sections that take place at the end of the song, after the verses have been sung—at a point where one could imagine the song going into a fadeout, were it a 45 rpm single.

For example, a typical performance of "Viola Lee Blues," a blues composed by Noah Lewis and first recorded by him with Cannon's Jug Stompers, would begin with the main groove, with some elaboration, perhaps in the form of a guitar solo, followed by the first verse.[32] Between the first and second verse, there would be more elaboration, again most likely in the form of a guitar solo, with the band getting somewhat more expansive; following this would come the third verse, and after this the jamming would begin in earnest.

At this early stage in their career, the Grateful Dead do not jam from one song into the next—or, at least, extant recordings have not preserved examples of this. Nor do they develop songs out of amorphous beginnings ("jam into a song," as a Deadhead would say); rather, songs will definitely start, following the clear finish of preceding songs, and they will begin with the form—or, if not the form, then at least with a statement of the main groove. This statement, if present, may be extended, but rarely for very long, and what jamming takes place stays fairly close to the original groove.

As a concrete example, take the version of "Cream Puff War" performed on October 7, 1966. The instrumental section begins (2:04) with Garcia soloing over a two-chord vamp. After four times through the progression, the band moves to slightly different territory, cued by Lesh's choice to extend the main chord slightly (2:28), to which Garcia responds by going up the neck into a higher, modal solo. They play the progression another four times through, as Lesh increases both his level of activity and the intensity of his playing. This rise in dynamics cues Kreutzmann to bring things together with some propulsive hits (3:16) as Lesh continues his driving bass line.

At several points in the jam (e.g., 3:36) it sounds as if Garcia and Lesh are thinking in terms of a one-chord structure, dropping the second chord of the vamp, but Pigpen's monotonous riffing on the organ prevents this change. Weir shows his willingness to suspend the chord progression (e.g., 4:16–19), and introduces a very effective high chord at 4:39, incorporating drone strings that move the jam into a more ambiguous, open, context before it returns to the vamp at 4:51. This in turn leads into the cue for the end of the song at 5:25, indicating that this open section—the high point of chaos and uncertainty in the improvisation—has been taken by the band to be the climax to the piece.

This piece clearly demonstrates the movement from the song proper into the jamming section and also shows how changes in harmonic motion can be used as markers. It is significant that the Grateful Dead's trajectory in this regard is toward simplicity and ambiguity. Although the main groove here involves a two-chord vamp, there is a tendency to break away from that vamp in favor of harmonic stasis (as in the case of Garcia and Lesh's tendencies to extend the first chord in the vamp) or, more subtly, in favor of creating a harmonically ambiguous area, essentially conceiving of the general tonal environment of the jam as a mode rather than a chord.

This tendency can be seen quite clearly in the band's treatment of blues and blues-related tunes, in which turnarounds and standard I–IV–I–V–I progressions are used during the verses and then often drop out of the improvisational sections. One striking example of this is their treatment of "Death Don't Have No Mercy" from March 19, 1966, in which the band chooses to understate the chord changes at 2:34–50, in order to keep the open drone on I going, or at 3:34–47, when they stay on the main chord following a turnaround, rather than immediately move into the form and its chord changes. The blues song "The Same Thing" is limited in harmonic motion, with no move to the IV chord in the middle of its progression (i.e., the change in harmony that usually happens on the second line of the verse in a blues song) and only a final turnaround from the V chord back to the I, but even this harmonic motion tends to be dropped as the band improvises, as can be heard in their performance on September 16, 1966. In fact, the Framework was in a developed state by that time, and the breakdown, in TABLE 3.2, of the version of "Dancing in the Streets" performed at that show illustrates how it was put to service in performance.

Jamming

As we just saw (and heard, if you are using the links in the footnotes to listen along), the jamming section will begin at the end of the form, at the point where a contemporary pop recording might go into a fadeout. As Bob Weir put it, in the Framework the improvisation comes in at the point where "we weren't done playing, but the tune was over."[33] The Grateful Dead do not introduce these sections abruptly; there is no jarring discontinuity or sudden change in basic musical parameters. Instead, they begin by simply continuing the main groove of the song, playing in a controlled, precise fashion, usually gradually bringing the dynamics up, and almost always with an introductory guitar statement by Garcia. They ease the listeners into the jam, keeping the dancers dancing and establishing a point of reference for later explorations.

As an example of this process, take the May 19, 1966, version of "Cream Puff War." As they vamp over the main riff, Kreutzmann begins smoothing out the song's pronounced 3–3–2 rhythmic accents into a straight 4/4 backbeat (at 2:22). As he is doing this, Garcia loops a lead figure above him as

TABLE 3.2. The Framework for Improvisation in Action:
"Dancing in the Streets" (9/16/1966)

Time	Event
0:01–0:08	Introduction, with the band playing the basic groove: a mid-tempo rock backbeat with a two-bar, two-chord pattern that moves from I–bVII; both the rhythm and the harmony create a call-and-response pattern, with the second bar responding to the first.
0:09–2:07	Body of the song, Weir singing lead throughout.
2:05–2:38	Beginning of the jamming: the band starts by playing the introductory groove while Garcia plays a lead, with emphasis on triplets; as time goes on, the rest of the band (led by Kreutzmann, cuing with a drum roll at approximately 2:20) begins smoothing out the rhythm so that the underlying feel is simply a backbeat, with less of the call-and-response feel.
2:39–2:42	Garcia pauses; Weir comes briefly to the forefront, calming the music down.
2:43–3:06	Garcia returns to soloing at the same high volume and with the same trebly timbre, but the rest of the band plays more quietly before coming up in volume and dynamics again at approximately 2:50, with Pigpen playing an offbeat pattern that drives the rhythm.
3:07–3:32	Pigpen moves away from an offbeat pattern to play sustained chords; when he ceases, the band brings the dynamics down somewhat, although Lesh gets more active throughout this section.
3:32–3:44	Garcia ends his lead and switches to playing a simple two-bar figure emphasizing A, B, and G over a droning A an octave below; Weir plays a high voicing over top of Garcia's rhythm; Pigpen fits his chords into this structure, creating a dense and disorienting texture.
3:40–4:04	Lesh moves into the forefront, no longer playing lines or establishing the rhythm, but playing over it with a strong triplet feel; Garcia breaks off briefly (3:46–3:52) from his riff to play a complementary line and then returns to the riff.
4:04–4:48	Garcia begins soloing again, while Lesh continues to play strong, active lines; Pigpen switches to playing a single note riff in a two-bar pattern with occasional chord pushes that sound haphazard, not in precise time with the rhythm.
4:49–4:57	Weir moves into the foreground with a high held note; following this, Weir creates harmonic tension by emphasizing the I strongly and builds rhythmic tension by playing against the rhythm.

TABLE 3.2. (*continued*)

Time	Event
4:56–5:26	Lesh moves into the upper register, creating the preclimax feeling; Weir keeps playing high chords, but places them even more jaggedly. At this point, only Pigpen is keeping the chord changes going; the combination of heightened dynamics, lack of harmonic motion, and movement of the bass into its upper register create a chaotic, climactic feeling.
5:27	The band settles down into the main groove again.
5:32	Weir starts singing the final chorus.

a holding pattern, providing stability while this rhythmic change is being worked out. After ten seconds of this, Kreutzmann starts incorporating the accents of Garcia's phrase into his playing; by 2:42, it is clear that the band has moved into the jamming section proper, and Garcia takes off into a solo.

What goes on while the band is jamming? It is not a question of riffing, of the rhythm section playing ostinatos while one member solos. Nor is it a question of the band settling into a solid groove and riding it the way that James Brown's band might have done. Rather, the Grateful Dead's practice in the midst of jamming can be likened to that of a jazz rhythm section. The parameters (e.g., tonal, rhythmic, melodic) of the piece are understood, the feel is broadly expressed, but within that context the players are free to play as they see fit, continually adjusting their lines and phrasing to express their take on what is happening at any given moment or to respond to what the other players are doing—and also, potentially, aspects of the song's harmony or rhythm.

The major point of potential difference would be that, most of the time, a jazz rhythm section is carrying out all of this activity against the backdrop of a more or less defined song structure, ranging in specificity from the rigidity of a standard to the openness of a piece based around modes and having few chord changes. When the Grateful Dead are jamming, the texture against which they are working at any given moment tends to be understood as a certain tonality, a certain dynamic level, and a certain rhythmic feel—keeping in mind that the band's tendency is to break down chord changes, thus emphasizing the bare, unadorned tonal centers of the songs more strongly. When they are jamming, the band creates an undulating, loosely unified space, filled by the different voices of the various band members making their own idiosyncratic contributions from moment to moment. We might say that the players are playing over top of a musical backdrop which they themselves are collectively engaged in creating; they're playing with form even as they are establishing it.[34]

The version of "Dancing in the Streets" performed on March 18, 1967, features a particularly elegant and illustrative entry into the improvisational section. The jamming starts (2:05) as a guitar solo played over the main groove, and the song continues in this vein for 20 seconds. At 2:24 Kreutzmann interjects a series of small drum fills that function as pointers, indicating that the texture is changing. Lesh responds to this at 2:30 with an extra few notes before returning to the main groove. By 2:40 the jam is in motion. Garcia finishes one statement and leaves a little bit of space; Weir immediately increases his volume and Kreutzmann also gets more active, driving the rhythm. Garcia then launches into another statement, playing more aggressively, picking up on Kreutzmann's increased energy; by 3:02 Weir joins in by playing open, ringing chords rather than clipped ones, and Lesh is beginning to roam more freely. Having moved through this gradual increase of dynamics, they coast on this level for 30 seconds or so until Garcia signals the move into a new context.

In this brief segment, we can hear the musical "ball" being passed from player to player, featuring the incremental intensification of the collective music through players responding to each other's markers, in this way moving from the main groove of the song into uncharted territory. The art of working successfully in this style lies in creating a musical space that is well enough defined to give the band something to play off of and the dancers something to dance to, and yet not so precisely defined that it inhibits spontaneous action and reactions. It is the combination of having boundaries *and* open space that they surround and protect.

The jamming sections are always full of motion, and this is particularly noticeable in terms of the rhythm section's playing. As we have discussed, the Grateful Dead do not work in terms of a lead guitarist soloing over a static backing band. Garcia is the lead voice, yes, but that just denotes his function, just as it is Weir's function to play the role of rhythm guitarist. The nature of the Dead's music is such that, while those roles or functions are maintained, people are free to jam within their roles. The overall group feel is created through continuous and independent although united movement in all the voices (Pigpen being the member most likely to simply riff through jams).

In addition to this continual motion of the individual band members, several characteristics of the group's playing are significant in keeping the jamming sections mobile and interesting. First of all, especially as the jams lengthen, there is an ongoing alternation between periods of expansion and contraction, particularly in terms of dynamics or rhythm. The band is continually moving to a high point—of intensity; of rhythmic drive; of volume; generally, of excitement—briefly sustaining it, and then moving back to a lower point. The rare exceptions to this principle (such as the extended, droning three-note riff in "Viola Lee Blues") are effective precisely because they are exceptions. When the riff does come in, you find yourself mesmerized partly because of the tremendous contrast between its stasis and the ongoing motion that is the more usual rule.

In addition to this rise and fall motion, there is also ongoing motion in terms of shifting the contexts of the jam. Broadly speaking, the band stays in any given "feel" for not less than fifteen seconds, and not more than a minute. At regular intervals, some aspect of the feel will change, whether that means someone introducing a new harmonic texture into the jam or dissolving harmonic progressions (often Weir's approach), tightening up or loosening the rhythm (typical of Kreutzmann), significant shifts in register or attack (Lesh), or looping riffs that are used as jumping-off points (Garcia).

Take, for example, the version of the blues standard "The Same Thing" performed on November 29, 1966. The improvisational section of this performance is carefully and subtly developed, offering a particularly translucent version of the band's process. The improvisational section begins (4:49) with Garcia's solo over a more or less static backdrop. By 5:15 the intensity of the band has definitely begun to increase, cued by Lesh. Garcia teasingly introduces a brief figure at 5:39, joined by Lesh to create a momentary respite from the main groove of the song. But he very soon drops the figure, only to bring it back again at 6:06, where it is looped and used as a marker to cue a leisurely intensification that smoothly turns into a double-time acceleration at 6:56. By 7:30 they have settled into a quick shuffle rhythm, with Garcia playing low notes and the whole band producing a very dense rhythmic structure, which Garcia eventually breaks out of (8:04), and then back into (at 8:24), quickly breaking out yet again to start another statement. At 8:51 comes what I think is the most interesting part of the jam. Garcia begins looping a triplet riff, holding it for close to 30 seconds as the rest of the band assimilates this new context—Lesh by droning; Weir by staying on one chord and moving from playing a counterrhythm to firmly supporting Garcia's rhythm; Pigpen by introducing a very effective high organ voicing. Overall, the effect is of something opening up, like a flower unfolding its petals. It is a lovely, evocative moment. Just as it threatens to become dissonant (with the dissonance led by Weir), Garcia breaks loose to continue his solo.

Here we have seen the regularity of the movement between sections, with significant changes in context taking place roughly every 30 seconds—enough time for the listener or dancer to get the feel of a new context, but not enough time for them to grow bored. Although many of the changes were cued by Garcia, the piece does not come off as a guitar showcase, but as a collective movement through different environments. Here, as elsewhere, Garcia is the leader, by virtue of his sensitivity to possibilities and his willingness to point the way to new adventures; this is more of a "first among equals" situation than the leadership often assumed by a lead guitarist.

Changes in feel will usually be signaled and initiated by one member briefly rising to the fore and making a musical statement, leading the other band members to echo or respond to it. These rise-with-statement moments we can understand as *markers*, and generally speaking they perform one of two functions.

Sometimes markers work as statements that lead the way to momentary interludes that involve focusing via playing a riff or tightening up the rhythm, as we find, for example, in the version of "Dancing in the Streets" played on September 3, 1967. From about 5:15 to around 6:38, the band is jamming in an open, free-floating conversational context that extant recordings suggest is unprecedented at this point in their career. At 6:38, however, things solidify: Lesh introduces a riff in 7/4 that is quickly picked up by Garcia; this marker serves as a grounding, in that it briefly anchors the jam, bringing them down to earth before they return to floating territory.

At other times, markers work as statements that inspire the band to change feels, whether to a great or small extent; in these cases, we could refer to them as *pointers*. An example of a pointer would be Lesh's bass run at 2:43–45 in the same version of "Dancing in the Streets," which problematizes the tonality of the jam and suggests a move into the "spacey" atmosphere that prevails in the next section of the jam.

Pointers may lead the way into new territory, or they may simply signal that someone thinks that the given feel has gone on long enough and is suggesting that things change, without necessarily taking a stand on how they should change, as is the case with Garcia's looped triplet riff in "The Same Thing."

Pointers lead to new musical territory, while groundings provide a momentary contrast to the more free-floating textures that are typical of the jamming section. Some markers are clearly intended to belong to a specific category when played, but often their ultimate function will be determined retrospectively, depending on the reception that the marker receives from

Ex. 3.1 & 3.2 . Phil Lesh's riff in 7/4 (*top*) at 6:38 and his bass run (*bottom*) at 2:43 in "Dancing in the Streets," both from the performance on 9/3/1967.

the rest of the band. An example of this can be found in the version of "Alligator," performed May 5, 1967. The jam begins at 3:15; by 3:59, Garcia has finished his introductory statement and Lesh has descended to an ominous low note. Garcia takes these markers as pointers, ushering in a somewhat new texture by playing lower and more quietly; Lesh, on the other hand, seems to take them as groundings, momentary respites before he returns to the fray, this time accompanied by Pigpen. Overall, markers can be, and are, played by any of the members of the band (with Pigpen using them least), usually in ways that reflect their traditional instrumental roles—for instance, Weir will usually play markers that involve harmonic changes or chordal riffs, whereas Garcia's markers involve melodic lines or single note riffs.

Jam sections end with a climax, built by the group as a whole, although their onset is frequently cued by Garcia. Typically, this climax will be at a high point in terms of the intensity and volume of the playing, but not necessarily the highest point in the jam. Rather, the climax is distinguished by the fact that it presents the most dissonant or chaotic playing in the song, the point where things come the closest to sounding out of control. While some climaxes may arise from spontaneous excitement, it is clear from other cases that this is a deliberate strategy—and an effective one, providing a moment of tension that is simultaneously a moment of destructive liberation, as the forms that the band has been manipulating momentarily dissolve and the listener is brought face to face with the raw sound that underlies all form.

It is typical of the Grateful Dead's aesthetic as a dance band, no matter how experimental, that such moments are nonetheless controlled, in two ways. First of all, the climaxes themselves are not as noisy, as extended, or as dissonant as they might have been, especially in the early period; they are mild compared with, for example, contemporary music made by the Velvet Underground or La Monte Young. Chaos is represented, but not enacted. Generally speaking, you can easily imagine them driving dancers into a frenzy, but they are not so disruptive as to make the dancers actually stop dancing, at least in this period—although one noteworthy exception to this is the climax to the "Viola Lee Blues" performed at Toronto's O'Keefe Centre on August 4, 1967, when the music turns into a howling mass of electronic sound, a harbinger of what is to come in the next phase of the band's development.

Secondly, the climaxes are followed by a return to the main groove of the song. This return initiates a settling-down period that is formally similar to the introduction to the jam in reverse—the groove is played, the musicians calm down, and often Garcia will take a solo before the song ends, sometimes with a sung coda that symbolizes a return to the song's form after the jamming section, as they do in "Dancing in the Streets" or "Viola Lee Blues."

Thus, the chaotic part of the jam—and, indeed, the jam as a whole—is encapsulated within the song, in an elegant chiastic structure.[35] We are never in doubt (at this point, anyway) as to what song the band is playing, but it is made clear that the structured, formal face of the song is only part of its identity, only the public face, so to speak; the Grateful Dead's practice unveils the private face as well, the part of the song that opens out into infinity, and that is (theoretically at least) always potentially present. As we will see later on, this desire to crack open forms, to reveal the secret and endlessly creative waves of change that flow through these forms and in fact constitute them, is directly related to their understanding of the religious aspects of their work.

Development of the Framework

The Framework was not the Grateful Dead's ultimate solution to the challenge of improvisation within a rock idiom. There are at least three other models that they developed out of it as their career progressed, including the aggressive "acid rock" approach that came out of the Framework and reached its height in 1968–69; the extremely flexible, layered, and nuanced "jazz-rock" approach that peaked in 1973–74; and a quite formalized and structured approach that was solidified by the end of the 1970s and in which they continued working for the rest of their career.

The Framework should be seen as but one step on a longer journey, and the time frame that we have covered enables us to see it as it is being developed, at its height, and then as it is in the process of being superseded by the next phase of the Grateful Dead's improvisational journey. We will look at these aspects in greater detail later on; here, I will summarize three especially significant alterations to the Framework that took place in 1967 and that eventually led to a new approach to improvisation, which occurred at the set list level, at the song level, and within the jamming sections. Fundamentally, these alterations have to do with the relation between the parts and the whole on different levels, and with a tendency to privilege the latter over the former—or, to put it another way, to see smaller forms as constituents of larger forms.

On the level of the set list, the band moves toward deemphasizing the autonomy of the individual piece. Whereas in the Framework pieces have definite beginnings and definite endings, in the next phase of the Grateful Dead's journey there is a tendency to have starts and endings of many (though not all) songs become amorphous, and frequently connected by jamming. In some cases, such as the "China Cat Sunflower"/ "I Know You Rider" combination, the pairings are consistent—which is the reason why that combo was inevitably referred to as "China/Rider" by Deadheads. But, in other cases, things are much more open, with potentially any song leading into any other—thus, for example, the shocking and (for me, anyway) profoundly disappointing move from "Dark Star," the band's most open and exploratory song, to Marty Robbins's leaden cowboy song "El Paso" that the band performed on August 27, 1972.

The effect of this unpredictable fusion of material, connected by jamming, is to shift the listener's focus up an order of magnitude, so that the set becomes perceived as the basic context, with its constituent songs being the pieces that make it up, rather than the other way around, as would be typical for a rock band. Conceptually, this has parallels with the relationship of the band members to the band as a whole: as the individual songs define but work very much within the collective identity of the set, so, too, the individual players define but work very much within the group spirit and essential unity of the Grateful Dead.

On the level of the individual songs, the old placement of improvisational parts in the "fadeout" section, following a period of grooving on the main riff of the song, is challenged compositionally as the band begins writing sections that function as taking-off spots for improvisation, or what I call *trap doors*. A trap door is a composed piece of music designed to serve as an escape from the song form, a scripted place to initiate the jamming; the classic example is a section of their anthem, "Uncle John's Band," which we will soon discuss. The placement of the jamming section in the song "Alligator"—at the end of the song, but within the song's form rather than in fadeout position over the main groove—is a clear step along this road, as is the placement of the jamming section in "New Potato Caboose."

This development allows for greater variety in terms of the placement and basic premises of improvisational activity, and it also has an effect on the perceived interaction of the composed and improvised sections of songs. The Framework model presents composed and improvised sections as being linked in their contexts of origin—that is, both develop out of the same basic rhythm and tonal area. They are linked by the fact that they come from the same place, and return to it.

On the other hand, the increasing use of compositional placement of improvisational sections unites composed and improvised sections in a different way. Although they may be different in rhythm or tonality, they are seen as constituent parts of the larger whole that they make up. Perhaps the clearest model would be the improvisational section of "Uncle John's Band," a song composed a little later than the period under discussion but sections of which pop up in jams long before the song itself is unveiled. The jamming section for this song is in a different key than the composed section (Dm versus G major), has a different time signature (7/4 versus 4/4), and ends with a bridging chord accompanied by a suspension of the rhythm to enable the players to return to the feel of the composed section of the song.

In all of these instances, the improvisational sections are joined with the composed section; they are not radically discontinuous. But, as was the case with the songs in relation to the set as a whole, so here within the songs we see a move toward deemphasizing the autonomy of the sections in favor of seeing them in terms of, and fitting them into, a larger whole.

Finally, within the improvisational sections we can hear distinct advances, having to do with changes in consistency and density. The tendency in the earlier material was for the jamming sections to be made up of more or less identifiable and distinct segments, with motion between them cued by markers and with the band playing in a relatively restrained manner, often one that was expressive of the dominant idiom of the given section. By mid-1967, however, the band is playing much more exuberantly, particularly Lesh, and they are playing at full tilt, all the time. At any given moment the playing will tend to be more exciting and impressive than before, but it is also true that the long jams can simply be exhausting, lacking in respite or change of atmosphere. The effect is to turn the jams into more homogeneous affairs, again reducing the separations between sections in favor of emphasizing the unity of the whole in which they are contained.

Improvisational Tactics, 1965–1974

ROADS TAKEN, AND SOME
THAT WERE NOT TAKEN

What we're thinking about is, we're thinking, we're trying to think away from solo lines. From the standard routine of *this* member comps, *this* member leads. We're trying to think of ensemble stuff, you know. Not like Dixieland ensemble stuff, [but rather] something which we don't know anything about. —JERRY GARCIA

The Grateful Dead's improvisational practice developed and changed over time, particularly in the first decade of their career. In this chapter I will argue that this practice can be broadly classified under eight headings, or approaches—although, of course, I acknowledge that these divisions are (hopefully) useful tools, not hard and fast rules.

They are also outsider formalizations, and, while I do believe that the analysis that I will present is accurate, I certainly do not intend to argue that the band members themselves formulated things in this way—although certainly they might have. My intent in this chapter is not to lock in our understandings of the Grateful Dead's improvisational practice, but to give us some new ways of looking at it, so as to increase our awareness of and appreciation for its flexibility and nuance, as well as to remind us of the conceptual and practical roots that supported it and made it possible.

Eight Approaches to Improvisation

At least according to what my ears tell me (yours may tell you differently), the eight approaches that the Grateful Dead used to guide their improvisation in their first decade are the following:

1   soloing over changes, in which a song's structure is maintained and a soloist improvises while the rest of the band follows the chord changes and keeps the rhythm flowing;
2   what I call a *dance tunes* model, in which dance songs are stripped down to their most fundamental structural elements and played with a great deal of emphasis on rhythm and dynamics;
3   what I call a *within songs* model, in which a prearranged and unaltered overall structure is nonetheless interpreted spontaneously as the band plays through it;
4   the Framework, which I discussed in chapter 3;
5   sounds, in which the band uses timbre and dynamics as the bases for improvisation;
6   what I call a *movement through sections* model, in which the band collectively improvises its way through a string of predetermined musical feels or environments;
7   what I call a *trap door* model, in which songs are written so as to include a section that dramatically shifts one or more elements of the song and provides a "launching pad" for improvisation; and
8   modules, in which the band, in the course of its improvisational playing, spontaneously invokes and works with small, precomposed musical patterns or progressions.

Two of these approaches—namely, soloing over changes and the dance tunes models—can be easily traced back to models common in popular music. Soloing over changes needs little explanation; basically, it is what people usually mean when they just say "soloing," and the Grateful Dead's use of this approach produced what was perhaps the most traditional of all their improvisational music: Garcia soloed, and the rest of the band played the changes behind him.

The dance tunes model refers to a style of jamming that the band would often engage in during two- and three-chord dance tunes, such as "Turn On your Lovelight" or "Scarlet Begonias." While Pigpen was still alive and appearing with the band, the Pigpen tunes would function as the "dance tunes"—that is, relatively simple songs that put the emphasis on maintaining danceable rhythms, while interest was provided primarily through dynamic changes and fairly subtle textural alterations of the basic feels of the songs. After Pigpen died, and coinciding with the band's move toward playing slower and more spacious music, the Grateful Dead composed or incorporated a number of songs that, it seems to me, filled the same role in the set that the Pigpen songs had, including "Eyes of the World" and "Fire on the Mountain," as well as "Scarlet Begonias": they were the extended dance tunes that rarely "went anywhere" beyond their fundamental grooves and chord changes.

The other improvisational approaches, though not without precedent in music generally, are less commonly found in popular music of the period. The "within songs" model refers to the band's tendency—or, better, their dogged commitment—not to play definite and precisely repeated lines in their pieces, but, rather, to improvise their accompaniments to their songs, even when playing set arrangements with vocal verses and choruses. Although the Grateful Dead as a whole and bassist Phil Lesh in particular take this approach to extremes, as we shall see, the model itself can be seen as a conceptually straightforward use of a jazz approach to rock- and folk-derived material, calling to mind Bob Weir's description of the Grateful Dead as playing rock music with jazz syntax.[1]

Conceptually, literally, or both, the five remaining approaches develop out of or can be related to the Framework, which was, as we have seen, the Grateful Dead's first step in creating a model for the spontaneous improvisation that they chose to practice. To begin with, the Framework itself continues to be recognizably present in their work, from its development in 1966 onward. Secondly, its tendency to climax in "noisy" or relatively open sonic exploration eventually results in the creation of more or less autonomous and improvised pieces of music. This begins with the feedback explorations that the band engaged in, starting in 1967, and continues with the expansive soundscapes that characterized many jams in the 1972–74 period, particularly those emerging from or around the songs "The Other One" and "Playing in the Band."

Another characteristic of the Framework is that it involves the band moving spontaneously through a succession of "feels" or "sections," playing improvisationally but with the overarching harmonic or rhythmic parameters being set in any given section. In such pieces as "New Potato Caboose," the band incorporated this sort of movement into their compositions, in the process adding to the detail and precision of the sections and taking advantage of the freedom offered by composition so that some songs or parts of songs were defined by a predetermined succession of open but precomposed sections.

In the Framework, improvisational jamming begins after the composed material of the song has been played, with the band looping the main riff or rhythmic feel and gradually moving away from it. The main riff, then, provides a "jumping-off point" for the band's improvisations. In the "trap door" approach to improvisation, the band varies the Framework approach, building in sections that lead to improvisation and that vary in placement or content from what we see in the Framework. Finally, when one listens to a number of Grateful Dead jams, one comes to note the presence of a number of themes, or, as I call them, "modules": independent sections that pop up in various songs, punctuating or giving definition to the improvisation.

Four Career Phases

The Grateful Dead's early career can be—needless to say, very roughly—divided into phases, marked by changes in emphases, musical approach and repertoire, lineup, and contextual issues with regard to the culture at large. I would argue that the period between the band's formation and its hiatus in 1974 can be usefully divided into four such phases.

1. In what we can call the "early phase" (late 1965–mid-1967), the band is developing the Framework and learning to jam interactively and spontaneously. During this phase, concerts are presented as collections of many discrete songs, and the band does not jam from one song into another. During the jams, the musicians' links to folk, rock, and blues traditions are very clear: the jams have the feeling of (potentially unlimited) extensions of and variations on older musical forms, rather than creating new forms of their own. In short, at this point they're still playing individual songs, and they are still a more or less "normal" band—they're just learning how to open things up. This matches with the broader context of "hip" culture (or the rock music scene more specifically) at the time: doors were opening, and possibilities were becoming apparent in many different aspects of life, but the backdrop remained "straight," and an entirely alternative lifestyle was not yet conceivable for most. If you watch the movie *A Hard Day's Night*, you'll get a feel for what I mean; in fact, as we saw earlier, Garcia identified this movie as a significant influence in his decision to start playing rock music.

2. In the acid rock phase (mid-1967–late 1969), the band shifts its focus to larger structures and a much greater use of improvisation, including integrating it with composition in novel ways; musical textures become increasingly dense as well. Concerts begin to take on the feeling of a small number of enormously extended pieces, with jamming being often used to obscure the distinctions between potentially or actually independent compositions— hence, for example, in the show performed on March 2, 1969, the second set begins with a four-minute version of "Alligator," followed by a seven-minute drum solo, a twenty-five-minute jam, and then a nine-minute version of "Caution (Do Not Stop on Tracks)," which at times is only distinguished from the preceding jam by its distinctive bass line.[2]

The texture of the band's jams is at its most dense in this period. Not only is the band itself as large (a septet) as it would ever be, but the players (particularly Lesh and Garcia, but also the drummers) play constantly and aggressively, filling in all the potential cracks in the musical texture. The band's sound systems were not as sophisticated as they would later become; thus the mix can frequently become cluttered and overly biased toward the mid-range, at least to judge from the extant recordings. The band's approach to playing in this period coheres with their approach to the set list: the overall effect is to submerge the listener in a totalizing musical experience operating both synchronically (in terms of texture) and diachronically (in terms of the merging together of songs).

Speaking from a broader social context, this period is when the counterculture and the hippie movement grew to their most extreme, with 1968 in particular touching off what could have been worldwide revolution. The Grateful Dead's music during this time captures that feeling of a new world being born, with all the chaos and energy that that implies. Furthermore, the way that it envelops the listener could be understood as creating a complete and alternate world to inhabit. I wasn't around to experience these shows, but they must have been intense, moving attendees (and the band!) into a new world.

3. In what I would call their "Americana phase" (late 1969–72), the band retreats somewhat from the apocalyptic excesses of the acid rock phase, now valorizing more traditional forms of rock, blues, country and folk-pop music. In a sense, they are returning to the approach of the early phase; one could also say that it is a return to their pre-Dead roots for all of the members, except Lesh and Hart. Concerts begin to take on a two-part structure, with more song-based material earlier in the evening, and more extended improvisation later.[3] Particularly in the first set, songs tend to be presented as separate, discrete entities.

Texturally, too, the band is more stripped down in this period than in the acid rock phase. They begin moving in this direction in 1970, even before the departure of drummer Mickey Hart, as can be heard, for example, in the comparatively restrained version of "Caution (Do Not Stop on Tracks)" performed September 20, 1970. When Hart left the band, they were reduced to a quintet (Garcia, Weir, Lesh, Pigpen, Kreutzmann), which, given Pigpen's recurrent illness and tendency to underplay, was often actually or effectively a quartet until Keith Godchaux joined on keyboards in October 1971. There was considerably less jamming in this period than in the acid rock phase: instead of building sets around three or four enormously extended songs, in this period the band would often play an assortment of short songs combined with one or two extended songs.[4]

This deemphasizing of the jamming can be related to the band's desire in this period to be seen as a straight-ahead roots rock group. As Garcia noted of *The Grateful Dead* (a.k.a. *Skull and Roses*), their 1971 live album, "People can see we're like a regular shoot-em-up saloon band"—at least, that is what they were trying to be at that point in the band's career.[5] Such a desire fits well into the context of rock as the 1960s turned into the 1970s. It was a period in which there was a degree of recoil on the part of many rock musicians and fans from the utopian ideals and rampant experimentalism of the late 1960s, in favor of claiming a traditional grounding for rock music and the rock scene, as can be seen from some of the later works of the Beatles, the success of Creedence Clearwater Revival, the Band's late-1960s rise to popularity, and Bob Dylan's turn to country music and his return to sparse, folky music with *John Wesley Harding*, released by Columbia Records in 1967.[6]

4. Just as the song-focused early phase was followed by the heavy-jamming acid rock phase, so, too, the Americana phase is succeeded by what I call the "jazz rock phase" (1972–74), in which improvisational playing again takes the fore. This time, however, the jamming is more leisurely and nuanced than was the case in the acid rock phase, and the band has a wider variety of material to jam on.

The influence of the first generation of jazz-rock or fusion music is evident in this phase, particularly the groundbreaking work of Miles Davis (who opened for the Grateful Dead in April 1970, and whose band included many of the players that performed on his seminal *Bitches Brew*).[7] This is also the period in which the Grateful Dead made considerable advances in their live sound, culminating in the development of the Wall of Sound, an elaborate sound system that presented their music with unparalleled clarity and fidelity.[8] It is quite likely that the improvements to the band's live sound contributed to their musical development, making it easier to conceptualize and deliver the sorts of drifting improvised playing that can be heard, for example, in the "Playing in the Band" performed on November 21, 1973.

As the Americana period was analogous to the early period, this period is reminiscent of the acid rock period, particularly in its renewed use of extended improvisation. However, the difference here is that the two-part structure to concerts, developed in the preceding phase, is still present; indeed, it continues on the road toward the quite formalized approach that will predominate for the rest of the band's career.

The Approaches

Before beginning our in-depth discussion of the approaches that we identified earlier, I should caution that they are not at all mutually exclusive; in fact, they overlap, sometimes considerably. It might be safest to say that they are tactics rather than rules. In this chapter, my goal is to advance the discussion of the Grateful Dead's improvisational approach in three ways—first, by shedding some new light on the specific tactics; second, by bringing these tactics together to create a somewhat comprehensive overview, something that to the best of my knowledge has not been done before; and, third, by discussing improvisational tactics that were *not* used by the Grateful Dead, and taking these roads not taken into consideration along with the roads that were taken.

SOLOING OVER CHANGES

This approach to improvisation needs little introduction, due to its widespread popularity in rock, pop, jazz, folk and blues music. It puts the focus on the lead player, who improvises lines over relatively subordinate and static accompaniment in which backing musicians play predetermined and set riffs, figures, or chord progressions. In rock performances, the soloist will typically be the lead guitarist or the keyboardist; in the Grateful Dead, Jerry Garcia is far and away the predominant soloist, with the keyboardists often working in an accompanist's role. Keith Godchaux, the keyboardist who joined the band in 1971 to replace Pigpen, did play more leads than his predecessor, but Garcia remained the primary soloist nonetheless.

In an interesting discussion with Ralph Gleason in 1969, Jefferson Airplane lead guitarist Jorma Kaukonen argued that the musical incapacity of many rock musicians had diminished the appeal of this traditional approach, saying that "rock rhythm sections are usually so sloppy in terms of laying down a solid foundation for a soloist to solo on, so they [the soloists] have to do other things."[9] Such technical incompetence may well have provided the spur for improvisational creativity for some bands, but this was not the case for the Grateful Dead, who were all competent or better players, especially by the standards of their time and context. In particular, Kreutzmann "was already a working band veteran" and drum teacher when he joined the Grateful Dead;[10] Pigpen was a competent and charismatic blues performer;[11] Garcia had years of experience playing bluegrass and folk music;[12] and Lesh had been trained in composition and had performing experience as a trumpeter.[13] Weir was a rudimentary rhythm guitarist in the band's early years, but his time was good, and he made innovative use of the musical resources that he possessed.

So, if the band did "other things" than just soloing over changes, it was not because they had to. As a band, the Grateful Dead thrived on interactive spontaneity; thus this soloistic approach to improvisation did not feature as strongly in their music as it did in the music of many other blues-influenced rock bands, such as the Allman Brothers. As Lesh noted in one interview, specifically with regard to his own solos but in words that are generally applicable to the band as a whole, "The concept of standing out there and doing a solo just seemed alien to the whole idea of what we were trying to do." The interviewer (Blair Jackson) responded: "It [the Grateful Dead] is an ensemble, first and foremost." Lesh agreed: "Yeah. Essentially, that's what I feel it is. Or that's what it is when it's at its best, because the whole is greater than the sum of its parts."[14]

Of the four chronological periods, the soloing over changes approach to improvisation is most notable in the first and third—that is, periods in which the band is focused on its roots, either because it had not yet developed beyond them (first period) or because it was engaged in a retrenchment, a step back from acid rock adventurousness (third period) and a reconceptualization of their mission, including the incorporation of more traditional approaches to music.

In terms of repertoire, this approach is most prominently found in songs that have clear and strong roots in rock, blues, or country traditions. However, a song's traditional rooting does not necessarily guarantee the adoption of this approach to improvisation. While the band approached such Chuck Berry classics as "Johnny B. Goode" and "Around and Around" as vehicles for Garcia's guitar solos, their playing on the equally iconic, equally traditional "Not Fade Away" (composed by Buddy Holly) was typically far more adventurous and collaborative, and its status as a "jamming song" meant that it would often be integrated into extended improvisational episodes arising from such songs as "The Other One," "Dark Star," or "St. Stephen," as on April 28, 1971, when it emerges from "St. Stephen," which itself emerged from "Dark Star."

We might be tempted to assume that the narrative, lyrical focus of the Berry tunes had something to do with the band's adoption of a conservative improvisational approach; this assumption must, however, be nuanced by taking the Johnny Cash song "Big River" into account. Also a strongly narrative piece, the band as a whole nonetheless tended to play this song more freely and spontaneously than they did the Chuck Berry songs, although, admittedly, never as freely as they played "Not Fade Away."[15]

I would suggest that the treatment of the Chuck Berry songs could be accounted for by Berry's reputation as an instrumentalist, as well as a songwriter. Although they both did play guitar, Cash and Holly were primarily known as singers and songwriters, while Berry, in addition to his work in these two roles, also stands as one of the canonical rock lead guitarists. When you play his songs, you are implicitly entering into a dialogue with the rock guitar tradition, staking your place in it: this might explain the focus on "straight" guitar soloing in the Grateful Dead's renditions of these songs. Berry, with his status within the rock canon, looms over anyone who plays these songs, and it is this sense of presence that evokes a traditional lead guitar solo approach as a response.

DANCE TUNES

As discussed, the Grateful Dead saw themselves, above all, as a dance band. Especially in their early years, they worked in a musical environment that put a strong emphasis on dancing. In his article "The Bands . . . That's Where It's At: The History of the San Francisco Rock Scene," Ralph Gleason notes that "what has marked the San Francisco bands from the beginning is that, unlike the bands in New York or Los Angeles, they are bands whose target is personal performances at dances and concerts."[16] Jerry Garcia, interviewed for a volume that included the above article, concurs: "We still feel that our function is as a dance band . . . and that's what we like to do. We like to play with dancers . . . nothing improves your time like having somebody dance. Just pulls the whole thing together. And it's also a nice little feedback thing."[17]

In conversation with Frank Kofsky, Garcia takes up this point again: "As far as I'm concerned, the ultimately responsive audience is a dancing audience"—and, as we have discussed, the San Francisco scene was a dancing scene.[18] People went out to the ballrooms to dance, and bands obliged them with dramatically extended songs.[19] Consequently, "the Dead, along with all the other successful psychedelic aggregates in the city, was first, foremost and finally a dance band," particularly with the Pigpen material— and, furthermore, a dance band whose mandate included playing for dancers who were young, excited, often high, and for all of these reasons comfortable dancing for ten or fifteen minutes at a stretch.

In his discussion with Kofsky, Garcia brings out an interesting difference between hippie and jazz-audience practice. Kofsky notes that "the jazz audience has tried for so long to overcome its feelings of inferiority that they put [dancing] down very strongly," to which Garcia assents: "You don't blow your cool. Well, here's the thing, is that everyone's so tired of keeping their cool— me, at any rate—that I would rather just blow it, you know? . . . Rather than concentrate on keeping my cool, I would rather have my mind blown."[20] This attitude helps to explain the popularity of ecstatic dancing at Grateful Dead shows. The band felt that they had moved past the jazz- and beatnik-derived sense of "cool" that had been one of the defining features of North American underground culture.

This emphasis on dancing, combined with the concurrent emphasis on the use of mind-altering and (potentially) ecstasy-inducing chemicals, produced an audience that was ready and eager to dance for a long time. This helps to explain the presence in the Grateful Dead's repertoire of a number of songs in which the band considerably adjusted its improvisational approach to suit the dancing needs of their fans.

We should note first of all that, for those who have a taste for the band's sense of rhythm, almost all of the Grateful Dead's music is quite danceable. By and large, the band did not sacrifice their groove on the altar of art— although this aspect of their music is not apparent to everyone; hence the need to state it explicitly. I make no judgment here as to whether the Grateful Dead "really" are or are not always danceable. Suffice it to say that, on the one hand, from a traditional perspective, there are numerous reasons why their music should be difficult to dance to, including the lack of a stable groove and Lesh's approach to bass; on the other hand, literally millions of people, including me, have found their music to be very danceable. But, in addition to this general truth, universally accepted by fans of the band, we can say specifically that there were a number of songs in which they put the improvisational accent firmly on the dancing side of things. There is a big difference between the transcendent improvisational space that the band enters in songs such as "Dark Star" or "Playing in the Band" and the "let's dance!" space in songs such as "Franklin's Tower" or "Turn On Your Lovelight": while the former might be more profound than the latter, it's the latter that really gets people out of their seats.

These songs, the ones that I have called the "dance tunes," are often extremely long, greatly improvised, but with that improvisation confined within strict musical boundaries. Dynamics may and do change considerably, but the basic chord changes and rhythms do not change during the jamming, and characteristic riffs will often be present or suggested throughout the improvisation. In the dance tunes, the band plays within very tight limits, but with a great deal of focus, in order to give the dancers music that is solidly anchored and yet variable enough not to be boring.

Precedents for this approach to music are particularly to be found in African American popular music, particularly R&B, funk, and soul, and yet the Grateful Dead took striking liberties with these precedents. Most notable of these, perhaps, is the absence of tightly organized rhythmic congrescence in the African-American sense as discussed by Earl Stewart, Richard Ripani, and Kevin Le Gendre.[21] As Stewart puts it, African American groove is based around contexts "when several melodies (or musical events) occur at the same time," forming "a rhythmic plexus: an interconnected network of musical events. The events that occur in a plexus are not arbitrary and consequently do not have the same function. Some events merge with other events. When this happens the listener does not hear the individual events, but instead hears the cumulative effect, or unison, of all of them. This effect is called *rhythmic congrescence*." It can also be described as "a type of rhythmic harmony."[22]

Stewart notes as well that the events making up the congrescence are "constant or mildly variable (they maintain the same basic shape) and generally form ostinatos." Variable elements of a plexus, on the other hand, provide rhythmic tension, another fundamental aspect of African American music—and "the most important of all inconstant events in African-American music is improvisation." In Stewart's view, the plexus is defined by the interaction between the congrescent and conflicting (variable) aspects of its constituent musical events, with the congrescent events being dominant: "Conflicting events are therefore parasitic on the underlying congrescent rhythm."[23]

As Ripani notes, the development of funk and R&B music in the mid-1960s and following highlights this emphasis on congrescence rather than conflict, moving in the direction of ever more complicated and precisely interlocking parts, and "an essential mind-set in this type of music is that *a musician is expected to play the exact same part throughout a song section, or perhaps even the entire song.*"[24]

James Brown is the classic innovator in this regard, and the breakthrough is found in his 1965 hit "Papa's Got a Brand New Bag." As Stewart describes the aesthetic: "Each aspect of the arrangement constitutes a distinct melodic idea: that is, the patterns played by the drums, the horns, the bass, the guitar, and of course the lead vocal . . . were distinct, with their own melodic and rhythmic character. Yet all the ideas blended with each other symbiotically, creating a higher rhythmical unity, an effect greater than the sum of its parts. This is the very definition of rhythmic congruence in the strict African sense."[25]

Despite the enormous influence of various strains of African American music on their own work, the Grateful Dead do not fit neatly onto this grid of musical practice in their improvisations, especially with regard to the groove tunes. Fundamentally, the band's music occupies a middle ground. When improvising, they work within a continually shifting musical space that is defined at any given point by a tonal center and a basic rhythm. In the non-groove tunes, the tonal center and the rhythm will be potentially subject to fluctuation and change, thus rendered more vague; in the groove songs, they will be made more stable through being incorporated into a motif (a riff, a chord progression, or the combination of the two) that underlies most or all of the jamming. So, in this sense, the dance tunes come closer to the idea of rhythmic congruence than do the nondance tunes. But to say that they "come closer" is a far cry indeed from saying that they model it, for the characteristic motif is spontaneously and independently variable by any member of the band or by the group as a whole, in practice as in theory. These motifs are not played as stable parts or as interlocking ostinatos; they are resources, bases for interactive experimentation.

Stewart identifies the primacy of congruent events as fundamental for African American music, and conflicting events as being parasitic. In the Grateful Dead's improvisational aesthetic for dance tunes, the point seems to be for the individual members to work in the borderlands where conflicting and congruent events overlap, and to fashion from that space a continuously changing mesh of sound that is roughly defined by the melody, harmony, and rhythm implied by the dominant motif.

I would argue that the Grateful Dead's practice could fit in with African American rhythmic congruence in a loose sense, particularly as it manifests in musical styles such as Dixieland—if we can imagine the heterophonic approach of the front line being extended to all the instruments. But the Grateful Dead's approach is not nearly so amenable to the stricter approach to rhythmic congruence that Stewart and Ripani identify as arising in the mid-1960s, a variety that has less place for group improvisation and spontaneity, especially on the part of the rhythm section. In other words, it seems to me that African American dance music and the Grateful Dead were coming from similar places but heading in different directions.

This might help to explain why, although they drew a great deal of their material and inspiration from traditions associated with African American culture, they did not incorporate African American songs composed after the mid-1960s into their repertoire. For the first two periods of the band's career, and into the third, the dance tunes would typically be led by Pigpen and would be drawn from African American popular material, especially blues (e.g., "Good Morning Little Schoolgirl") or R&B ("In the Midnight Hour," "Turn On Your Lovelight"). After Pigpen left the band, most of the dance tunes associated with him were dropped from the repertoire; some would later reappear (such as "Good Lovin'," sung by Weir), while others were permanently abandoned. In the meantime, the Grateful Dead introduced several new dance tunes of their own. These songs showed the influence of African American dance music (such as the disco rhythm in "Eyes of the World"); however, they were original songs rather than covers, and they did not feature the vocal call-and-response approach that was so characteristic of Pigpen's songs. Furthermore, these songs were often played considerably more slowly than was the case with the first wave of dance tunes—a characteristic that might be related to the much larger venues and audiences in which and to which they played, contexts that privileged mid-tempo grooving over manic velocity.

In short, this new crop of dance tunes (including most notably "Franklin's Tower," "Scarlet Begonias," and "Fire on the Mountain," in addition to "Eyes of the World") differ considerably in some regards from the first wave of Pigpen-led songs. Nonetheless, it seems to me that the two groups can be legitimately coupled, given their similarities in terms of function, improvisational method, and their common use of African American musical references, particularly in terms of their rhythms.

The dance tunes give the most straightforward presentation of the Grateful Dead as an improvising dance band, and thus as a band working with and on behalf of its audience, accentuating the celebratory and communal ethos that lay at the heart of their music and doubtless helped to account for their long popularity. The Framework was employed by the Grateful Dead in their explorations of the original material in their repertoire, as well as the more pop or folk cover material. But it was not used to guide the band in their improvisational work on much of their blues-, soul-, or R&B-oriented material. In their work with this material, they often took a distinctly different approach, less formally sophisticated and idiosyncratic than the Framework.

Understanding this approach to open rock improvisation over blues, R&B, and soul songs is significant not only for our understanding of the Grateful Dead specifically but also for our grasp of the rock improvisational tradition more generally. This is because a great deal of the earliest extended rock improvising on record was set in musical contexts that owed a great deal to precisely these musical genres. Listen, for example, to the earliest extended rock pieces, such as the Rolling Stones' "Going Home" (*Aftermath*, Decca, 1966) or Love's "Revelation" (*Da Capo*, Elektra, released January 1967), which are both essentially blues songs—and, even as time went on, playing blues or blues-related music was a characteristic of many improvising rock bands, such as the Allman Brothers or, later, Blues Traveler.

It is not hard to see why rock bands would choose to "stretch out" over blues- or R&B-related songs or feels. These songs offered circular, repetitive forms over which soloists could play as long as they felt inclined, and their regularity and rhythmic consistency gave the band support when rhythm section members took chances. Jazz standards, of course, would have offered equally circular forms, but they were also a great deal more difficult to play for novice or informally trained players (remember Kaukonen's point, which we discussed earlier). There was already a strong tradition within blues and R&B performance practice of open-ended songs, rather than the stereotypical three-minute limit for pop songs, giving support and a model to rock musicians as they began to work in extended forms. Also, the majority of pre-British Invasion rock and roll was based on such forms, and even into the 1960s and 1970s a great deal of rock music used them; they would thus have been familiar territory for rock players, and the work of players in these styles would have provided accessible and comprehensible models for rock musicians' developing interest in instrumental virtuosity.[26]

In addition to these musical advantages, the use of blues-, soul-, and R&B-related material gained cultural capital for rock bands, in that such material bore (not unproblematically) connotations of authenticity, naturalness, and soulfulness for the predominantly white audience that supported such improvising rock bands. For example, it was said that in bringing blues songs into the Grateful Dead's repertoire, keyboardist/vocalist Ron McKernan (a.k.a. "Pigpen") "brought to the Dead blues roots [and] genuine soulfulness," an argument that takes a well-trodden line in equating "soulfulness" and "roots" with invocations of African-American musical tropes.[27] The ramifications, both oppressive and liberatory, of such equations are beyond our present scope; for better or worse, however, they played a significant part in making playing "bluesy" music attractive for rock musicians.

Given the importance of this sort of material to improvising rock bands, and given, too, the Grateful Dead's status as one of the foremost such bands, it is interesting to examine the ways in which they approached this sort of material, working with it so as to create potential vehicles for extended improvisation and models for the many groups that came after them. This is all the more true in that it is an area that has not been addressed at length by Grateful Dead scholars. Musicological analyses of the band's work tend to avoid the Pigpen songs and focus on their acid rock material, such as the iconic "Dark Star."[28] The most extensive such analysis, David Malvinni's *Grateful Dead and the Art of Rock Improvisation*, focuses on the Grateful Dead's work in the early 1970s, when Pigpen was ill and less present than he had been. In this book, I have chosen to focus on the band's first few years, in which the dance tunes are mostly sung by Pigpen.

Malvinni's concern in discussing the Pigpen-sung material differs from mine in two other regards. In terms of context, Malvinni presents the Pigpen material as it relates to the Grateful Dead's other improvisational material, whereas here I am interested in showing how the band's improvisational strategies differ from Framework-related strategies. In terms of trajectory, Malvinni presents the early Pigpen material as steps on the road to what he considers to be the band's most fully realized music, which was produced in the early 1970s—in fact, his second chapter is entitled "Primal Grateful Dead Improvisation: From R&B Covers to Originals Like 'That's It for the Other One.'" For my part, I don't consider this music to be primal in the sense of leading up to something; rather, I am concerned with the material itself. That said, Malvinni's work will be referenced as necessary and will be of interest to any who seek to take their investigation of the Grateful Dead's improvisational strategies further.

When the Grateful Dead performed contemporary blues, R&B, and soul songs, it was usually Pigpen who sang lead.[29] Some of these songs (e.g., "Smokestack Lightning") were performed "straight"—that is, with little structural improvisation beyond guitar soloing and hence will not be discussed here. Other songs, however, became contexts for extended workouts, during which the band jammed at length while audiences danced. These songs included "Turn On Your Lovelight," "In the Midnight Hour," and "Good Morning Little Schoolgirl."

As mentioned earlier, the band's improvisational practice when backing Pigpen on these considerably extended songs differs significantly from their Framework-related work. The consistency of the harmony, rhythm, and implicit or explicit presence of a structuring riff or chord progression marks these songs as different from the Framework material, in which the musical textures are much more changeable and fluid; so, too, does their structure.

As we saw in the discussion of the Framework, when the Grateful Dead are using this approach the jamming starts up at the end of the song, with a final return to the song after the jamming has finished; thus a typical Framework-structured song will go for two to three minutes, as a pop song would; briefly establish the sort of groove that one might hear in a fadeout on a record; and then develop improvised structures of increasing complexity and diversity out of that groove, before eventually returning to the groove. With the Pigpen songs, on the other hand, the band never really moves away from the song. The formal boundaries of the Pigpen songs remain tight—in other words, the underlying harmony and rhythm are almost never challenged, and the focus is firmly on providing a danceable backdrop for Pigpen's showmanship.[30]

February 14, 1968

In this section, I will examine three of the classic Pigpen dance songs, namely "Good Morning Little Schoolgirl," "In the Midnight Hour," and "Turn On Your Lovelight," songs originally associated respectively with Junior Wells, Wilson Pickett, and Bobby "Blue" Bland. I will begin by discussing the versions performed by these artists, and then will discuss the Grateful Dead's versions of the songs. My goal will be to show how the Grateful Dead transformed these pieces so as to make them amenable to extensive jamming.

The Grateful Dead performed these songs many times; for the sake of clarity and simplicity, I will be drawing on the versions heard on the night of February 14, 1968.[31] That show has come to be regarded as one of the greatest of the band's performances. As Lesh writes in his autobiography, "When we listened back to the [tapes of the] show, it was spectacular—vivid, protean and relentless."[32] Michael M. Getz, writing in *The Deadhead's Taping Compendium*, says that "serious listening to this show reveals such a sheer depth of soul-wakening power that it astonishes me to remember just how young a band they were at the time."[33] For what it's worth, I feel the same—this was a truly superb show. Additionally, working from a show this early in the band's career helps to challenge the tendency in previous writings noted above to ignore or downplay the achievements of the band's earliest years.

"Good Morning Little Schoolgirl"

"ORIGINAL" VERSION: This song was first recorded in 1937 by Sonny Boy Williamson in country blues style and was recorded many times afterward.[34] In 1965, Junior Wells recorded it for his extremely influential *Hoodoo Man*

Blues album on Delmark in an electric Chicago blues style, with the tune being defined by its repeated and propulsive pentatonic bass riff. It is this form of the song that was picked up by the Grateful Dead.[35]

Wells's version of the song, here titled "Good Morning Schoolgirl," begins with a snare hit that ushers in the rest of the band, playing the song's main riff, a simple walk down the blues scale. Its arrangement is simple; there are five choruses of twelve-bar blues (one instrumental, two vocal, one instrumental, one vocal), followed by an extended vocal outro section, where Wells gets playful while the band drones on the main riff.

The rhythmic feel of the song is "half swing," a term that "is often used to designate swing that is somewhere between the straight-eighth feel and triplet swing" frequently employed in early rock and blues songs.[36] Billy Warren, the drummer, expresses this alternation through his hi-hat playing, which goes back and forth between a swing and straight feel. Jack Myers, the bass player, "holds it down," playing very straight rhythmically and with a dull, flat tone, producing the main riff with no fills. Buddy Guy, the guitarist, on the other hand, consistently uses a swinging feel.

Guy's playing illustrates a fundamental structural issue of the song. Throughout the piece, movement away from the I chord is accompanied by looser, more expressive playing. Thus Guy plays a repetitive riff on the I chord, but when the progression moves to the IV and V–IV sections he moves away from that riff, first playing melodic lines, and then, as the song progresses, switching to soloistic lines with variations on the melody. These changes in approach give the song a back and forth feel, moving from tightness to momentary looseness, then back to tightness.

We can describe the main body of the song as a series of repeated twelve-bar cycles, with movement within these cycles being governed rhythmically by the alternation between—or the tension generated by—the simultaneous coexistence of swing and straight feel. In terms of the musicians' playing, the harmonic progression translates into movement from a solid, riff-based texture (on the I chord) to movements of greater expressivity (on the IV, and then more so on the V–IV progression) and, finally, back "home" again to the I.

The song ends with an outro section, stretching from 3:05 to the end, roughly 15 percent of the song. In this section the band sits on the riff and brings down the dynamics, while Wells talk/sings over top. The guitar does play some fills in this section (at 3:29 and 3:34, both times as responses to the vocal line) but the bass and drums play the same line throughout.

GRATEFUL DEAD VERSION: In their version of the song, the Grateful Dead take the same approach to the verses as Junior Wells, in terms of playing tightly on the I chords and loosening up on the others, bringing the tension and drive of the music up and down in a cyclical motion. The Grateful Dead also retain the idea of ending the song with a lead vocal rap over a static I chord, as well as using this technique between verses. Throughout these sections, the band frequently follows Pigpen's lead, although the way in which they do this varies—sometimes through responding to his calls, sometimes using his vocals as cues to raise or lower the intensity, sometimes taking up and working with melodic or harmonic ideas derived from his vocal lines. However, there are just as many times when the instrumentalists turn to each other for their ideas rather than to Pigpen's cues, as we see, for example, in the section starting at 10:26, when Weir begins a phrase, and Lesh immediately picks it up.

Also noteworthy is the fact that the Grateful Dead ease into the song, using the main riff and variations on it, just as they ease out of it with the main riff. The twelve-bar blues section of the song is thus introduced by, interspersed with, and completed by jamming based on the tonality, contour, and rhythm of the main riff. In dealing with this riff, its duration and broad melodic outline are kept unvarying, while the riff itself can be played, developed, excerpted, or ignored. The riff is always potentially present, but it is not always actively present.

In terms of call and response, the band does respond to Pigpen's cues, but not in a mechanical or predetermined way; the cues are used as the basis for improvisation and taken as guides rather than orders, indications of musical direction that invite active and spontaneous interpretation on the band's part. This can be heard in the instrumental section following the last of the vocal verses, as the band moves into what was, in the Junior Wells version, the ending of the song, holding the I chord while Pigpen vocalizes (starting at 4:48).

As Pigpen talk/sings, the band improvises, steadily increasing their volume and the complexity of their interplay for the next thirty seconds (to approximately 5:27), when they settle back into a groove related to the main riff and then move into a response after each of his lines. Pigpen starts playing harmonica at 6:00; this seems to be a sign for things to get unsettled and complex again, which they do for the next 30 seconds, until Garcia moves into the lead role. His solo soon takes on a call and response flavor, with the band including Pigpen (on harmonica) responding to his phrases. In all this time, the band has stayed on the I chord, as they do until the song's end.

"In the Midnight Hour"

ORIGINAL VERSION: The original version of the song, recorded in 1965 by Wilson Pickett, possesses a rolling, majestic feel that owes a great deal to its "minutely delayed beat two and four."[37] The majority of the song consists of a simple I-IV groove, played under the verses and most of the instrumental material. The solidity of this inexorable progression is emphasized by the "delayed" feel and the song's unchanging bass line. Only in the horn-led introductory material, in the chorus, and in the bridge does the song move away from this groove.

In the first half of the song (up to the bridge), interesting variations on the basic groove are introduced. In this section the drummer (Al Jackson) very subtly varies his snare drum hits, playing them with a different degree of intensity each time. Similarly, while guitarist Steve Cropper largely restricts himself to chopped chords on the 2 and 4 for the verses, with more flowing playing for the choruses, nonetheless he does get slightly more energetic and ragged as the song goes on; at 0:50, the sound of his guitar strings ringing out is audible, and at 1:06 and 1:22 his single note lines are played more vigorously than in the first verse.

The horn section, too, contributes to these variations. In the first part of the first verse, a saxophone line plays a response to the vocalist's call, with the horns switching to chording for the second half of the verse. In the second verse, the response line is gone, but now the horn section plays a countermelody line that outlines the chords, but does so with more movement than in the second half of verse line. With all of this taking place against the backdrop of an unchanging bass line, the effect is that of a slow, staggered build in intensity.

This slow build leads the listener into the bridge, which presents a new level of intensity as the drummer doubles up on the snare drum, the bassist likewise doubles up to phrase in eighth notes rather than quarters, and the guitarist starts playing on every note, rather than just 2 and 4 (although his playing is different on 1 and 3 than on 2 and 4, thus preserving the emphases of the original feel). The horns take the lead here.

When Pickett returns with the vocals, the drummer and guitarist play less intensely, but this loss of energy is compensated for by an increase in complexity, with two different horn lines playing new melodic calls and responses, Pickett singing a different melodic line over top, and the interlocked groove of the rhythm section continuing to drive home the two-chord main progression—which has become the simple constant in the midst of ongoing musical development.

GRATEFUL DEAD VERSION: The Grateful Dead begin their version of this song in the same manner as the Pickett version—that is, with a drum roll, followed by a four-bar-chord progression leading into the two-chord groove of the song. It seems, in fact, as though one of the drummers is being extremely faithful to the Pickett version, to the point of replicating the characteristic solid, delayed thud for the first few bars (to 0:08). However, as the song develops, the feel changes, with the other drummer bringing in off-beats and fills, while Lesh plays with a dancing, exuberant approach that is quite different from the stolid approach on the original.

It is also significant to note that the way that the Grateful Dead's rhythm section plays lends the song its own, instrumental, call and response feel, with the second half of each bar leading back to and responding to the first half. It is over top of this back-and-forth interplay that Pigpen sings. Whereas the Pickett version of the song was marked by a slow increase in energy and raggedness, taking place over top of a static bass and drum pattern, here we have the reverse situation; the drums and bass provide dynamic and not always predictable forward motion, the second half of the bar completing the phrase in the first half and leading the listener on, while the guitars by and large serve as the stabilizers. The band plays two verses and choruses before heading into the bridge, and the second verse and chorus are approached no differently than the first verse and chorus; there is no gradual build as in the Pickett version.

In the bridge (1:27–45), Garcia plays a version of the horn melody line from the Pickett version. There is a switch to doubling up on the snare on the part of one of the drummers, but this fidelity to the original version is nuanced, or undercut, by the fact that the other drummer does not join in, but keeps playing around the beat. The original arrangement is acknowledged, but not strictly followed.

Three more verses follow, in which Garcia and Lesh play more and more independently. The fifth verse is marked by call and response interplay between Garcia and Lesh, and by the fact that the band does not go into the turnaround; instead, Pigpen keeps singing and the band sings responses until they all eventually drop out (by 3:40), leaving Pigpen to rap over top of instrumental music.

Although they have stopped singing, the band does not come down in intensity here; they stay up, jamming energetically and independently. Pigpen's vocals thus function as part of the overall sonic web, rather than as the dominant voice. By around 3:59 the band has begun taking off in a number of directions; however, throughout the jam that follows, the band never leaves the basic two-chord progression behind, nor do they fundamentally alter the underlying groove. Throughout the jam, then, the band manages its improvisations so as to keep constant the basic harmonic and rhythmic kernel of the song.

Pigpen has returned to singing by 7:25, but, again, his vocals function as a backdrop to Garcia's chording and Lesh's energetic playing. The band does calm down by 7:42, but then, as Pigpen makes it clear that he is not going to sing another verse right away, Lesh gets active again, sounding eager to keep jamming. Note that, in this section, Pigpen is still singing, contributing interjections to the jam, more textural and rhythmic than melodic. From 8:00–30, it again seems as though the band is making space for Pigpen to take a more active role, looping a quiet riff. By 8:38 one gets the impression that Garcia has tired of waiting and is preparing to take off again, but he is countermanded by Pigpen, who brings the verse back in at 8:44, finishing the song.

In this song, we have seen the importance of the basic two-chord pattern. Although it is no longer linked to a specific and repeated bass line as it was in the Wilson Pickett version, nonetheless it remains the fundamental organizing principle of the song. For this reason, I cannot agree with David Malvinni's presentation of the improvisation in this song (working from a version performed on September 3, 1967) as "the epitome of controlled chaos . . . with Deleuzian lines of flight expanding on the source material to the extent that the source disappears."[38] The source does not disappear, but is stripped down to its most fundamental—and, significantly, most danceable—level and used as a basis for the band's interactive improvisation. With regard to Pigpen, we have seen how he functions here as a member of an improvising ensemble; the band plays with and around him, making space for him when necessary but prepared to go on without him should he choose not to enter.

"Turn On Your Lovelight"

ORIGINAL VERSION: This song, written by Deadric Malone and Joseph Scott, was first recorded by Bobby "Blue" Bland in 1961.[39] It was also covered in 1966 by the Irish band Them for their second album, *Them Again*, on Parrot Records. Although some members of the Grateful Dead were influenced by Them's music—enough so that their early original "Caution (Do Not Stop on Tracks)" is clearly derived from Them's "Mystic Eyes"—the Grateful Dead's version of "Turn On Your Lovelight" draws on Bland's original arrangement, and not Them's more laid back and less sharply defined version.

In Bland's version, the song's basic, jaunty rhythm does not vary at all, and its I-IV harmony pattern is constant, with the sole exception of a four-bar section in which the drums play alone. The bassist and pianist also play their simple parts with little variation. The guitarist alternates between three approaches. When the horns play their punches at the very start of the song, he plays a chord-based riff that accompanies them; following these, he switches to a "shave and a haircut"/clave chord rhythm that he plays until Bland has sung his first line; at this point, he switches to single-note melodic lines, which he continues until Bland reaches the climax of the verse, at which point he briefly returns to the "shave and a haircut" line, and then the riff that accompanies the return of the horn punches. After this there is a drum solo, and then the pattern continues: he riffs when the horns are punching, plays the rhythmic chords until Bland has finished his first line, and then plays the melodic single-note line under the rest of Bland's singing.

In terms of the rhythm section, this alternation of guitar patterns provides the only contrast in the arrangement. As the guitar is not foregrounded and does not change exactly in synch with Bland's vocals, the alternation has a subtle effect: the listener feels that something is changing, but is not immediately sure what it is, especially given the driving constancy of the bass, drum, and piano playing. Bland's vocal takes the lead for the majority of the song, the only exception being the saxophone solo from 1:43 to 2:02. The song ends with a fadeout as Bland sings, "I feel all right! Let it shine!"

GRATEFUL DEAD VERSION: At this show, "Turn On Your Lovelight" emerged out of a band composition called "The Eleven," with Garcia signaling the move to a new song by playing the distinctive single-note guitar riff. As the song begins, Lesh switches to his "Lovelight" bass line, showing that he has understood Garcia's signal, and Garcia moves to a chord-based figure. For the first twenty-five seconds, Garcia, Lesh, and Weir play interlocking lines, establishing the song, before coming down in volume and moving to a more ragged and minimal feel for Pigpen's vocal entry.

The band brings up the dynamics as the verse proceeds, until, by the time Pigpen has hit the chorus (0:44), they are almost back to their former level, and playing the interlocking parts. The chorus ends with a drum break, as in the Bland version of the song, although this break is twelve bars long. Pigpen sings another verse, with only the drums accompanying him, and there is an interesting moment at 1:30, when one of the drummers plays a response to Pigpen's vocal on his kick drum and then crosses the bar line with this response, extending it into a full phrase of its own.

At end of the vocal verse they move into an improvisational section, in which the underlying I-IV progression and groove are maintained by Pigpen's organ playing. At around 3:01, Garcia starts playing a descending chord line that seems to be a cue to bring things down—at least, it is interpreted as such by Weir, who drops the intensity and volume of his own playing, soon followed by the rest of the band. After this, Garcia leads the way back into the main riff, as he did at the start of the song, but Pigpen reenters before the band is ready for him; they have not yet come down as low as they did in the introduction to the song (3:16). Their response to this is simply to keep playing, while Pigpen sings over top.

The song's second drum break, starting at 3:50, is considerably longer than the first. Pigpen starts singing again at 4:08, but sounds uncertain, so he retreats, tries again at 4:12 and 4:14, and retreats again both times. The drummers have brought things down at 4:14 to make a space for him to enter. But when he does not come in, they get more active again, apparently shifting their plans and intending to extend the drum break (4:16), just before Pigpen definitively decides to reenter (4:19). This time, when Pigpen gets to the chorus, the rest of the band joins in singing responses to his calls. He, in turn, extends this section, talk/singing over top as the instrumentalists bring things down, following his cues. When he then sings "Turn it on up, bring it on up" (5:28), Garcia responds by coming in quietly on guitar (5:32), with the backing vocals spontaneously dropping out to facilitate this. Garcia continues playing leads as Weir's vocals return, now singing a different line ("Little bit higher"; 5:37). As the song's intensity rises, Weir sings louder, Garcia plays louder, and Lesh plays more firmly over the underlying two-chord progression, Pigpen talk/singing all the while.

At 6:06, Pigpen drops out, and Garcia plays a riff where Pigpen's vocal would have been. After Garcia plays the riff a second time, Lesh begins responding to it in his own playing; following this, Lesh integrates the riff into his bass line and starts working with it (6:12) just as Pigpen starts singing again, with Weir providing responses. Garcia then shifts to play the introductory single note riff, and the band starts to build things up again, with Pigpen leading them on. At 7:09 Garcia takes off on a solo, starting out in a high register but shortly afterward (7:20) dropping down and getting more active as Weir heightens the activity of his own playing. At around 7:28 Garcia pauses; at 7:32 Garcia comes in with a lead riff that interlocks with Weir's rhythm guitar riff. After establishing this pattern, Weir breaks from it, switching his line so that it includes a response to Garcia (7:40). They continue in this fashion until 7:49, when Garcia brings the song to a close (7:56).

The guiding principle underlying the Bland version of the song was the idea of building the piece up through the successive introduction of lines. The essential core of the song (the groove and the harmony) never changes, but provides the stable basis over which the song develops and changes. This is also the case with the Grateful Dead's version, except less so. In theirs, while the essential groove and harmony do not change, there is much more that is "up for grabs." No member or members of the band are responsible for expressing the fundamental elements; rather, they are conceptual aspects of the piece that can be manifested by different members at different times. Moreover, whereas the Bland version introduced its variations and developments in what seems to be a predetermined order, the Grateful Dead's variations are, as we have seen, frequently the result of spontaneous interaction between the band members.

Just as there is no one member responsible for "holding it down" in the background of the Grateful Dead's version of "Turn On Your Lovelight," so there is no unambiguously foregrounded member. Certainly, Pigpen is the "leader" of the band during this song, but his leadership is of the "first among equals" variety: he signals changes, but does not control how those changes are expressed.

Playing the Main Groove

The songs just examined are not tremendously complex in their essential structures. In their original versions, they all consist of a repeated main element—whether a riff, or a chord progression over a groove—that plays through the majority of the song, with one or more periodically occurring interludes that move away from, and then back to, this element.

In "Good Morning Little Schoolgirl," the main element is the song's riff, and the moves to the IV and V–IV chords are the interludes that contrast with it, not only by virtue of the change in harmony but also because the playing gets (somewhat) looser and more expressive in these sections. In "In the Midnight Hour," the main element is a two-chord vamp, and there are two interludes—namely, the four-bar series of chords that open the song, and the V–IV chord progression that ends the verses, both of which differ dramatically from the vamp. In "Turn On Your Lovelight," the main element again is a I-IV vamp, with the interlude being the horn shots that are played over it before verses and during the saxophone solo.

The Grateful Dead's tendency when playing these Pigpen songs is to render these interludes more or less faithfully; they do not use them as vehicles for wide-ranging improvisation. This is most clear with respect to "In the Midnight Hour," in which their use of the interlude figures conforms with the way that these figures are used in the original version of the song, and they are dropped during the improvisation. In "Good Morning Little Schoolgirl," when the band shifts from guitar solo to group improvisation, the chord changes. In other words, the interludes are dropped; all that remains is the main riff and what the band makes of it. In "Turn On Your Lovelight," the interlude figure is brought in more frequently than in the original—a necessary step if one is to maintain interest and danceability in a piece this long—but otherwise is kept much the same.

Thus, in both the Grateful Dead's versions of the songs and those performed by the original artists, the interludes fulfill roughly the same function: to give the listener some sort of contrast to the main elements, the riffs or vamps that make up the majority of the piece. The Grateful Dead's versions differ from the originals in their treatment of these main elements, which are a) enormously elongated, and b) considerably varied. When the band is improvising, they work exclusively with the main riffs or vamp.

The band's use of these vamps or riffs contrasts with their improvisational practice in the non-Pigpen, Framework-based songs. As we discussed, their practice in the non-Pigpen songs is to move from section to section of the improvisation, changing feels and working within musical areas loosely defined by a tonality and a rhythmic sensibility. Chord changes are dropped; riffs may be picked up, but are sure to be dropped as well, and there is a gradual but continual flow through a variety of musical environments. Everyone is listening to their fellow musicians to pick up hints of possible new directions to go in, new places to explore. And such exploration, of course, runs the risk of taking the band into places where their audience's desire to dance would be sidelined.

Here, though, the situation is different, and it is the band's inventiveness that is tested, their ability to work within strict limits as they stretch these looped one- and two-bar cells out to great length. While this approach places great demands upon its practitioners, it is nonetheless a more straightforward approach than the Framework, and more clearly related to mainstream rock approaches, such as the "rave-up" pioneered by the Yardbirds. Therefore, it presented a model that could relatively clearly and accessibly guide other bands as they developed their improvisations on the basis of blues-related songs.

"WITHIN SONGS" IMPROVISATION

What it means to "play a song" varies greatly between musical contexts and involves dealing with challenging questions having to do with the very definition of songs. The question is complicated, and only becomes more so the more improvisation is brought into the picture.

Fortunately, for our immediate purposes, we need not go tremendously far away from the common understanding of "songs"; in most of their music, the Grateful Dead seem to have adopted a definition of vocal songs as composed of definite melodies, sung over fairly definite if sometimes implicit harmonic and rhythmic accompaniment. What differentiates them is the fact that within these guidelines the band members had the liberty to improvise their accompaniment, to a much greater degree than is typical with rock bands—as mentioned, the band approached their material in a way that can be compared to a jazz band, rather than a typical pop band. The impetus in taking this very open approach to accompaniment can be traced back to developments taking place in the rhythm section, and there are several aspects of these developments.

To start with the drummers: in the fall of 1967, drummer/percussionist Mickey Hart joined the band, playing alongside drummer Bill Kreutzmann. The idea of a rock band having two drummers (as opposed to a drummer and a percussionist) was unprecedented at the time. The approach that the Grateful Dead took to this situation was an interesting and intuitive one. Rather than constructing their rhythms so as to feature precise and predetermined interlocking parts—that is, heading in the direction of rhythmic congrescence—the band opted to keep the rhythms fundamentally the same, but greatly augment their density and flow. Hart and Kreutzmann, playing off and around each other, thickened and nuanced the basic pulse. In the Grateful Dead's context, having two drummers did not profoundly change the basic grooves that they played; what the change did instead was to enable them to do more playing with and around those grooves.

This approach produced a constant flow of rhythmic commentary, in which the basic beat was technically maintained, but was at times almost submerged by the elaborations and subject to endless discussion and spontaneous alteration. The effect was to produce a web of rhythm, or an ever-flowing current of guided improvisation that both expressed and commented on the beat being played, as can be heard, for example, on the version of "The Eleven" performed August 23, 1968, and released in 1992 on *Two From the Vault* on the Grateful Dead label. At all times, the rhythm is maintained by at least one drummer, while the other one is free to play fills or lines that layer other rhythms over top (such as the triplet and offbeat feels heard on the bell at the start of the performance), or that thicken the percussive texture (as happens at 4:00–4:15).

The effect of this approach was not to call the rhythm into doubt. There is no question of such ecstatic deconstructions of the beat such as we find in the work of many of the contemporary free jazz rhythm sections—for instance, Gary Peacock (bass) and Sunny Murray (drums) on Albert Ayler's *Spiritual Unity*.[40] In all but a very few Grateful Dead songs, by contrast, the rhythm may be lost at most for seconds, or in very rare cases as long as a minute or two, in the climax of songs.[41]

The effect of the Grateful Dead's drum section, from their second chronological period onward, was to establish the fundamental groove as a basic principle and then add layer upon layer of skittering commentary, playing with and around it as well as simply playing it. This principle applies, in theory and often in practice, to any of the Grateful Dead's songs. Speaking in reference to the "cowboy songs" that the band would cover, including "El Paso" (by Marty Robbins) or "Mama Tried" (by Merle Haggard)—the most fixed songs in the band's repertoire—Kreutzmann would still point out that playing them "is not ever mechanical . . . even though we play a lot of songs of more or less the same lengths, we really do change the interiors of them all the time—change the carpet, so to speak; paint the walls."[42]

Another development that increased the potential for improvisation within songs was Bob Weir's growth as a rhythm guitarist. He was the youngest member of the band, and indeed had at one time been a student of lead guitarist Jerry Garcia. His earliest work draws heavily, obviously, and not always comfortably on folk, rock, and blues licks and riffs. But, as time went on, he developed a unique and powerful voice on his instrument. Rather than, in typical rock rhythm guitarist fashion, focusing on barre chords and steady patterns, Weir kept his parts open and flowing, making innovative use of unexpected chord voicings, at times jagged rhythmic pushes, and a willingness to play less and to freely move about the fretboard. If this sounds more like jazz than rock, rest assured that Weir was aware of that: in a video clip published by *Relix* magazine, he cites Coltrane Quartet pianist McCoy Tyner as the major influence on his style.[43] The underlying principle behind Weir's playing is the same as with the drummers: Weir usually does not challenge or contradict the basic beat or chord changes, but nuances and interprets them, doing so differently each time he plays a given song.

But the most significant break from tradition in terms of improvisation within songs comes from bassist Phil Lesh, who asserted a degree of melodic, harmonic, and rhythmic freedom that is unprecedented (then or since) for a rock bassist. Lesh's adventurous, contrapuntal approach to bass playing seems likely to have derived from two main sources. First, there is his own experience in classical music and early training as a trumpeter—that is, a lead instrumentalist. Second, it was enabled by his appreciation for jazz, a genre in which bassists are typically granted a much greater degree of musical freedom than their popular music counterparts. Playing a walking bass line, the mainstay of jazz bass playing, does, after all, produce a continuous string of improvised lines, although, admittedly, within tighter rhythmic parameters than Lesh himself would work.

We should also note that the period in which the Grateful Dead formed and defined their musical vision was one that was marked by the liberation of the bass guitar. The rise of such inventive and influential players as Paul McCartney, Jack Casady, Jack Bruce, James Jamerson, Carol Kaye, John Cale, and John Entwhistle, to name only a few, along with developments in amplification and sound manipulation, demonstrated the increased potential for the bass guitar in a rock context and also legitimated the sort of experimentation that Lesh engaged in. Electric bass guitar is a fundamentally different instrument than upright bass, and the mid-1960s saw a generation of rock musicians coming to terms with this insight.

All of these factors came together to inspire Lesh to develop a bass guitar style that was, and still is, unique to him. Its expression was hampered at first by his lack of fluency on his new instrument (Lesh only took up bass upon joining the Grateful Dead), but by mid-1967 he had gained sufficient command of his instrument to present his vision, which was one of a spontaneous and improvised approach to bass.[44] Just as was the case with Weir, Kreutzmann, and Hart, so, too, Lesh acknowledged the formal structure of the song as a framework, but instead of clearly and unambiguously expressing this framework, he played with and through it, producing a liquid flow of notes that curled around it. As a jazz player would, Lesh improvised his way through all of the band's material, vocal or instrumental, only very rarely playing the definite lines or stock phrases that typically are the rock bassist's responsibility. His playing represents a significant transgression of the standard role for rock bassists; his age, personality, and training gave him the authority that he needed to carry out this transgression, and he was fortunate enough to be working in a social and musical environment that, as we have seen, encouraged the taking of artistic liberties.

The cumulative effect of all these liberatory gestures from the rhythm section was to move the band away from the concept of playing set parts and instead to turn Grateful Dead songs into an ever-shifting web of music, in which the composed aspects of the music were understood but not necessarily played, and in which specific lines were collectively and spontaneously negotiated by the players. This approach was just as applicable (theoretically if not always practically) to the instrumental accompaniment to the sung verses and choruses of the songs as to the instrumental jamming.

The vocals, too, are variable, but to a much lesser extent than the instrumental aspects of the songs. Lyrics are never changed (unless by accident); melodies, inflections, and timbral approaches do not vary more than would be the case with any other band—and considerably less so than in some bands, such as the Jefferson Airplane. There may have been many reasons for this, including the band's lack of a truly commanding and versatile lead vocalist. Another possible reason that comes to mind, however, has to do with the band's identity as a pop/rock band; in such a context, I wonder if the vocal melodies and lyrics as written might be considered to be essential defining features of the songs and hence not easily changeable.

I have discussed this issue at length, because I feel that it is one of the more significant yet unheralded aspects of the Grateful Dead's improvisation. It shifts our understanding of them and helps us to see them not as a band that plays songs and frequently jams, but as a band that is committed to improvisational playing in all contexts, whether they are in the throes of voyages into outer space, or playing a cowboy ballad such as "Me and My Uncle." This aesthetic is common in jazz, but it is considerably less so in rock. When it is approximated by rock bands, there is often a sharp divide between the amount of freedom permitted to the lead instruments and that permitted to the other instrumentalists, as we will see, for instance, when we discuss the Paul Butterfield band's "East/West." In that piece, the bass and drums stay locked into ostinatos while the guitarists are free to solo over top of their foundation. The liberation of the rhythm section that the Grateful Dead practiced was a crucial step forward for rock improvisational playing; it was also a step forward for this improvising rock band, integrating both the "rock" and the "improvising" sides of its nature. Finally, it permitted the band to provide a living demonstration of the fact that freedom—and even potentially transcendence—could, given the right spirit, be found or created anywhere. As they sang, "Once in a while you can get shown the light / In the strangest of places if you look at it right."[45]

THE FRAMEWORK

We have already discussed the Framework at length, so we only need to briefly recap that discussion here. The Framework is a model for the approach to improvisation developed in the Grateful Dead's earliest period (1965–mid-1967).

Pivotal experiences, both musical and spiritual in nature, in late 1965 and early 1966 convinced the band that they could play—and, in fact, needed to play—in an improvisational, open style. At that time, however, there were few models for rock musicians as to how to accomplish this in a manner that was faithful to rock music as a form in itself, rather than borrowing from jazz or new music practice. The Framework was the Grateful Dead's first original solution to the problem of how to integrate substantial amounts of group improvisation into their music.

This was indeed an elegant solution, and one that suits the band's chosen identity as a rock dance band. The placement of the improvisational material at the end of their shows ensured that the band was warmed up by the time the jamming began and also satisfied the audience's desire to hear the song—lyrics, chorus, and hooks—before getting down to just dancing.

The placement also brings up associations with fade-outs, a popular way at that time to end singles. The purpose of the fade-out is to symbolically dissolve temporality, making it seem as if the song can overleap its finite boundaries and enter eternity. Properly executed and properly heard, a fade-out can give the impression that the song never ends, but merely moves away from the listener until it is inaudible. The Framework evokes a world in which the listener can keep following the fade-out as it recedes, bringing its tantalizing promise of eternal musical pleasures into reality.

It is often the case that musicians will play more expressively or more freely in the fade-out than in the song proper. This makes sense, especially in contexts with an emphasis on capturing live performances, as was generally the case in pop/rock recording of the mid-1960s. During the body of the song, the musicians would be constrained by the need to record a "keeper" take and would not want to risk making a mistake or playing something that didn't gel with the other musicians, or that took away from the main melody or the focus on lyrics and hooks. Having made it safely to the end of the song, however, with the singer either silent or repeating an already-heard chorus, or using their voice as an instrument, the other musicians had a brief grace period in which to experiment or play more expressively. Also, the gradually diminishing volume in fade-outs can be used to render mistakes unnoticeable, which would further encourage musicians to take chances. As the fade-out recedes, then, it can change subtly, with players taking more liberties, just as in the Framework.

However, the point of a fade-out is that it fades away. Eventually, no matter how attentively one listens, the song ends, or, better, vanishes. This is not the case in the Framework. There, instead of fading to nothing, the song makes a return. Following a climax, a point of maximum separation from the original tune, the band falls back into the defining groove of the song and sings one last chorus.

This can have a profound effect on the listener. First of all, it gives a sense of finality. There is a definite ending. Second—and, to my mind, more significantly—it serves to encapsulate the improvisation within the song as a whole. No matter how strange or distinct the jamming may have been, the final return to the main groove suggests that we never really left the song. All that transpired during the jamming section, all the changes and potential that it contained, are thus symbolically present within the song itself. The Framework's placement of the jamming section, and its return to the song's theme, takes that feeling one step further, showing that a song can be elastic enough to contain anything that the band, working together, could conceive of. There are strong parallels here to the experience of taking LSD, an experience that most of the members of the Grateful Dead knew well: one moves away from one's normal experience of life through the gradual and organic emergence of adventures or ruminations, and then, in the end, one returns to one's baseline state.

The Framework was a first step, and by mid-1967 the band was already engaged in developing new models or tactics that would facilitate their improvisational activity. However, they would still make use of the Framework, both in the songs that originally featured it, such as "Dancing in the Streets," and in some newer songs.

SOUNDS

Manipulation of sound is what a musician does, and amplified music permits access to a new world of sounds. In this new world, not only can never-before-heard sounds be experienced, but they and more mundane sounds can also be made to transcend previously definitive limitations of volume, sustain, and timbre. The Grateful Dead, like other groups of their generation, were pioneers in terms of exploring these new realms, in their songs as well as in their jams. When I speak of sounds here, however, I will be referring only to the points in the Grateful Dead's improvisations when melodies, chords, and other normal delineations of music dropped away, along with the conventional uses of their instruments, and when the band focused on creating sound collages, especially making use of feedback (particularly in the acid rock phase) and musical space (particularly in the jazz rock phase). These sound collages tend to be identified on set lists as "Feedback" (in the 1960s shows, although feedback is only one of the sonic options) or "Space" in later set lists.

As we saw, one characteristic of the Framework was that jams would build up to a climax before returning to the main groove. This climax could be defined simply by dynamics and intensity, as was the case in 1966 and early 1967. However, as time went on, and the climaxes grew more extreme, there was a tendency for them to become more dissonant as well—pushing at the boundaries of conventional tonality and melody, and disintegrating the fixed beat. By mid-or-late 1967, climaxes could go even further, into sonic realms that many would have considered to be altogether nonmusical, in which feedback and distortion played a major musical role. A case in point, mentioned above, would be the Grateful Dead's twenty-minute performance of "Viola Lee Blues" in Toronto on August 8, 1967.

I suggest that we see in such climaxes the origins of the "sounds" approach to improvisation. However, we should note as well that the development of such an approach necessarily requires the willingness, and the ability, to hear such sounds as music. Contemporary developments in European art music would have developed this ability in listeners, as would developments in "out" or free jazz and even in popular music as well; this was a period in which artists of all sorts were experimenting with the increases in timbral potential made possible by electricity. The Beatles' "I Feel Fine," for example, with its introductory feedback, was released in 1964, while the Who made use of "noisy" guitar sounds in their songs "Anyway, Anyhow, Anywhere" and "My Generation," both released in 1965; at the same time, John Cale was incorporating his heavily amplified and dissonant approach to playing viola in the Velvet Underground's music, while in England Pink Floyd were creating electronic soundscapes as elements of their live performances, influenced by the experimental music group AMM.[46]

Tracing the early development of the Grateful Dead's use of sound in this sense is difficult. After all, they were not only an experimental music ensemble; they were also a commercial dance band, and as such they had to take into account the expectations of their listeners, the owners of the venues in which they played, and the promoters that organized the shows. Hence it is reasonable to assume that their performance practice in commercial environments was, at least in the very early years, more conservative than their practice in rehearsal or in noncommercial settings, particularly with regard to such nonmusical, noisy sounds. Garcia points this out in discussing the appeal for the band of the Acid Tests, the multimedia parties at which the band's religious vision came about: in 1965, "we got more into wanting . . . to take it farther. In the nightclubs, in the bars, mostly what they want to hear is short, fast stuff . . . so our trip with the Acid Test was to be able to play long and loud. . . . Of course, we were improvising cosmically too."[47]

By late 1967, the band's popularity had grown considerably. Also, and probably more importantly, the band was performing in contexts in which all sorts of "trippy" or strange sounds were permissible as music, and in front of audiences who enjoyed hearing extremely loud music. In these contexts, the Grateful Dead could indulge to the fullest their desire to work with sound—although, as it happened, that desire did not extend quite as far into the realms of dissonance as, for example, the Velvet Underground or AMM. It is not impossible to work compositionally with this sort of sound, even live (although it is a great deal easier to do in the studio). Nonetheless, such sounds by their nature are difficult to control, or to preconceive beyond a general idea, and they thus encourage an improvisational and spontaneous approach—which is the approach that the Grateful Dead took.

As I suggested, improvised sounds sections seem to have begun as the climaxes to jams, but they quickly expanded beyond this role. At a show on November 10, 1967, we can hear the "sounds" emerging *out of* the climax to the preceding piece—namely "Caution (Do Not Stop on Tracks)." In a show played on January 22, 1968, the sounds arise *after* the climax to the preceding piece ("Born Cross-Eyed"), creating what seems clearly intended to be a new piece, although with its roots in the old; this approach will be generally followed in the rest of the acid rock period.

Sounds episodes are less common in the Americana period, although not entirely absent. When they return in full force for the jazz-rock period, the tendency is for them to take place in the middle of longer and more conventional musical jams that would arise out of such songs as "The Other One," "Playing in the Band," or "Dark Star." A good case in point is the performance from April 26, 1972, released as *Hundred Year Hall* in 1995 on the Grateful Dead's label. On disc 2 of the performance, the band jams from "Truckin'" into an extended version of "The Other One." By 21:30, they have wound down the momentum of the previous jamming and moved into playing very open, spacious music, with Lesh taking the lead; the playing becomes more abstract and at times dissonant, until by 25:00 they are fully into a "sounds" section. By around 28:00 they have begun to pull out of it; by 28:25 they are again playing non–sounds music, albeit still improvising; by 33:30 they have returned to the main theme of "The Other One."

One of the most interesting characteristics of the Grateful Dead as an improvising band is their flowing nature. Many of their contemporaries embraced discontinuity and the creation of jarring effects, which often somehow ceased to jar as their novelty value evaporated. Indeed, the use of such features, abetted by the new possibilities of the recording studio, would become characteristic of the emergent genre of psychedelic music, with the Beatles' "Revolution 9" from the *White Album* being perhaps the most famous example.[48] The Grateful Dead's overall preference was for continuous but nonmechanical, ever-fluctuating movement. Even when that continuous movement led the listener to some very odd and distant places indeed, as on their tour de force *Anthem of the Sun* album, still, the operative verb is *lead*, rather than, say, *catapult*.

This tendency extends to their live use of sounds as well. Although, as noted, parts of these sections could be quite jarring, the Grateful Dead tended to lead up to them, gradually increasing the intensity or dissonance of the sounds—listen, for example, to the buildup to dissonance in the latter half of "Playing in the Band" from December 2, 1973. By 12 minutes in, the song's rhythm has been abandoned, although a pulse still remains; by 13 minutes, the musicians are playing jarring fragments of lines, and Kreutzmann has largely abandoned timekeeping. At 14:30, Lesh cues a move into even less traditionally "musical" space by striking his bass (or so it sounds to me), producing a crackle of low-end sound, and scrabbling at his strings; Garcia picks up on this by increasing the intensity of his playing, making use of his wah pedal and producing a flurry of indistinguishable notes that turns into a climax at 15:20 while Weir manipulates feedback. From this point on, the music is very open, without a clear rhythm or structure, while the musicians use harmonics and effects (such as Lesh's jarring use of distortion starting around 17:45) to produce a very dissonant sonic texture.

It is important to note in this regard that sounds sections generally arose out of preceding songs, rather than beginning sets; they were places that the listener was taken to. Just as the improvisation in the Framework arose out of the main riff of the song, so here the movement is from normality to strangeness, the impression being that of a sudden change of perspective, so that what was normal is now revealed to be strange. But the perception of the strange is presented as being liberatory rather than basic; in other words, it follows, rather than precedes, the perception of normality, revealing what lies behind that facade.

The Grateful Dead's willingness to experiment with sounds gave them the opportunity to take their improvisations beyond the limits of "songs" and many conventionally accepted aspects of music. It is important to note, however, that such conventions were implicitly supported in a general sense even when violated in a specific sense through the restricted use of the sounds— that is, the sounds episodes provided a designated space for the violation of convention within an overarching and broadly conventional structure. As

Garcia puts it, "Now that we have this new thing, these electronic sounds, it's a question of how can you use them in such a way so that they are musical instead of a racket?"[49] For the Grateful Dead, by and large, in the period under discussion, such sonic explorations were reserved for their own sections and would not intrude when the band was playing more conventional songs.

This distinguishes them from other bands that were exploring nonstandard sounds. The early Pink Floyd, for example, would keep a steady flow of them happening, using them as permanent parts of the context of the song, as can be heard on their soundtrack to the film *Tonite Let's All Make Love in London . . . Plus*.[50] The Grateful Dead, on the other hand, did not tend to integrate these sounds with their other songs, thus implicitly validating the distinction between the two approaches to playing music, and, moreover, increasing the sense of motion in the music. Rather than putting the listener in an entirely normal or entirely spacey or noisy context, the Grateful Dead would lead their fans through one context and into another. As we've seen elsewhere, here, too, the band's method is to respect formal, conventional structures, even as they are used as jumping-off points for improvised adventures.

MOVEMENT THROUGH SECTIONS

Another approach to improvisation that seems related to the Framework involves striking a balance between improvisation and composition by structuring music around the improvised movement through somewhat predetermined sections. A given section may be identified by its tonality, basic rhythm, melodic elements, harmony, motifs, or riffs. In a sense, it is fixed, with definite outlines. But these outlines are less apparent, less specific, and less restrictive than the outlines of songs proper. The outlines mark out the musical space in which the band works; they do not provide a road map of specific paths through that space.

Although there is no evidence of a direct causal linkage, this practice of movement through sections can be seen as the spiritual descendent of the Framework's tendency to work in a certain feel for a period of time before moving into another feel. It is an extension of the idea of taking voyages, of moving consecutively through different musical environments, which, as we will see, was tremendously important for the band. However, the sections tend to be more sharply differentiated from one another and to last longer than the feels that the band will move through when playing according to the Framework. Additionally, the sections function on a higher level of organization: they are macro-organizing principles that oversee large sections of jams, not micro-organizing ones.

Now, whatever its links to the Framework, this approach to improvisation does owe obvious debts to contemporary jazz practice. There is an especially striking parallel in the John Coltrane Quartet's *A Love Supreme* album, an enormously and widely influential work at the time.[51] Although Coltrane's career had many highlights, *A Love Supreme* has generally been seen as his masterpiece, especially by those who are not jazz insiders: it is epic in scope and has a spiritual, almost sanctified, feel, standing midway between the "straight" jazz of *Giant Steps* and the freer, less accessible music that would follow it.[52] *A Love Supreme* was released in early 1965, immediately prior to the Grateful Dead's formation. The album is structured as a suite, with several different movements. Like the "movement through sections" approach, it involves the band improvising its way through these movements, these different musical territories.

Blair Jackson notes that with the development of the suite idea and jamming between tunes, the Grateful Dead "could play for an hour or more without stopping between songs. . . . This had never been done before in rock. Even in jazz . . . there were rarely attempts at fusing pieces together the way the Dead did, much less figuring on the spot, through inspired improvisation, ways to create transitions between songs that hadn't previously been joined."[53] This formal innovation took their music in different directions from those pursued by Coltrane.

But Coltrane was not the only jazz musician exploring such extended forms at the time. Ekkehard Jost's discussion of Don Cherry's work shows that from the mid-1960s on Cherry was moving in similar directions to the Grateful Dead, using "themes" (as Jost calls them; I would call them "sections") as fundamental structuring principles for his music, giving the underlying material over which and through which his bands improvise.[54] But, given Coltrane's iconic status generally, and specifically his importance for the Grateful Dead, and combined with the fact that his greatest work using this approach was done just shortly before the Grateful Dead's formation (from *Africa/Brass* [Impulse!] in 1961 to *A Love Supreme* in 1965), it is likely that his work would have been primarily influential as the Grateful Dead moved to larger but still improvisational forms, a progression in musical approach that would eventually find them structuring whole sets as "suites" made up of sections to be played through successively.

A related approach is that taken by the Butterfield Blues Band in their "East/West," released by Elektra in 1966 on the album of the same name.

"East/West" was an important work, for its concept as for its execution: it was extremely long by the standards of its day and possessed a power and sophistication that impressed contemporaries, as did the band's lead guitarist, Mike Bloomfield. Bloomfield was "the first American guitar hero";[55] both Eric Clapton and Jorma Kaukonen cited him as an influence, and the influence of his tone and approach are clearly audible in Garcia's early work.[56] John Kahn, the bassist for the Jerry Garcia Band, said that "Jerry told me that when he was first playing in San Francisco, Bloomfield was the one guitarist who really impressed him."[57] David Brackett writes that "as reminiscences of participants make clear, the Butterfield band's tour of the West Coast in early 1966 and their relatively advanced abilities as improvisers played a major role in the spread of improvisational practices, and in the blending of blues, jazz, and classical Indian music, especially in the San Francisco Bay area."[58] This is why, as Peter Prown and H. P. Newquist write, "East/West" "had a dramatic influence on nearly every guitarist in San Francisco and clearly anticipated the days when long, exotic solos and psychedelic jams would be commonplace in rock and roll."[59]

The song is divided into sections, each one underpinned by a single bass riff with improvisation over top, gradually building in dynamics until a climax is reached, at which point another improvisatory cycle begins. Each section is underpinned by a subtly different bass riff (played by Jerome Arnold) which serves as a bed for the improvisation, establishing the atmosphere for the section.

This was an innovative piece, possibly inspired by Miles Davis's "Flamenco Steps," in which each of the soloists moves through a series of modes as they solo. Jerome Arnold, serving as the fulcrum for the band, stayed locked into one set pattern at a time, but his periodic changes of the pattern maintained interest and allowed the band to explore new areas without the song being fundamentally destabilized. Band member Mark Naftalin says that "[guitarist] Elvin Bishop started with a long solo, then retreated to tamboura-like droning while Mike [Bloomfield] soloed on a sequence of sections, using a different mode in each section. Some of the modes were more Eastern, some more Western."[60]

The Butterfield Blues Band was a well-respected and well-known band in the mid-1960s. There is no evidence that "East/West" was directly taken as a model by the Grateful Dead, but the way that it moves through environments while maintaining a strong basic tonality and rhythm makes it comparable to, and possibly influential on, the development of the Framework. Naftalin argues that it was inspired by an acid trip that Bloomfield took, in the course of which Bloomfield "had a revelation and told me that he now understood how

Ex 4.1 Basslines
from Butterfield
Blues Band's "East-
West," 1966.

Indian music worked. On our next gigs . . . we began performing the improvisation that we called 'The Raga' for a while, until it was given a name: 'East-
West.'"[61] If this story is true, and if it was known to the Grateful Dead, one can
easily imagine that it would have been inspiring to them as they worked out
their own approach to improvisation based on the contents of their acid trips.

The "movement through sections" approach to composition mixed with
improvisation is ambitious and complex, placing great demands on the musicians; therefore, it is not surprising that the band's use of it was limited. It is
most prevalent in the second, acid rock period; one of its classic presentations
is found in the complete "That's It for the Other One" suite, as found on
the band's second album, 1968's *Anthem of the Sun*. As mentioned earlier, the
band's tendency in this period was to merge songs together, creating continuous pieces of music that could last entire sets. Lesh speaks of these as
"sequences," with the "Dark Star"—"St. Stephen"—"The Eleven"—"Turn On
Your Lovelight" progression being their "major" sequence in 1968–69.[62]

This tendency can make it difficult at times to distinguish between songs,
multisection songs, and modules; it must have been especially difficult for
people in the audience, and this should caution us against being too hasty to
draw distinctions between songs. To take an example, technically, the song
called "New Potato Caboose" is distinct from "That's It for the Other One,"
but, both in the recording on the *Anthem of the Sun* studio album and in the
live performance of August 24, 1968 (released by the Grateful Dead in 1993
on their own label as *Two from the Vault*), there is nothing to tell the listener
that "New Potato Caboose" is a separate song, rather than simply being part
of the overall "That's It for the Other One" composition.

Similarly, the band could move seamlessly through songs from "Dark
Star" to "St. Stephen" to "The Eleven" and into "Turn On Your Lovelight," as
they did on their *Live/Dead* album, with a song-fragment inserted between
the second and third pieces—although this album is made up of material
drawn from several different shows, the progression reflects their actual concert practice at the time. How would this music have been perceived, and
how did the band intend it to be heard? As four pieces? Five? As one very

long piece? Perhaps as all or none of the above, depending on the listener, their mindset, and their familiarity with the band's music. As David Malvinni reports, "We know from accounts of these early shows that the audience in many instances and especially under the influence of LSD had no idea what they were actually hearing—it was truly an aural journey into uncharted territory for many."[63]

The band's practice indicates that they were comfortable with a certain degree of ambiguity in terms of distinguishing songs, and, indeed, even courted it. In this period, the set as a whole seems to be the band's focus; thus distinctions between songs, sections in songs, and modules is not as clearly marked as it would be in the early and mid-1970s, when the band returned to this approach for such epic compositions as "Terrapin Station" and "Weather Report Suite." Both of these songs are extended works with a great deal of jamming in the sections, but those sections are clearly divided through obvious changes in such musical parameters as feel, tonality, and rhythm. There is far less ambiguity, far less interweaving of modules, sections, and songs in these pieces than in the band's live practice in 1968 and 1969.

Another shared aspect of these compositions is their susceptibility to being stripped down as time went on and the band rehearsed less. On the one hand, it was only fairly rarely that the full versions of any of these three songs would be performed; on the other hand, excerpted segments of these compositions *would* be regularly performed.[64] Indeed, "The Other One" would become one of the band's most sturdy musical workhorses, along with "Let It Grow," a section of "Weather Report Suite."

The movement through sections approach incorporates predetermined, composed features to the improvisational playing. One always knows where one is going, even if there is some uncertainty about how one will get there. It is a challenging and intricate way of organizing larger pieces, one that (when done well) enabled the band to play extended but coherently unified works without the "burnout" factor from overcomplexity that is an occupational hazard of progressive rock bands. Use of this tactic causes these longer pieces to be heard not as a collection of lines or riffs, but as the sum of several large musical environments within which the band is free to move about.

TRAP DOORS

In situations involving movement between composed material and improvisation, the question "When do I start improvising?" will naturally arise. Another, equally natural question is, "How do I start?" Granted that once the improvisation has begun the musicians can rely on spontaneous interband reaction, nonetheless they still need strategies for determining the initial content of the improvisation—that is, the material that will be their point of departure.

As we have seen, a number of options are available in terms of negotiating the placement and initial characteristics of improvisation. In the case of the Framework, the main location is set as the end of the song, and the initial content is set as the basic groove of the song. The improvisation thus follows and develops out of the song. In the movement through sections approach, the improvisations are guided and structured by the overarching characteristics of the sections in which they are found, with one section following another in a predetermined pattern.

The "trap door" approach is another way to solve this problem. In this approach, paradigmatically audible in the songs "Uncle John's Band" and "Playing in the Band," there is a distinctive and repeated phrase found within the song that identifies the location and initial characteristics of the improvisation. These phrases stand in marked contrast to the feel of the rest of the songs in which they are found: to borrow an expression used in an interview with Garcia in a different context, they could be described as "signposts to new space."[65] In "Uncle John's Band," for instance, the phrase over which jamming takes place is in Dm, while the rest of the song is in G; it is 7/4, while the rest of the song is in 4/4; and it possesses a very tight and distinctive rhythmic structure, while the rest of the song tends more toward a loose, open rhythmic feel.

In naming this approach, the image of a trap door appealed to me because it brings to mind the ideas of revelation and exploration of unsuspected potential; a trap door is a way to get out of the obvious levels of the structure one is in and to explore previously hidden areas. After these explorations, of course, one returns to the original structure, just as the wardrobe in C. S. Lewis's *The Lion, the Witch, and the Wardrobe* is the means by which the children both enter and leave Narnia.

To the best of my knowledge, the earliest use of the trap door approach— or at least an intriguing precursor to it—is to be found in one of the earliest of the second wave of band-composed pieces, "Alligator." In this song, there is a sudden and radical change of rhythm and harmony at the very end of the song, taking place under the last section of vocals, where the band repeatedly sings "Alligator." One notable difference, however, is that this section never returns to the main body of the song; it is the end of the piece, thus representing something of a compromise between Framework standards (end the song with extended improvisation taking off from a basic groove) and trap door standards (introduce a different riff or feel as a jumping-off point for improvisation).

"Alligator" was one of the first of the band's more sophisticated compositions, having been introduced by January 1967. The Grateful Dead always performed at least some originals, but early compositions such as "The Only Time Is Now," "Cream Puff War," and "Can't Come Down" are derivative, drawing, respectively, on earnest folk balladry, garage rock (particularly Love's version of "Hey Joe," from their first album), and Dylanesque folk rock. The band's second wave of original material, including "Alligator," "Cardboard Cowboy," and "Dark Star," features songs that are much more original and idiosyncratic, incorporating the musical developments that the band had made in the meantime—in the case under discussion, the early application of the trap door approach.

These trap doors have a dramatic effect on the listener. One's expectations and understanding of the musical context are first shifted rapidly—by the jump to the trap door riff or feel, which usually contrasts in one or more ways with the rest of the song—and then more slowly, as the band begins jamming in this new musical space. One is introduced to a new and exciting musical world that is to be found hidden within the old world.

The impression created by the trap door songs is not so much that of a journey, as in the movement through sections approach, but, rather, one of the juxtaposition of two worlds: an esoteric and usually longer, stranger, and more disconcerting one nestled within an exoteric one. It is reasonable to suspect that we have here a homological invocation of the sort of sudden enlightenment experience that was so important for the band, and for their community and fans (we will discuss these in chapter 7). We start in more or less mundane, discursive reality; suddenly we are somewhere else, having unpredictable adventures, and then one returns to mundane reality, but with our understanding of this context altered and nuanced by our experiences "through the looking glass."

MODULES

Finally, there is the way in which jams can be punctuated through the use of more or less independent modules—that is, chord progressions with associated melodies and rhythms. These modules, which are often several bars in length, are related to the sections just discussed; indeed, they can be conceptualized as free-floating sections, mini-compositions that were, whether for a period or permanently, allowed to drift free rather than being integrated into a composition.[66]

Such integration could come later, of course; in fact, these modules can represent nascent forms of what will become fully developed songs, as is the case with a module in 10/4 known as "The Main Ten," which later became incorporated into a song called "Playing in the Band." Tom Constanten, who played keyboards with the band at the time that module was developed, notes that "there was a slow ten figure that we'd run through from time to time. . . . It was amusing to notice it later in the middle section to 'Playing in the Band.'"[67] Similarly, drummer Bill Kreutzmann reports that their song "The Eleven" "was really designed to be a rhythm trip. It wasn't designed to be a song. That more or less came later, as a way to give it more justification or something, to work in a rock 'n' roll set. We could've used it just as a transition, which is what it was, really."[68]

Another example of this approach concerns one of the band's most-loved songs, "Uncle John's Band," in which an instrumental version of the verse and chorus arose out of a jam on November 1, 1969, a full month before the song was premiered (December 4, 1969). Interestingly, the band moves into the "Uncle John's Band" module from another one, which would often serve as the coda to their version of the folk tune "Going Down the Road Feeling Bad." In this performance, then, we hear the invocation of both of these modules before they acquired their more or less permanent forms/locations.

On a somewhat different note, it can also happen that a module becomes associated with a given improvisational segment, as is the case with the "Feeling Groovy Jam," based around a descending D major scale and inspired by the Simon and Garfunkel song "The 59th St. Bridge Song," which was very often played in the jamming that led from "China Cat Sunflower" to "I Know You Rider."[69] Such modules have ambiguous associations. While not fully incorporated into a song, they do become associated with a specific song or combination of songs.

On the other hand, many of these modules never became songs of their own. In some cases, the movement goes in the other direction, and they are rather to be described as stripped-down versions of other songs, as musical borrowings—thus the "Mind Left Body Jam," an A7-Dadd9-Dmadd9-A progression which frequently appeared in jams from the early 1970s, was based on Paul Kantner's song "Mind Left Body." And in other cases, the modules simply represent familiar territory, comfortable musical environments that the band would choose to revisit from time to time, such as the E-F-E progression of the "Spanish Jam."

Whether they are potential sections of as-yet-unwritten songs, musical orphans, or borrowings from other artists, the modules provide moveable composed segments that can be brought in—or hit upon—in the course of improvisation; indeed, in some cases they probably result from the remembering and repeating of particularly fortuitous moments in other jams. They serve to ground improvisational sections, to give them a touch of stability and a temporary destination—but a destination whose appearance does not also invoke a whole chain of other musical associations. The use of these modules develops in the second, acid rock phase, logically enough, as the band builds up its musical vocabulary and "road tests" new or as-yet-unfinished pieces.

In addition to functioning as temporary destinations, the use of modules also helps, for band and audience, to integrate the immediate musical context with the larger musical context. The appearance of a theme that is familiar, but not specifically or necessarily attached to the song that the band is playing, serves as a reminder that all of the Grateful Dead's specific songs are played within a larger musical universe that also contains wandering musical elements in addition to the sorts of fixed systems represented by the songs as such. To extend the image: if, in this musical universe, the songs can be seen as solar systems, and the purely improvisational sections as the space between systems, the modules could be compared to asteroids, points of solidity moving through space, occasionally intersecting the star systems but then going their own way again. On a more prosaic level, these modules also work as tools for the band, giving them a context in which they can rekindle their inspiration for further exploration or providing a signal that a return to some sort of stability is needed or imminent. Modules, then, signal both familiarity and otherness, stability and change: they ground the band and listener while reminding them that the context in which one is grounded is one that includes more than just songs and space.

Excursus on "Dark Star"

Of all the Grateful Dead's songs, "Dark Star" best epitomizes the band's spirit of adventure and improvisation, especially in the band's early years, and the song has attracted more critical attention than any other single song in the

Grateful Dead's repertoire;[70] the reader is referred to these discussions for in-depth analysis of the song.[71]

Starting as a peppy, short number and even released as a single, the song expanded in length and slowed down in tempo over the first year of its performance. By late 1968 it had become a lilting, at times languid piece of music over which the band could jam for half an hour or more. Dodd notes that "generally the version from [the band's 1969 album] *Live/Dead* . . . is the acknowledged standard"—a summation that I think most people would agree with, certainly in terms of the song's rhythm and overall feel.[72] Some features of the song could and did change dramatically whenever it was played, but by the time *Live/Dead* was recorded (in early 1969), "Dark Star" had acquired the following characteristics:

1   A brief introductory flourish, played mainly on the bass guitar, leading into
2   a two-chord progression played over a mid-tempo rhythm, which was the main point of departure for improvisation, interrupted by
3   two sung verses with choruses. The verses are largely played over the main progression and rhythm; the chorus changes the rhythm, time signature, and harmony.[73]

Of these three characteristics, only the two-chord progression and the improvisations arising from it are absolutely essential to identify the song as "Dark Star." The second verse and chorus, in particular, were often dropped in concert, as the band moved from jamming directly into another song. "Dark Star" can be best understood, then, as a fairly open improvisational field, whose initial parameters are roughly defined rhythmically and harmonically and that are then potentially interrupted by the precomposed verses and choruses, when present.

When we try to categorize this piece, the way that the musically set verse/chorus combinations arise from improvisation and then sink back into it tempts us to see them as modules that have been attached to this specific song. But, upon closer examination, we see that this impression is misleading. As mentioned, the verses begin by using the same harmony and rhythm that underlies the improvisational section. Only as the verse progresses—and especially as we enter the chorus—do distinctions emerge. This creates a slow and understated move away from the main groove into new territory, led by the vocal.

We can see, then, the verse/chorus combinations as a slow and organically arising buildup to a momentary suspension of the main feel of the song, creating anticipation for the return to the main feel or (as would be the case after the second verse/chorus) creating an open space in which a new song can be brought in. Overall, the effect is quite elegant, an inspired solution to the problem of how to navigate between composed and improvised sections.

Conclusion

In this discussion, we have examined some of the tactics used by the Grateful Dead to facilitate, structure, and nuance their improvisational practice. Just as improvisations based on the Framework start and end at the same place, I would like to end this discussion as I began it, by stressing the heuristic and somewhat arbitrary emphasis of this examination. These various tactics are, for one thing, not exclusive. We have seen how trap door pieces arose from modules; modules themselves can be the free-floating stuff of sections, when and if they are set into definite orders; even the most pro forma solo over changes will include "within song" improvisation on the part of the rhythm section; and, of course, the links of most of these approaches with the Framework is clear as well, so there is no question of using these categories exclusively. Their sole purpose is to give some points in a multidimensional continuum, consideration of which might enhance our ability to discuss of the Grateful Dead's improvisational practice.

In so doing, I have chosen not to examine the actual in-the-moment act of improvisation—that is, I have not discussed precisely how, for example, Lesh responded to Garcia's response to Kreutzmann at 12:14 of "Playing in the Band" on June 19, 1973. Instead, my focus has been on looking at some of the formal parameters within which these moment-to-moment decisions are made. My choice in this regard was determined by my desire to express a rock-derived conceptuality and aesthetics, rather than one derived from jazz scholarship.

With the exception of Garcia, none of the Grateful Dead were consummate individualistic "improvisers" such as one finds among musicians coming out of the jazz or new music traditions—we might think of Steve Lacey or William Parker. As we discussed, one of the distinctive aspects of rock—and one that is often underappreciated—is the fact that it is profoundly a group endeavor, groups being in many ways the fundamental elements of rock music, rather than compositions or specific players. The ability (or lack of ability) of individual players is much less the point in rock than the way in which they fuse together into a group—thus, for example, collections of fairly untalented players such as the Ramones or the Stooges can come together and create masterpieces. Group activity is guided by shared assumptions or understandings, whether explicit or implicit. In this chapter, I have tried to lay out some of these understandings

THE TURNING POINT

In looking at a band's career, it is necessary to harmonize two conflicting but equally essential aspects. On the one hand, retrospective examination often shows clearly that there are phases to a band's career. It becomes apparent that at such and such a point, the band had such and such an approach (to aspects of its songwriting, or performance, or whatever the case may be); at another point, things have changed, and now the band had a distinctly different approach. It's often the case that given characteristics of a band's playing or writing will, when examined carefully, fit unproblematically into one phase and will either not be found in another, or will acquire a different resonance.

On the other hand, bands are organic groupings working within commercial and social structures that affect both their development and the perception and manifestation of that development. What this means is that we can say when a new approach is presented to the public, but often we cannot say how long it may have preexisted in the intentions or dreams of band members, and it is also often the case that the inaugural steps of a new direction are not perceived as such at the time that they are made.

It is necessary, then, to be both nuanced and cautious when discussing the way that bands change and develop. We simply don't have all the evidence, and we have only one side of the story. With these caveats in mind, I would like to suggest, in a nuanced and cautious manner, that there are two foundational periods, or—to change the image—two absolutely crucial turning points for the Grateful Dead as an improvising rock band. The first took place in late 1965, when, under the influence of transcendent experiences, tendencies in jazz and modern classical music, and a mystical belief in the band's distinctiveness and musical potential, the group opened their music up to collective improvisation and spontaneity. It is from this period that the Framework, the development of the dance tunes model, and the soloing over changes approach date.

The second turning point, as I see it, is to be found in early-to-mid-1967, with the introduction of a "second wave" of original compositions (including "Dark Star," "Alligator," "New Potato Caboose," and "That's It for the Other One") that facilitated or inaugurated the rest of the improvisational techniques that I have discussed in this chapter. The band's songwriting took several leaps forward, and new songs were brought in that use the "sections" approach, such as "New Potato Caboose."

As I have argued, "Alligator" can be seen as using a proto–trap door approach, thus inaugurating this particular tactic. It is during this period that the band's jamming, especially on "Viola Lee Blues," begins to enter the realms of pure sound during climaxes. And, finally, steady gigging over the past year and a half have developed Weir's and Lesh's competence and loosened up Kreutzmann, to the point where they can improvise "within songs" more freely.[74] By the middle of 1967, then, the band had had a year and a half to become comfortable with their musical direction and had the confidence that pursuing it would not prevent them from finding an audience; this conjunction of familiarity and security might explain why they were able to take these steps forward. At this point, I would argue that the foundations for the Grateful Dead's future improvisational work had been laid; the thematic outlines were in place. What followed in subsequent years involved working out and nuancing these broad approaches.

MOTION: CONTINUAL, IF NOT STEADY

So far in this chapter, we have discussed a number of tactics that the Grateful Dead used in order to facilitate, organize, and indeed render possible the improvisational approach to rock music that they adopted. Our understanding of the band's approach and values can also be furthered through examination of some tactics that they did not use. This might seem a unusual approach to take, and I freely grant that arguments from silence are intrinsically weak. Nonetheless, "weak" and "insignificant" are not synonyms. There is value in examining some of the roads that the Grateful Dead did not choose to take, especially when these are roads that their contemporaries, successors, or influences did take: we see the Grateful Dead's motivations more clearly when we understand the options that they eschewed. An illustration might be useful here: if no one I know reads Hemingway, and I don't read Hemingway, that is not surprising. But if many people I know and respect read Hemingway, and my friends talk about him a lot, and I still choose not to read him . . . well, maybe that is a sign that there is something to be learned from my refusal to read him.

Turning back to music, there are three tactics that immediately come to mind as ones that other improvising bands made use of, but that the Dead did not use.

Drones

The improvisational use of drones of various sorts and taken to various degrees would have been a familiar part of the Grateful Dead's musical environment, coming from a number of directions. One of these would have
been Phil Lesh's exposure to minimalist music. In the early 1960s, composer
Terry Riley points out, "Phil Lesh was always around the [San Francisco]
Tape Music Center, and he and Steve Reich bought a tape recorder together and shared it."[75] Bernstein also notes that "both Lesh and [Grateful
Dead keyboardist Tom] Constanten were active participants in the Bay
Area new music scene," a point brought out by Lesh himself as well in
his autobiography.[76] Several members of the Grateful Dead—Mickey Hart
foremost among them—showed a strong interest in Indian classical music,
in which drones are extensively used.[77] We also cannot rule out the possible influence of the improvisational experiments of such contemporaries
as the Velvet Underground (with whom the Grateful Dead shared several
bills in 1969).[78]

Of course, depending on how loosely one interprets the term, *drone* can
mean a great many things, and certainly there are aspects of the Grateful
Dead's improvisational practice that could loosely be described as *droning*.
But we do not find any extended use of drones such as would be provided by
the tambura player in a Hindustani classical ensemble, for instance, nor of
the sort that one encounters in the music of La Monte Young or the Velvet
Underground (particularly in live performance, but also on record in such
songs as "Venus in Furs," from their first album). As I mentioned, it is possible that minimalist aesthetics had an effect on the Grateful Dead's improvisational approach, but the minimalism in question was what Fink describes as
"pulse pattern minimalism": minimalism as "repetition with a regular pulse,
a pulse that underlies the complex evolution of musical patterns" rather than
the drone minimalism of a composer such as La Monte Young.[79] In short, the
idea of a constantly held long tone that underpins a song or improvisational
section is, interestingly, not found in the Grateful Dead's music.

This is particularly striking, considering that drones would have already
been linked to improvisation for various members, and that drones are especially simple to produce and effective with the use of electrically amplified instruments played at high volume. It can be difficult to play a really sustained
drone on a Western acoustic instrument (bagpipes and a few other exceptions aside), but with an electric keyboard or sufficiently amplified guitar, it
is easy. This absence, then, needs to be seen as a road that was seen, but not

taken; it cannot have been due to ignorance of the technique on the band's part, nor the inability to produce effective drones.

Riffs

For a band as influenced by blues, especially electric Chicago blues, as the Grateful Dead, their avoidance of riffs (by which I mean short, precisely repeated figures that provide the backbone for a song) is striking. Perhaps the clearest example of this can be seen when we compare their versions of the traditional blues tune "Good Morning Little Schoolgirl" with the roughly contemporary version found on Junior Wells's influential *Hoodoo Man Blues* album. As we discussed, this latter version is absolutely underpinned by the defining bass riff, which the bassist repeats unchangingly throughout the vast majority of the song. When the Grateful Dead played this song, however, they would use this riff to introduce and identify the song and would work with it as a motif during the song, but it was never simply replicated with the same mechanical repetition as that employed by bassist Jack Myers in the Junior Wells version. Even when Lesh was playing it, the riff would be continually varied to greater or lesser degrees, and it was quite common for him to abandon it altogether, and for the motif to be passed around the band members to be played or suggested.

As this discussion shows, on the one hand Grateful Dead songs do possess characteristic motifs, progressions, and even the sort of figures that could be used for riffs, but on the other hand they lack the unison riffing approach that underlies the improvisational playing of many of their hard-rock and blues-rock brethren and sistren. You will never hear all the members of the rhythm section come together to repeat a figure in the way that is so common with other early improvising rock bands such as, for example, Hawkwind, the MC5, or the Stooges.

Noise

Finally, we come to noise. I use the word *noise* to distinguish it from the *sounds* to which I referred earlier. I must stress, though, that the two are not absolutely distinct, but separate points on a continuum. When I speak of noise here, I am referring to the sort of chaotic, often energetic, so-to-speak "unmusical" soundscapes created by musicians playing in the "energy music" approach to free jazz (e.g., Albert and Don Ayler), as well as by musicians who can be linked to the emergent "free improvisation" scene, such as the members of AMM.

At their most frenzied, the Grateful Dead would occasionally approach these extremes, but this was rare and almost never sustained. When it did occur, it took place either at the climaxes of jams, or in the "feedback" sections that sometimes closed their shows, especially in their acid rock phase—again, as a sort of climax, but this time to the set rather than to the song. Such noise was at no point the group's main purpose, as it so frequently was for Albert Ayler, for example. The idea of building entire songs much of whose raison d'être is the generation of a noisy, assaultive tumult that tries to break down the boundaries of music altogether is foreign to their approach.

As we have seen in discussing the Framework, the Grateful Dead as a general rule are musically experimental, but only to a point: basic, traditional conceptions of music are affirmed and rarely undermined in their songs and in their approach to instrumental practice and roles. No doubt this has to do both with their personal inclinations, and with their status as a working rock band with a large audience and also large overheads. Melvin Backstrom notes that "although . . . creating music of a highly challenging nature was not foreign to the band, the intention in doing so was rarely of the antagonistic—vis-à-vis the audience—kind that Greene celebrates in performances by the Mothers or the Velvet Underground. It was intended, largely understood, and realized as a collaborative experience of heightened, even transcendent, aesthetic experiences realized through the temporary merging of performers and audience members."[80]

Their practice on many levels—from instrumental roles to songwriting to staging of concerts—shows that the band was interested in traditional forms and in devising ways to work freely within them rather than abandoning them. Furthermore, as a band they were not commercially marginal, as were most of the free jazz musicians, and they thus needed to appeal to a popular audience as "entertainers" as well as "artists," unlike many of the early free improvisation players. The need (and, one suspects, the genuine desire) to play for a large, popular audience also placed certain constraints on their practice. As former soundman Augustus "Bear" Owsley notes, the members of the Grateful Dead "have always had a sense of responsibility to a paying audience."[81] What the Grateful Dead were trying to do was truly challenging and strange, often as magical as music gets, but, as we have seen, they believed that the extraordinary was something that underlay, and occasionally arose out of, the conventional.

One thing that all three of these eschewed approaches have in common is that they create a feeling of stasis: they eliminate or relativize motion. The drone creates an unchanging sonic space, a constant to which the rest of the piece responds and by which it is defined. When bands focus on riffing, they create a defined and tight and theoretically never-ending space within which the music is set. Finally, noise either eliminates motion by carrying it to its frenzied extremes, to chaos, or prevents it by creating a context of such indeterminacy that it rules motion out.

This is not to say, of course, that change, including development, is impossible when any of these approaches are used. Old sections or lines can collapse into a drone, and new ones can be born out of it; riffs can change; noise can change texture. In all of these cases, it is possible to make and move between large structural elements and distinctions. However, these approaches do rule out the sort of ongoing and flowing change on a microscopic level that is so characteristic of the Grateful Dead's aesthetic, in which nothing is ever repeated exactly, although at times the changes are extremely subtle.

The Grateful Dead are always traveling, negotiating new musical environments, exploring them, and moving on. The movement tends to be gradual and dialogic, but it is always present, and it is usually relatively smooth. The improvisational approaches that we have discussed in this chapter are ways of structuring and contextualizing, but not eliminating, such motion; it flows through everything that the band played.

JOURNEYS AND ENVIRONMENTS

The Grateful Dead's valorization of this sort of movement can be seen, then, not only in their practice but also in what they do not practice—that is, their eschewal of improvisational tactics such as droning, riffing, or noise that are opposed to it. The lack of use of these tactics links up with what I have noted relating to the tactics that they do use, to give us an overall picture of a band whose musical focus is on creating environments in which spontaneous but nonetheless gradual, flowing improvisation is facilitated, often involving relatively smooth motion through a succession of "fields" or sections rather than sudden jumps. The trap door approach may seem in some ways to be a contradiction to this general principle, but in fact it is not: it provides an abrupt starting point, true, that is often in contrast to the rest of the piece, but all it really does is to provide the improvisation with a distinct starting point. From this point, the jamming develops as freely in trap door songs as in any other material.

Ultimately, the Grateful Dead's jamming is about the gradual, connected unfolding of new musical contexts that arise from the ones that precede them. They take the audience on journeys, rather than teleport them to new musical environments. You may end up sightseeing on Mars, but you will have gotten there step by step, not just by teleporting in, and you will know that on some level Mars is reachable from your front door. And when you get home again, you will never be able to forget that in some way Mars is potentially present even in the most mundane of contexts.

This approach is well grounded in psychedelic aesthetics: as Patrick Lundborg discusses, psychedelia involves the recognition that there are multiple states of being, and thus "the experienced psychedelicist may feel able to move between various expressions of 'reality.' . . . This wilful motion between states of equal actualization but differing content was one of the key concepts that Ken Kesey and the Merry Pranksters developed," although it goes further back, at least as far as "William James' pioneering insight of the presence of multiple realities, from which we are blocked only by habit." However, Lundborg argues, "the crucial condition [for truly psychedelic art] . . . is that the other plane or state must be somehow adjacent to the plane currently inhabited, so that the transition becomes no more radical than taking an elevator ride."[82] Alternate states of being emerge out of each other in psychedelic art, just as reality gradually warps rather than abruptly shifts when one is under the influence of LSD. For a nuanced and detailed expression of this, listen to the first side of the Grateful Dead's second album, *Anthem of the Sun*, as different sounds and different approaches to the music, excerpted from several different live performances as well as studio recordings, arise and unfold. Although the Grateful Dead were not able to pursue this approach as thoroughly live as they did in the studio for that album (recorded in 1968 at the peak of the psychedelic movement), the overall commitment to ongoing, flowing motion remains at the heart of their practice.

Writing about Improvisation

APPROACHES TO UNDERSTANDING SPONTANEOUS PLAYING

How relevant is an analysis of recorded improvisations made on a certain date and under certain circumstances (the group involved, the improviser's physical and mental disposition, the conditions imposed by the producer, etc.)? This will depend upon the extent to which these improvisations can be taken, beyond the immediate musical facts, as indicative of the specific musicians' or groups' creative principles.
—EKKEHARD JOST, *Free Jazz* (1994)

Having taken a look at the Grateful Dead's improvisational practice and its development, now it is time to integrate this firsthand perspective with some of the theoretical discussions that have swirled around improvisation. In his canonical article on the topic, Bruno Nettl notes that, while "we feel that we know intuitively what improvisation is," still "we find that there is confusion regarding its essence."[1] He devotes the first half of his article to arguing that improvisation is to be viewed as a point on a continuum, at the opposite end of composition, rather than as something utterly unique. He then goes on to say that

> having apparently done what we could to demolish the improvisation as a concept separate from composition, we must now reinstate it for the purpose of examining certain performance wherein the musician is free to contribute of his own spontaneous making. The improviser, let us hypothesize, always has something given to work from—certain things at the base of the performance, that he [*sic*] uses as the ground he builds. We may call it his model. In some cultures theoretical terms are used to designate the model . . . On the other hand, the model may be a specific composition. . . . Or, again, styles indicating some specific pitch or content (figured bass in Western music, or abadja and kpanlogo, rhythmically distinctive styles of West African drumming) can reveal the existence of an improvisatory model and its recognition as such by its culture.[2]

Improvisational Models

This model is often implicit, described by Richard Widdess as "a set of (usually unconscious) assumptions about what things look like and/or the order in which they occur" that is always to be approached with caution so as to avoid reification.[3] As improvising guitarist Derek Bailey notes, "I would have thought it self-evident that improvisation has no existence outside of its practice."[4] This practice always takes place within contexts, which bring their own constraints—thus Leslie Tilley, a researcher of collective improvisation, points out that "only by discovering both the model and the technical, aesthetic, and social guidelines shaping its idiomatic performance do we reveal the fullest possible conceptual space of any improvised practice."[5]

Models need specific characteristics that enable listeners to identify them. As Nettl writes, "Thus we may take it that each model, be it a tune, a theoretical construct, or a mode with typical melodic turns, consists of a series of obligatory musical events which must be observed, either absolutely or with some sort of frequency, in order that the model remain."[6] Nettl uses the word "density" to refer to the frequency with which these "obligatory musical events" occur and observes that density varies greatly depending on the genre. In this light, Tilley refers specifically to "the relatively free improvisation of psychedelic or acid rock bands. . . . Here, models take the form of very broad schemas for exploration that encourage almost unlimited creative flexibility."[7] From our earlier discussion, it would seem that this openness arises from the process-based nature of the Framework that the band built between 1966 and 1967: the Grateful Dead lead the listener by steps into their improvisations, with each step building off the last.

This emphasis on process—and, as we saw, the emergence of improvisation as a tactic to keep dancers engaged—permits us to see many sorts of improvisation as fundamentally being about "keeping it going," as Stephen Slawek puts it: "Keeping it going means that something has to be there to do next. And since what is there is not concrete or written down, it must be something remembered and reproduced intact on the spot, or something created extemporaneously."[8] Stephen Blum, referring to how improvisation is required in order to have musical events continue, writes that "in every part of the world we can observe activities that would fail to achieve their ends if performers were unable to improvise effectively in the presence of other participants. . . . When one purpose of repeating a sequence of motions in dance or ritual is to generate feelings of euphoria, one or more participants may need to decide when to replace one pattern with another. When one of the aims of a ceremony is to invite gods or ancestors to take part, the performers must know how to react appropriately at any sign that the invited guests have arrived."[9] While there has been a great deal of highly theoretical or abstract definition of improvisation, it is important to keep in mind that improvisational playing can also simply arise from the sheer enjoyment or appreciation of the moment and the desire to keep the moment going. The Grateful Dead's improvisation cannot be understood outside of the context of a concert venue filled with happy, dancing people.

One very typical characteristic of discussion of improvisation is the invocation of the idea of "freedom." Ali Jihad Racy observes that "improvising has been viewed as a metaphor for freedom," while Jeff Titon argues that "perhaps at some deep level we prize improvisation not just because of the skills involved but because we think it exemplifies human freedom," and the very names of genres such as "free jazz" and "free improvisation" testify to the importance of the concept.[10] But what is meant by *freedom*? In his discussion of jazz-derived free improvisation, Mike Heffley makes some interesting and useful distinctions. He speaks of three aspects of musical freedom with regard to the form or tradition within which the musician is working:

1 freedom from form, the revolutionary act of "shaking off constraints";
2 freedom to form, "the simple access by one body of information to another" that enables someone working in one genre to draw on aspects of another genre; and

3   freedom in form, which involves knowledge and "mastery" of the conventions of a given form and "fulfilling [its] potential in new ways."[11]

The first and third of these correspond, respectively, to what Derek Bailey describes as "idiomatic" and "non-idiomatic" improvisation. The former approach is "concerned with the expression of an idiom"; the latter, "while it can be highly stylized, is not usually tied to representing an idiomatic identity."[12]

The Grateful Dead were, if revolutionary, quietly so. As I will discuss, the majority of their music and the principles upon which that music was based fit into broad understandings of "rock" music, unlike, for example, more noisily transgressive contemporary groups such as the Red Krayola or the Velvet Underground. And, although the Grateful Dead were clearly aware of other musical traditions, we do not hear in their music the sort of wholesale and explicit adoption of characteristics of these traditions that are found in blues-rock bands such as Cream, or jazz-rock bands such as Blood, Sweat, and Tears.

Thus, the Grateful Dead's improvisational approach is an example of Heffley's third category, freedom in form, with the form being 1960s rock music. As we saw in chapter 4, in the Grateful Dead's improvisational practice the expected roles of the various instruments are not challenged: there is usually a tonal center and an implicit groove, and, in the earliest period the jamming itself emerges out of an area in the song—the fadeout—that would already have been marked as a more open and exploratory section.

Especially in their earliest years, the Grateful Dead performed many common folk-rock and blues songs, including "Hard to Handle," "Good Morning Little Schoolgirl," "Morning Dew," and "I Know You Rider," all songs that would have been common currency among working bands of the period. These, along with their own compositions, particularly their extremely derivative early works—such as "Can't Come Down," "Mindbender," "Tastebud," and "Cream Puff War"—show the Grateful Dead's knowledge of the conventions of their field.[13] Just as their early improvisations emerged out of already complete songs, so their improvisational practice builds on and develops the musical genre in which they work, rather than abandoning it or grafting it onto other forms.

To speak of the Grateful Dead's context of origin leads us to the issue of the interaction between culture and improvisation. As mentioned, improvisation—like language itself—is a universal practice that manifests in different contexts and responds to the exigencies of those contexts.[14] Therefore, discussions of improvisation are most useful when they clearly articulate and respond to the concerns of the context that they deal with, as it is only within such contexts that the meaning of the musical event can be determined. Even musical approaches such as "free improv," which seem to (or strive to seem to) recreate music ex nihilo, arose out of a definite artistic and intellectual context, one that blossomed in the fertile avant-garde subcultures of the 1960s and 1970s.

As one example, Regula Qureshi's detailed and fascinating discussion of qawwali improvisation is integrally linked to the musical, social, and (Sufi) religious context in which it is performed. She assesses the various improvisational acts of the musicians with regard to how those acts are chosen so as to increase, maintain, or control the degree of religious ecstasy aroused in listeners, and how they serve to guide the listeners through a complex and complete religious and aesthetic experience. Her goal is "to develop for Qawwali a musical grammar that includes programming Qawwali in performance."[15] To this end she presents the religious and theoretical underpinnings of the qawwali performance and then guides the reader through the actual unfolding of a performance, linking the performers' choices in terms of musical changes and their ritualized movement to the arousal and maintenance of the desired spiritual states in the listeners.

For example, Qureshi notes at one point that "Meraj's [a musician] focus [during the performance] has remained on several other special listeners who are showing incipient [spiritual] arousal. To intensify the impact of the repeated statements he therefore employs the higher-pitched alternate tune (A alt) and also restates the responsorial repetitions of A1. But no increase of their arousal occurs, so he decides to insert a *girah* [extra verse]."[16] Qureshi's analysis and discussion make it clear that there is no abstract improvisational nature here; the performers' choices cannot be understood without considering the social and religious contexts in which they are working, as well as the musical context.

Working from a very different perspective, David Borgo's analysis of improvisation, with its emphasis on systems theory, is based around the goals and approaches validated in modern free improvised music. Implicit in his discussion of such "difficult" artists as Evan Parker and Peter Brötzmann is an affirmation of the ideal of the autonomous experimental artist wrestling with "pure" sound and the expectation of audience passivity and assimilation of the artistic experience that is provided by the musician. In his analyses of musical examples, Borgo is extremely attentive to such parameters as musical density, textures, and the ways that musicians navigate through textures. He also discusses some of the theoretical explanations that musicians give for their practice, but, in contrast with Qureshi's work, he leaves the needs or desires of audiences and social imperatives undiscussed. In his concluding overview, he makes the claim that "the process of improvising music can teach us a way of being," but that "way of being" is one in which the musician is presented as a model figure for audiences to emulate instead of interact with.[17]

It is clear, then, that appropriate ways of talking about improvisation vary greatly depending on the context. In my discussion of the Grateful Dead's music, I have therefore been concerned not to discuss "improvisation" as its own category, but as the process by which the band facilitated improvisational playing and the reasons for which they did so.

While the European classical music tradition has been granted a privileged position in European and North American music instruction over the past several centuries, this has been mainly with regard to music that falls on the composed side of the composition-improvisation musical continuum. It is true that, for the past century, there has been more use of improvisation in classical or European-descended art music, particularly in the avant-garde (where it is sometimes referred to as "chance" or "aleatoric" methods), but, when it comes to teaching or thinking about improvisational playing, jazz is the privileged form, due to the combination of its valorization of improvisation with the strong emphasis placed on reflective practice, knowledge of historical context, and astounding technical virtuosity. When writing or teaching about improvisation, particularly in a North American context, it is typical to default to a jazz lens. Now, jazz and rock share a variety of characteristics—typical ensemble sizes; links to popular tradition as well as ties to the "art" world; an American popular culture context of origin—and so it is tempting to examine rock improvisation using tools developed for the study of jazz. However, there are two significant differences between the traditions that raise problems in this regard.

First of all, as we discussed, rock as a form tends to privilege the group, not the individual or the tradition within which the individual works. And group improvisation, particularly outside of high art contexts, tends to be overlooked in discussions of improvisation: as Tilley notes, "the musicology of improvisation . . . often depicts the strategies and schemas of individual musicians." But, she continues, this is unrealistic: "From jazz and Javanese gamelan to Shona mbira music . . . many improvisational practices have been shown to rely on the close interaction of multiple musicians." Drawing on Sawyer's *Group Genius*, she notes that "human beings, then, are often at their most creative in collaboration . . . yet 'there are very few comparative studies of improvised music traditions' . . . and even fewer specifically comparing group improvised practices." She argues that, "outside of New Orleans jazz, then, it seems that the notion of *collective improvisation* is reserved for . . . performances loosely exploring a structure, not those bound by melodic, rhythmic, or harmonic constraints," as the Grateful Dead usually were.[18]

If we want to understand how the Grateful Dead worked, though, we need an understanding of improvisation as a group practice, with the group as a structured whole (i.e., with the different instrumental roles maintained) that moves spontaneously through musical contexts. This understanding differs significantly from what we see in mainstream jazz, where the individual player rather than the group is the focus of attention, and the form is usually understood as being broadly established for any given piece, or art music, where the individual composer and his or her intentions (or, in the case of "aleatoric" composers, deliberate lack of intentions) for the piece tend to be the focus of attention. This is not to say that there are no exceptions, but the general rule is that rock tends to be about groups, while jazz tends to be about individual players, and art music tends to be about composers. And, by the way, the amount of intellectual and aesthetic status given to these three traditions just might have something to do with why, as Tilley observes, there is a lot more writing about improvisation from the perspective of an individual performer or someone who is engaging with an abstract tradition than there is from a group perspective.

We should also keep in mind that the Grateful Dead stand at the head of a tradition. They belong to the first generation of rock bands to seriously engage with improvisation; they also formed just a decade after rock came into being, during a period of immense development in the genre: it is not an exaggeration to say that the mid-to-late 1960s were a period when rock's fundamental parameters were being defined. For this reason, the sorts of analyses that one often finds of jazz improvisational practice, relying as they do on the existence of an acknowledged tradition of jazz improvisation, are not appropriate to the Grateful Dead's contemporary situation, nor can we use these methods as models for retrospective looks back at the rock improvising tradition, which has not developed in anything like the same way that the jazz tradition has developed.

For example, the sort of approach taken by Paul Berliner in his truly exhaustive and canonical book on jazz improvisation, *Thinking in Jazz*, in which he details the many and varied aspects of the jazz tradition so as to provide "documentation of traditional learning practices," will not work here.[19] First of all, rock music did not have an improvising tradition in the period I am discussing, secondly, rock—at least until the mid-1990s—did not develop the same sort of reverence for tradition or construction of traditional, authoritative standards that have marked jazz since the start of bebop, if not earlier. Let us recall the advice from Hal Crook's guide to jazz improvisation in which we find a typical emphasis on the individual soloist (rather than the group) and the weight of tradition: "A soloist's search for originality must be balanced and tempered with authenticity and tradition."[20] "Fuck it, let's rock" is a sentiment that defines rock, but it does not translate at all to jazz.

Interestingly, one jazz-related approach that does illuminate our present situation is that taken by Ekkehard Jost in his *Free Jazz*. This is precisely because he is not talking about the mainstream jazz tradition, but about free jazz musicians. Jost points out that the first and second waves of free jazz, motivated by "a mixture of musical and ideological factors," produced "a large number of divergent personal styles. . . . Their only point of agreement lay in a negation of traditional norms; otherwise, they exhibited such heterogeneous formative principles that any reduction to a common denominator was bound to be an over-simplification." Like me, Jost sees his subjects as standing at the head of their traditions and thus deals with their innovations in their own terms, with the (strong but not sole) emphasis on their status as unique creations rather than evolutionary developments of a tradition. In his analyses, he focuses on creating "style portraits" of the major groups or leaders, showing the ways in which their unique approaches to musical organization were created and describing these approaches.[21] For Jost, each group or artist that he examines is to be understood as motivated by a distinct vision, whatever its debts to tradition, and his concern is to describe this vision.

For instance, in speaking of trumpeter Don Cherry's "endless melodies" approach, which draws on repetition of themes, and in which the thematic material no longer "acts as a trigger for improvisation" but "itself is an object of improvisation," Jost identifies the goal as being to "create a new attitude towards time," diminishing the aspect of development and instead creating "a situation of repose in which movement is reduced to cycles of the smallest possible dimension."[22] In speaking of Archie Shepp's creative practice and the wide range of Shepp's collaborators and the creative contexts in which he works, Jost notes Shepp's "conviction that his duty as a musician must go beyond creative self-realization."[23] Jost's approach has been very influential on my analysis of the Grateful Dead's practice, and my efforts to link it to their spiritual beliefs and experiences (which I will discuss at length in chapters 7–9); Jost's is an exemplary method for discussing large-scale and coherent innovatory endeavors.

Discussion of the Grateful Dead's Practice

Over the past several decades since Graeme Boone's groundbreaking analysis of a canonical performance of "Dark Star"—perhaps the band's most emblematic song—Grateful Dead scholars have refined and nuanced their musical analyses of the band with great skill.[24] Although a tradition of serious critical discussion of rock-related music dates back to the 1960s, it was in the 1980s and 1990s that the tradition started to significantly break into academic domains, particularly with regard to analyses of the music itself. For the Grateful Dead, this breakthrough moment came, ironically, at the same time as the band's dissolution.

Boone's article examines the harmonic underpinnings and improvisational interactions of the version of "Dark Star" that was immortalized on the *Live/Dead* album, as well as giving a solid and detailed interpretation of both the specific song and, more generally, the Grateful Dead's improvisational practice. Boone presents the band's work (music, lyrics, and improvisational practice) as an integrated, unified whole, oriented around the pursuit of a spiritual experience he calls "virtuality." He writes: "Virtuality, as I am using it, emphasizes the far more open-ended approximation of an internal, intuitive reality, distinct from the externally tangible and the mundanely real." He concludes that "for the Dead, music is a doorway to a different, heightened reality—what its detractors would surely call an *unreality*, opposed to everyday reality. Through the vernacular spirituality of the group and its fans, that other reality can be a positive, uplifting thing, and the doorway to it becomes an essential, permanent Sign."[25] His article is thus pivotal for this book in the way that it explicitly links its analysis of the Grateful Dead's practice to the pursuit and evocation of an extraordinary level of being, and its use of musicological language and the analysis of improvisational practice to outline this pursuit. This connection, then, is not a novelty: it extends back to the start of serious published critical discussion of the band's music.

Although it is now over twenty years old, Robert Freeman's "Other People Play the Music: Improvisation as Social Interaction" offers the best model I have encountered thus far for how to examine the practice of an improvising rock band such as the Grateful Dead.[26] This is understandable, as his article presents a summary of his research on the Other People, a jam band formed directly and consciously in the lineage of the Grateful Dead, and whose goal was to induce a state of intense interaction and unity among the musicians, a state that they saw the Grateful Dead (at their best) as modeling.

Freeman's perceptive analysis provides a taxonomy for assessing improvisation in a rock idiom. He discusses songs as models, including the relative density or openness of required material for any given piece, the moods that the piece evokes, and typical approaches in playing it. He then moves on to address musical role conventions, including the usual function of each of the instrumentalists, both in terms of rock's common practice and the developments of that practice made by the Grateful Dead and picked up by the Other Ones. An examination of how players work within and around those conventions, how they affect the band's improvisational practice and how they help to structure it, leads into an analysis of how they *accomplish* structure (the cues and keys that provide structure to otherwise less structured sections), *push* structure (the way that the band negotiates in open sections and in passage points between songs, places where things are theoretically up for grabs), and their use of transitional strategies that communicate or disrupt emergent structure.

Finally, Freeman takes apart the improvisational passages with a typology of their musical elements: melody, counterpoint, rhythm, and symbolic interaction (cues), with the manipulation or interaction of these elements creating tendencies that come together into formalized approaches or structures, which then must themselves be contested in the interest of maintaining improvisational freedom. His analysis is both perceptive and compelling, and its application goes far beyond the Other People. Indeed, Freeman's conclusion could apply equally to the Grateful Dead:

> Creativity is not simply a product of the initiative or abilities of individuals. Rather, it may be a systemic outgrowth of organizational forms that institutionalize playful and deconstructive processes rather than enforce rigid hierarchies. Such social forms reshape themselves in response to both external inputs and the creative solutions and contributions of individual elements. By allowing lower-level elements to self-referentially reprogram upper-level processes, flexible social forms open their very structures up to adaptation. . . . The lesson is to build porous forms with room for individual contributions rather than rigid structures to ward off chaos.[27]

I hope to have corroborated and furthered Freeman's conclusion by outlining the "porous form" that the Grateful Dead constructed early in their career and by tracing some of the ways that it was "reprogrammed" as time went on. Although the way that the Dead developed their signature approach to improvisation evokes and deeply reflects the complex cultural ferment of their times, there are far broader lessons in the Dead's work for scholars studying improvisation, as Freeman's article suggests.

Another analysis of Grateful Dead–style improvisation is provided by Jim Tuedio and Stan Spector in their introduction to *The Grateful Dead in Concert: Essays on Live Improvisation*, in which they argue that there are three forms of improvising. "Hierarchical improvisation operates whenever musicians play spontaneously and extemporaneously in front, or against the background, of an underlying structural framework," they write, giving as an example a soloist playing over the chord changes of a jazz standard. "In contrast," they continue, "associative improvisation is more free-flowing, insofar as the underlying structure and framework are abandoned by musicians busy setting in motion suggestive new ideas."[28]

In addition to these more common forms of improvisation, the Grateful Dead, they argue, improvised in a way that they describe as "fusion" or "psychedelic." The band "had to practice: first to learn the structure of the songs; then to learn how each player could solo within the structure (hierarchical improvisation); then to learn how each instrument and player could participate in a free-flowing musical conversation no longer tethered to the structural framework of the song (associative improvisation), and finally, to play the song as a Grateful Dead song in which each player makes a musical statement not so much in response to another player's statement as in response to *the song itself*."[29]

Their division is interesting, but it raises some real concerns. First of all, the consistent use of the word "solo" is problematic, as it evokes associations that are only rarely applicable to any of the players except Garcia: the Grateful Dead's conception deemphasizes soloing in terms of group interplay— indeed, this is one of its characteristic elements. Second, the sequential presentation that Tuedio and Spector make is potentially deceptive. In some cases, we have clear evidence of parts of songs arising from the band's jams before being incorporated into specific songs, thus inverting Tuedio and Spector's third and first steps. For instance, in an interview with David Gans, Bob Weir says that "about half the songs I write have their basis in some jam somewhere."[30] A good example is the way that the main motif for the song "Playing in the Band" was played in jams and identified as "The Main Ten" before being incorporated into "Playing in the Band."[31] Another example can be found in a performance from September 3, 1967, in which you can hear musical elements that would be incorporated into "Dark Star" developing out of a "Dancing in the Streets" jam. These instances support my argument that the "free-flowing musical conversation" was the basic level of Grateful

Dead music-making, whether fitted into the contexts of the various songs or exposed freely on its own in jamming sections. In this regard, the way that the Grateful Dead played their songs would be somewhat reminiscent of how a jazz rhythm section typically interprets a standard—which also does not fit into Tuedio and Spector's categorization.

In *The Grateful Dead and the Art of Rock Improvisation*—the longest and most detailed examination of the band's music to date—David Malvinni looks at an aspect of the band's style of playing that he calls "Deadness." This "aesthetic category" involves the creation of performance rituals and musical codes, but it is nonetheless open to "free play, improvisation, and the unknown in a paradoxical attempt to reach the unreachable."[32] In his book, Malvinni attempts to outline some of the rituals and codes that gave the Grateful Dead a structural underpinning for their evocation of "Deadness." Although he does discuss song or jam structure to a limited extent, he is mainly concerned with the band's use of modal approaches to playing: modal jams are "the foundation of the Dead as a psychedelic band."[33] Thus, where I hear and discuss the band's progression through jams as a succession of sections that develop from preceding sections, and where I present the Framework (discussed in chapter 3) as a "musical code" that permits the band to achieve "Deadness," Malvinni argues that it is the group's overall modal understanding that is key to their playing: "Remaining constant through these years . . . is the modal organizing principle behind a Dead jam, where the tendency is to dwell on a chord or two and explore the linear application of the scale or mode."[34]

This small example illustrates another aspect of Malvinni's work that distinguishes it from my own—namely, his synchronic focus. Whereas my concern is to illustrate a particular phase in the broad historical narrative of the Grateful Dead's career, Malvinni views that career as finding its fulfilment, its true realization, in a specific period (1972–74) in which true "Deadness" came the closest to being realized. "Shows from 1972 to 1974 represent the pinnacle of the Grateful Dead live concert," he contends, whereas earlier he describes jamming as "primal Dead."[35] As a Deadhead, I would find it hard to disagree with Malvinni in terms of his preferences—for all the many joys found in earlier or later periods, there is something absolutely fundamental about much of the band's playing in 1972–74; one really does see this period as the band's peak. Where we differ is in the idea of seeing the Grateful Dead as pursuing some specific quality that they were working up to and then managed to fairly consistently deliver for those three years. I think that the development of the Grateful Dead's music is much more about the process than the product, and, to understand the process, we need to look at the band's music as the process developed.

In addition to his modal analyses of the Grateful Dead's music, Malvinni explores the philosophical ramifications that he sees in the band's pursuit of the "unreachable." His work is informed by the philosophy of Heidegger and his followers, especially Deleuze and Derrida, which he justifies on the basis of the "open-ended quality of the Grateful Dead [that] invites such a substantive approximation to continental philosophy."[36] Although Grateful Dead jams are incorporated into more or less conventionalized structures, Malvinni argues that these jams are Derridean aporias, "unresolvable contradictions that present a double bind for analysis," as they oblige us to consider the jams as "stable, repeatable entities," on the one hand, and as things that exist "outside and beyond these familiar . . . categories, as existing without a *telos*," on the other. Jams thus represent efforts to overcome the "limits of convention" and, in so doing, can lead audiences to "ponder the unlimited, dynamically expanding and infinite nature of the cosmos" as well as the inherent paradoxicality of improvisation. The jam creates "a singular event indeterminable by analysis."[37] For my part, I would argue that this "singular event" is only "indeterminable" when it is removed from its temporal context—or, to put it another way, when it is stripped of its connection to process. When we observe the ways in which jams develop, we can see clear pathways leading from the known into the unknown.

When we combine Malvinni's approach to jams with the presentation of the Dead's development as a more or less successful pursuit of "Deadness," Malvinni's work can be seen as an attempt to divorce the idea of "Deadness" from history, turning it instead into a timeless and fascinating cipher that remains distinct from history while interacting with it. This understanding resonates quite strongly with me, and I suspect with anyone who has ever been a Deadhead: that said, I suspect that most non-Deadhead readers will find that the idea of Deadness and the band's special access to it requires a large leap of faith. (I should add that this faith, in my view, would not at all be misplaced. But it's a lot to ask.)

In any case, Malvinni's book discusses the Grateful Dead from a point of view that is very different from the one that I am using here; reading it clarified a great deal of my thought, and I encourage anyone who is really interested in how the Grateful Dead's music worked to give Malvinni a try. My own concern, though, is to ground the band's musical developments in a firmly diachronic context, showing the band's musical development and their relationship to their context: following in Jost's footsteps, my interest is less Deadness in the abstract, and more how and why the band chose to pursue Deadness in the first place. We will discuss this aspect at great length, but, before we do that, it will be useful to contextualize the Grateful Dead by examining the practice of improvisation, and its motivations, for some of their contemporaries.

Other Improvising Rock Bands

SIMILAR DIRECTIONS,
DIFFERENT MOTIVATIONS

"In musical cultures that distinguish between improvised and precomposed music, the improvisor—or groups of improvisors—is inevitably making a statement . . . And in their discourse about improvisation, musicians, the audience, and scholars are saying something about social relations . . ." —BRUNO NETTL, in *Musical Improvisation* (2009)

A Comparative Look

Earlier, we discussed some of the reasons why rock music developed an improvisational imperative in the mid-1960s, and the Grateful Dead were, of course, not the only band to go this route. In this section, I want to take up that conversation again—specifically, to discuss several other significant improvising rock groups that formed in the mid-1960s, and, as part of each discussion, I will look at how their musical practice relates to that of the Grateful Dead, thus contextualizing the band's unique developments within their musical and professional context. Doing this will not only shed light on the approaches to improvisation that these contemporary groups devised (thus giving us a better understanding of this weird and underdiscussed mid-1960s musical development) but will also enable us to better understand the Grateful Dead's practice in particular.

As we will see, the improvisational approaches that these bands developed had a great deal to do with the respective groups' status and reputation—in other words, their context within the world of popular music. As we now know, improvisation, even when it is only a matter of improvisation within a given genre, is not a "one size fits all" approach to playing; rather, it establishes a general field, within which a variety of specific strategies can be devised, depending on the requirements of the context and the group in question. By looking at other improvising rock bands, arising from somewhat different contexts, we will get a bit more of an idea of the parameters within which the Grateful Dead were working, and we will gain a bit more understanding of the uniqueness of their approach. We will also be able to see how broadly applicable an improvisational approach to rock could be—that is, we'll see that it wasn't *just* a tool for religious-minded hippies, but could also serve as a means of identifying with a new culture, filling a showbiz niche, establishing one's musical credentials, or making capital-A Artistic statements.

The groups that I will examine—the Grateful Dead's companions in the creation of an improvisational tradition for rock music—are the Jefferson Airplane, who will give us a contrasting example from within the Grateful Dead's own San Francisco scene; the Velvet Underground, from New York, who came out of a very different aesthetic background and with different musical goals from the San Francisco bands; the English band Cream, whose take on improvising music draws from a jazz- and blues-influenced validation of soloistic virtuosity; and Pink Floyd, the iconic representatives of the London-based psychedelic rock scene.[1] I must stress that this is not the place for a fully detailed examination of these groups' improvisational work; each of them easily deserves a book of its own in that regard. My concern here is to draw out some of the broad parallels or contrasts between these groups and the Grateful Dead, in order to present a picture of the range of approaches that were taken up in these early days.

THE JEFFERSON AIRPLANE

The Jefferson Airplane, along with the Grateful Dead, Quicksilver Messenger Service, and Big Brother and the Holding Company, were one of the main bands in the San Francisco scene—a scene that vocalist Marty Balin helped to start by cofounding the Matrix Club.[2] Drawing on similar folk/rock roots to the Grateful Dead, the Jefferson Airplane can in many ways be seen as the Grateful Dead's "big brother" band: they were actively playing before the Grateful Dead, they established themselves on the scene before the Grateful Dead did, and they quickly achieved a level of commercial success that would elude the Grateful Dead until the 1980s.[3] They also shared with the Grateful Dead a drug-fueled willingness to experiment musically; both bands used a wide variety of drugs, and indeed acquired well-deserved reputations as drug bands. But, whether it was through their work at the Acid Tests, their association with famed LSD chemist Augustus Owsley Stanley (a.k.a. "Bear") or the perfect aptness of their music for tripping (according to acidheads, anyway), the Grateful Dead became particularly associated with LSD, an association that would remain consistent throughout their career, even as band members moved on to focus on relative sobriety.[4] The Jefferson Airplane's attitude, as expressed by guitarist Paul Kantner, was that "acid for us was just a tool rather than a religion, like a good dessert after a fine eight-course meal. It was as good as several other tools."[5]

Both bands built their musical experimentation on the foundation of a basic folk/rock template, and there seem to have been musical influences going both ways: Garcia made significant musical contributions to the Airplane's *Surrealistic Pillow* album and was credited by them on the album's back cover as their "musical and spiritual advisor." Going the other way, the Airplane's bassist, Jack Casady, seems to have been a profound influence on Lesh: he played the same style of Gibson Starfire bass that Lesh would adopt, he showed an eagerness to explore nonconventional (particularly distorted) timbres, and his playing was aggressive and unconventional (although Casady was more firmly rooted in blues or folk tropes than Lesh would be).[6] In his autobiography, Lesh credits Casady with showing him a model for the rhythm/lead style of bass playing that he sought to develop.[7]

The Jefferson Airplane, then, present an interesting case. On the one hand, they were musically, professionally, and socially linked to the Grateful Dead; they shared the Grateful Dead's appreciation for taking drugs; and both bands worked in an environment in which improvised jamming of some sort was taken as a normal, expected way of playing. On the other hand, there is no record of their having had the sort of religious conversion experiences that (as I will argue in chapters 7–9) were understood by the Grateful Dead to have led them to their particular approach to improvisational playing. The Jefferson Airplane were an allegedly and often incoherently revolutionary band, but they were not a mystical or religiously inspired band. Thus, the musical and religious conclusions that guided the Grateful Dead were not inevitable for San Francisco folk-rock musicians with a penchant for drug use, especially LSD. In other words, you can't entirely blame the Grateful Dead on LSD.

In the fall of 1967, the Jefferson Airplane recorded *Bless Its Pointed Little Head*, a live album drawn from performances at the Fillmore West (in San Francisco) and the Fillmore East (in New York).[8] This album displays the band's aggressive, but also ramshackle, approach to live performance: because it is an easily accessible and well-known document, I will use it to illustrate my discussion of their improvisational approach. Other live recordings of the band from the mid- or late 1960s circulate, whether as bootlegs or as official releases (e.g., *1966 Jefferson Airplane Early and Late Shows*), and they display similar characteristics to the music on *Bless Its Pointed Little Head*.[9] Members of the Jefferson Airplane (mainly bassist Casady and guitarist Jorma Kaukonen) did get involved with jamming with other San Francisco musicians, as in fall 1968, when, for example, Casady played along with Garcia and Mickey Hart in the ad hoc group Mickey and the Hartbeats, and Casady and Kaukonnen formed the (still extant as of this writing) blues-rock band Hot Tuna in early 1969, but, in what follows, I will be discussing only the work of the Jefferson Airplane.[10]

Interestingly, the music on *Bless Its Pointed Little Head* shows the Jefferson Airplane to be simultaneously tighter and looser than the Grateful Dead. They are *tighter*, in that their songs remain themselves. With the exception of "Bear Melt," a loose jam that is related to the piece called "The Thing" on other recordings, the Jefferson Airplane do not venture far away from the basic structure and feel of their material. They may extend introductory sections of songs as in the extended, layered introduction to "3/5's of a Mile in 10 Seconds," in which the drums play alone for 16 seconds, after which the bass joins in, shortly followed by the guitar, with the vocalists coming in to start the verse at 00:30; similarly, the band improvises over the introductory chords and rhythms of "Somebody to Love" for 55 seconds before the vocals enter. In those two songs, they also incorporate instrumental sections played over the chord progressions of the verse. However, the Jefferson Airplane do not perform anything comparable to the extended, developmental improvisatory excursions that one finds in the Grateful Dead's Framework and post-Framework music.

Rather than the song proper being superseded by the jamming section, in the Jefferson Airplane's live performances the song is always present, albeit elaborated. As Grateful Dead manager Rock Scully has put it, "The Jefferson

Airplane certainly never [performed] anything they didn't have down cold. The Dead would play stuff that they didn't even remember having written that day."[11] We can surmise that this was not always the case in rehearsal, as Casady's work with the Grateful Dead spinoff group Mickey and the Hartbeats is considerably more open than the Jefferson Airplane tended to be.[12] There is, furthermore, a widely available bootlegged studio outtake from sessions for the Jefferson Airplane's third album, *After Bathing at Baxters,* that features Casady, Kaukonen, and Dryden jamming quite freely, only loosely adhering to an Am-Bb progression.[13] The last nine minutes of this outtake were released on *After Bathing at Baxters* as "Spare Chaynge"; the first fifteen minutes have never been officially released.[14] However, in their live work as the Jefferson Airplane, with the exception of "Bear Melt"/"The Thing," they play their songs as songs.

This leads us to the way in which the Jefferson Airplane are *looser* than the Grateful Dead. While the song is always present, the Jefferson Airplane play with a more aggressive and informal feel than the Grateful Dead—rather than the Grateful Dead's "electric chamber music" effect, which Phil Lesh has spoken of, with its thoughtful and deliberate interlocking of parts, the Jefferson Airplane's performances in this period are reminiscent of jam sessions, or of the sort of "go for the throat" intensity that would be raised to a high art by the MC5, with Casady in particular taking the lead in this regard.[15]

Moreover, while in the Grateful Dead's music the vocals tend to be stable and presented the same way every time, defining the song and serving as structured sections in contrast with the open jams, with the Jefferson Airplane the vocals, too, are subject to considerable spontaneous reinterpretation. Live, lead singers Marty Balin and Grace Slick interact heterophonically, contrapuntally, and in call-and-response style, as well as harmonically, taking chances that are not always successful, and there is a ragged edge to their voices that intensifies the feeling of being "in the moment," as can be heard, for instance, on "3/5 of a Mile in Ten Seconds," the first song on *Bless Its Pointed Little Head.* The Grateful Dead's vocals could be ragged as well, but with the exception of established repeated chants (e.g., the backing vocals in "Lovelight"; the "anymore" chant that ends "Bertha"; the "You know our love will not fade away" chant in "Not Fade Away"), one suspects that this was more often due to failed attempts to sing the song correctly than to vocal improvising.

Overall, then, this Jefferson Airplane album and the other live material from the mid-to-late 1960s that I have heard shows a powerful, driving band that is willing to take chances and "stretch out" on their material, but one that is not (again, with the exception of "Bear Melt"/"The Thing") willing to take its songs into entirely new realms, as the Grateful Dead was doing at that time. In keeping with this is the more individualistic feel of the musicians in the Jefferson Airplane, producing the impression of an excited and exciting interplay of distinct voices rather than the creation of a polyphonically unified band sound.

It is quite possible that part of this difference in approach was due to the Jefferson Airplane's status as a commercially successful rock band with hit singles and the audience expectations in terms of "delivering the hits" that this status led to. However, we could also note that the Grateful Dead adhered to their improvisational approach even at such enormous and significant venues as Woodstock, and even when they became rock stars in the 1980s, so the difference might well have more to do with basic artistic differences between the two bands. But, overall, what we see when we compare the improvisational practice of the Jefferson Airplane and the Grateful Dead is an aspiration on the part of the latter toward greater band coherence and a willingness to grant autonomy to spontaneous musical developments. The Grateful Dead work as a group to create and explore new musical territory, whereas the Jefferson Airplane explosively jam on or over already existing songs.

As I have mentioned and will discuss at greater length, both of these distinctive aspects of the Grateful Dead's improvisational practice can be linked to their understandings of the significance of the foundational religious experiences that they underwent in 1965 and 1966. It is clear from their similarities that the two bands emerged from very similar musical contexts; their differences, on the other hand, show their contrasting motivations. The Jefferson Airplane presented itself as an explicitly revolutionary countercultural band, fond of brash (at least in hindsight), deeply entitled and privileged rhetoric about cultural and political upheaval, such as their allegedly revolutionary "Up against the wall, motherfucker!" lyric in "We Can Be Together," from their 1969 *Volunteers* album on RCA.[16] This support for individualistic, chaotic, "revolutionary" activity, it seems to me, finds a counterpart in the band's improvisational approach, where the emphasis is more on an aggressive self-expression than on weaving multiple voices into a coherent polyphonic structure.

THE VELVET UNDERGROUND

The Grateful Dead and the Velvet Underground knew, or knew of, each other: they played on the same bill several times (February 7 and April 25–26, 1969), and members of the Velvet Underground were openly scornful of the

Grateful Dead.[17] As lead singer and guitarist Lou Reed put it, the San Francisco scene was "just tedious, a lie and untalented. . . . You know, people like Jefferson Airplane, Grateful Dead are just the most untalented bores that ever came up."[18]

This disdain, although to be expected of the famously cranky Reed, is ironic, as the improvisational strategies followed by the two bands have a great deal in common. Both groups drew extended and at times extremely "outside" jams out of basic rock songs, built on basic rock rhythms and melodies, and, in both cases, were strongly influenced by garage rock. Furthermore, these basic rock songs were performed more or less "straight"—that is, the song would usually be rendered in what seems to be a standard and predetermined form, with the major variations and spontaneous contributions being reserved for the jamming section. With the Grateful Dead, as noted, improvisational developments take place even within these structured segments, while the Velvet Underground play them a good deal straighter.

Also, while it is difficult to quantify this observation, I get the impression in listening to both the Velvet Underground and the Grateful Dead that there is in their improvisations a pursuit of something more significant than simply a good jam. One feels that they are making capital S Statements, that they are deliberately moving the listener into a different conceptual world from the one that they would normally inhabit, rather than simply playing well.

As I argue throughout this book, in the case of the Grateful Dead, this aspect can be understood religiously: it can be seen as a movement into a Turnerian liminal state appropriate to their transformative/spiritual mission.[19] In the case of the Velvet Underground, I would suggest that it is due to their self-understanding as, among other things, an art rock band, in a period when such a designation was something of a novelty, as well as being a means of acquiring cultural capital for rock as it matured. Founding member John Cale came into the band with a strong grounding in the Western art music tradition, albeit working within a very modern and underground stream; Lou Reed brought his "poetic" sensibility to the group, having studied with and been influenced by poet Delmore Schwartz; and vocalist Nico had worked for film director Federico Fellini and was associated with Andy Warhol's Pop Art scene, which adopted the band.[20]

Consequently, the Velvet Underground can be seen and were understood at least in part as an Art-with-a-capital-A band, whose medium was (ironically) primitivist rock. To take one example: Detroit's MC5 played with the Velvet Underground at the Boston Tea Party on December 12–14, 1967. The MC5's public image at that time was trendily "revolutionary"; when guitarist Wayne Kramer was asked by Victor Bockris if the Velvet Underground also had a "revolutionary rep," he responded: "No, I think they had more of a rep with people who were into art, a cultish kind of a thing."[21]

John Cale, in a 1967 interview with the *New York World Journal Tribune*, said that "we're putting everything together—lights and film and music—and we're reducing it to its lowest common denominator. We're musical primitives."[22] But, of course, there is inevitably some level of artistic irony present when a classically trained, avant-garde musician refers to himself as "primitive." Real musical primitives do not refer to themselves as such, nor do they associate or work with La Monte Young, Xenakis, and Morton Feldman, as Cale did (although Cale's claims to have worked with John Cage have been called into question).[23] As drummer Maureen Tucker notes, "Most of the places we played were for older art people.... At first, when we were with Andy, we played places like art shows."[24]

For both the Grateful Dead and the Velvet Underground, then, there was a palpable sense of (aesthetic or religious) significance that surrounds their music, a sense of mission—which is all the more striking given that both bands also embraced the modernist collapse of distinctions between high and low art, juxtaposing the influences of classical and experimental music of European and Indian descent with popular rock and roll songs and a determinedly irreverent attitude.

For all their similarities, however, the Velvet Underground differ strongly from the Grateful Dead in two major aspects: their use of dissonance, and their love of drones. I have noted that the Grateful Dead tend to gradually work their way up to dissonant sections in their improvisation, and that these sections tend not to be unduly extended. The Velvet Underground made a great deal more use of strong dissonances and outright noise in their music, and, while they could work their way up to it, they also reveled in the shock that could be produced through its sudden imposition (as can be heard in "European Son" on their first album, *The Velvet Underground and Nico*, and "I Heard Her Call My Name" on their second album, *White Light/White Heat*), or through its prolongation, as can be heard on versions of "Sister Ray" from the *Bootleg Series, Vol. 1: The Quine Tapes* (recorded in 1969 but released on Polydor in 2001).[25] David Brackett has described the way that different routes could end in the same place: "A comparison between a Velvet Underground recording such as 'European Son' and a Grateful Dead tune from the same time, such as 'Viola Lee Blues' (both released in March 1967 but performed and recorded in 1966) reveals a good number of similarities, particularly in the near-atonal, improvised climaxes of both songs. *The difference lies more in the way of arriving at these sounds*: for the Velvet Underground, the path runs through avant-garde minimalism and the rejection of conventional virtuosity; a group like the Dead arrives at noise through the evolution of dissonance within a trajectory of increasing musical complexity during a performance."[26]

Especially in their early days, the Velvet Underground seem to have regarded destabilization and disorientation as valued goals of improvisational playing—a confrontational aesthetic that coheres with their approach to their early staging of their shows, performing at high volume, obscured by blinding lights, and potentially accompanied by staged S/M performances.[27] Part of this was no doubt due to the assaultive aesthetics favored by many avant-garde artists at that time; part of it can also be ascribed to a desire to homologically model their noisy, urban environment; and part of it can be understood as a musical evocation of the rampant amphetamine abuse in Warhol's scene.[28]

The band's emphasis on disorientation might seem paradoxical when we take into account its simultaneous love of drones and stasis. Some of this emphasis is easily explainable, as bassist/violinist John Cale had worked with LaMonte Young in his drone-based Theater of Eternal Music, while, in their early day, the Velvet Underground were closely associated with Andy Warhol and his stasis-based approach to film. As Martin Torgoff notes, "In all of Warhol's early films, the camera never once moved, and the sense of time was . . . slowed down even more by the techniques of loop printing, frozen frames, and retarded projection speeds. The effect was to take something completely static to begin with and render it trancelike, otherworldly."[29]

There is evidence that bandleader Lou Reed was also independently interested in drones even before his association with Warhol, to judge by his early (pre–Velvet Underground) composition "Do the Ostrich," in which all six strings of the guitar were tuned to the same note. Musician and filmmaker Tony Conrad, who was selected to play in the ad hoc band that Pickwick Records assembled to promote the song, writes that Reed "said, 'Don't worry, it's easy to play because all the strings are tuned to the same note,' which blew our minds because that was what we were doing with La Monte [Young] in the Dream Syndicate."[30] But John Cale left the band in 1968, while the band's association with Warhol ended in 1967, and Reed's tuning experiments with the Primitives were not repeated in the Velvet Underground. The one constant drone element throughout the Velvet Underground's career was drummer Maureen Tucker, who took musical minimalism to previously unknown levels.

Tucker was unquestionably a *rock* drummer, not an avant-gardist like Cale or her predecessor in the band, Angus MacLise. She laid down solid, powerful rock rhythms, but these rhythms were stripped to their bare essentials, as was her kit; she notes that "I think I had a bass, a tom-tom, and a snare, and maybe I had one cymbal."[31] Complementing her minimal setup, Tucker was prone to playing extremely long songs with few variations or even fills, as her performances on *Bootleg Series, Vol. 1: The Quine Tapes* show very clearly. On the 17-minute long version of "Follow the Leader," she plays two fills in the first minute and a half; following this, with the exception of adding brief snare hits to cue the chorus at 4:30, 6:06, and 7:51, she plays no fills or variations on her driving rock backbeat until 11:05.[32] From here until 11:29, she responds to the rhythm guitar's accents by briefly playing a Bo Diddley beat; following this, she returns to the backbeat, and plays it without fills or variations until 14:50, where she interjects a few extra snare hits to emphasize the chorus; following this, she returns to her basic beat and plays it without change until the end of the song.

So, it is clear that Tucker was perfectly capable of maintaining a metronomic rock beat for extended periods of time, but she never created the sorts of complex rhythmic webs that Grateful Dead drummers Bill Kreutzmann or Mickey Hart delighted in, which meant that, at its bottom level, the Velvet Underground's sound was profoundly static: things did not change or develop. As Tucker puts it, "Now, playing the drums, I didn't learn to do a roll for five years. I was lucky, because if I was Ginger Baker, the music would not have sounded the way it did. . . . Since all I could do was beat [the drums], that's what I did, and it made a certain style."[33] Her stolid determination as a player may also have partly derived from her awareness of gender issues: as a woman working in a male-dominated context, she was determined not to show weakness. She has said, "I guess I always had it in the back of my mind that it wasn't gonna be me who had to stop the song. If they lasted twenty minutes, so was I going to last twenty minutes."[34]

But precisely because this stasis was so profound and so simple, it had the potential to be endlessly involving, rather than boring. Her lack of fills and elaboration enabled Tucker to create a conceptual space that felt timeless and eternal, an endearingly human and yet also robotic emptiness in which anything might happen, because it ruled nothing out—something like the effect created by the endless drone of the tambura in Hindustani classical music. Wayne McGuire, in "The Boston Sound," a 1967 article for *Crawdaddy*, noted the comparison with Indian drones: "Essential to [the Velvet Underground's music] is the drone. Not the pencil thick drone of Indian music which emanates from spirits and nervous systems which think they've found it and probably have within their limited structure of things, but a drone which is as broad as a house, a drone which is produced by New World Citizen nervous systems plugging into the Cosmic Whirl."[35]

This connection is particularly apt given Cale's work with La Monte Young, who was hugely influenced by Indian music especially as regards drones, to the point of issuing a recording of himself and his wife Marian Zazeela playing tambura drones on *The Tamburas of Pandit Pran Nath* (released in 2004 on the Just Dreams label). Another comparison would be the relentless and somehow transcendent pulse of the *motorik* rhythm developed by German drummers in the "krautrock," or "cosmic music," scene, which began toward the end of the Velvet Underground's career, and in which the Velvet Underground were regarded as "seminal" pioneers.[36] By eschewing variation, Tucker also liberated her band's music from ever needing to end, bringing it into contact with eternity.

The liberatory significance of her drumming style has been noted by others. In his article "The Velvet Underground: Musique and Mystique Unveiled," published in *Circus* magazine in June 1970, Phil Morris writes that "Maureen's drumming was a distillation of all the rock that had gone before, and yet she played with mallets on two kettle drums while standing up. She's methodical and steady like some entranced Zulu witch doctor [*sic*]."[37] Similarly, Wayne McGuire writes that "no other drummer in the world could play the archetypal 1234 with such perfection, with a weight that verges on religious ritual."[38] M. C. Kostek, who edited the pioneering Velvet Underground fanzine *What Goes On*, strikes a similar note when he recounts his first experience of Tucker's drumming: "And the drummer—not only has she stood all night, but she's pounded steadily with those big mallets all the while, raising one up over her head for the big BAMP-BAMP-BAMP. Steady. I'm not quite sure how long this went on. It seemed a half hour—but time, space . . . meant nothing. I was gone. No drink or drugs, I was flattened by the raw power."[39]

In this context, with its emphasis on timelessness, the Velvet Underground's use of noise and dissonance takes on a new aspect. They were shocking, but also profoundly alienating, in the sense of separating the listener from their customary sonic environment and moving them to a new or alien perspective. In combination with the monumental and monotonous rhythms, they had the potential to put their audience in a different and affectively eternal sonic context. As Wayne McGuire puts it, "The feedback at peak moments is a suspended mystical ecstasy."[40]

This focus on creating such timeless structures through repetition and droning remained even in cases where the music was less abrasive. Whether one thinks of the chordless droning of the early piece "The Nothing Song," or the seemingly endless alternation between the I and IV chords in "The Ocean," the effect is the same.[41] While their studio albums were driven by a variety of different, more cerebral, and abstract motivations, in their live performances the Velvet Underground sought to stop time, to invite their listeners to enter an unchanging realm that they created in the middle of the modern world, using such archetypally modern tools as avant-garde art, classic Brill Building pop songwriting, and electrically generated instrumental timbres. As Jon Savage aptly summarizes, "Their drones evoked both the eternal Now of the drug experience and the possibilities opened up by the incredible acceleration of Western culture."[42]

This, finally, is the key to the distinction between the Velvet Underground and the Grateful Dead in terms of improvisation. Although they started in many ways from similar places—a modernist appreciation for the musical potential of new instruments; an understanding of their performances as significant events rather than just gigs; a desire to integrate these new perceptions into their popular music tradition; a love for extended forms—they were headed in different directions. The Velvet Underground, in their improvisations, worked to stop time and to reveal the unchanging repetitions that lie at the heart of the world; the Grateful Dead, by contrast, witnessed and manifested the incursion of an endlessly active and fertile power into our world.

CREAM

Most bands build their reputations as they develop; Cream, on the other hand, began their career as a "super group." As Welch puts it, "each member of Cream came to the group with a formidable reputation for musical excellence, hard-won on the thriving British R&B scene."[43] Guitarist Eric Clapton had come to fame as a member of the Yardbirds, a group that he left over issues of musical "authenticity" and blues purism and then worked with John Mayall's more traditional Bluesbreakers; drummer Ginger Baker was well known for his work with the Graham Bond Organization, also a blues and R&B band; and bassist Jack Bruce had worked with Graham Bond, Mayall's Bluesbreakers, and the blues-rock group Manfred Mann.

As befitted the traditionalist associations of its three members, Cream played an important role in terms of rock's increasing legitimation in the 1960s by modeling a standard of rock virtuosity that borrowed heavily from already-established blues and jazz standards. Hence, while not conceptually radical, their approach was impressive; while their virtuosity was not easily attainable, it was familiar and comprehensible in a way that, for instance, Bob Weir's own distinctive musical contributions were not. To put it simply, in their live performances Cream took jazz and (especially) blues and blues-rock clichés and performed them at great length and high volume, extending rather than altering genre-based expectations. As Clapton has said, "It became a question of finding something that had a riff, a form that could be interpreted, simply, in a band format."[44] If, as mentioned, the Jefferson Airplane used their songs as a canopy to cover and delineate their aggressive individual interplay, it could be said that Cream used the blues-rock tonality and rhythms in the same way: in other words, they jammed over top of their chosen *genre*, and it is the genre-linked characteristics of their playing that make their music coherent as a group effort.

In listening to the improvisation on the widely available bootleg recording of their show at Detroit's Grande Ballroom on October 15, 1967, for instance, it is striking to note how similar Jack Bruce and Eric Clapton's lines often are.[45] Although they are playing an octave or two apart, their moments of real togetherness frequently come about when their lines overlap or mirror each other (rather than being complementary), because they are playing the same sorts of licks, or even the very same licks, based on the same pentatonic blues scales (e.g., at 5:15 on "N.S.U." or in the tradeoff in "Spoonful" where Clapton introduces a riff at approximately 3:15, and Bruce then picks it up).[46]

This is all the more striking when the harmonic motion is reduced to a single chord, as during the long jam on "N.S.U." (stretching from 2:01–15:19) or in "Spoonful" (from 3:10–17:20). Stripped even of the stereotypical twelve-bar progression and its goal-oriented movement, we are left with nothing more than essential "bluesiness" in its rawest form. Dynamics rise and fall

Ex. 6.1 Jack Bruce and Eric Clapton's Bass and guitar unison riffs from Cream's "N.S.U." and "Spoonful" (as performed 10/15/67).

throughout the performance—although the overriding tendency is for all three members to play very loudly and very busily when jamming—but the band stays within its chosen genre, key, and overall rhythmic feel. The variations that arise in the jams, while powerful, are not subtle and do not change the overall parameters of a given piece in the way that changes in the Grateful Dead's jams have the potential to do.

This need not be taken as an aesthetic failing on Cream's part. Rather, it shows very clearly the value that their approach assigns to, for lack of a better word, purity. As we have seen, all three members of the band had been strongly associated with blues-rock before joining Cream, and blues-rock at that time in England tended to have strong purist associations.[47] Early Rolling Stones bassist Dick Taylor's description of their first gig gives the feeling: "You could hear people saying . . . 'Ah, rock and roll, are they?' Before we'd played a note, we could feel the hostility."[48] Indeed, Clapton's departure from the Yardbirds had been precipitated by concerns on his part that their single "For Your Love" was too "pop." Bassist Paul Samwell-Smith recalls that Clapton "hated 'For Your Love' because he thought we were selling out to market pressures—which we were." The decision to use it as their single instead of an Otis Redding song left him "very disappointed, disillusioned."[49]

Cream's improvisational approach, then, can be best understood when looked at in the context of a concern for genre-based purity. Although in many regards (including their instrumental volume and timbres, the length of their jams, their sartorial flamboyance and cult of personality, and their privileging of original and pop-influenced material) they left the purist standards of mid-1960s British blues behind, they made clear through their playing that they were proceeding along a trajectory that extended directly outward from the blues.

This strongly distinguishes their improvisational work from the Grateful Dead, who enthusiastically embraced an almost postmodern hybridity, in which the band was free to invoke an extraordinarily wide range of generic signifiers, including those associated with folk, blues, jazz, pop, avant-garde classical, musique concrète, and rock. This made the band difficult to categorize and probably had an adverse effect on their popularity in their early days, although it also most likely contributed to their longevity; Cream, by contrast, was easy to categorize as a blues-rock band—even the *archetypal* blues-rock band, especially live.

The Grateful Dead's transgressive hybridity, which relied on the extremely wide range of musical experience of the various members, was made possible through the band's commitment to being open to the moment in their playing, to following what arose in the act of collective improvisation whether or not it transgressed genre boundaries. In pursuing the aesthetic of living in the now, responding to the music being played in a given moment, the band was obliged to turn their backs on the predetermined purity that enabled Cream to play in such a powerful, striking, and conceptually unified way.

PINK FLOYD

Pink Floyd drummer Nick Mason writes about their early exposure to the London underground scene when they played at the Marquee in March 1966: "I found the whole event pretty strange. We were used to playing R&B parties where the entry fee was a keg of bitter. Suddenly we were performing for a 'happening' and being encouraged to develop the extended solos that we'd only really put into the songs to pad them out."[50]

The solos that Mason refers to, which were originally intended only to make songs longer and fill up sets, became something quite different from standard rock solos. Discussing this period, manager Peter Jenner notes that "what intrigued me [about Pink Floyd in 1966] was that instead of wailing guitar solos in the middle, they made this weird noise. For a while I couldn't work out what it was. Then it turned out to be [guitarist] Syd [Barrett] and [keyboard player] Rick [Wright]. Syd . . . was doing weird things with feedback. Rick was also producing strange, long shifting chords. Nick was using mallets. . . . This was avant garde!"[51] Their avant-garde tendencies were encouraged in the shows at the All Saints Hall in the summer of 1966, where they were playing for full-fledged "freaks," and, as Mason recalls, "the effect on us was terrific. They responded so well and so uncritically to the improvised sections in our set that we began to concentrate on extending those rather than simply running through a sequence of cover versions."[52]

These discussions of the early Pink Floyd make it clear that they wanted very much to belong to the underground scene and to suit their music to this social context. The starting point of their early music was R&B, particularly Bo Diddley; added to this, you can clearly hear the inspiration of surf and spy theme music in the guitar and keyboard tones, respectively. But, as Palacios points out, in lead guitarist Syd Barrett's approach you can also hear the influence of the pioneering sonic explorations of such British rock guitarists as Jeff Beck and the Who, and experimentalist Keith Rowe, whose group, AMM, played many of the London underground events.[53] The result was a "freeform R&B" that arose out of a desire to fit into a context in which beat music and avant-garde explorations were fused.[54]

Peter Jenner observes that "even the Grateful Dead, they had improvisations but they seemed a perfectly ordinary group, playing with chords. The Floyd didn't play with chords."[55] This impression is borne out by early recordings of the band improvising, such as the versions of "Interstellar Overdrive" and "Nick's Boogie" found on the soundtrack for the movie *Tonite Let's All Make Love in London* and recorded in 1967, in which odd, unfamiliar, and definitely science-fiction sounds pulse and fade in and out over top of a throbbing beat.[56]

This music truly is "space rock" avant la lettre, music that combines the kitsch appeal and the genuine strangeness of 1950s and 1960s science-fiction movies and television shows.[57] It is also profoundly environmental music, made to create an evocative sonic space, and it is easy to see how the band arrived at it through tailoring their experimentations to the multimedia psychedelic events at which they made their reputation. Manager Peter Brown remembers that at these events Barrett was "inspired. He would constantly manage to get past his limitations and into areas that were very, very interesting. Which none of the others could do."[58] Wynne Wilson, a friend of the band, recalls that "it was at UFO that everything started to gel. There's no doubt that the music they played at UFO was the best they ever did. . . . Syd's improvisations would go on for extended periods, but would be absolutely immaculate."[59] Their improvisations originally arose out of necessity, but when they proved to be Pink Floyd's ticket to a large, hip, and receptive audience, Pink Floyd (or, at least, Barrett, during his brief tenure with the band) rose to the challenge.

Making It Work

When considering improvisational strategies—or any artistically experimental strategies—with working rock bands such as these, we need to take at least a moment to consider their economic and professional impacts. Rock musicians do not have access to the same amount of institutional support that is enjoyed by classical or other "serious" musicians, and that nowadays is also accessible to jazz artists: there are and have always been major biases in funding and support that reflect broader societal biases. Rock musicians, one segment of music's "blue collar" workers, are expected to earn their income from paying customers in noninstitutional settings to a far greater degree than "art" musicians, who are presumed to be at least potentially white collar "professionals" or "refined" artists and hence worthy of institutional financial support for their efforts.

This situation, for all its bias, has benefited rock music (if not individual rock musicians) in many ways. When rock musicians start taking themselves too seriously as "artists," their music tends to lose its power—take the last two Replacements albums as examples of this. However, it does pose challenges to musicians who seek to take artistic chances and who nonetheless need to hang on to fans who might not be primarily interested in supporting their heroes' experiments. It is interesting, therefore, to look at the ways in which these improvising bands integrated their practice into their professional lives.

From its inception, Cream based its appeal on its members' reputations for instrumental virtuosity. Contemporary accounts show that people went to see Cream precisely because of the musicians' chops: Jorma Kaukonen of the Jefferson Airplane, for example, said that "when I saw Cream for the first time, I thought they were the most incredible performing band I had ever seen in my life. That may still be true."[60] As I have discussed, Cream's improvisations displayed those chops in a blunt and easily accessible manner, one clearly related to blues standards. Thus, the improvisational activity that Cream engaged in could actually be seen as fulfilling rather than challenging its audience's expectations. Clapton has himself acknowledged that the band sometimes got lost in "endless meaningless solos . . . [in which] we were not indulging ourselves so much as our audience, because that's what they wanted."[61] Cream did the expected, and they did it at high volumes, at great length, and with consummate skill.

The Jefferson Airplane, on the other hand, were stars because they represented the "poppy" side of the San Francisco music scene. With their hit singles ("White Rabbit" and "Somebody to Love" being the most successful) and hit albums, they were working in the mainstream popular music market; on the other hand, what made them distinctive in that market was the way that they represented "hip" values and musical directions associated with the influential San Francisco scene. In concert, they lived up to their multifaceted image by giving their fans the hits, but not straight: their aggressive jamming fit into their public persona by emphasizing that they were not just a pop band like the Monkees.[62]

For Pink Floyd, the turn to improvisation enabled them to fit in with what was at the time the most active and exciting scene in their London milieu. As a conventional R&B band, they were one of hundreds; by being willing to get "weird" in their playing and moving away from standard pop music, their music became an appropriate backdrop for multimedia events. The existing documentation leaves no reason to doubt that for Syd Barrett, at least, the decision to play this sort of abstract, explicitly "spacey" music was heartfelt. His ongoing experimentation and sonic exploration strongly suggests that he was genuinely excited by the new possibilities for the spontaneous creation of otherworldly sound. As Palacios puts it, "Syd put great amounts of energy into illuminating his performances with the vibrant and immutable [sic] magic that was his trademark. Blinding lights, visions of space, AMM's spontaneous jazz, Cantabrigian folk, mutated Bo Diddley riffs, the jangle of the Byrds, Bloomfield's blues-raga epics. . . . Experiment, whimsy and spontaneity were his great contribution to the new music."[63] Nonetheless, it cannot be denied that it was an extremely good career move for the band as a whole, enabling them to establish a unique brand in an extremely crowded popular music market. And, of course, it is significant that the band's improvisational approach became much less radical as time went on, especially following Barrett's departure, when they became rock stars and acquired an audience that would follow them, rather than vice versa. Later Pink Floyd has many virtues, but it does not challenge listeners' expectations in the way that the music produced in 1966 and 1967 still has the power to do.

As for the Velvet Underground, they were a band who aspired to—and briefly enjoyed—the status and patronage accorded to "art" musicians, at least in a New York pop and avant-garde art sense, and in their early attempts to work their way into the rock scene they strike me as coming very definitely and very deliberately from a pop art perspective, reaching out from the art world into the rock world as an artistic statement at least as much as a desire to be working rock musicians. As Cale, for example, describes the band's early motivations: "The idea that kept us struggling with rock and roll as the medium of choice was the combination of the study of time through sonic backdrop from La Monte [Young], and the venomous subconscious of Lou [Reed]. It was an attempt to control the unconscious with the hypnotic."[64] Such an understanding of the group's motivation shows the influence of a conceptual, classically artistic approach on the band's music and sense of mission.

The Velvet Underground's extended improvisations fit into this approach, marking them as the sort of "artistic" and "difficult" band whose claims to high-art legitimacy are intended to earn them their audience's respect and indulgence. Their early improvisational activity is both transgressive in its simultaneous embrace of stasis and dissonance, and at the same time grounded in legitimating high-art tradition, invoking La Monte Young's musical experimentation and Andy Warhol's cinematic and, more broadly, philosophical contributions to pop art. They make clear that, in listening to the Velvet Underground, one is listening to artistic music with a pedigree.

This changed as the band moved away from its high-art associations. After breaking with Warhol and the departure of Cale and singer Nico, the group continued to improvise droningly at great length, but those improvisations were much more grounded in rock tradition. Instead of the chordless, pulsing jams of "The Nothing Song" or "Melody Laughter," we find the use of extended repetitions of rock riffs (as in "Sister Ray") or chord patterns, over which the band plays, as can be heard on *Bootleg Series, Vol. 1*. This much more rock-based approach to improvisation accompanied the band's move to a popular music context of performance, stepping away from the Warholian or Youngian art context of their genesis in order to play for younger and less sophisticated audiences.

In all of these cases, a band's use of extended improvisation, as radical an idea as it might have seemed to be, was made to fit into their overall professional context—and, indeed, it was affected by that context. How, then, do the Grateful Dead fit in here? In this regard, the band's dance songs (the Pigpen songs) are much more directly comprehensible than the Framework songs. We have seen that the San Francisco audiences liked to dance, and that the Grateful Dead enjoyed playing the part of a dance band. The approach that they took in these songs is ideally suited for dancing, combining the exhortations of a charismatic front man with extended dance grooves that vary little except in terms of dynamics.

The Framework is at first sight more difficult to explain in terms of its rapport with the group's working context, until we realize the importance that they placed on professionalism, on giving the audience a good performance. As Grateful Dead soundman and associate Augustus Owsley Stanley ("Bear") has noted, the Grateful Dead "always had a sense of responsibility to a paying audience."[65] Manager Rock Scully points out that "though we considered ourselves hippies, we weren't the hippie movement. We were musicians first . . . we wanted to be recognized as musicians."[66] Nicholas Meriwether suggests that "you could say that [people] might be surprised at the degree to which the Dead were enormously thoughtful, reflective and careful businessmen," and this applies to their approach to music as well.[67] Recall, too, Brackett's observation that, while the Grateful Dead and the Velvet Underground might sometimes go to the same places, their routes were different—and that professional virtuosity was one of the means by which the Grateful Dead arrived at their destination.

Brackett's observation, which is deeply, profoundly correct, brings out an aspect of the Grateful Dead's music that is rarely noted but nonetheless extremely important. As we listen to the almost exhaustive documentation of the Grateful Dead's performances, we can hear this commitment to professionalism very clearly in the astonishing rarity of flubbed notes or obvious mistakes (instrumentally speaking, at least: the band was far more hit or miss vocally). There are many reasons why that should not have been the case:

1 the Grateful Dead was committed to improvising, to taking enormous musical chances;
2 shows were long, potentially running up to three or more hours of solid playing;
3 the composed parts of the music often had tricky rhythmic and melodic shifts (e.g., the sung part of "Dark Star") or worked in unusual time signatures or feels (e.g., the 11/4 time of "The Eleven," which has the feeling of a waltz with a missed beat every four bars and with the waltz 3/4 combined with a rock 4/4); and
4 the band was on the road constantly, a lifestyle that brings with it fatigue and disorientation.

For these reasons alone, we ought to expect a much larger number of clear mistakes than we hear on the surviving tapes.[68]

Oh, and let's not forget the drugs. It's fairly well known that the band enjoyed using drugs—particularly LSD, in the early period. Now, with regard to this, Grace Slick of the Jefferson Airplane has argued that "if you talk to the Dead, they didn't really play that much on acid. . . . Break off little bits with your fingernail and snort it, and you got high rather than so blazing you couldn't play. That's how people like the Dead would do it, but not full-bore."[69] Part of this, no doubt, is Slick's competitive desire to portray her band as the real, go-for-broke drug band by downplaying the Grateful Dead's drug habits. But, given the Grateful Dead's commitment on the one hand to LSD-inspired musical exploration, and on the other hand to professionalism, her story does not seem implausible, as it would have given them the best of both worlds. (We should also note, however, that LSD was not the only drug circulating in the San Francisco scene, and, while I do not know of any formal studies of this, I have found that large amounts of marijuana or alcohol can make it more difficult to perform competently than up to moderate sized doses of LSD.)

But, despite all these factors—playing a lot of sometimes tricky music, with significant amounts of spontaneous improvisation, on grueling road trips, while high—when you listen to their early live performances, you hear remarkably few actual mistakes in their playing. This is not to say that every musician is "on" at every moment, nor is it to say that there are not questionable artistic decisions being made on the fly. It is merely to say that the

Grateful Dead seem to have committed themselves to maintaining a certain baseline level of musical professionalism in their playing.

This is all the more impressive, given the number of extant recordings of the band. While there are intonation and tuning issues and minor errors scattered throughout their work, glaring mistakes—such as the clearly miscued introduction to "Dark Star" from their show of January 20, 1968, at the Eureka Municipal Ballroom—are disconcerting not so much for the error itself, as for the rarity of errors of that degree.

The Framework, I believe, should be seen in light of this commitment to professionalism. It was a supple form that nonetheless gave some degree of structure and guidance to the band, so that they could dedicate themselves to the pursuit of improvisational transcendence even on evenings when inspiration was in short supply, or when one or more of the musicians simply wasn't feeling it. The Framework and its developments gave them support when they needed it, serving as a tool that enabled them to go out and play upward of a hundred shows a year, year after year, as they furthered their dual imperatives of giving professional performances and following their improvisational muse. What the Grateful Dead were doing was challenging and unexpected, and the Framework and its developments, not being consciously expressed, did not directly or obviously affect their public image—unlike, for example, Cream's virtuosic displays of blues-rock. What it did do was enable them to live up to that image.

Conclusion

In this brief examination, we have seen a variety of approaches that were supported by improvisation. The Jefferson Airplane used it as a way of bringing their songs to life onstage; Cream used it as a means to create an extension of the blues tradition, moving it into the psychedelic era. Both the Velvet Underground and Pink Floyd used it to generate profoundly alien musical contexts—in the one case, drawing on a contemporary high-art appreciation of drones and an invocation of immobility; in the other, drawing on contemporary popular art evocations of interstellar travel and sonic experimentation.

All of these examples overlap in some ways with the Grateful Dead's practice. The virtuosic and thunderously loud conversations between the members of Cream bring to mind some of the interplay between Lesh and Garcia; the Jefferson Airplane's spontaneous group recreations of their songs are comparable to the Grateful Dead's fundamental understanding of ragged ensemble playing; the Velvet Underground's movement from popular songs into extended jams is reminiscent of the Framework; and Pink Floyd's exploration of truly alien sonic realms is comparable to some of the places that the Grateful Dead's music would go at its most extreme, particularly in the early 1970s—for example, in the half-hour-long version of "The Other One" performed on April 26, 1972, in Frankfurt, Germany. For all their similarities, however, in none of these bands do we find the sense of developmental group exploration of spontaneously generated musical contexts that we hear in the Grateful Dead's music, the parameters of which I have attempted to outline.

Another difference lies in the range permitted by the respective approaches to improvisation. All of the approaches that I have discussed are in some way absolutist and limiting. They all stop at some point; they all carry with them inherent conceptual boundaries. For the Jefferson Airplane, the limits are imposed by the songs that they are playing. For Cream, they are imposed by the tradition within which they work (although they did extend that tradition as far as they could take it). For the Velvet Underground, the limits were imposed by their drive to static eternity, while, finally, for Pink Floyd, the limits are to be found in their science fictional and atmospheric aesthetic.

The Grateful Dead, by contrast, prioritized continual motion and continual conversation. Their limits were human ones—namely, the limits of the musicians in the band. Beyond that, they were free to ramble wherever their pursuit of their muse took them. It could be argued that this made their work less coherent as a group artistic expression than the work of the other groups that I have mentioned, but, even if so, this deemphasizing of formal coherence in favor of perpetual motion is by no means necessarily an aesthetic failing. The world is a big place, with room for finished masterpieces as well as gloriously messy works in progress; indeed, depending on the point of view that you take, the one can easily morph into the other, allowing us to see a career spent in dedicated pursuit of the ineffable as itself a masterpiece. Even on an aesthetic level, then, it would be unwise to write off the Grateful Dead's approach; as I will discuss, it could even and also be seen as a religious necessity.

However we regard it, it is also clear that the Grateful Dead's approach to improvisation was both more nuanced, and less commercially comprehensible, than the approaches of the other bands that we have examined. While the logic behind it is not clear or straightforward, when actually heard in concert it makes perfect sense and seems the most natural thing in the world—a typical situation when dealing with the Grateful Dead.

Music, Transcendent Spiritual Experience, and the Grateful Dead

HOW THEY CAME TOGETHER

Let it be known
There is a fountain
That was not made
By the hands of men.
—ROBERT HUNTER,
"Brokedown Palace" (1970)

Music has always been paradoxical, a deeply powerful force that is none-theless completely ephemeral. Painting, architecture, or writing all produce things; they all leave things behind them. But from the earliest stages of human development until the latter half of the nineteenth century, music left nothing behind except, occasionally, in some cases, its score, which was at best merely a blueprint. As jazz saxophonist Eric Dolphy put it in a spoken-word passage at the end of *Last Date*, a live album recorded in 1964: "When you hear music, after it's over, it's gone in the air. You can never capture it again."[1] Of course, this is also the case with dance and acting, but, at the very least, those art forms manifest in space and occupy space; music, by contrast, takes up no space (although the musicians themselves do).

And yet, despite—or perhaps because of—music's evocative ephemerality, traditions from across the world attest to its vast power. Jericho's walls were allegedly destroyed by music; Orpheus was said to have rescued Eurydice from the realm of the dead with it; the pre-Socratic Pythagoreans argued that music revealed the principles that underlie all of existence; shamans ride their music up to celestial realms; voodoo priests use it to open the way for the gods to descend to the human realm. In short, people in a wide variety of contexts make enormous claims about the power of music. Even in contexts where music or a type of music is prohibited, the very existence of the prohibition itself testifies to the power that music is believed to have. Plato would not have been as concerned as he was about the allegedly harmful effects of certain modes if he didn't believe that, as Bonds puts it, "no other human endeavor is as deeply embedded in the construction of the universe as music";[2] similarly, the fulminations of twentieth-century Christians against rock music show respect for the power that they ascribed to it—and later sought to harness for their own ends.[3]

I don't imagine that most of the people reading this will believe in the power of music to literally bring down walls or take us up to heaven, but that does not mean that the modern world lacks a profound appreciation for music's potential, even when that appreciation gets expressed—as in the case of Christian resistance to rock—as racialized fear.[4] On a more positive note, there are abundant testimonies to the power of music as a pedagogical tool, as a source of healing, or as a way of representing the divine, while others stress its ability to build community; some even argue that tuning principles have profound effects on our psychological and social well-being. For example, Mark Bonds speaks of the use of music in education as well as the revelation of abstract universal principles; Joachim-Ernst Berendt speaks of its links to fundamental levels of reality; Joscelyn Godwin collects numerous discussions of its alleged mystical and magical powers; Thomas Turino, among many others, links it to social formation; and Deborah Kapchan discusses its use in healing spirit possession. Personally, I have found W. A. Mathieu a useful guide in terms of sorting out the various ways in which—and levels on which—music creates meaning.[5]

With music being ascribed such vast and broad powers, it is natural that it would be seen as overlapping with beliefs about religious or spiritual aspects of existence.[6] Music is often understood as being an ineffable phenomenon—as a quote of uncertain origin puts it, "writing about music is like dancing about architecture"—that nonetheless can provide access to fundamental aspects of reality.[7] Depending on the tradition, these can be understood as the structural underpinnings of existence itself, as in Pythagoreanism;[8] contact with the divine, as in some Sufi thought;[9] or an aesthetic level of reality that is sui generis and transcends everyday reality.[10] In any case, their parallel to spiritual or religious conceptions is clear.

In both cases, we are speaking of an experience that can be linked to a specific community, and that is understood to lead to ultimate things while creating unique representations of the group in the light of eternity. In other words, while the specific form of the music or the religious experience is culturally bound, the transcendence to which it can lead its listeners is often seen as a manifestation of universal principles. Furthermore, participation in musical or religious activities can produce dramatic physiological changes that can be associated with experiences of transcendence; for example, both religious and musical activity often feature distinct and repetitive movements that are often prolonged and can lead to altered states of consciousness, just as both sorts of activity can involve group settings in which a common mindset is evoked among the participants. In short, it is no wonder that music and religion are very often considered together, whether it is a question of music arousing religious or spiritual feelings, or of music being integrated into a religious or spiritual worldview. They overlap at numerous places, seeming to do similar things or respond to similar needs.

If we turn to thinking about *how* music creates the effects it is alleged to produce, we can see a spectrum of potential causes, ranging from the more or less objective to the more or less subjective. It is clear, for instance, that such things as high volume, very low tones, and extended repetition have effects on the human body and on thought processes—as Coggins notes, religious aspects of musical experience are "rooted in the mediation of powerful sounds in the vibrating body, and in events which emphasize the materiality of sonic mediation itself."[11] However, as Gilbert Rouget has argued, it seems that much of music's ability to induce extraordinary experiences has to do with the way it is perceived in a given cultural context.[12] In other words, it appears that the effectiveness of certain melodies or rhythms or instruments or texts has less to do with anything intrinsic to them than it does with the associations built up around them in their cultures. The same, of course, might be said of many aspects of religious practice and religious experience: the sound of a church organ can have radically different associations for Christians and for Buddhists, while mystics raised in Catholic environments are more likely to have visions of the Virgin Mary than of Kali. So we can sum up by saying that music is often understood to have the potential to do some very special things, and that these special things often overlap with the kinds of special things that religious or spiritual experience are said to do; moreover, those special things are linked to the surrounding culture in terms of how they manifest.

Having spoken on a general level, I now want to focus more closely on improvised music specifically. This is because it is in their jams that the Grateful Dead and their fans tended to see the clearest connection between the band and the transcendent. We saw this, for example, in David Malvinni's location of the purest expression of "Deadness" in their improvised work; similarly, in *The Deadhead's Taping Compendium*, John Dwork describes the Grateful Dead's improvisation by "liken[ing the jamming] to the progression of perceptions that advanced Tibetan Buddhist lamas say one experiences at the moment of death."[13] In *Skeleton Key: A Dictionary for Deadheads*, the entry that describes the ultimate Grateful Dead state, "The Zone," identifies it as "the state of being to which bandmembers and audience 'travel' together when the music is at its most intense, exploratory, and collective" and goes on to quote from fan Gary Greenberg: "The zone is hard to define, but unmistakable when encountered, a sacred space that lies behind and beyond the world we inhabit. It is where the Other lives, a place without time, but filled with consciousness."[14]

This association between musical improvisation and religious experience is not unique to the Dead and Deadheads. The sort of powerful experiences that are likely to be understood as "religious" or "spiritual" are not completely under the control of the one experiencing them; we cannot simply choose to have an emotionally powerful experience, although we can set up contexts in which such experiences are more likely to happen. By its very nature, improvisation brings in a number of features that are extremely helpful in generating contexts in which religious experience can occur. These include a deliberate surrendering of control on the part of the participants, the cultivation of an openness to inspiration, and the use of flexible strategies within a formal structure that allow participants to respond to whatever arises.

We have seen how improvisation served as a tool to invoke religious experience among the listeners in qawwali ritual contexts; in his discussion of the generation of *saltanah*, "modal ecstasy," in Arabic *tarab* music, Ali Jihad Racy demonstrates that these characteristics also apply in a context where the experience is generated in the musician, rather than the listener: that saltanah involves an "ecstatically transformed artist gain[ing] artistic and physical powers that are mysterious and awe-inspiring."[15] Racy also notes that, while there are conditions that can make it more likely to happen, "the idea of forcing inspiration to descend upon the musicians is truly absurd," and that the sorts of "musical triggers" that can generate it can be "unexpected or incidental"; a musician must be prepared to respond improvisationally to triggers as they arise.[16]

Given improvisation's importance for such endeavors, another attempt to create religious or spiritual experience through improvised music, or with its aid, would not be unusual in world history, and, as we will see very clearly in the following pages, this is exactly what the Grateful Dead's fans and the band members themselves thought they were doing. In this particular case, it would, however, differ from many otherwise comparable situations in that there was no one tradition that the Grateful Dead were drawing on: they were standing at the head of their own tradition, and so we are in the very rare situation of being able to observe a musical tradition as it develops. Of course, there is no such thing as creation ex nihilo in culture: as we discussed, members of the Grateful Dead drew on their knowledge of blues, classical, folk, jazz, and raga traditions. But the Grateful Dead themselves were not a blues band, a folk band, or a jazz band: they were a new thing, an improvising rock band. When they formed, they had to build their own tradition.

When reading about the Grateful Dead, it is possible to overlook the significance of religious or spiritual connections to their music. This isn't because of any absence of such references—in fact, quite the reverse. Rather, it is because these sorts of references are so common that they can just become background noise, things that one automatically expects and hence tunes out when reading about the band. It might be a Deadhead talking about the spiritual insights they had while listening to "Dark Star"; it might be a newspaper reporter describing Deadheads as cultish; it might be an academic looking at the sociological overlaps between Deadhead culture and religion; it might even be Jesse Jarnow writing a tremendously important book that puts the Grateful Dead at the center of a whole new way of thinking about spirituality.[17] The idea that the Grateful Dead are in some way linked to an often naive, charismatic take on spirituality or religion is so omnipresent that it ceases to even stand out.

There has been a great deal of scholarly discussion of the Grateful Dead with regard to links to religion or religious experience or spirituality.[18] In this work, a variety of approaches have been taken to the topic, but the two most popular are:

1   interpreting Grateful Dead songs (usually lyrics) through the lens of an established religious tradition,[19] and
2   taking a sociological approach to analyzing the band or (especially) the behavior of their fans.[20]

By contrast, the views or statements of the band members themselves have not been subjected to as much scrutiny: the emphasis is on the reception or interpretation of the music or listeners. This applies as well to more popular accounts of the Grateful Dead's performances or fans, where it is extremely common to find references to fans' "cultish" behavior or "religious" devotion to the group.

This is not at all an unfair perspective to present—rather, it accurately captures the way that many fans view the band. For some, in fact, this perspective can become the sole way in which the band is understood: there has been at least one religious organization that was created by Deadheads, and that puts the band at the center of its theology. The Church of Unlimited Devotion— whose members are colloquially known as the "Spinners," because of the circular dancing they would do at shows—developed a fascinating understanding of the Grateful Dead and their music and its relationship to fundamental principles of the universe in which the Grateful Dead, and particularly Garcia, "were viewed as channels through which God's energy moved."[21]

So it is common for both writers and fans to make strong religious or spiritual associations with the music of the Grateful Dead, particularly in terms of their improvisational practices. Such an approach has both emic and etic roots and is validated and reinforced through conversation with Deadheads and through the writings of respected insiders. This spiritual focus is part of the ideology surrounding the Grateful Dead; it's impossible to get away from it, and new members of the community are encouraged through multiple inputs to view the band from this perspective (in addition to other perspectives, of course). However, we should not forget that this discussion largely overlooks the band members themselves: Did they share the perspectives of their fans in terms of the power and efficacy of their music?

There is a short answer to that question: yes, they (or some of them, anyway) absolutely did. Over the next few pages, I have collected a number of quotes from the band members—this is by no means an exhaustive list— both to show that they had this understanding of their music and to give us some idea of how they conceived of their music's religious power. What we see here is that the fan/writer perspective is exactly right in a broad sense, even if details may differ: there was a religious or spiritual motivation there for the band members as well. Both the community and the band agree that Grateful Dead music was intended to be religious and soteriological. That said, there are a lot of aspects to this that need to be unpacked.

The spiritual understandings of the band from the perspective of its audience are interesting and valid topics for discussion; however, in the present context I am curious not only about the way that the band's music was *received* but also about the way that it was *conceived*. If we think of music as a process extending from performers to audience, my interpretive goals in this book are focused more at the performers' than the audience's end. This isn't a better or worse place to start than any other; there is meaning to be found at every point along the trajectory. But it is a relatively unexplored approach, one that I think deserves a great deal more attention than it has received in the past.

Testimonies

In their comments in interviews and discussions dealing with the band's spiritual or religious importance, members of the Grateful Dead invoked several key themes, which I will briefly discuss and illustrate through quotes below. Bringing their discussions together, we find that they describe the following stages:

1   There was a dramatic introduction to the power of the band's music, revealing that the music caused or was related to something unique and potent.
2   They found that their music gave access to a normally imperceptible level of reality.
3   Playing their music allowed this level to manifest in the world.
4   This manifestation had positive—or even soteriological—effects on listeners and potentially for the entire world.
5   There was something fundamentally uncontrollable about this manifestation, both in terms of whether or not it took place and in terms of how it played out: the musicians were not in control.

My purpose in allowing the band members themselves to lead us through these themes is to clearly demonstrate that a spiritual or religious understanding of the band's music and mission is something that the Grateful Dead shared with many fans and scholars. Whatever one's views of the accuracy of this understanding, it is one that is found at the very heart of the band.

1   There was a dramatic introduction to the power of the band's music, revealing that it caused or was related to something unique and potent:

LESH: "I couldn't walk away from this. It was too good, too interesting. Not interesting in the sense that you say about a new play or paperback novel. I mean really *interesting*—and fraught with meaning, dare I say, of greater breadth and scope than I had ever imagined, even in other forms of music."[22]

HART: when he began playing with the band, the music "felt like some kind of force field from another planet, some incredible energy that was driving the band. . . . It was prayer-like music."[23]

2   They found that their music gave access to a normally imperceptible or unattainable level of reality:

GARCIA: "Music goes back way before language does. And music is like the key to a whole spiritual experience, which this society doesn't even talk about. We know it's there. The Grateful Dead plays at religious services essentially. We play at the religious services of the new age. Everybody gets high and that's what's it all about, really."[24]

GARCIA: "[The state created by the music] might be a completely functioning, already existing reality which has always been energized by humans for this purpose—which is largely invisible or largely magical. . . . It might have always been there . . . and still is, and that's what we're involved in: the rediscovery of it. As long as life goes on, as long as there's energy, this thing might always want to express itself."[25]

HART: "It wasn't songs, or entertainment. Most of the time we were playing for salvation."[26]

GARCIA: "Music is the key to a whole spiritual existence which this society doesn't talk about. The Grateful Dead play at the religious services of the new age."[27]

HART: "Sometimes I think of what happens in a shamanistic sense of embarking on a collective journey. . . . Other times I think of our music as something almost organic that we've grown over the past twenty-five years, a living entity that exists in another time-world."[28]

3   Playing their music allowed this level to manifest in the world:

INTERVIEWER DAVID GANS: "One time I came home from a concert and wrote, 'The Grateful Dead is immortal, but the men who play in the band are not.'"

GARCIA: "That's exactly right, and that's the way we feel. It takes the responsibility out of our hands, which is comfortable. It's scary if you feel like you're responsible for it—that's a lot of energy to be responsible for."[29]

GARCIA: "We know from our own experience that enough things happen [in performance] that aren't the result of signals or planning or communication that we're aware of, but that are miraculous manifestations, that just keep proving it out, that there's no way to deny it. We're involved in something that has a very high incidence of synchronicity. You know the Jungian idea of synchronicity? Well shit, that's day to day reality for us."[30]

LESH: "Ever since the Acid Tests we've been into that power. That's what powered the Acid Tests behind the acid, and it later became apparent that you didn't need drugs. . . . It was a rawer order of energy, less information riding on that raw carrier wave of power, but the power was always there."[31]

HART: "The music is everything; it is a musical organization. But we're not necessarily involved primarily in music."[32]

LESH: "After this many years there's nothing awesome about it at all, except those moments—when you're not a musician anymore, you're not even human. You're just *there* . . . when 'it' plays instead of me."[33]

4   This manifestation had positive—or even soteriological—effects on listeners and potentially for the entire world:

LESH: "To make music for dancers like [the ones at the Fillmore in the 1960s] is the rarest honor—to be coresponsible for what really is the dance of the cosmos. . . . The fervent belief we shared then, and that perseveres today, is that the energy liberated by this combination of music and ecstatic dancing is somehow making the world *better*."[34]

GARCIA: "I think basically the Grateful Dead is not for cranking out rock and roll . . . it's to get high. To get really high is to forget yourself. To forget yourself is to see everything else. And to see everything else is to become an understanding molecule in evolution, a conscious tool of the universe. And I think every human should be a conscious tool of the universe. . . . I'm not talking about being unconscious or zonked out. I'm talking about becoming fully conscious."[35]

LESH: "The Grateful Dead are trying to save the world."[36]

HART: "We've got transformation going here. We don't have a popular musical group. That's what the trappings may look like . . . but that ain't what we have. . . . People come to be changed and we change 'em."[37]

LESH: "The Grateful Dead group mind was in essence an engine of transformation. . . . It felt then as if we were an integral part of some cosmic plan to help transform human consciousness."[38]

LESH: "I've always felt we could do something that was not necessarily extramusical, but something where the music would be only the first step, something even close to religion, not in the sense that 'the Beatles are more popular than Jesus,' but in the sense of the actual communing. We used to say that every place we play is a church . . . the core of followers is not the reason it feels like church, it's that other thing, 'it.'"[39]

GARCIA: "Magic is what we do. Music is how we do it."[40]

5   There was something fundamentally uncontrollable about this manifestation, both in terms of whether or not it took place and in terms of how it played out: the musicians were not in control:

LESH: "We didn't declare it. It declared us."[41]

LESH (*speaking about the Grateful Dead "thing"*): "We're just a piece of it, too."

GARCIA: "That's right . . . we're not *it*—"

LESH: "No. *It* is informing all of us."

GARCIA: "That's exactly right. So our opinions are just that. They're our opinions, in our tradition. . . . But everybody who experiences it, on whatever terms anyone experiences it, is right about it."[42]

LESH: "When we play, we're praying. . . . And then you have to hope that the dove descends."[43]

GARCIA: "The thing we do depends so much upon the situation that we're in and upon a sort of magic thing. . . . Whether [a given performance will be] magic or not is something we can't predict . . . there's a certain phenomenon that *can* happen."[44]

LESH: "I have faith in this thing, whatever the fuck it is."[45]

Talking Religiously

It should be clear from the quoted testimonies that at least some of the members of the Grateful Dead had a spiritual or religious understanding of their music that corresponded to the understanding of many of their followers. But was this understanding "spiritual," or was it "religious"? In this book, I will be speaking of the Grateful Dead as relating to religion, rather than just to spirituality. As *religion* is a contested word, one whose definition is in play, I want to make it clear what I mean by it. In what follows, *religion* will be understood here as having to do with

1   fundamental attitudes toward life and values,
2   particularly insofar as those attitudes and values are related to or derived from a supramundane or transcendental level of existence, as well as
3   the mediations between this supramundane level of existence and the individual person, and
4   the organizations or rites founded to regulate these mediations.

In *Comparing Religions*, religious studies scholar Jeffrey Kripal defines religion as "any set of established stories, ritual performances, mind disciplines, bodily practices, and social institutions that have been built up over time around extreme encounters with some anomalous presence, energy, hidden order, or power that is experienced as radically Other or More." He specifies that "religion is not that original anomalous experience, revelation, or salvation event. Religion is the total psychological and social response to that breaking-in. Religion is the taking of that More and transforming it into narratives, performances, social structures, material objects [etc.] . . . that are certainly less than that original More but can publicly point to, remember, re-enact and above all make contact with it."[46]

Thus, from this perspective, religion is not simply to be identified with what is often described as "religious experience," coming into contact with some powerful Other; rather, religion is firmly planted in this world and represents the way that we express or deal with the memories of, or faith in, that contact. As the title of one of sociologist Peter Berger's books puts it, religion is the "sacred canopy" that relates our world with the normally unperceived realms understood to be beyond or above or within it.[47]

Unfortunately, *religion* can be something of a dirty word in popular usage, sometimes being associated with oppression and closed-mindedness, and this is certainly the case within Grateful Dead circles.[48] To take a very specific and personal example, at the 2010 meeting of the Grateful Dead Caucus at the Southwest Texas Popular Culture and American Culture Association convention, I spoke of "religious" aspects of the ways in which the members of the Grateful Dead and Deadheads regarded Grateful Dead music. When I did, I was met at first with blank incomprehension, and then with the strong response that there was nothing "religious" about any aspect of the Grateful Dead phenomenon, although it was "spiritual"—a view shared, as we will see, by members of the Grateful Dead.

I respect where this point of view is coming from, but I do not subscribe to it myself. Here is why: *spirituality* as a heading loosely covers noninstitutionalized approaches to religion, particularly those that emphasis personal religious experience and the priority of feeling over dogmatic systems. In a North American context it can often be traced back to Transcendentalist and other nineteenth-century thought.[49] While American religiosity in general has not decreased over time, "spirituality" (as opposed to "formal" or institutionalized religiosity) has been particularly important for the baby boom generation, which has been explained by reasons including post–World War II optimism with regard to the ability to remake the world, the popularity of mind-altering drugs, an increasingly ethnically and hence religiously diverse society, the modern spread of knowledge about the world's religious traditions, and the impact of mass media.[50]

In contemporary nonscholarly discussion, spirituality is often presented as the positively valued counterpart to heavily critiqued institutionalized religion, particularly among baby boom "seekers." As Wade Clark Roof writes, "Intense seekers prefer to think of themselves as 'spiritual' rather than 'religious.' They feel most acutely the tension that exists between spiritual experience and its expression in conventional religious forms."[51] In this quote, Roof identifies another characteristic aspect of discourse about "spirituality"—namely, an emphasis on personal experience. In a later work, Roof aptly notes that "for a considerable number of people . . . 'religion' appeared to be in disfavor, and 'spirituality' was in vogue. It was not always clear what was meant by the latter term, but its usage to refer to something distinct from religion and deeply subjective was obvious. . . . Talk about spirituality was often rambling and far-ranging."[52]

This is borne out in Anna King's attempt to summarize the range of potential meanings of the term, which she wrote in the heyday of the "spiritual but not religious" discussion. I will quote it at length in order to illustrate the "rambling and far-ranging" nature of such discourse:

> Speakers "choose" how to define the term to indicate inwardness or to emphasize relationship. They may understand spirituality to refer primarily to the great religious traditions or in a way that includes any religious-like phenomena (which may well include the growth of popular beliefs in corn circles, extra-terrestrials, near death experiences, regression to earlier lives, magic, etc.). People can detach spirituality from institutionalized religion or regard it as its essence. They can define the spiritual in opposition to the material, the corporeal, the rational, the scientific, the secular or stress their fusion and interconnectedness. And of course none of these usages need be exclusive. They are contextual—that is to say, they reflect the situation in which people find themselves.
>
> What spirituality means is very much bound up with who uses it. The word has a long history but it has acquired new associations from its use by New Age writers, by psychotherapists, by ecologists, by feminists, by gays, by black people, by ethnic minorities. It has been linked with protest and with the creation of new paradigms. If "religion" is seen in terms of inherited structures and institutional externals and "worldview" has cognitive associations, spirituality has become a term that firmly engages with the feminine, with green issues, with ideas of wholeness, creativity, and interdependence, with the interfusion of the spiritual, the aesthetic and the moral.[53]

The vagueness of such a definition is typical, and both frustrating and comprehensible. It is comprehensible because this vagueness serves well to guard against the possibility of spirituality becoming an institutionalized, organized, or potentially repressive phenomenon; however, the vagueness renders the term effectively unusable for precise talk.

Roof attempts to resolve this problem by changing the spirituality/religion dichotomy to a contrast between spirit and institutions, carried out on the playing field of religion: "'Spirit' is the inner, experiential aspect of religion; institution is the outer, established form of religion."[54] But this is not simply to valorize spirit—as he points out, "this fluid, less contained form of spirituality does have its limitations. If official religion can become encrusted and rigid, highly personal religion easily suffers from a lack of institutionalization. Mystical experiences, so much a part of religious life, are highly sporadic and volatile; they tend not to encourage lasting loyalty to social organizations, privileging instead the individual's own inner world.[55] But without an institutional and communal context, it is difficult to regularize religious life around a set of practices and unifying experiences . . . or even to sustain personal religious identity."[56]

Another writer on contemporary North American religion, Robert Wuthnow, takes the opposite approach, folding both institutionalized religion and "spiritual" religion (i.e., religion that emphasizes subjectivity, individualism, and experience) into the category of "spirituality," but arguing that there has been a move over the past half century from a spirituality of dwelling that "requires sharp symbolic boundaries to protect sacred space from its surroundings" to a spirituality of seeking which draws "fewer distinctions."[57] He writes, "One type of spirituality seems more secure; the other appears to be less constraining . . . both types of spirituality offer freedom, but the meaning of freedom is quite different. . . . Places that are familiar offer the freedom of not having to worry about where one's next meal is coming from."[58]

I find Wuthnow's discussion of these two sorts of spirituality interesting, but of questionable value in the present context, given the strong associations in modern usage between the term *spirituality* and what Wuthnow would describe as "spirituality of seeking." His "spirituality of dwelling" is fundamentally equivalent to what is often condemned as "religion" or "institutionalized religion." However, Wuthnow's discussion does do good work in reminding us that there can be freedom in stability and familiarity, even in "institutions," no matter how maligned they may be by some spiritual seekers.

This reminder is particularly relevant in the present example, for the Grateful Dead were clearly engaged in founding an institution, even if it was to be a remarkably mobile one, and this institution contained all the features that one would naturally associate with a religious movement. The Grateful Dead and their fans created

1 a *social network* (whose folkways and distinctive language were spread through oral communication, example, and such publications as Shenk and Silberman's *Skeleton Key*), in which there was
2 an interest in transcendent spiritual experience;[59]
3 a rudimentary *ethics* (although lacking for the most part in *paraenetic* discourse, or moral guidance) along with
4 equally rudimentary but strong *soteriological* and *ontological* speculations (i.e., speculation about the ultimate goals of life and the nature of being);[60]
5 characteristic *iconography* or images (tie-dyes, the use of skull and roses imagery, the dancing bears, the ubiquitous "steal your face" or "stealie" logo);
6 a somewhat nomadic lifestyle that involved medium-grade tension with mainstream society (i.e., Deadheads were usually more welcome in communities than bikers or Scientologists, less welcome than Shriners);[61]
7 a belief in the potential *manifestation of supernatural forces*, particularly in the context of the *ritual* and *cultic* activities related to the band;[62]
8 a unique and distinctive *artistic* (especially musical) *sensibility*, as shown in the idiosyncrasies of the Grateful Dead's style, picked up by numerous groups arising from or playing for the Grateful Dead's audience;
9 a foundational *"myth of origins"* centering around the Acid Tests;
10 a collection of more or less *authoritative writings* subject to endless exegetical work and interpretation—namely the lyrics of songs, especially those written by Robert Hunter;[63] and, most importantly of all, perhaps,
11 a *shared ritual* experience, the band's concerts, that took place literally thousands of times over a period of three decades.[64]

If this collection does not entitle us to call the Grateful Dead a religious movement, it is difficult to imagine what would. From the Acid Tests on, the band's explorations of potential relations with a transcendent power were set within a formal context with a definite institutional or ritual cast, borrowing the structures (physical, social, and musical) of popular music performance contexts (concert halls, outdoor festivals, and, eventually, sports arenas), organizing performances into sets (with the sets becoming more and more defined as the years went on), having definite points in the sets in which certain definite kinds of transcendent manifestations were held to be likely to occur (songs amenable for extended improvisation were slotted in towards the end of the first set and throughout the second set), devising strategies for facilitating such occurrences (as we have discussed), and building up a repertoire of motifs to express the significances of the occurrences (the "steal your face" or "stealie" logo; tie-dyed clothing). As lyricist John Barlow writes, "There was a religious aspect to it. That cannot be denied. Nor can it be denied that it was a fundamental element of both our commercial success and our longevity."[65]

The similarity between the Grateful Dead's activity and religion was strong enough to be explicitly addressed by Barlow and the band's other lyricist, Robert Hunter, as we will discuss; their resolution not to provide dogma for this religious movement does not remove the religious connection, but it does show that they took that religious connection seriously and treated it with respect, if in an idiosyncratic manner.

It could be argued that the individual band members, with their wide range of reading interests, fascination with such topics as ancient Egypt and shamanism, and more generally "gnostic" interests in esoteric learning, are typical of the broad lines of American unchurched religiosity or spirituality that has been chronicled by Fuller and others.[66] Furthermore, the scene that developed *around* their music and their concerts could be described as a miniature cultic milieu in the sense defined by sociologist Colin Campbell, who found that traditional sociological organizations of religious movements into churches, sects, and cults was inadequate to deal with the reality of nonmainstream religious change and development.[67] Instead, he considered it more useful to speak of a "cultic milieu" from which many new religious movements arise and into which they dissolve again.

The cultic milieu, Campbell writes, is "the cultural underground of society. . . . It includes all deviant belief-systems and their associated practices. Unorthodox science, alien and heretical religion, deviant medicine, all comprise elements of such an underground. . . . In addition, it includes the collectivities, institutions, individuals and media of communication associated with these beliefs."[68] According to Robert Balch and David Taylor, the cultic milieu "consists of a loosely integrated network of seekers who drift from one philosophy to another in search of metaphysical truth. . . . Members of the cultic milieu tend to be avid readers, continually exploring different metaphysical movements and philosophies. . . . A significant part of their lives is devoted to the pursuit of intellectual growth, however undisciplined that may be in conventional academic terms."[69]

From this point of view, Grateful Dead shows would provide a physical, cultural, and ritual center that held together a very wide and shifting constellation of elements, manifested by fans, concerned with various aspects of spirituality or religiosity, albeit of the unchurched variety. The fans would come together at shows, and particularly in the parking lot outside of the venues in which the band performed, to recreate each night a Deadhead cultic milieu.[70]

These are valid descriptions of the social context either within which the Grateful Dead lived, or that their fans created. But when we are speaking specifically with regard to the Grateful Dead's approach to music—which, as we have seen, was inspired by the hopes of contact with, or actual contact with, a higher power through the medium of a ritual event that was at least theoretically duplicable and whose outlines were broadly formalized—it is clear that these activities can and should be described as properly (if unconventionally) religious activities.

So, to sum up: on a general level, the "spirituality" label is too fuzzy for nuanced work, and in this specific case, it does not apply.

"RELIGION" PROBLEMATIZED

There is another potential challenge to my use of the term *religion*, one that comes not from participants but from scholars of religious studies. Over the past several decades, some scholars have developed a critique of the very concept of religion. Such scholars argue that the creation of such a category is an attempt by defenders of religion, and particularly members of powerful religions, to create a conceptual space that would be immune to deconstructive and other forms of criticism. Relating to this critique, Ann Taves has argued that speaking of "religious experiences" is improper, as it creates a special category of "experience" and thus implicitly supports the heavily contested idea of "religion" as a sui generis phenomenon. She would prefer to speak of "experiences *deemed* religious," thereby putting the emphasis on the process by which an experience is interpreted as being religiously significant.[71]

In Taves's view, people do not have religious experiences per se; rather, they have experiences that are marked as being special through their uniqueness or anomalous nature, experiences that the subject feels "stand out" from the rest of his or her life. In defining these "special" experiences as "religious" experiences, subjects are not recognizing the nature of the experiences, but are constructing a religious meaning for them, consciously or not.[72]

Coming, so to speak, from the opposite side of the problem, Patrick Lundborg—who, before his untimely death, became perhaps the preeminent modern writer on psychedelia—argues that the tendency of many authors to ascribe religious significance to drug-aided psychedelic experience is illegitimate, forcing this experience into a grid and leading to misinterpretation. He notes that "it is difficult to disentangle the psychedelic experience from the various religious frameworks that have been wrapped around it over the past century."[73]

This emphasis on the *construction* of religious meaning is an important one. But it does not seem to me that such an emphasis necessarily requires us to abandon the use of the term *religion* in general or with reference to psychedelic experience when we are speaking—as we are here—of the subjects' own attitudes toward their experiences. I am not arguing that the events claimed by the members of the Grateful Dead did (or did not) take place; neither am I working through the process by which an intellectual context for the experiences was created. More modestly, I simply contend that the band members themselves believed that their experiences were of a sort that could legitimately be described as religious, according to the rough definition I have sketched out, which corresponds to a "lowest common denominator" definition of religion. Thus, they participated in what Alan Segal would describe as "a religiously interpreted state of consciousness."[74]

This being the case, the "deeming" to which Taves refers—the ascribing of these experiences to a religious conceptual space—is a definitional move that has already been made by the subjects. Were we to refuse to speak of these events as "religious," we would be privileging our armchair scholarly perspective over the testimonies and experiences of the subjects in question. There is a long history of scholars doing exactly this; we ought not to perpetuate it.

One way of avoiding the simple religion/spirituality dichotomy might be to speak instead of the category of "outsider religion," just as we speak of "outsider art." Timothy Beal uses this term to describe the eccentric, idiosyncratic, and physically and socially rooted manifestations of religious feeling that he investigates.[75] Beal argues that these outsider statements allow us to "explore themes and issues that are central for American religious life, such as pilgrimage, the nostalgia for lost origins, the desire to recreate sacred space and time, creativity as religious devotion, apocalypticism, spectacle, exile, and the relation between religious vision and social marginality"—all themes and issues that apply to the Grateful Dead as well. In Beal's view, these outsider religious creators are trying "to create a place that is set apart from ordinary space, from the homogeneity of everyday life, an otherworldly realm governed by rules 'other' than those of normal profane space. . . . In the outsider religious spaces we explore here . . . such meanings are more personal, located in the particular and peculiar experiences and beliefs and practices of the individuals responsible for each space."[76] This also applies to the Grateful Dead's approach, which remained to some degree informed by an outsider vision even as they became a hugely successful musical group.

UNDERSTANDING RELIGIOUS EXPERIENCE

As we have seen, many have found it valuable to use religious themes and approaches in speaking of the Grateful Dead. This outsider perspective coheres with the insider perspective. There are testimonies from Deadheads describing the band in clearly religious terms, from the banal ("Jerry is God, man!") to the quite detailed. Steve Silberman speaks, for example, of a "Grateful Dead deity" that was "both wrathful and benevolent. . . . It was partly lizard, partly mammal. . . . It definitely had big teeth. And it would just sit there and look out at you. I would say that all serious, longtime Deadheads have had some experience of that creepy alligator in the nighttime sun that would look out at you from the music and was not altogether good."[77] At least one formal religious organization, the Unlimited Devotion Family, was dedicated to the band.[78] However, it is important to note that the tenets of this organization did not hold that the band members were divine, but that they (especially Garcia) could serve as conduits for divine energy. In other words, the members of the Unlimited Devotion Family "did not believe that the persons in the band were divine persons, but they did believe that the process of Grateful Dead music was a channel of divine intelligence"—a point of view shared by some of the band members themselves, as can be seen from the assembled quotes earlier in the chapter.[79]

Most importantly for our present purposes, there is evidence that at least some of the band members had what we can describe as a religious view of the Grateful Dead and its mission. The most outspoken members on religious issues were Lesh, Garcia, and Hart. In this discussion, I will be focusing on Lesh, as his interviews and autobiography provide the most extensive discussions of these issues, but, before I do, it will be interesting to briefly note the differences between the three spiritually outspoken members in terms of how they discuss this issue; I will do this in chapter 9.

It must also be explicitly stated that there is no question in my discussion of establishing the "facts" of the situation, of detailing "what really happened." Speaking from the outside, in my role as a scholar of music and religion, I have no way of knowing whether or not the claims made by Lesh, Garcia, or Hart are "correct," "or correct if properly understood," or "incorrect"—nor can I say whether any of these judgments are even potentially applicable to the situation. This concern is important, because it relates to larger areas of controversy within the field of religious studies. Over the past thirty-five years, there have been extensive debates over the nature and status of "religious experience," with few definitive conclusions having been reached. The battles were primarily waged between those who felt that there was some element of religious experience that was common to all or many religious traditions and the supporters of what is often called *constructivism*, who felt that religious experience was socially constructed and inextricably linked to (strong constructivists would say solely created by) the experiencer's social or physical context of origin. The first shot was fired by Stephen Katz in 1978, but the battle heated up in the 1980s and continued thereafter.[80]

Constructivism has become the more or less de facto fallback position for the non–religiously affiliated academic study of religion, but advances in neuroscience and psychedelics research over the past several decades have provided unexpected support for the perennialist position.[81] Clearly they do so not in the sense that they have given any proof to the objective existence of a transcendent level of existence (nor have they disproved it), but, rather, in their suggestion that the capacity for some sorts of religious experience are "hardwired" into the human brain, and thus at least potentially independently accessible to people in very different times and places.[82]

The great virtue of the battles in the field of religious experience between supporters of perennialism or essentialism and supporters of constructivism is that they reminded scholars—of whatever stripe—that the content carried by or ascribed to transcendent religious experiences is to some degree created after or before the fact, based on prior expectations, social environment, and the subsequent interpretation of whatever "significant" experiences people may have had.

Whatever validity there may be to a claimed religious experience, this validity is never directly, transparently accessible to the claimant or her audience. Rather, it is profoundly affected by and emerges from prior expectations and post facto constructions. We thus have to do with a continuum, stretching from whatever basis there may be for the claimed experience, through the way in which it is clothed in language or meaning, or integrated into a system, and on through the way in which it is received and transmitted by others. As Earl Waugh writes, "At bottom, [the tradition-producing experience] is an experience that is brought out of a context and made conscious as an authoritative memory." Waugh argues that "the experience is not [necessarily] invented, but rather the process of it becoming a tradition reflects the 'religifying' capabilities of one's psychology and culture. It also signifies the importance of the formative for us, since that formation is the apparent grounds for further interpretation."[83]

As in so many things, one's approach must depend on one's position. As mentioned earlier, in this book I am not discussing what "actually" took place in the religious experiences that various members of the Grateful Dead underwent. Indeed, I share with the constructivists a conviction that as scholars we will never be able to access the experiences themselves, unfiltered by pre- and post facto constructions and interpretations. My goal is simply to discuss the ways in which these experiences were constructed by the members of the Grateful Dead, and the ways their constructions affected their musical practice.

My approach, then, is phenomenological, in the sense described by Jason Blum, in that it is "designed to disclose the meaning of religion, as understood and experienced from the religious consciousness. Conceptualized in this fashion, phenomenology of religion does not posit the existence of transcendent, religious or sacred realities. . . . Rather, it employs epoché and suspends judgment concerning these matters, and instead focuses on interpreting the consciousness and experience of the immanent religious subject."[84]

In this context, the ascription of religious status to these experiences can be seen as a move that has already been made, by the subjects. My role is merely to interpret that move, not critique it. This relates back to Kripal's definition of religion: that it consists of the practices and institutions that are "built up over time around extreme encounters with some anomalous presence, energy, hidden order, or power that is experienced as radically Other or More." In other words, religion is the traces of the original More as they express themselves in culture: the More is undefinable, but the traces are expressed in, and are created by, specific cultural contexts. It is precisely for this reason that I feel it is appropriate to describe the Grateful Dead's work as "religious"; it literally is their attempt to point to, remember, reenact, and make contact with the More that they encountered. You do not need to agree with me about this to enjoy this book, but I do think it's important to put my own cards on the table.

I trust that it will not come as a shock to anyone when I note that the Grateful Dead's religious experiences came about when they were under the influence of LSD, and that the band members freely acknowledged the tremendous significance of the drug for their religious development. This ascription of chemical origins to their religious experiences would lead some—perhaps many—to argue that the experiences themselves were thus necessarily invalid.[85] In other words, it is tempting to argue that whatever they thought they perceived, it wasn't "authentic," it was not "real," because it was drug induced.

There are several good arguments, however, against adopting this approach. First of all, the association of drugs with various sorts of religious experience is widespread. Were we to rule that drug use alone invalidates religious experience, we would be obliged to rule out a priori the experiences of all Rastafarians, some Sufi groups, some Hindu traditions, and many Indigenous American religious traditions, at the very least—and, indeed, writers on drug use throughout history make claims of varying strength for drug use in many other religious contexts.[86] In fact, there is hardly a religious tradition that would emerge entirely unscathed if we took drugs out of the religious mix.

We would also have to rule out the extrainstitutional experiences of the many people in the 1950s and 1960s who found that drug use did or could have a legitimately religious impact, including such reputable figures as Aldous Huxley, Alan Watts, Walter Pahnke, and Huston Smith, who, very sensibly, points to the distinction between religious experience and the religious life, arguing that drug-inspired experience is valid, but not apt to lead to anything more lasting unless combined with faith and discipline.[87] I would argue that the Grateful Dead's vision of creating a concert experience in which transcendent experience could be facilitated, and their commitment to building a musical form that permitted them to achieve this and then touring with it, demonstrate both their faith in the religious experiences that drugs brought them, and their discipline in pursuing those experiences.

I would even go one step further and argue that to treat "drug-produced experience" as a special category is itself an illegitimate move. Drugs are chemicals that are used to induce altered states of consciousness, and there are many ways of creating altered states of consciousness, including fasting, prolonged repetitive action, prolonged immobility, or unusually intense physical exercise such as dancing.[88] Were we to argue that any religious practice that associates self-imposed physical or physiological alterations with religious experience is invalid, what would we be left with? Abnormal contexts do seem to be fertile grounds for religious experience: it arises out of extreme situations, whether or not those situations are self-induced.

Jeffrey Kripal refers to this as "the traumatic secret" and writes that "by the traumatic secret I mean to signal the observation that in many cases the mystical event or altered state of consciousness appears to have been 'let in' through the temporary suppression or dissolution of the socialized ego, which was opened up or fractured (either at the moment of the mystical event or earlier in the lifecycle) through extreme physical, emotional, and/ or sexual suffering, that is, through what we would today call in our new psychological code 'trauma.'" This is not a reductionist perspective; Kripal's approach "does not reduce the mystical event to the traumatic fracture but rather understands the trauma as a psychological correlate or catalyst of the mystical state of consciousness."[89] The idea of the "traumatic secret" thus simply acknowledges that extreme circumstances can be the catalysts for extreme experiences.

Additionally, the very word *legitimate* brings up problems. Speaking as interested outsiders, as I have mentioned, we are not competent to discuss whether or not a given religious experience "really" (i.e., objectively) took place. Our concerns here should address more pragmatic issues: What does the person claim to have happened? How do these claims relate to the person's social and intellectual contexts? Does the person's postexperience life show that the experience was important to them, and do they continue to construe it as being religiously important?

It is clear from their religious uses that drugs have the potential to create "special" experiences in those who take them, and LSD is no exception to this rule. As Charles Hayes's collection of trip accounts makes clear,[90] LSD can provide a "trigger" for special experiences, but whether or not drug-inspired experiences will be taken as religious in nature depends on the person undergoing them, the specific context in which they take them, the dosage that they take, and their intellectual, social, religious and historical context.[91] (Different drugs do, however, tend to encourage, if not cause, different sorts of experiences, and I will argue that characteristic aspects of the LSD experience affected the religious understanding that members of the Grateful Dead derived from their experiences.)

As Hartogsohn puts it, "LSD . . . is a psychopharmological chameleon, one that changes its psychoactive pigmentation in relation to the cultural set [the experiencer's expectations and understandings] or setting [the context of use] into which it is introduced."[92] This is because "despite the extreme malleability of psychedelic effects . . . their one common and crucial characteristic is their ability to magnify and amplify the content of one's experience."[93] There are, he argues, "recurring elements" such as "the dissolution of boundaries, the intensification of sensations, and a hyperassociative . . . possibly irrational or magical mode of thinking," but these elements do not necessarily have to be interpreted as being part of a religious experience.[94] Nonetheless, this interpretive move toward a religious or spiritual association has frequently been made, and it is one that, once made, will affect how one understands one's experiences.

So far, we have seen evidence that the members of the Grateful Dead, as well as fans and scholars, felt that there was at least potentially a supranormal experience associated with their music. I have argued that this experience can be best described as "religious," rather than merely "spiritual." Against those who would argue that "religious" is a reifying category rather than a sui generis one—that is, it freezes experience rather than arising naturally out of the experience—I have argued that, whatever the merits of their case, this specific ascription of transcendent experience to a sacred realm is not one that I am carrying out, but one that the Grateful Dead themselves accomplished. Thus, my analysis is situated in a context in which the religious ascription has already been made. Against those who would argue that the source of the band's religious inspiration renders it unworthy of respect, I have argued that if we refuse to grant legitimacy to any religious experiences that took place in a deliberately altered state of consciousness, we must rule out the vast majority of the world's religious traditions—clearly a case of throwing the baby out with the bathwater.

The Grateful Dead's
Spiritual Context

THE ACID TESTS AND AFTERWARDS

The first time that music and LSD interacted in a way that really came to life for us as a band was one day when we went out and got extremely high . . . and we went that night to Lovin' Spoonful. . . . It was just truly fantastic. We began to see that vision of a truly fantastic thing. It became clear to us that working in bars was not going to be right for us to be able to expand into this new idea. And about that time the Acid Test [*sic*] was just starting to happen. —JERRY GARCIA (1970)

It is probably an understatement to say that the 1960s was a time of spiritual and religious experimentation on all levels, and in many cases we see the inchoate beginnings of traditions or intellectual explorations that would become more defined later, in the early 1970s and 1980s—for example, spiritual teacher Stephen Gaskin's weekly Monday Night Classes led to his and his followers' exodus from San Francisco and the creation of the spiritual commune the Farm.[1] Similarly, Aidan Kelly and others formed the New Reformed Orthodox Order of the Golden Dawn, which helped to spur and define the revival of paganism and witchcraft in the 1970s. The so-called Jesus Freaks or Jesus People are another example of a case in which 1960s drug-related spiritual exploration served as the seed for clearly organized religious expression.[2]

The Grateful Dead's religious practice also arose out of a broader context of spiritual beliefs and practices. While there was a bewildering variety of modes of spiritual expression and traditions at play in the (specifically San Francisco) hippie scene, there do seem to have been some core principles that relate especially strongly to the Grateful Dead's own work, particularly the emphasis on the experience of merging telepathically together with others as a fundamental spiritual aspiration.

Stephen Gaskin was an enormously influential figure in the Haight-Ashbury spiritual scene who worked with hundreds of hippies every week in his Monday Night Class.[3] From his perspective, the pursuit of telepathic union with others was the core of all authentic spirituality and religion.[4] Gaskin did not start out with the intention of becoming a spiritual leader. Indeed, he claims not to have been seriously involved in religion in his earlier life: "I . . . had no religious upbringing and was on a completely materialistic trip."[5] As Gaskin tells it, his spirituality was something that he developed for practical reasons, with the goal of making certain sorts of highly valued experiences more possible. Specifically, his spirituality was designed to support and interpret the experiences of telepathy that he felt he'd had while under the influence of entheogens. For him, moral action and spiritual development are necessary in order to permit telepathy and other miracles to happen. He learned to see religion not as arbitrary beliefs, but as an eminently practical guide to life: "I got into religion in the early days of the hip thing in San Francisco, and I had experiences that convinced me that religion was real and that what I thought was an empty morality structure was a description of how the universe works."[6]

These "experiences" included, most prominently, telepathy, for which he felt that religion (properly understood) provides the basic principles that allows it to operate. While Gaskin and his group were pursuing telepathic abilities, "we said, there's probably some kind of a best system that you could run this kind of a thing on that works good for everybody. . . . We started putting this thing together, and then it started getting recognizable as the pieces fell in. And we saw that it looked just like Christianity, and it looked just like Buddhism, and it looked just like every religion, because that's what a religion is."[7] The link between religious ethics and telepathy is logical because, from Gaskin's point of view, what he and his fellow hippies were doing is what all the religions were originally about anyway. "Just do it like it says in the book," he states. "Really, just like it says in the book. Sermon on the Mount is tripping instructions and will carry you through. If you have read the Sermon on the Mount so many times that it doesn't mean anything to you anymore, read the 81 poems of Lao Tzu and they'll tell you the same thing."[8]

For this reason, Gaskin felt that his group's attempts to become telepathic were, in fact, at the core of what religion—every religion—is really about. "Well, the thing about all those religions is that you can stack them all up together like IBM punch cards and you can look at them and see which holes go all the way through. And that's the trip we're trying to do, the one with the holes that go all the way through."[9] Technically, this attitude can be described as reductionistic and perennialist. To start with, it is reductionistic because it reduces the infinite complexity and diversity of religious expression to a search for one sort of experience. There are many forms of reductionism— currently, religious studies tends to favor a sociological reductionism—but Gaskin's own reductionism is related to perennialism, a philosophy of religion that argues that a common core underlies all religions. A version of perennialism, inspired by Aldous Huxley's *The Perennial Philosophy,* was often used as a fallback position in the Consciousness Revolution of the 1960s in order to contextualize and legitimize experiences prompted by entheogens, coding them as "religious" and presenting users of entheogens as mystical seekers rather than, for instance, drug-addled hedonists.

So, Gaskin's perennialism is timely and to be expected from someone in his social and intellectual context. Further, his idea that psychedelics permitted the realization of religious goals through the creation of a telepathic group mind that is the real goal of all religion is fundamental to the development of hippie spirituality and has been well analyzed by Daniel Merkur in his two contributions to *Seeking the Sacred with Psychoactive Substances.* Merkur writes that, for the hippies, "telepathic occurrences were mystical events that proceeded within the group mind" and notes Gaskin's spiritual and intellectual influence in the San Francisco hip scene of his day. Merkur's discussion makes clear that Gaskin was both helping to create this understanding of spirituality and responding to it.[10] In addition, Merkur's discussion emphasizes how hippie spirituality developed to incorporate character development and utopian or millenarian transformative goals into the "group mysticism" that characterized its early days. While these goals led "many people" to liken "the hippies to the early Christian community," however, "Gaskin reversed priorities," arguing instead that the hippies were an authentic and current manifestation of the same impulses that had driven all other religious communities, including early Christianity, with a fundamental emphasis on telepathic interaction as the core transcendent experience.[11]

As we have discussed and will continue to discuss, this was also a musical goal for the Grateful Dead: the band felt that their music acquired its transcendent power when they were able to "blesh"—to come together in a musical group consciousness.[12] Daniel Merkur has perceptively argued that much of hippie spirituality, and especially this emphasis on telepathic union, arose from the scene around author Ken Kesey: "The crucial element in the formation of hippie spirituality, which moved it beyond bohemia to occupy a social location of its own, was the contribution of Ken Kesey and his Merry Pranksters."[13] It is certainly the case that involvement in his scene, and particularly the Acid Tests that he organized, was pivotal for the Grateful Dead.

The Acid Tests

The Acid Tests were events in 1965 and 1966 organized by the Merry Pranksters, a guerilla art group led by author Ken Kesey and best described in Tom Wolfe's *The Electric Kool-Aid Acid Test*. The Merry Pranksters possessed a strong, almost messianic, sense of mission and a high commitment to mind expansion, to be achieved with the aid of sensory overstimulation and psychedelic drugs. Their goal—insofar as they had one—seems to have been to enable people to break through the normal limits of consciousness and attain a state of inspired intuitive oneness with universal forces. As Kesey wrote, "We have to do something to break us out of that rut, the rut of our minds. . . . You can't have a new idea. You can't strain . . . and go forward and find a new idea . . . [but] you can be enlightened, which is, like, 'Ah!' But to do that, though, you have to wander into a new area."[14] There are clear overlaps here with Stephen Gaskin's discussion of the "sudden school" of Zen, as he understood it: he felt that the universe was being recreated in every moment, and so there was always the possibility for sudden enlightenment.[15] Like him, the Pranksters believed in the potential for immediate spiritual awakening.

The Acid Tests were of pivotal importance for the Grateful Dead. The band's career did not literally begin at the Acid Tests, but it was at these events that the Grateful Dead collectively discovered its vocation, its defining environment. When asked in an interview in 1983, "When did you start realizing that there might be something of greater human significance available to the Grateful Dead?," Lesh was quick to respond: "[At the] Acid Tests. That's when it really hit me." Later in the interview, he added: "I know that if the Acid Tests had never happened, we would have been just another band."[16]

When asked, in the same conversation, "How did the personal, collective quest [for musical transcendence] turn into this incredible myth?," Jerry Garcia responded that it happened "as soon as we were playing at the Acid Tests."[17] In an earlier interview, in 1972, Garcia had presented it very clearly: "The Acid Test was the prototype for our whole basic trip. But nothing [that the band had done since] has ever come up to the level of the way that the Acid Test was."[18] The Acid Tests were where the Grateful Dead felt that they had glimpsed transcendence; as Garcia put it, "that Acid Test experience gave us glimpses into the form that follows chaos."[19] Given the significance of the Acid Tests for the band, the ways that they crystallized and revealed the group's spiritual or religious mission, the Acid Tests and the meanings that were derived from them can reasonably be described as the Grateful Dead's foundation story. It is in that light that I will now examine them.

Religions need myth, and they need in particular foundational myth, the creation of which involves the establishment of a "year zero" that is crucial to any religious movement (providing the axis mundi that supports the religious world, as William Paden might have put it) from which aspirations can be derived, aesthetic and ethical standards set up, and the future predicted or preenacted.[20]

Since foundation stories describe the establishment of the sacred period from out of its secular historical context, it logically follows that they delineate three situations: a state of potential that sets the stage for the foundation story; the foundation period, in which a particular period is liberated from history and moved into an archetypal realm, and in which the bases for the religious movement and its values are set; and the move out of the liminal realm and back into history, which presents particular challenges for the new religious movement. In the discussion that follows, we will see how this tripartite delineation played into the Grateful Dead's relationship to the Acid Tests.

To illustrate the importance of foundation stories for the understanding of religious movements, we could look at such works as the gnostic writings found near Nag Hammadi in Egypt, in which challenging reconstructions or re-presentations of mainstream Christianity are very often legitimized through their ascription to the apostolic period.[21] The foundational period is where religious power comes from.

Foundation stories derive from the historical period that marks the beginning of the religious movement in question. They lift this period out of history, turning it into normative myth and the template for future ritual. In this way, "the actual processes of human agency . . . are overlaid with a historiography that confers legitimacy to religious claims and practices."[22] As Paden notes, "Each religious world has its own past . . . these pasts and histories are given form . . . through the memory and continuity of tradition. Every past rises up around key events and exemplary figures." Myths and foundation stories arise from "prototypical time in which divine events and words have been definitively posited."[23] Or, as Roland Barthes more jadedly put it, this sort of myth "has the task of giving an historical intention a natural justification and making contingency seem eternal."[24]

Whether or not these myths are literally true is not the point. As Mikael Rothstein puts it, when discussing issues of truth/history from religious points of view, "It is necessary to acknowledge that the mythical rendering of time and history is much more important than 'history' in the everyday (secular) sense of the word. Here I have to emphasize that 'mythical formations' are different from 'lies.' . . . Things that are not factual may easily be appreciated as true in religious contexts."[25] And, indeed, they may do religious work, making them "authentic fakes," a concept that we will discuss.

The Creation and Maintenance of a Foundational Myth

I have been arguing that the Grateful Dead's inspiration can in some sense be described as religious. As for when and how this aspect of things enters the picture, there is no evidence in any of the sources that I have examined for any of the original members having had strong attachments to organized religious groups prior to the band's formation, nor in the interviews that I have read do band members speak of spiritual crises or religious concerns before 1965.[26] It does not seem, either, that the mere fact of playing rock music was religiously fraught for them—a notable difference from the experiences of many earlier rock and rollers such as Jerry Lee Lewis, Little Richard, and Elvis Presley. Steve Turner brings out this difference between many of the first-wave rock and roll musicians and their successors when he notes of the Beatles that "they were typically second-generation rock and rollers in that none of them suffered any anxiety over a secular-sacred split in their lives" with regard to their music.[27]

To speak generally, and to judge by the extant accounts—as well as by the band's musical developments—it was the Grateful Dead's use of LSD, beginning in 1965, that led several of the band's members to start feeling that their music was potentially of religious significance. It was, however, at the Merry Pranksters' Acid Tests that these more or less inchoate feelings turned into something more definite. At the Acid Tests, the Grateful Dead found a community, and with it an identity and a legend: they were no longer merely a folk-rock-blues group, but became Ken Kesey's "faster than light drive," the house band for a new kind of public experience.[28] In *The Electric Kool-Aid Acid Test*, Wolfe presents the Grateful Dead as, essentially, the Acid Tests' house band. It might be argued that Wolfe, as a non-hippie New Yorker, could easily have been ignorant of the real situation, but, as band insider Augustus Owsley Stanley III (better known as "Bear") has said: "Grateful Dead were Pranksters. They were musicians, but they were also Pranksters."[29] He adds that "all I know is, I joined up with a band that were Pranksters; they were part of the scene that was doing something that was right on the edge."[30] It is with their association with the Pranksters, and specifically their role at the Acid Tests, that the band's distinctive myth really begins.

The Acid Tests were all-night, drug-fueled multimedia parties, a source of inspiration for psychedelic "happenings" and the later rave scene. The point of these parties was to encourage people to be as picturesquely weird and open to the moment as they could be, all in an environment that combined unpredictability with sensory overload and as much of an absence of control as was possible for events sometimes drawing thousands of people. Many of the participants would have taken LSD, and so a night at an Acid Test would be passed in the company of very stoned, often oddly dressed or oddly acting people while strange music played, often provided by the Grateful Dead, ambient sounds and conversation were fed into the PA, and images and lights were projected on screens.[31] By all accounts, attendance at an Acid Test could have a tremendously powerful impact on the participant, often changing lives, for good or for ill.

Based on that description alone, the Acid Tests could have been no more significant than great parties. What turned these parties into foundation stories was the way that they were mythologized after the fact—or, to put it another way, the sorts of meaning that were ascribed to them, and the future activities that were suggested or rendered possible by them. For example, the hippie spiritual teacher Ram Dass (born Richard Alpert) writes that "the Acid Tests were extraordinary. I felt that they were sheer magic. And they were scary magic. In many ways I saw it as religious ritual."[32]

While the impact that the Acid Tests had on at least some of their participants is clear, their meaning is less clear—perhaps by design. They were carnivalesque events at which participants were encouraged to "freak freely," to express themselves as fully, flamboyantly, and spontaneously as they liked, responding to the sensory overload environment and drugs, and at which magic was felt to arise from the conjunction of spontaneous events, particularly when enhanced by the Grateful Dead's music. One of the main Pranksters, Ken Babbs, notes that "we always thought of the Grateful Dead as being the engine that was driving the spaceship that we were on."[33]

The Acid Tests bear strong similarities to some of Victor Turner's ideas about liminal spaces, in which social roles are altered or suspended and a ludic approach to life is privileged. But, for some participants, they were significant in ways that transcended sociology. As Farber writes, the Acid Tests were "geared toward maximizing psychic, sensual input, loading up the mind and pushing tripsters toward a vast collective experience that roared toward the unknown. The Acid Tests pointed toward the creation of enclaves, social spaces in which visionaries played out new collective games."[34] In a 1969 interview in *Rolling Stone*, Garcia said that the purpose of the Acid Tests were to "do away with old forms, with old ideas. . . . Nobody was doing something, y'know. It was everybody doing bits and pieces of something, the result of which was something else . . . when it was moving right you could dig that there was something that it was moving toward, something like ordered chaos."[35] Garcia did not elaborate on the origins of the order in this "ordered chaos," but later comments from him and Lesh suggest that the order arose through the visible manifestation of universal consciousness—the "uncontrolled anarchy" that took place at the Acid Tests was actually, when properly understood, "the dance of the cosmos."[36]

This freely occurring magic—the overwhelming presence of what was felt to be deeply meaningful, if often inexpressible, coincidence—was interpreted by several band members as signs of the manifestation of a divine energy, invoked by this most modern and ad hoc of rituals. Lesh concludes his autobiography by writing that "it's safe to say that in the 90 days or so that the Acid Tests existed, our band took more and longer strides into another realm of musical consciousness, not to mention pure awareness, than ever before or since. At the beginning we were a band playing a gig. At the end we had become shamans helping to channel the transcendent into our mundane lives and those of our listeners."[37]

Thomas Wolfe was a close but nonconverted observer of the Acid Tests and Kesey's scene. In *The Electric Kool-Aid Acid Test* Wolfe makes it very clear that the Merry Pranksters, the loose organization that Kesey founded and that hosted the Acid Tests, took on some of the characteristics of a new religious movement. These were not—or were not just—a bunch of deranged bohemians getting high in the woods. The craziness was enfolded in or justified by a sense of religious mission, a pursuit of fleeting contacts with something large and meaningful. As Wolfe notes, although the Pranksters scrupulously avoided religious language, nonetheless "there was something . . . religious in the air, in the very atmosphere of the Prankster life."[38] Kesey served as the charismatic leader, and there was a shared view of their activities as being spiritually significant, a sense that in their daily lives they were taking part in extremely important immanent metaphysical explorations. William Plummer speaks of the sense that a "new church" was being founded: "The landscape was littered with portents. . . . Increasingly, [the Pranksters] were coming to believe they were in an I-Thou relationship to the universe."[39]

Looking back, Kesey argues that "when we got into acid with a group of people, we felt that we were dealing with the end of time."[40] Garcia points out that "I've been lucky enough to meet people like Kesey, who've been able to illuminate some sense that this is not just a drug induced fantasy, but part of the larger picture of consciousness which we're making an effort to map and . . . well, we're making an effort to evolve. . . . [Without the influence of people like Kesey] I tend not to believe that the voice I hear is the voice of God."[41] The religious nature of the events, and Kesey's dominant role in them, is clear.

In *The Electric Kool-Aid Acid Test*, Wolfe cites Joachim Wach's theory of the primacy of the religious experience in founding new religions: the experience is brokered by a leader, and those who have undergone this life-changing experience come to recognize themselves as a unique new group, in need of new means of expressing and accessing transcendence.[42] Although this theory is not universally applicable—there are other ways in which new religions can form—it certainly does apply here. This is the purpose that the Acid Tests served for Kesey and the Pranksters; also, the tests were the group's major public statements, their first steps outside of their own tight scene to engage the outside world and build a place for themselves there. Very literally, the Acid Tests were laying the foundations for Kesey's new movement, and Wolfe presents them in his book as the ultimately unsuccessful attempts to found a new religion (more on that later). Plummer concurs: "There was an undisguised messianic purpose behind the Tests"—or, as Kesey put it at the time, "The millennium started some months ago."[43]

In the quotes from Jerry Garcia or Phil Lesh that I have presented, we can hear the mythologization of the Acid Tests: they have become archetypal events sufficient to provide the starting point, the legitimation, for an approach to music that sustained the Grateful Dead through a thirty-year-long career: "The Dead's drive for improvisation is quintessentially American . . . but their practice of it is the most audible legacy of their experience with the

Acid Tests."[44] Although the musicians were by no means as accomplished as they would later become, nonetheless it was at the Acid Tests that the transcendent potential of their music became clear to them. In later years they would discuss the Acid Tests as their soteriological high point, as the purest manifestation of what their music could and was intended to do.

It is clear that the Acid Tests were fundamental experiences for the band, particularly when the Grateful Dead is considered as a religiously motivated organization. They functioned in the band's mythology much as did the period of Jesus's earthly ministry for later generations of Christians—that is, they represented a time when the parameters and standards for the new movement were established, when miracles were possible and utopia dimly visible, when the walls between the transcendent and human realms were thinnest. Thus, the tale of the Acid Tests represents a foundation story for the Grateful Dead seen as a religious organization.

David G. Bromley and Douglas E. Cowan note that "because they are literally religions-in-the-making, new religious movements (NRMs) offer a particularly fruitful source of insight into the processes by which religion is socially constructed."[45] In this case, the Acid Tests provide us with a reminder of the unexpected ways in which religious feeling can manifest. But, when we think about what we do or do not expect, we should keep in mind that the aura of reverence, of sanctity, that is often cast over religious beginnings comes later. Things happen, and then later people realize—or decide—that they were extremely significant, and they backdate that feeling of significance, so that the memory of the primal event expresses the understanding of that event that developed since it happened. The Acid Tests, whatever they were at the time, have been remembered by the members of the Grateful Dead and many Deadheads as profound, significant experiences, just as what may have been a somewhat drunken party at a place called Cana has been remembered by generations of Christians as being deeply sacred and significant.

The End of the Beginning

By necessity, foundation stories require some kind of delimitation. Logically speaking, if the apostolic period, the golden age, is forever, then how can it be perceived as a golden age? Furthermore, life and history being what they are, sooner or later things fall apart in some way for any movement, let alone one that presents radical new understandings about religious matters and hence poses challenges to the established orders of its period. Therefore, the foundation story also needs to make religious sense out of the end of the golden age and to explain how the religious movement is still, or could still be, legitimate.

In many foundation stories, this is done by presenting the founder as laying down authoritative moral codes, rules of succession, and guidelines during or at the end of the golden age. Mohammed, for example, received the Koran, which was later passed on to his followers; Jesus appeared to and instructed his disciples after the resurrection; Mani codified his teachings into several books; and the Buddha's sayings were remembered and orally passed on.

The Grateful Dead and the Acid Tests were different, however, in that the leading figure most qualified to fit into the role of founder—namely, Ken Kesey—had lost a great deal of his prophetic charisma by the time of the last Acid Test. This was the "acid graduation" ceremony, at which even the Grateful Dead deserted him in order to play a different show—as Wolfe brings out quite clearly in *The Electric Kool-Aid Acid Test*, itself a work of mythologization, of course, but the general details of which are regarded as being historically reliable.[46] By this point, Kesey had lost the respect of—or been superseded by—the San Francisco hippie community whose expression and aesthetics he had influenced so strongly, and even his group of Merry Pranksters had splintered. "The hippies, at the last moment, rejected Kesey," making the Acid Graduation "one of those pivotal moments that you find in myths, when the hero fails a crucial test because he lacks faith."[47]

Although Kesey remained part of the Grateful Dead family, and they did perform to support his family-owned creamery in Oregon, where he retired after the collapse of his charisma, their discussions of him and other presentations of his impact show that his role as a potential mass-movement leader ends with the Acid Tests.[48] His group was fractured; his ideas had been taken up and popularized by others, not least the Grateful Dead; he was not trusted by such power brokers as Bill Graham and Chet Helms; on a popular level, he and the Pranksters seem to have lost the respect of a hippie movement that was considerably younger and less focused than he; and he was embroiled in legal troubles that led to him serving jail time, after which he moved away from San Francisco entirely.

In short, Kesey and the Pranksters created a new and at least partly religious phenomenon, the Acid Tests, which had a profound influence on the Grateful Dead's aesthetics, design, and aspirations. And yet, despite this, the collapse of his prophetic charisma did not cause the collapse of the spiritual psychedelic movement that first manifested in the Acid Tests and with which the Grateful Dead identified themselves. This counterintuitive result might well arise from the Grateful Dead's well-known distrust of authority figures and would-be leaders, but it also supports James R. Lewis's argument that the importance of prophetic figures is often overstated. As Olsson writes, "Basically, the Acid Tests were initiation rites, separating those who took the Test from the rest of the world. Those inside would form part of the charismatic group, and outsiders were excluded. When the Acid Tests became impossible to uphold, the Grateful Dead took up the mantle of charismatic authority through their performances—although playing down the 'authority' aspect as much as they could."[49]

In an article focused on the Native American Ghost Dance tradition, James Lewis notes that

> a key factor in causing academics to attribute ephemerality to messianic movements is a mistaken theological perspective that portrays the personal charisma of the founder as the "glue" holding together alternative views of reality. Such a perspective misconstrues the role of charisma. In the first place, no matter how charismatic a prophet, his message must somehow address the concerns of the community in a satisfactory manner if he is to convince more than a handful of close associates. In other words, a contagious new vision has more going for it than merely the personality of the revealer. In the second place . . . the actual adoption of an emergent religion by a human community recruits the forces of social consensus to the side of the new revelation. . . . Because social consensus is the real glue that maintains the plausibility of any given worldview, potential sources of crisis in the life of a religious movement lie in the areas of breakdown of social consensus, not the passing away [or loss of charisma] of the prophet.[50]

Lewis's point is valid, and evidently there was enough of a social consensus within the Grateful Dead community that Kesey's innovations were valuable enough to keep them going. At least in his early days, Kesey felt that one could find transcendence through LSD-inspired visionary experience set in a very public context that encouraged sensory overload and was joined with an aesthetic of spontaneity and a hyperactive Zen reveling in the moment. The messianic significance of this idea survived Kesey's own passing as a prophetic leader.

However, my present concern is not so much with the actual continuation of the movement as with the way that that continuation is rhetorically constructed. In other words, here as with our discussions of transcendent religious experience, I am less concerned with what "really" happened than with how events were understood—what kind of a story they were built into.

Working in that spirit, I would like to discuss the ways in which the Grateful Dead's Acid Tests foundation story deals with these issues, protecting the band's mission from the collapse of Kesey's own mission.

The Grateful Dead's lack of public discussion of the end of the Acid Tests is in itself one way of doing this: in their accounts and in the writings of their fans, the Tests are remembered as the glorious events that spawned the Grateful Dead's way of approaching music and life, and their ending is glossed over or ignored. We might compare this to the way that John the Baptist's story is incorporated into the story of Jesus in the New Testament, with his fall and death being an addendum to what is presented as being his real significance as forerunner.[51]

We can see another way in which the Grateful Dead safeguarded their foundation by turning our examination from the end of the golden age to its start—the period in which the new religious movement began. Titus Hjelm makes an interesting and relevant point when he discusses "'conversion' as an implicit legitimating strategy" and argues that "the religious group a person affiliates with conditions the depictions of the 'past life' and the conversion experience itself."[52] He gives as an example his work among Wiccans, in which most of the respondents presented entry into Wicca as being a question of manifesting or realizing something they already felt, and notes that "the 'logic of conversion' in Wicca seems to be the opposite compared to, for example, evangelical Christianity. Whereas the evangelical Christian is 'born again' and sees her previous life behind her, with a sharp break between it and her current status, the Wiccan finds her past life in front of her: the past is defined as something which now has a name."[53] This strategy, Hjelm argues, foregrounds individualism and "relegates tradition to a less important . . . position"; it also enables the respondents to "identify with Wicca, while at the same time distancing themselves from it."[54] New Wiccans are not indebted to the tradition, nor have they changed so as to affiliate themselves with it: the tradition's power derives solely from its correspondence to the convert's sense of self.

Hjelm's presentation of Wicca casts light on the way that Phil Lesh and Jerry Garcia have discussed their introduction to the Pranksters and the Acid Tests. Although they acknowledged the Acid Tests as in some sense the beginnings of the Grateful Dead's spiritual mission, nonetheless in several accounts both of them can be heard to emphasize not only that the band and its scene existed prior to the Acid Tests but also that its mission was in some way present then as well. As both Lesh and Garcia have presented it, the Grateful Dead's religious significance arose from the time when the band was exposed to, and started playing under the influence of, entheogonic drugs, including most prominently LSD, well before their participation in the Acid Tests.

Thus, for Lesh, it is the two-month period of gigless rehearsal in the fall of 1965 that enabled the band "to meld our consciousnesses together in the unity of a group mind," the necessary precondition for musical transcendence, and they had already played their first "big gig" before Lesh "wangled invitations for the band to the first [Acid] Test"—to attend as guests, not to play. Lesh describes this first Acid Test as being "subdued," in need of "some kind of focus" to "transform diffuse individual energies into coherent collectives. Clearly, music was the answer," and it is when the Grateful Dead bring their music to the second test that the tests become truly magical. As Lesh recounts, "We knew we had something, but we didn't know how deep it was. We directed and focused it through these parties."[55]

Garcia, for his part, made it clear in his interview with Charles Reich and Jann Wenner that the fundamental changes in his attitude toward life and music that LSD caused had all taken place well before the first Acid Test, and that the Acid Tests, for all their mystical powers, were ways for him to continue in the musical direction that he had already mapped out.[56] As he described it, "In the night clubs, in bars, mostly what they want to hear is short fast stuff . . . and we were always trying to play a little, stretch out a little. . . . So our trip with the Acid Test was to be able to play long and loud. Man, we can play as long and loud as we wanted and no one would stop us."[57]

When the Acid Tests started happening, Garcia said, "we were ready for something completely free-form. It kind of *went along with where we were going*, which is we were experimenting with psychedelics, as much as we were playing music."[58] When asked directly, "Were you under Ken Kesey's tutelage?," Garcia responded, "Not really. I was getting high with those guys, but 'it' wasn't coming from them—it was coming from 'it,' whatever 'it' was."[59] Lesh has stated that "we were always more aware of ourselves as a unit, as a band, than as representatives of the culture, or any other abstract—that's why we didn't stick with the Acid Tests, because we wanted to be the Grateful Dead, and not the Acid Tests house band. . . . I remember that as an unspoken but totally conscious thought."[60]

As Hjelm might put it, the band's past is being presented as something that was defined at the Acid Tests as something that now had a name, but that nonetheless existed before it acquired that name. In Lesh and Garcia's presentations of the Acid Tests, they become a glorious, definitional moment, but a moment into which they enter as a group, to get a foretaste of apocalyptic perfection and validation of their direction. The Acid Tests are integrated into a longer spiritual voyage, being seen as the early, revelatory stage of a journey that extends before and after them. My point is not that this is factually incorrect—indeed, I am inclined to believe that it is a correct representation of the band's situation. I merely want to emphasize that it is also *rhetorically useful* for navigating the presentation of the Grateful Dead's history between the Acid Tests' undeniable importance and their equally undeniable demise with the collapse of Kesey's charisma.

The complicated attitude that the Grateful Dead took with regard to the Acid Tests is expressed by their associate and sometime manager "Bear." He notes that, when the Acid Tests were going on, "no matter what else we were doing, we *had* to be at the Acid Tests every week," but that his own view was that "here was this band of incredible musicians making this magic music which I thought was more important to do than [the Acid Tests]."[61]

Although he presents his view as having been controversial within the band's scene at the time, it was the one that prevailed, once the undeniable excitement of the Tests was done. As Lesh notes, "When the Acid Tests went their way, we still had a band to operate."[62] As Kesey's "faster than light drive," the Grateful Dead had been one of the means to the Acid Tests' ends (as Joel Selvin writes, "the Dead played house band to the dawning of the psychedelic apocalypse"); with the collapse of the Acid Tests, the situation was reversed.[63]

This validation of the band and its career serves two purposes: it shields them from the effects of the Acid Tests' collapse, while in so doing transferring the ultimate spiritual authority from the Acid Tests to the band. Rather than the Grateful Dead being known for taking part in the Acid Tests, as contemporary accounts suggest was the case, the Acid Tests become significant insofar as they fit into the Grateful Dead's career. The parallels with the presentation of the career of John the Baptist in the New Testament are again clear: the authors of the canonical gospels, or the traditions they pass on, have significantly diminished his contemporary significance, so as to cast more light on the career of his most famous disciple, Jesus.

In this section, I have addressed some of the ways in which the Grateful Dead used the Acid Tests as a foundation story, as well as the ways in which they defined themselves separately from the tests, seeing them as the place where their mission was revealed to them, but maintaining enough distance from the tests so that their eventual collapse and Kesey's loss of charismatic authority did not cause insurmountable difficulties for the band.

While the Grateful Dead recognized the fact that Kesey and the Pranksters functioned as incubators and innovators, bringing to light a new vision and a new context that achieved social consensus (as witness, e.g., the influence of light shows, psychedelia), their integration of that vision into their overall context freed them from too much dependence on the Acid Tests' founder, thus giving support to the argument that James Lewis makes specifically with regard to the Ghost Dance.

On a broader theoretical level, this examination has presented foundation stories as consisting of essentially three parts: (1) a state of potential that sets the stage for the foundation story; (2) the foundation period, in which a particular period is liberated from history and moved into an archetypal realm, and in which the bases for the religious movement and its values are set; and (3) the move out of the liminal realm and back into history, which presents particular challenges for the new religious movement. We have seen how the Grateful Dead navigated these phases, how they drew upon the Acid Tests as a foundation period, but kept their own identity to some degree separate, so as to allow them to survive the collapse of the golden age and continue on into the brave new world that they helped to build for the remainder of their career.

What They Did

HOW THE GRATEFUL DEAD
JOINED THEIR MUSICAL
AND SPIRITUAL IMPERATIVES

Half a century on, acid is still a secret staircase that lets
ghosts into the machine.
—CHRISTOPHER HILL, *Into the Mystic* (2017)

To this point, we have established that there was indeed a religious impulse behind the Grateful Dead's work, and we have seen how that impulse fits in with their broader social and artistic environment. We have also seen the foundational importance of the Acid Tests for the band: they were where the Grateful Dead discovered their mission. Now it is time to examine the nature of this mission: What religious work did the band feel that they were doing? How did the band understand transcendence and their relationship to it?

We can start with the testimony of drummer Mickey Hart. Although he was not present at the Acid Tests, he was nonetheless an outspoken advocate for the Grateful Dead's mission. In his autobiography, *Drumming on the Edge of Magic*, he suggests that the Grateful Dead stand in the lineage of shamanic journeys, at least as conceived in the modern, popular, and Western context. As Hart says, "Sometimes I think of what happens in a shamanistic sense of embarking upon a collective journey in which we are all allies. Other times I think of our music as something almost organic that we've grown over the past 25 years, a living entity that exists in another time world . . . and that can only be accessed when all of us are on stage."[1] According to this view, the Grateful Dead's music provides the soundtrack, even the engine, for religious and intellectual traveling, and it is natural that such traveling would pass through a variety of regions. The journey begins and ends at fixed points—you start from home, and you return home—but, in-between these points, the goal is to travel, to keep moving, and the person who returns home is not exactly the same person who left. As he put it in an interview: "We've got transformation going here. We don't have a popular musical group. That's what the trappings may look like . . . but that ain't what we have. . . . People come to be changed and we change 'em."[2]

In his discussion of the Grateful Dead's music in particular, and music in general, Hart often invokes the powers of entrainment: the tendency for rhythms to link up, both in terms of how the band members link up to one another, and how the audience links to the band. He writes, "From the stage you can feel it happening—group mind, entrainment, find your own word for it."[3] Technically, this idea is at odds with his invocation of shamanic ideas, properly speaking; in a shamanic context, the shaman does the traveling on their own, while the "audience" watches and awaits their return.[4] However, "shamanism" has been the subject of a great deal of loose discussion over the past century (partly due to its evocative but uncritical adoption by folks such as Hart), and it is clear that Hart does not use the term in a strict sense.[5] What he seems to want to take from it is the idea of a journey, a voyage, that the music makes possible.

Jerry Garcia, too, emphasized the traveling aspect of the band's music, although it seems from the sources that I have read that his understanding is not focused on the goals of the journey or its overriding rationale as much as on the journey itself. As Garcia notes, speaking of John Coltrane's improvising, "I've been impressed by that thing of flow, and of making statements that to my ears sound like a paragraph—he'll play along stylistically with a certain kind of tone, in a certain syntax, for X amount of time, then he'll like change the subject, then play along with this other personality. . . . Perceptually, an idea that's been very important to me in playing has been the whole 'odyssey' idea—journeys, voyages, you know? And adventures along the way."[6]

This view coheres with a more general view frequently expressed by Garcia elsewhere, emphasizing that he was far more interested in the act of musical exploration, including the transcendent moments that this would entail for the members and audience of the Grateful Dead, than in laying out goals or explanations for this exploration. He argues,

> From the point of view of being a player it's this thing that you can't make happen, but when it's happening you can't stop it from happening. . . . I've tried to analyze it on every level that I can gather together, and all the intellectual exercise in the world doesn't do a fucking thing, doesn't help a bit, doesn't explain it one way or another. The Grateful Dead has some kind of intuitive thing. . . . We talk about it, but all those things are by way of agreeing that we'll continue to keep trying to do this thing, whatever it is, and that our best attitude to it is sort of this stewardship, in which we are the custodians of this thing.[7]

Garcia was often seen as the spiritual spokesperson for the band, as the incarnation of the Grateful Dead's principles—a prophetic or charismatic figure, in other words. But his comments on the religious aspects of their project, the ineffable "it" that the Grateful Dead pursued, are noteworthy for their humble, personal, and nonsystematizing nature. While he was perfectly willing to acknowledge that the Grateful Dead did have spiritual goals that extended beyond the band's function as an amazingly popular dance band, Garcia was extremely leery of precise definitions. As he characteristically said in 1983, "Everybody who experiences 'it,' on whatever terms, is right about it. . . . I want 'it' to surprise me, to continue to surprise me. I don't want to know anything about it."[8] While acknowledging a spiritual, transcendent element to the band's music, he consistently opposed attempts at a precise definition or limitation of that element.

This attitude is exemplified by his explanation of the band's choice not to get involved in political or social causes, religious or otherwise. He contends that "it's our responsibility to keep ourselves free of those connotations. I want the Grateful Dead experience to be one of those things that doesn't come with a hook. We're all very antiauthoritarian. There's nothing that we believe so uniformly and so totally that we could use the Grateful Dead to advertise it."[9]

Garcia was not alone in this refusal. Members of the inner Grateful Dead community seem to have been quite aware of the potential dangers of religious organization, both in terms of its tendency to impede access to transcendent experience, and its potential for creating rigidity and oppression on the social level. In discussions by Grateful Dead members, one often finds the word *religion* being used to express only these negative connotations. For example, Garcia states that "I don't like the word *religion*. It's a bad word. I'd like to not have that concept." But, in the same discussion, he acknowledges the ambiguity of his position: "On a certain level, it's a religion to me too."[10] It seems to be the association of "religion" with the creation of dogmatic belief systems and hierarchical power structures that he is objecting to.

Also illustrative of this attitude are remarks delivered by John Barlow, one of the band's two lyricists, in an unpublished keynote address delivered at the 28th Southwest/Texas American and Popular Culture Conference in Albuquerque, New Mexico, on February 16, 2007. Barlow notes that, at some point early in the band's career, "we realized that [fans of the Grateful Dead] were assembling themselves into something that had certain cult-like characteristics." Recounting a conversation that he had in the early 1970s with the Grateful Dead's other lyricist, Robert Hunter, Barlow went on to say:

> I said [to Hunter], "This [i.e., the perception of the band by some of its fans] is turning into a cult, or a religion, or something." And he said, "Yeah." And I said, "So far it doesn't have any dogma, which makes it kind of okay as a religion, but it's got ritual, it's got iconography, it's got all these characteristics of religion, it just doesn't seem to have a belief system." And he said, "Well, I've been thinking about that. If it's going to get a belief system, it's going to be because of us. . . . But you don't want to do that and I don't want to do that." . . . And so we agreed that we would never write anything that could be taken as dogma.[11]

In this passage, Barlow makes very clear that his discomfort with "religion" comes from its link to "dogma" and "belief systems," a point of view that seems to have been shared with other members—that is, the fans' appreciation of the Grateful Dead is "kind of okay as a religion" because it has no dogma.[12] I should note here that Barlow, like Hart, was not present for the first two years of the Grateful Dead's existence; he was an old school friend of guitarist Bob Weir, but they lost touch in the early 1960s and did not meet again until mid-1967.[13] While, in this section, I am discussing spiritual and musical developments that took place before he reappeared on the scene, Barlow's attitude does fit in with comments made in interviews with Garcia and Lesh.

To sum up, we can say that while Hart placed the band's musical journeys within a (popularized understanding of a) shamanic context, Garcia seems to have tried not to place them into any such ritual, teleological context. Where Hart sees the band as leading the audience on a mission, Garcia sees it as going off on a ramble.

As for Lesh, he does indeed have a prescriptive conceptual framework worked out, as we will see. But, whereas Hart's framework is based on entrainment and the concept of the shamanistic *journey*, Lesh's concept is phenomenological: it is based upon *experience*. In this regard it coheres with Garcia's understanding of the religious aspects of the Grateful Dead's music. However, where Garcia is content (in his public remarks, at least) to leave things as open as possible, Lesh has a much more detailed understanding of the situation.

Lesh's conception of the band's music is focused less on the journey and more on the experience as a guiding image, the experience in question being that of contact with, and the manifestation of, a mobile, ever-changing, transcendent level of reality. Lesh has said: "I've always felt, from the very beginning—even before the Acid Tests—that we could do something that was, not necessarily extramusical, but something where music would be only the first step. Something maybe even close to religion . . . in the sense of the actual communing. We used to say that every place we play is church." Hence, it is logical that he would refer to improvising as "praying" and says that you play and then "hope" that "the dove descends"—that is, that the band will touch upon transcendence.[14]

The Christian references in Lesh's comment are especially interesting. It was common within the 1960s counterculture to ascribe "exotic" origins to transcendent experience, leading, for example, to descriptions of Indian classical music, with its tight connection to Indian religio-philosophical teachings, as presenting a more "spiritual" avenue for Western musicians to explore. The Grateful Dead, unlike many of their contemporaries, did not do this (nor did their mentor, Ken Kesey, although Timothy Leary certainly did): one listens in vain to hear a "hip" use of sitars, tablas, or harmoniums on their recordings, or self-consciously exotic references in their song titles. Rather, the band, in this period as in their later work, emphasized their ties to various strands of American artistic and musical traditions. To my knowledge, drummer Mickey Hart is the only member of the band who has published his views on Indian music, and in these comments he speaks of it as a source of technical ideas, a tradition, and as a musical inspiration, but not as a source of transcendent religious experience.[15] Hart invoked India for musical but not religious purposes: the band's explicit religious references tend to be Christian, with "St. Stephen" being the classic example (although the song's lyrics do not seem to have a great deal to do with the saint who was the first recorded Christian martyr), or to express a vaguer point of view that fits in well with American religious traditions such as transcendentalism.

As Lesh's use of the verb *hope* suggests, the transcendent experiences that the band pursued cannot be compelled, but one can increase the likelihood of this taking place by creating conditions favorable to it, foremost among which is the attitude of openness. The band's efforts to pursue this manifestation, and its adventures in the continually shifting reality that the manifestation reveals when present, correspond to the journeying that Garcia and Hart speak of. Lesh's view can thus be seen as enfolding Garcia's and Hart's views, but expanding on them, as well as modifying them by putting the accent on the strictly religious focus of the interplay between ethical and practical issues, ritual, and the divine (with strong soteriological overtones, in the form of a realized, or intermittently realizable, eschatology—which is a fancy way of saying that people felt as though the world had already ended or been transcended).

In what follows, we will be dealing mainly with Lesh's point of view. For the purposes of this discussion I will narrow the focus even more and deal primarily with the material found in Lesh's autobiography, *Searching for the Sound*, which provides a look back over Lesh's career with the Grateful Dead.

The religious theme enters Lesh's narrative along with drugs. He first gets high while at university with poet and lyricist Bobby Peterson, whom he sees as "a true artist, following an artistic and spiritual quest"—a quest that, in Lesh's view, was incorporated into the efforts of those involved in the 1960s cultural revolutions to work toward "a culture built on love, respect, and the quest for spiritual values."[16] This journey involved the use of cannabis and psychedelic drugs, which Lesh sees as (at least potentially) entheogens: substances that can have valid religious and spiritual effects. Entheogens have been used "to manifest the numinous and sacred, tools that had been in use for thousands of years by shamans, by oracles, in the ancient mystery schools, by all whose mission was to penetrate beyond the veil of illusion," Lesh writes; the trips that these shamans and oracles took "were explorations into the super-real, voyages designed to bring a larger sense of reality back into human consciousness, which had become irredeemably bogged down in the material world."[17]

In this passage, Lesh links the Grateful Dead to a tradition beloved of esotericists—namely the alleged "Golden Chain" of enlightened teachers allegedly stretching back to prehistory.[18] In Lesh's telling, human existence is characterized as being "bogged down" in the material world and thus separated from the realm of the "super-real," a separation that must be overcome, at least temporarily or intermittently, through mystical experience triggered by ritual, meditation, magic, or—as in the case of the Grateful Dead—drugs and music. On this level, Lesh's presentation shares obvious features with Platonic and gnostic traditions in the Abrahamic/Hellenistic religious world, as with Hinduism and Buddhism further east.

In the previous chapter, we discussed what took place at the Acid Tests, and the way that they were constructed so as to serve as foundation stories for the Grateful Dead. Having established their status as the key to the Grateful Dead's mission, I would like at this point to look at their meaning for Phil Lesh, who seems to have engaged in the most detailed and coherent reflections on the Grateful Dead's religious significance of any of the core members. (As one might expect, Garcia's published comments on the Acid Tests emphasize their importance as "magic" events, but do not pin down the nature of this magic.) He has left us a more detailed interpretation of the meaning of the Acid Tests—and thus, by extension, the meaning of the religious experiences produced by or facilitated by the Grateful Dead.

Again, I want to stress that his interpretation is not necessarily "true," or truer than anyone else's interpretation (and that goes at least double for my interpretation of his interpretation). When we work with religious experience, we cannot access any sort of absolute meaning; all we can do is present our own understandings of how meaning was constructed by the participants in the events that we study. In his autobiography, Lesh makes his own construction accessible to us in considerable detail, which makes it appropriate to focus on, all the more so because it does not contradict and is not incompatible with any of the other extant testimonies about the Acid Tests that I have encountered. On a personal note from an emic perspective, I will add that, speaking as a Deadhead, Lesh's discussion works for me: it feels acceptable, although I would not go so far as to say that it (or any other single perspective) is necessarily "right."

In *Searching for the Sound*, Lesh describes the Acid Tests as an attempt to let go of all humanly imposed control over the flow of events and open oneself up instead to the universe and to whatever arises. For this to take place, it was necessary to have an environment in which there was enough freedom, or fluidity, to permit the spontaneous emergence of structure principles, such as patterns and waves. The Acid Tests, which, in Lesh's view, were such an environment, were "ordered only by those same mysterious laws that govern the evolution of weather patterns, or the turbulence in a rising column of smoke."[19]

To Lesh, this same characteristic applies to the dancers at early Grateful Dead shows (which, to some degree, overlapped with the Acid Tests). These dancers manifest "the same sort of spontaneous consensus seen in flocks of birds, schools of fish, or clusters of galaxies." Indeed, as they dance they are both modeling and enacting the creation and perfection of the universe itself: as Lesh puts it, in a passage whose importance demands that it be quoted at length,

> to make music for dancers like these is the greatest honor—to be responsible for what really is the dance of the cosmos. If, as some savants of consciousness suggest, we are actually agreeing to create, from moment to moment, everything we perceive as real, then it stands to reason that we're also responsible for keeping it going in some harmonious manner. The fervent belief we shared then, and that perseveres today, is that the energy liberated by the combination of music and ecstatic dancing is somehow making the world better, or at least holding the line against the depredations of entropy and ignorance.[20]

This is an absolutely enormous amount of salvific energy to be ascribed to a rock band playing for dancers, and it turns successful performances into events that profoundly affect the universe itself. It also fundamentally validates a theology of perpetual motion: in a conception of the universe as an ever-changing dance that is organized only by the manifestation through spontaneous rhythmic action and interplay guided by "mysterious laws," there is no room for stasis or solidity.

I said earlier that Lesh's theology as expressed in passages such as this resonates with aspects of Platonic and gnostic traditions, but there are striking differences as well. Rather than presenting the divine realm as having a fixed structure, being made up of a realm of unchanging Forms (to speak Platonically) or a higher pleroma of fixed emanations proceeding from an unchanging Source (to speak gnostically or Neoplatonically), Lesh presents the "super-real" level as energetic but changeable. It sends out or moves through structures, but it is not defined by these structures; it is defined by its dynamism, creativity, and inherent experiential rightness. As we will see, this description coheres very strongly with aspects of the LSD experience, which presumably inspired it, as well as with Catherine Albanese's study of metaphysical religion (to be discussed).

Fittingly, considering the influence of the Beats on the Grateful Dead and its scene, Lesh's conception provides a theological counterpart to the intense, energetic drive to be found in works such as *On the Road* or *Howl*.[21] In a classically American approach—one that contrasts strongly with the Platonists and most gnostic authors—Lesh does not show any essential discomfort with the material world. In his view, it is admittedly intrinsically less real than the higher realm and needs regular connection to that realm, but it is not necessarily flawed. His is a dualistic but fundamentally irenic view, in which the role of the Grateful Dead is to create a vital connection between the two realms, which they do through their music.

The soteriological note in all this is clear, as is the messianic tone, which intensifies as Lesh continues to speak of the Acid Tests. He adds that,

> by this time [1966], everyone in the band, except for Pigpen [who did not enjoy psychedelics], had been taking acid at least once a week for more than six months. It's safe to say that in the ninety days or so that the Acid Tests existed, our band took more and longer strides into another realm of musical consciousness, not to mention pure awareness, than ever before or since. At the beginning, we were a band playing a gig. At the end, we had become shamans helping to channel the transcendent out of our mundane lives and those of our listeners. We felt, all of us—band, Pranksters, participants—privileged to be at the arrow's point of human evolution, and from that standpoint, everything was possible.[22]

Aided by LSD, which he calls "the sacrament," the Grateful Dead's music thus takes on a "hymnlike" character, and the band begins to have "fuzzy visions" of "the Meaning of It All" and to experience "ecstatic ego loss."[23] There are also deliberate attempts to encourage this ego loss through forming a group mind: "The unique organicity of our music reflects the fact that each of us consciously personalized his playing: to fit with what the others were playing and to fit with who each man was as an individual, allowing us to meld our consciousnesses together in the unity of a group mind."[24] This links up to what Garcia had to say in 1969 about the Acid Tests: "Nobody was doing *something*, you know, it was everybody doing bits and pieces of something, the result of which was something else."[25]

Summarizing what Lesh has to say, we come up with the following: Lesh is first of all arguing for the existence of a deeper, hidden level of universal structure or active structuring principle, which, to his mind, became apparent or manifested during the course of the Acid Tests. Access to this level is desirable because a) it is intrinsically fascinating; b) it is ontologically "truer" than the everyday level; and c) it has the potential to improve existence on the everyday level. One cannot guarantee access to this level, but, by constructing an external environment that has some degree of form, yet is designed to facilitate open, creative expression, and by coming to this external environment with an internal, subjective mindset of enhanced receptivity to events, one makes it possible for these otherwise hidden aspects of underlying universal structures to manifest themselves spontaneously. As Hart puts it in *Drumming on the Edge of Magic*, "The unexpected is . . . courted; magic won't happen unless you set a place at the table for it."[26]

These structures are not slow, but quick, changeable, and evocative. They come and go, forming patterns out of chaos. Evoking or properly seeing these patterns has to do with having a certain mindset. In one sense, it cannot be deliberately done, but, in another sense, it can—at the very least, one can encourage these experiences to take place by creating the space for them to occur, and by keeping oneself unfixed and open so as to be a perceptive conduit for them. The participant's power has to do with this creation of environment: they cannot compel the desired manifestation, but they can construct a situation in which it *might* take place.

Ideally, it seems, participants in the ritual environment will join together, linking their efforts toward transcendence and pattern realization, and this will increase the potential for universal manifestation. This most definitely applies to the musicians as well. As Lesh points out, the Grateful Dead's goal was to unify their voices in the band so as to form a group mind. This unification within the band, however, does not have to do with everyone playing the same thing, nor with creating and reproducing stable interlocking patterns. The goal, rather, is to be fully, individually, and spontaneously expressive in the context of a group effort aimed at facilitating religious manifestation. United in goal and approach, the players need not be strictly, literally unified— or, as the song "Truckin'" puts it, "together, more or less in line."[27]

There is, in fact, an aesthetic of raggedness to be found throughout the Grateful Dead's music and lyrics, and Lesh's deliberations in his autobiography enable us to see how it can be understood theologically. Some degree of concerted effort, and some amount of organizing structure, is necessary to create the space in which "it," the spontaneous manifestation of transcendence, can take place, but an overly rigid unity would involve approaching the experiment in an inappropriate state of mind and thus ruling out the proper, spontaneous unity that allows for cosmic manifestation. Similarly, an overly determined or controlled environment would not provide the most fertile ground for this manifestation. We can, perhaps, understand Garcia's reluctance to be too precise in his discussions of such matters as arising from the fear of reifying the experience, of trying to capture it within an ideological construct that would ultimately prevent it from functioning.

It is important to keep in mind that when Lesh speaks of the Acid Tests, or of Grateful Dead concerts, he is not describing scenes of purely spontaneous transcendence. The Acid Tests, the templates for Lesh's vision, were deliberately (if eccentrically) organized events. There were people running the show (the Pranksters), a cover charge (albeit only one dollar) was collected, and the Tests were promoted. With regard to the setting, the external space in which they were to take place was prepared beforehand, as we saw in the previous chapter, with elaborate sound and light equipment that took time and planning to set up; with regard to the set (i.e., participants' understanding of what was to happen), advance expectations were guided through word of mouth and print publicity and iconographical resources (flyers), and people were urged to prepare their internal space through drug taking.

In other words, although the mindset and immediate environment were to be informal and unfixed, there was nonetheless an organized, defined border around this liminal zone in which the transcendent events were to take place. This border created the social, physical, ritual, and psychological space within which the spontaneous manifestation that was the goal of the event could take place. As Ulf Olsson notes, while

> the Acid Tests have been nostalgically recalled by band members and Pranksters, most of whom characterize the Acid Test as a free space in which there was no division between performers and audience: every participant was performing, making the event more important than any performance. But the Tests were also manipulated—the event was observed from the inside; there was a control center, manned by Kesey and others, connected to speakers, cameras, and lights, all feeding the sensorium, even if largely unplanned.[28]

They were largely unplanned by design, but the spontaneity was limited and bordered.

The concept of this border is perhaps the strongest element distinguishing Lesh's view of the Grateful Dead's theological significance from what we can discern of Garcia's. Garcia has claimed that his preference for playing contexts was "total and utter anarchy. Indoor anarchy . . . our experience with these scenes is that's where you get the highest."[29] Although this is not, for Garcia, an isolated claim, there is room to question whether this claim about his values reflects his real desires, or whether it is simply a beloved self-image. Nothing that I am aware of in Garcia's career suggests that he was really interested in "total and utter anarchy" in his music, and indeed, it could be strongly argued that it was the Grateful Dead that pulled him as close as he ever got to "anarchy"; his solo and side projects (e.g., his solo albums, the Jerry Garcia Band, Old and In the Way) are considerably more disciplined and controlled in their approach than the Grateful Dead, even in their most conservative years.

In fact, of all the Grateful Dead members, it is Lesh who seems to have had the most appreciation for music that flirted with chaos or anarchy, whether we are speaking of his early avant-garde orchestral compositions, his "soundscape" work with Ned Lagin, or some of his bass solos during Grateful Dead performances in the early 1970s. But it is noteworthy that Lesh's taste for "anarchy" is a privileged one that relies on boundaries and protections to delimit the "anarchy" and protect its creators—as he notes with refreshing honesty regarding the sort of anarchy he advocated, "You can't have it without a whole lot of money."[30] Neal Cassady and the other Merry Pranksters really did operate "without a net" (to quote the title of a Grateful Dead live album), taking their anarchy into truly open, unsafe situations with unpredictable outcomes and the potential for disaster on levels beyond the simply aesthetic. Lesh, by contrast, understood the Grateful Dead's musical and religious phenomenon, no matter how chaotic, as being one that existed within a definite and limited context, and one in which the band was sure to be the main attraction as a commercially successful rock band, with all the security and protection that that implies.

The Model

The religious model that we can derive from Lesh's autobiography is not unique. The formal, explicit creation of a liminal space, a protected and established environment in which the normal rules of day to day life are suspended, is common to almost all religious ritual activity: Victor Turner's work deals with it extensively.[31] However, the structural similarity between the Grateful Dead experience and many other religious manifestations should not blind us to their profound differences in terms of content.

The creation of a space that is deliberately intended to be anarchic so as to avoid preconceptions that might interfere with the manifestation of the divine—instead of one having its own set of divinely sponsored rules and customs—is perhaps the most striking difference. The idea of divine manifestation being played out through the spontaneous creation, and perception, of structures by the participants is likewise unusual. Both of these aspects are atypical of religious ritual as practiced in many contexts, although they are clearly related to the artistic concept of "happenings" that circulated in the 1960s.

Charles Glock and Rodney Stark have created a taxonomy of religious experience that might be usefully invoked here.[32] They argue that the essential thing about religious experience is *some sense of contact with a supernatural agency*.[33] They divide such experiences into four categories having to do with the relation between the human actor and divine actor. Rising from most common to least common, these categories consist of (1) experiences in which the human actor simply senses the presence of the divine actor; (2) experiences in which the perception is felt to be reciprocal; (3) experiences in which perception is reciprocal and an affective component (love, affection) is sensed as present in the divine actor; and (4) experiences in which the human actor feels herself to be "a confidant of or a fellow participant in action with the divine actor."[34] It is clear that Lesh is speaking of experiences that fit into this fourth category. However, the significant thing is that his conception of the divine actor is itself rather impersonal—it consists of improvisationally structured, significant activity, rather than personality.

When we turn our attention back to the Grateful Dead's musical practice, we note that a very similar juxtaposition of structure and freedom is to be found in the way that the band incorporates improvisation into their rock practice, as discussed. There was, as Garcia has pointed out, a framework to the band's improvisational activity. Song structures, considered broadly, were usually fixed. It is true that introductions to songs and their endings might be improvised (the band would "jam into" or "jam out of" songs), sections within songs might be extended, and occasionally one song would move to another without finishing.[35] This aside, verses, choruses, and bridges or interludes were presented in a predetermined order, when presented.

But although Grateful Dead songs do possess specific chords, riffs, lines, rhythms, and so forth, and although a certain consistency of performance practice did exist, it is true nonetheless that in theory and often in practice the songs were open to interpretation by the individual players as they worked within these general limits, especially in the first decade of the band's career. The musicians could play what they wanted, as long as it fit within these larger, but quite flexible and expandable, structures.

The sort of interpretation that was thus privileged was not primarily soloistic, nor was it about individual self-assertion. Rather, it involved displaying sensitivity to the other band members in the construction of a group sound, as well as to the overall "flow" of the particular moment. The point was to be open to the spontaneous musical impulses of the moment and to express those impulses as a group in a harmonious if not necessarily uniform fashion, with all of this taking place within a definite, organized structure—that of the songs themselves.

This approach plays out particularly clearly in Lesh's approach to the music. In many musical forms, and especially in rock and blues music, the bass is usually the most restricted instrument in the band. The bassist is typically obliged to clearly and stably outline the fundamental harmonic and rhythmic structure, and to do little else. Thus stability ("Just lay it down, man!"—or, less politely, "Keep it simple, stupid!") is especially prized for bassists. This general expectation highlights Lesh's extremely contrasting approach—and this is particularly the case considering his historical context, having begun his bass-playing career coincident with or even before the careers of many of the emancipators of rock bass, such as Paul McCartney, Jack Bruce, or Chris Squire.

As a player, Lesh works improvisationally within the rhythmic, melodic, and harmonic structures of the songs, instead of by preconstructing repeatable, definite lines. The outlines of the songs are set, by and large, as are certain architecturally significant riffs. But what precisely happens within those outlines is not; it varies from bar to bar, song to song, and performance to performance, determined partly by Lesh's background and convictions, but also very much by his perception of, and spontaneous response to, the overall group context.

In this regard, the way the songs are approached replicates in miniature the structure of the Acid Tests as presented in Lesh's religious vision of the band. In both cases, one creates a flexible but present structure to provide boundaries to the liminal experience. With these boundaries, the transcendent experience can take place, and its effects can become manifest if the participants are in the correct mindset, which involves an openness to improvisation, valued not so much in itself as for its ability to permit the spontaneous revelation of hitherto-unsuspected structures that correspond to the deep, and ordinarily hidden, formal underpinnings of the cosmos. The band's music is not intended simply to represent the transcendent experience, to present it or proselytize for it; at its height, the music *is* the transcendent experience, which reaches its fullest expression when "the music plays the band" (to quote a line from their song "The Music Never Stopped"), not vice versa.[36]

As Lesh's writing suggests, the band's choice of improvisational practice was prompted by spiritual, even religious, imperatives. Their practice both models and enables the sort of spiritual experiences that they underwent in the Acid Tests. As Garcia notes, "We play rock and roll music and it's part of our form—our vehicle so to speak—but it's not who we are."[37] In creating an artistic form corresponding to their religious experiences, they weren't just making a flag to express their allegiance: they were also building a machine that could reproduce that experience.

We see in the history of the Grateful Dead a progression commonly found in the broader history of religions. For one thing, we have a group of people who share experiences of overwhelming power and significance. These experiences lead the members of the group to question and recreate their old ways of thinking and living, with the goals of aligning their lives and work with the values revealed or suggested by the experiences, or of creating conditions in which the experiences are more likely to recur, thus blurring the lines between ethical, ritual, and social/practical issues.

Many such groups have existed throughout history, and it is common for them to have as their center a charismatic leader who takes the lead in determining the conditions under which the new community will live. The Grateful Dead, however, did not have such a leader. Beat hero Neal Cassady (immortalized as "Dean Moriarty" in Jack Kerouac's *On the Road*) was an associate of the Pranksters and an icon to the Grateful Dead (he was the "Cowboy Neal" immortalized in the Grateful Dead's song "The Other One"), but hardly a leader or a systematic thinker; Ken Kesey does not seem to have exerted the same authority over the Grateful Dead that he did over the Merry Pranksters; Garcia himself was the closest thing that the band had to a leader, but as such he seems to have made active efforts to undermine his status, acting as a nonleader. As his then-partner and future wife, Mountain Girl, has noted, "We also had this commitment to a group decision-making process," except for cases where Garcia had "already made a decision about things."[38]

This lack of a clearly acknowledged leader did not mean the band was without guidance, however. They found this guidance in their music. The Grateful Dead was a band first and foremost, and so instead they had their music and their identity as a rock band to give them focus as a young religious community, both on an earthly and on a transcendent level (as the music was seen as the way of accessing transcendence). With regard to the former point, manager Rock Scully points out that "though we considered ourselves hippies, we weren't the hippie movement. We were musicians first. . . . We wanted to be recognized as musicians."[39] With regard to the latter, as Garcia put it: "Magic is what we do. Music is how we do it."[40]

The great challenge for the Grateful Dead, as for any such group, was to find ways of creating the conditions—social and personal—in which the conversional experiences could be recreated and communicated to others, a task that they undertook as a group of musicians. Earlier, we looked at some of the musical tactics that the band adopted in order to do so, most of which derive from the Framework: their pioneering invention that enabled them to turn rock into an improvisational art form.

A Coherent Spiritual/Musical Phenomenon

It is no novelty to argue that there is some kind of religious dimension to the Grateful Dead, but in this discussion we have been able to take that insight further than it is usually taken. We have seen, first of all, that in Lesh's mind this religious understanding is fairly clearly conceived, and, second, that this conception plays out in terms of the band's musical practice. We can now perceive the Grateful Dead phenomenon as a more or less coherent whole, with a theological level that is in harmony with its musical level—a degree of coherence that suggests more seriousness of purpose than is often attributed to rock bands.

Not only this: we also see that this coherence did not come about by chance, or without sustained reflection on the parts of at least some of the band members. The Grateful Dead's improvisational practice—its development of a unique mode of playing that enabled them to work spontaneously within a dance/rock band context—is inextricably linked with this religious dimension. It is not, however, linked homologically, which means that it does not seek to mirror or represent the religious conception on which it is based. Instead, it is linked causally or functionally: the music is as it is so that it can do the religious work that it is intended to do, create the context for a divine manifestation.

As pointed out in the classic works of Max Weber and Joachim Wach on the sociology of religion, it often happens that new religious movements come together on the basis of shared ecstatic or transcendent experience among the members.[41] Not always, but sometimes, new religions get started by people who have been brought together through having shared something utterly overwhelming. For example, in the Grateful Dead's immediate context, we might cite the way that the Merry Pranksters bonded through their LSD experiences; we might also consider the testimony of Californian Aidan Kelly, who in this period was engaged in founding the New Reformed Orthodox Order of the Golden Dawn (NROOGD), one of the most influential organizations in the Neopagan revival. He writes that after their first ritual "we wandered about the gardens, laughing and clowning, drunk on the very air itself, babbling to each other: 'It worked!' No one asked again, that day or later, whether the ritual was worth going on with: we were hooked. As Judy Foster later commented to me, 'When Marx said 'Religion is the opium of the people,' he never imagined that someday people would say, `Groovy! Let's get stoned!'"[42] In short, "NROOGD started out as an experiment in ritual and celebration. We found that when we did it right, something strange happened, a kind of buzz," and it was only after the group was united on the basis of the buzz that they started thinking about ethics, metaphysics, or other aspects of their religious identity.[43]

In the more recent study of new religious movements, however, the importance of religious experience for the creation and growth of such movements has been overlooked, at least in academic circles—an oversight that James Lewis argues can be traced to the fact that the field of religious studies itself is fairly new and, consequently, has been struggling for legitimation. "As members of a discipline generally perceived as marginal," he writes, "most religion scholars were reluctant to further marginalize themselves by giving serious attention to what at the time [the 1970s and 1980s] seemed a transitory social phenomenon. . . . As a consequence of this situation, the study of new religions was left to sociologists until relatively recently."[44] This resulted in an emphasis on the role of social interaction and social conflict rather than religious experience, as brought out, for example, in Rodney Stark and William Bainbridge's canonical *The Future of Religion*, in which analysis of the formation of religious groups focuses on doctrinal innovation, social ties, and the degree of tension between the new group and its context, but not on the role played by religious experience.

Social factors are certainly important, but, as Lewis notes, "many alternative religions hold out the possibility of life-transforming experiences. . . . Is the attraction of transformational experiences really so hard to comprehend? What if we actually could let go of the burden of our past and be reborn as new people? Such transformation may or may not be attainable, but the attractiveness of the possibility is certainly understandable."[45] Let us also think about the social costs that attach to membership in new religious movements, such as losing your spouse, job, or friends: heartfelt religious experience would help to explain the evident willingness of members to incur such costs if necessary.

Lewis concludes by arguing that "an important aspect of the phenomenological method as it is properly deployed in religious studies is that religious experiences are taken seriously. Without pronouncing judgment on the ontological status of spiritual agencies encountered in such experiences, a disciplined effort is made to understand the consciousness of those for whom the encounter with the sacred is ultimately real and meaningful."[46] Such an encounter, which is often felt to be of overwhelming importance, is associated with a new worldview or set of priorities. It is what binds the members to each other. This period, in which the experience forms the basis of the religious community, is later seen as the "golden age" for that religion (if the religion survives)—as, for instance, the period of Jesus's ministry and the Spirit-infused period immediately following (as detailed in Acts) are for most Christian groups.

The problem is that this period inevitably fades: either the charismatic leader leaves or dies, taking with them the gift of the spirit, or rigidity and, with it, staleness set in, and again the original spirit is lost. As they lose this inspiration, and as they become more organizational in focus, new religious movements must deal with what is called the "routinization of charisma," which involves formalizing the group's innovations and establishing set lines of authority and doctrine.[47] This helps to ensure the movement's survival and grants it consistency and focus, but at the expense of that transcendent experience that originally lay at its heart.

Now, it will be clear from the foregoing that the transcendent experience is what the Grateful Dead were originally all about, at least from Lesh's point of view—and Garcia's as well. As Garcia notes: "We were doing the Acid Test, which was our first exposure to formlessness. Formlessness and chaos lead to new forms. And new order. Closer to, probably, what the real order is. . . . What we're really dedicated to is not so much *telling* people, but to *doing* that thing and getting high. That's the thing; that's the payoff and that's the whole reason for doing it, right there."[48]

I would like to raise the possibility that the band's valorization of this ineffable experience, combined with their ongoing determination to keep it ineffable rather than defining it too precisely, and their commitment to creating a space (musical, social, and spatial) in which this experience could be modeled and enacted, can be seen as attempts to resist the routinization of the Acid Tests' spiritual and charismatic gifts, to keep the magic alive. In other words, the band did not want the experience to turn into the sort of religion to which Garcia refers when he says, "That word *religion* has a whole lot of . . . negative to it. . . . I don't like the word *religion*, it's a bad word. I'd like not to have that concept."[49] In his view, "I think basically the Grateful Dead is not for cranking out rock and roll. . . . It's to get high. To get really high is to forget yourself. And to forget yourself is to see everything else. And to see everything else is to become an understanding molecule in evolution, a conscious tool of the universe. I'm not talking about being unconscious or zonked out, I'm talking about being fully conscious."[50] Or as Lesh writes, "Every time I walked out on that stage, I knew in my heart that the infinite potential present in that moment was available to us all, if we could only reach out and take it. That remained my goal—to walk out every night and play as if life itself depended on my every note, to wrest meaning from the jaws of entropy and decay, and to transform every place we played into a shrine of expanded consciousness."[51]

If this is the case, we can sum up by saying that certainly Phil Lesh, and possibly other members of the Grateful Dead, do seem to have been interested in being a part of a new movement that in many ways can be described as having religious aspects. But we are not speaking here of religion in the sense of a solid monument to a primordial and unrepeatable inspiration, from which dogmas and doctrines proceed. Rather, for Lesh, religious organization reaches its peak when it clears a space for the ever-present possibility of the spontaneous manifestation of transcendence. This is what Lesh and others saw happening in the Acid Tests, and this was the incentive that led the band to develop their unprecedented approach to rock improvisation. The Grateful Dead did not leave any churches behind them, but maybe they never meant to: what they did offer was less concerned with the past or future than with helping people to see how intimately Right Now is linked to the ceaselessly creative nature of Eternity.

This is perhaps best brought out in Dennis McNally's description of Garcia's reaction to the Watts Towers, a collection of structures erected by outsider artist Simon Rodia in Watts, Los Angeles. Garcia notes that "my thoughts about [the Towers] were something like, 'Well, if you work by yourself as hard as you can, every day, after you're dead, you've left something behind that they can't tear down, you know. If you work real hard, that's the payoff. The individual artist's payoff, that thing that exists after you're dead. . . . I thought, 'Wow, that's not it for me.' Instead of making something that lasts forever, I thought, I think I'd rather have fun. For me it was more important to be involved in something that was *flowing and dynamic* and not so solid that you couldn't tear it down."[52]

Building a Transcendence Machine

Churches represent things: machines do things. I have suggested that the Grateful Dead's improvisational practice could be understood as a transcendence machine, a means of more or less artificially creating the conditions in which transcendence could (but did not have to) occur. I suggested, too, that such a machine is necessary if your job involves creating transcendent experiences night after night, gig after gig. You cannot rely on inspiration all the time, so you build the machine and figure out ways to make it work.

But that leads to the question of legitimacy. I used to find it odd to talk about a "transcendence machine": it felt as though the transcendence it helps to produce must be faked—we can't get real transcendence from a machine, can we? And yet I could not deny the sense of transcendence I'd felt in the Grateful Dead's music, at the same time that I also could not deny the evidence that it was carefully organized, planned out, and designed (consciously or not) to produce the sorts of experiences that it gave me. It was a trick, but it seemed to be an effective one.

I was helped past this impasse by comments made by one of the band's associates, David Gans. Years ago he published a truly wonderful and detailed book of interviews with the band. In one interview with Lesh, Gans speaks of his own initiation into the "backstage" scene of the Grateful Dead. He writes that "from time to time I'm sorry I . . . learned how the Wizard of Oz really works . . . [but now] I've gone past being embarrassed about having seen that it is a machine, not a miracle. *Now I can see the miraculous nature of the machine itself*."[53]

This is beautiful. And, I think, true. Maybe you, the reader, do not feel that way about the Grateful Dead, but I am sure that something in your life is magic to you, or religious, or transcendent—take whatever word you want. You and your world get bigger and more interesting because of this thing, which lifts you out of mundane reality. And yet . . . whatever it is, it arises from mundane reality, and it takes on its specific form on the basis of its mundane origins, and it has the effect that it does at least partly because of the mundane context that surrounds it, and you as you encounter it. It really is a mystery.

Sometimes it is even more than a mystery. Sometimes it really is a trick. Sometimes people put on an act; sometimes an act nonetheless produces real experiences in the people who take part in it or witness it. Sometimes you just do not know if what you are seeing or feeling is real or fake, and maybe sometimes that does not even matter so much. The paranormal researcher Jess Hollenback speaks of "materialization," in which the religious imagination can be so strong—so "empowered," to use his term—that it can even affect things in the material world.[54] The empowerment needs a "trigger," but the legitimacy of the empowering trigger might not be the point: whatever works, works. Drawing on Hollenback, Jeffrey Kripal argues that sometimes the mind "needs to trick itself" into using its full powers: he notes that there may be truths "that will sometimes only manifest . . . through, or with the help of, a trick." And he adds the following: "Which, come to think about it, is not a bad definition of religion."[55] We might also say that it is not the trick itself, but, rather, the headspace that the trick produces. Either way, if it works—and the Dead and Deadheads clearly felt that it did work, at least sometimes—then it works.

That is one side of the coin. The other side is this: the Grateful Dead have always had a strongly American identity. They have invoked the nation and its pantheon of cultural heroes countless times, to the point where Garcia could sing, with his tongue only partly in his cheek,

I'm Uncle Sam
That's who I am
Been hiding out
In a rock and roll band.[56]

They waved the flag for the beatniks, visionaries, con men, and dreamers who make up the America of Twain, Whitman, Emerson, Kerouac, and Moondog. Alongside that noble, if sometimes ragged and disreputable, lineage, there is a vigorous American religious tradition of—to put it bluntly—making sure that religion is effective. Although this emphasis on effectiveness manifests throughout the American religious scene, it is especially prominent in the various streams of religiosity that make up what Catherine Albanese refers to as "American Metaphysical Religion," a broad tradition that helps to unify all the more or less unchurched movements of seekers in American life from Theosophists to Spiritualists to the modern New Age and beyond.

Albanese argues that this religious tradition has four unifying emphases: a concern with consciousness and its powers; a belief in correspondence between this world and higher worlds, which can be consciously made use of; understanding existence at every level as dynamic and mobile rather than static; and a "pragmatism" that always has "a point and purpose on earth." As she sees it, American metaphysical religion is "above all a work of the practical imagination" in which "being aligned with the spirit (the goal) meant standing in the free flow of spirit energy."[57] The Grateful Dead, with their transcendence machine, fit right into this American spiritual tradition.

Or, looking at it a little differently, you can say that the Grateful Dead's story is as American as L. Frank Baum's *The Wizard of Oz*. The Great and Powerful Oz didn't get to the magic world and his position through prayers or righteous conduct; no, it was an experimental flying machine, a balloon, that got him there, and it was his command of high-tech theatrical special effects that gave him his role there—and, in the end, even if he was a humbug, he was a pretty nice person who made wonderful things happen. That, I think, is a perfectly valid—and perfectly American—way to look at the Grateful Dead. As David Chidester puts it, "Even fake religions can be doing a kind of symbolic, cultural and religious work that is real."[58] He stresses that, "as a matter of urgency, in order to recover the religious, creative, and imaginative capacity of America, we need to understand and appreciate the religious work and religious play of "authentic fakes" in American popular culture."[59]

Nor is this a fringe approach. Indeed, Tanya Luhrman's work over the past several decades has explored the ways in which religious or spiritual movements enable their adherents to develop practical, ideological, and narrative processes by which they can "bootstrap" themselves into experiences of transcendence—see in particular her *When God Talks Back: Understanding the American Evangelical Relationship with God*. These "technologies of the self" (to follow Foucault) or "anthropotechnics," as Peter Sloterdijk refers to them, are "techniques of the body and mind that enable individuals to mold and experiment with their own existence."[60] The Grateful Dead seem to have been using their music in this way; such technologies also have a history of being associated with psychedelic drugs, as, for example, in Aldous Huxley's blueprint for a perfect society in *Island*, or in the various contexts within which LSD was understood as laid out by Ido Hartogsohn.[61]

Religious Understandings of Avant-Garde Musical Improvisation

I have been focusing in this work on the Grateful Dead's religious inspiration for their improvisational practice. It is clear, however, that musical improvisation and religious concerns have been frequently associated—as happens, for instance, in the Near Eastern concepts of tarab and saltanah, the creation of transcendent states through Pakistani qawwali music, the expression of fundamental cosmic principles through Indian raga-based improvisations, or the invocation of the Holy Spirit through gospel music.[62]

All of these approaches to improvised music bear some similarities to the Grateful Dead's practice, thus suggesting that a link between improvised music and religious experience exists worldwide. Murphy's quoted description of an African American gospel meeting in the 1930s, for instance, is surprisingly and strongly reminiscent of the Grateful Dead's improvisational practice: "Scraps of other words and tunes were flung into the medley of sound by individual singers from time to time, but the general trend was carried on by a deep undercurrent, which appeared to be stronger than the mind of any individual present, for it bore the mass of improvised harmony and rhythms into the most effective climax of incremental repetition that I have ever heard. I felt as if some conscious plan or purpose were carrying us along, call it mob-mind, communal composition, or what you will."[63] From an entirely different cultural background, Racy's description of tarab musical procedure is also applicable to the Grateful Dead's work: "Flexible musical interpretations produce tremendous ecstasy through the use of highly evocative musical devices. . . . The interpreter teases out the compositional form without breaking it, tantalizes musical expectations without totally violating them, and presents refreshing departures without obfuscating their essential points of references. In all, the manipulation of preconceived structures renders the musical message more potent. Ecstatically speaking, it brings out the 'real music.'"[64]

Furthermore, the joyful playfulness that is characteristic of the Grateful Dead's music is mirrored in Indian attitudes that combine hedonism and deeply religious understandings. Annette Wilke and Oliver Moebus note that in contrast to Western discourse from Plato on that emphasizes the possible dangers of music, Indian discourse often simply regards it as a good thing.[65] In this context, musical mysticism is "the conscious cultivation of the 'void' of great transcendency experience, which is linked with the sensory experience of music, and the connection between emotional fusion and cognitive abstraction. Music, musicians and musical experience are socially coded with 'incorporeality,' 'superindividuality' and 'detachment from the world' while at the same time they make the Brahman accessible in a sensorily affective and substantial fashion in the audible, musical Nada. One should note that this occurs very simply as delight, untrammeled joy, and immersion in the music—without being overloaded with theology."[66]

However, the Grateful Dead's social or institutional position is fundamentally different from all the groups just mentioned. For one thing, the Grateful Dead were not anchored in an established religious position and, indeed, took care to decrease the possibility of such a position being created around them. For another, the Grateful Dead started up in a truly interesting, unique period for American music that produced a number of avant-garde artists who used improvisational tactics that were carried to extreme levels, with explicitly religious motivations, including Albert Ayler, Sun Ra, John Coltrane, Alice Coltrane, Pharoah Sanders, Terry Riley, and La Monte Young— in other words, many of the most significant improvisers of the 1960s. I have discussed this issue at length elsewhere, but for now we just need to be aware that at this time there were a lot of people combining extended improvisation as a musical technique with explicitly religious references and goals.[67] John Coltrane was naming songs after "the Father, the Son, and the Holy Ghost"; Albert Ayler was releasing albums with titles like *Spiritual Unity*; Pharoah Sanders used his song titles to tell everyone that "the creator has a master plan"; Sun Ra was speaking of Other Planes of There; Alice Coltrane was investigating Hinduism and preparing for her future career as a guru; and the list goes on.

Why did all of this happen just then? Broadly speaking, during the 1960s several streams came together to create a welcoming conceptual environment for such religious/improvisational crossover. There was an increased interest in artistic improvisation and spontaneity, alongside an "unchurching" tendency for North Americans to look for spiritual or religious significance in nontraditional settings.[68] They were more likely than ever before to look for this significance in non-Western cultural and religious influences.[69] This was backed up by the tendency of jazz artists, especially, to validate and contextualize experimentation through religious ascriptions, so that "mantra-like melodies, static harmonies, pentatonic improvisations, dynamic ensemble interactions and increasing freedom from metre constraints came to signify both a religious attitude and a new ecstatic spiritual practice in its own right."[70]

The music made by such religiously motivated artists as the Grateful Dead or John Coltrane was distinctive, different than traditional religious music: it was experimental, it often didn't even sound like "normal music," it was made outside of established religious movements and cultural contexts, and people often made huge claims about its powers (we'll hear about some of those shortly).

The artists producing this sort of improvisational religious music were not all tightly linked, aside from the fact that they were exploring experimental improvisation-based music at roughly the same time and in the same country. A number of artists—including Ayler, Coltrane, and Sun Ra—did work in the same avant-garde jazz scene; Terry Riley and Ra were also performing in rock contexts as, of course, were the Grateful Dead.[71] I am considering these artists together because their respective deployments of experimental improvisational music in their respective religious contexts harmonize with each other in interesting ways, giving an overview of how this versatile tool was applied to the artistic realization of religious ideals. So, the Grateful Dead were not alone in their general approach; they were, however, unique in the interpretation that they made of their musical/spiritual interaction, and I think a lot of that uniqueness should be linked to their use of LSD.

LSD and Music

As we have seen, the ritual aspects of Grateful Dead performances were of a very fluid nature, delineating a space of musical or spiritual openness instead of prescribing the order or nature of activities to take place within that space.[72] Rather, the potential for transcendence to happen was created by the band members' willingness to open themselves up to the moment and to spontaneous interaction with their fellow musicians—in other words, to improvise. The band could not guarantee by doing this that transcendent experiences could take place; their approach merely created the necessary preconditions for them to happen. For the Grateful Dead, then—or, at least, for Lesh and Garcia, who were the most willing to discuss these aspects of the band's career—improvisation provided a musical and ritual space where the divine can manifest, a field within which participants can be immersed in the ever-changing nature of ultimate reality.

The Grateful Dead were far from alone in viewing experimental, avant-garde approaches to improvisation as having the potential to be religiously significant. But their religious understanding of improvisation differed from the understandings of other religiously motivated improvising artists. One of the best known of these, for instance, was saxophonist Albert Ayler, one of the founders of free jazz, whose enormous tone and gorgeous melodic sense coexisted with a willingness to explore the extremes of shrieking noise in his solos. More, perhaps, than anyone else, he showed how sheets of sound and a fully liberated rhythm section could be used to establish a new improvisational aesthetic for jazz.

But, in fact, this was more than a merely aesthetic concern for Ayler. He understood his music in a Christian, eschatological context: the world was moving into a new phase, and his music would somehow both symbolize and help to create that shift. "When there's chaos, which is now," he has said, "only a relatively few people can listen to the music that tells of what will be. You see, everyone is screaming 'Freedom' now, but mentally, most are under a great strain. But now the truth is marching in . . . and that truth is that there must be peace and joy on Earth. I believe music can help bring that truth into being." Thus, "in my music, I'm trying to look far ahead. . . . This is about post-war cries; I mean the cries of love that are already in the young and that will emerge as people seeking spiritual freedom come to spiritual freedom."[73]

For the Grateful Dead, on the other hand, improvisational activity was not linked to future-oriented eschatological fervor, as it was for Ayler; indeed, such apocalyptic enlightenment is described and critiqued in the Grateful Dead song "Estimated Prophet." Guitarist Bob Weir describes the song's inspiration: "Every time we play anywhere there's always some guy that's taken a lot of dope, and he's really bug-eyed, and he's having some kind of vision. Somehow I work into that vision, or the band works into his vision, or something like that. He's got a rave that he's got to deliver. . . . If there's a point to 'Estimated Prophet' it is that no matter what you do, perhaps you shouldn't take it all that seriously. No matter what."[74]

Other radically improvising artists, such as the visionary jazz keyboardist and bandleader Sun Ra, believed that the secret, esoteric underpinnings of the universe could be exposed through radical improvisation. Over a long and enormously productive career, Ra and his ever-changing Arkestra attempted to demonstrate the real nature of the universe—or, as he might say, the Omniverse—through their unsettling, frequently dissonant improvisations interspersed with outer space chants and evocations of swing-era jazz.

The idea that music reveals or models the principles that structure all of existence is venerable, going back at least to Pythagoras in the West and to the foundations of raga theory in India. Ra continued in this tradition, but his pessimistic view of human capacity meant that he doubted musicians' ability to deliberately create valid music or understand its principles; instead, they had to be led beyond their planning, beyond their conscious intentions. As he has said, "I came from somewhere else, but it [the Creator's voice] reached me through the maze and dullness of human existence. But if I hadn't been [from someplace else] it couldn't have reached me and I'd be like the rest of the people on the planet who are dancing in their ignorance."[75]

Improvisation was a tool to enable his musicians to transcend the limitations of their consciousness, so that they could access and represent structures that were truer than they could have known. "What I'm doing," Ra claims, "is stuff that's beyond human knowledge and on a higher plane. So therefore it can't really be explained, but it can be felt. That's everything I'm about—feeling—because people have lost that direction as far as intellect is concerned, so they make a lot of mistakes. It is time to eliminate mistakes, and true feelings would never make a mistake. If people could activate that part of themselves that is their true feelings, then they can strive for something on a greater plane."[76] Because "the idea or being of jazz is based upon the spontaneous improvisation principle," it was able to be "a bridge to something else"; it can function as a "bridge" to lead the player to "intergalactic music . . . because it is a spontaneous creative form of art."[77]

The Grateful Dead do not seem to have linked improvisation to the creation of representations of the existent but hidden and separated universal order, as Ra did—and I read several lines from the Grateful Dead's song "Cosmic Charlie" as a critique of excessive concern for this level of being. The song's unnamed narrator, speaking to Cosmic Charlie, says that "I just wonder if you shouldn't feel / Less concern about the deep unreal." According to the narrator, things are much simpler than this: "The very first word is 'How do you do' / The last, 'Go home, your mama's calling you.'"[78]

Extended, radical improvisation could also be seen as a means to personal spiritual development, as it was for tenor saxophonist John Coltrane, the highly respected jazz superstar whose albums such as *A Love Supreme* and *Meditations* made him the figurehead for the radical approach to improvisation that emerged in the early 1960s.[79] As he put it in 1966, "I believe that men are here to grow themselves into the full—into the best good that they can be."[80] Coltrane felt that his role in this process was "to uplift people, as much as I can. To inspire them to realize more and more of their capacities for living meaningful lives."[81] Nor was he only to be of service to others. Rather, his playing helped to sanctify him as well, getting him closer to his long-term goal: "I would like to be a saint."[82]

But improvisation for the Grateful Dead was not a field within which one could struggle one's way to spiritual perfection. Indeed, Bob Weir has stressed the lack of spiritual mastery of his bandmates: "We aren't accomplished masters of any sort of spiritual realm. . . . I know the guys in the band pretty well, I think. By and large they are some philosophically adept individuals. But I wouldn't go so far as to call any of them spiritual masters."[83] The band was a vessel for the divine spirit; as Garcia put it, "from the point of view of being a player it's this thing that you can't make happen, but when it's happening you can't stop it from happening. . . . The Grateful Dead has some kind of intuitive thing. . . . We talk about it, but all those things are by way of agreeing that we'll continue to keep trying to do this thing, whatever it is, and that our best attitude to it is sort of this stewardship, in which we are the custodians of this thing."[84]

The necessary elements were the presence of these specific people onstage, and their willingness to engage with divine inspiration and follow where it led; it was not necessary that they be in a ritually or morally pure state, and members were not granted spiritual privileges. As Garcia puts it, "You don't gain an improved position just by virtue of being in the Grateful Dead. We're frequently seen as being privileged somehow, but being in the Grateful Dead is by no means a privilege. It doesn't exempt you from anything particularly, and the reward is a fleeting existential kind of reality."[85]

So, to sum up, we can say that the Grateful Dead's religious vision was not a prophetic, monastic, or Pythagorean one, unlike those of Ayler, Ra, and Coltrane. Open improvisation was the means through which the Grateful Dead and their audience could participate in a moment of realized eschatology, by opening themselves up to an incursion of divine significance, even when that significance is without specific content. Testimonies from band members reveal that this significance was perceived as meaningful, but not as possessing definite meaning. It was not incorporated into a clear doctrinal or ideological system, but represented an unfixed sense of importance, a tantalizing awareness that one had entered a liminal zone whose very atmosphere was magical.

Generally speaking, this feeling is a common reaction to strong art. When powerfully moved in an aesthetic sense, one often feels transported into another world that is in some indefinable way special—the work is felt to be powerful even when the meaning is not understood. Greil Marcus and Simon Frith draw on the work of Roland Barthes on *signifiance* to argue that, when listening to powerful music "we do not respond to symbols . . . though we seize on such symbols and connect them to historical events or personal situations in order to explain our response"; rather, "we respond to symbol creation."[86] As Frith puts it, "What is involved in musical pleasure is . . . the work of signification; our joyous response to music is a response not to meanings but to the making of meanings . . . as the terms we usually use to construct and hold ourselves together suddenly seem to float free."[87] We recognize something as being powerful, fascinating, or important even before we have figured out (or decided) *why* it feels that way to us. In addition to this explanation (which is true, but would apply equally well to other music), I would argue that there could be another inspiration for this sense of meaningfulness-stripped-of-attached-meaning, associated with ceaseless change—namely, drugs.

As we have seen, the Grateful Dead discovered their sense of mission in a context that was saturated with LSD. The band's foundation period was at the Acid Tests; their early manager and patron was LSD manufacturer Augustus Owsley "Bear" Stanley; LSD experiences had huge effects on the band's development; and the countercultural scene in which they worked was symbolized and partially defined through LSD use. We must, then, consider the Grateful Dead in the context of LSD—which has, of course, very frequently been associated with religious experience, for its "capacity reliably to induce states of altered perception, thought and feeling that are not experienced otherwise except in dreams or at times of religious exaltation."[88] As

Christopher Hill puts it (in a book that to my mind contains some of the best writing about the Grateful Dead and what they were doing), "It was acid. The Dead can't be seriously talked about without talking about acid."[89]

I do follow Patrick Lundborg in his argument that psychedelic experiences need to be treated phenomenologically, rather than having religious categorizations simply imposed upon them: "The religious model is an interpretation, whereas the psychedelic experience, if registered according to the proper phenomenology, is simply a description."[90] The very fact that he has to make this argument, though, is an implicit acknowledgment of the fact that psychedelic drugs and religious experience have been frequently—indeed, almost inevitably—associated.[91] Nick Bromell puts it extremely clearly: "Psychedelics are powerful. Psychedelics are distinctive. As research in the fields of psychopharmacology, religion, and anthropology makes perfectly clear, psychedelics do something no other drugs can, and that mysterious something lies very close to the human sense of wonder that is formalized in the world's religions."[92]

This association is a natural one to make, due to the ability of psychedelic drugs to produce "experiences of ultimacy."[93] Religious systems derive their authority from claims to represent or define the "true," fundamental, or ultimate nature of existence; thus any experience that strikes the experiencer as being of unparalleled meaningfulness, significance, or power will have a quite understandable tendency to be understood as falling within the religious realm. This is all the more true given that the middle of the twentieth century was a time in North America "when a great deal of the educated reading public shared psychologist Abraham Maslow's view that all religions have their origins in the 'peak experiences' of certain extraordinary individuals. . . . In this view, the primary datum of all religion is the attainment of altered states of consciousness," arguably (and it was a very popular argument) similar to those attained under the influence of LSD.[94]

Michael Hicks argues that LSD, especially in terms of its artistic ramifications, has "three fundamental effects . . . dechronicization, depersonalization, and dynamization. Dechronicization permits the drug user to move outside of conventional perceptions of time. Depersonalization permits the user to lose the self and gain an 'awareness of undifferentiated unity.'"[95] Dynamization involves the perception that everything that one sees or hears is, in Albert Hoffmann's words, "in constant motion, animated, as if driven by an inner restlessness."[96] This description overlaps with Alan Watts's argument that LSD leads the user to focus on the present and to become aware of polarity, relativity, and eternal, unceasing energy in his or her environment.[97]

I would add to Hicks's and Watts's breakdowns a further—and very important—element, defined by D. X. Freedman as "portentousness—the capacity of the mind to see more than it can tell, to experience more than it can explicate . . . from the banal to the profound."[98] In other words, LSD can create the impression that whatever the subject experiences is deeply significant, encouraging them to invest it with meaning, no matter how far-fetched the meaning may seem to observers. This sense of meaningfulness without connection to any specific meaning has been compared to Rudolph Otto's concept of the "numinous" as an essential quality of divinity, thus enhancing the LSD/religious experience overlap.[99]

All of these aspects can be understood as subsumed under the general presentation of LSD as a corrosive and facilitating, rather than inherently creative, agent. It functions by disabling the mental mechanisms that use categories and distinctions to organize the flow of impressions that the brain perceives. In so doing, it allows the mind to construct new interpretations of those impressions and vests the new constructions with a feeling of profound meaningfulness or significance. As Humphry Osmond, an early researcher of LSD, writes, "The brain, although its functioning is impaired, acts more subtly and complexly than when it is normal."[100] Moreover, subjective, internal impressions may be present quite as strongly as externally created ones: "Signals arising from introspective and interoceptive processes, virtually imperceptible during waking consciousness, may then represent a significant portion of the incoming data available for processing during the actions of a hallucinogen."[101]

Charles Tart, a prominent researcher into altered states of consciousness, argues that powerful psychedelics, including LSD, break down normal states of consciousness, but do not permit the creation of a stable altered state of consciousness, instead keeping the subject floating and unable to stabilize.[102] Nichols and Chemell contend that "psychedelics perturb key brain structures that inform us about our world, tell us when to pay attention, and interpret what is real."[103] For this reason, as Jay Stevens notes, "the hippies used LSD as a deconditioning agent"—which probably explains the CIA's interest in it as well.[104] As neuroscientist Marc Lewis puts it, "LSD (lysergic acid diethylamide) goes to work in the brain by blocking serotonin receptors. Serotonin's job is to reduce the firing rate of neurons that get too excited because of the volume or intensity of incoming information. Serotonin filters out unwanted noise, and normal brains rely on that. So, by blocking serotonin, LSD allows information to flow through the brain unchecked," leaving the brain scrambling to build meaningful constructions that will explain and contain this information.[105]

In an impressively lucid discussion, Charles Perry takes up this approach, arguing that "LSD suppresses the mind's ability to discriminate according to levels of importance and to form persisting notions about reality. . . . In a sea of perpetually changing impressions, the meaning of anything can differ wildly from moment to moment. The exaltation of being stoned might be the dawn of birth, the moment of death or a mystical unity of the two. The world might be the play of eternal archetypes or nothing but the moment-to-moment flashing of spontaneous energy." Thus, LSD hallucinations are "not full-fledged visions of things that are not there, but extraordinary and uncontrollably shifting interpretations of things that are."[106] In the San Francisco scene, these experiences were taken as "a gateway to experience itself, to spontaneity, to visions of unsuspected connections between things; an equivalent of the contemporary avant-garde art project that combined ritual, psychodrama, political amelioration and the expounding of secret things."[107] LSD provided "the experience of seeing everything disappear into a ceaseless froth of change."[108] Under the influence of LSD, "life could become a fathomless and evanescent flow of events, which you were supposed to trust," and out of which one spontaneously built meanings and interpretations that could be used as guides until the flow of events transformed them into new meanings and interpretations.[109]

We have seen that the Grateful Dead did trust this evanescent flow of events; indeed, the Framework's ceaseless motion, and the band's dislike of formalized religion, can both be viewed as showing a desire to valorize continual revelatory experience, rather than settle down into a given context, whether intellectual or musical. In the Grateful Dead's jams, as in the experience of the world when one is under the influence of LSD, one can follow structures of meaning as they arise from the "ceaseless froth of change," only to dissolve back into it again as new structures take their place. In this regard, the Grateful Dead's liberation of the rhythm section—the liberties that, as we have discussed, Lesh felt free to take—plays a huge role in that it opens up the underlying harmonic and rhythmic structures that would otherwise define and lock in the band's music. Freeing the rhythm section is what distinguishes jamming, moving into newly created musical spaces, from simply soloing over a static backdrop.

This is particularly true in the band's acid rock period (1967–70), at the height of the counterculture and the public fascination with LSD and its effects. Performances during this period usually feature successions of songs that fade into one another by means of extended jamming, to the point where the songs themselves can take on the aspect of temporary structures arising from and disappearing into the waves of change. As Garcia describes it, their approach was "inspired by the psychedelic experience. . . . It's taking chances, and going all to pieces, and coming back, and reassembling. You don't despair about letting yourself go to pieces—you just let it go."[110]

Overall, then, both the band's improvisational practice, and their religious understanding of that practice, can be plausibly linked to their use of LSD— all three things work together. The popular association of the Grateful Dead with LSD is thus justified, and not only because of the band's early performing contexts or the fondness of Deadheads for hallucinogens, although these are significant as well. The Grateful Dead, particularly in their early years, can also be seen as taking an impressively coherent and developed approach to working through or working from the implications of the LSD experience, with those implications developed both on the level of craft (the band's music) and theory (their theology).

This fidelity to their understandings of their LSD experiences is what makes the difference between the use of LSD as a trope or motif, as did so many late 1960s groups, and using it as a foundational element of the religious and musical world that the Grateful Dead constructed. For example, John Coltrane is said to have taken LSD, and his *Om* album was said to have been recorded while he was under the drug's influence, but Coltrane did not allow the drug to define his musical worldview in the thoroughgoing way that the Grateful Dead did: "Coltrane's LSD experiences confirmed spiritual insights he had already discovered rather than radically changing his perspective. . . . Books, however, continued to be the main source for Coltrane's intellectual and spiritual search."[111]

I have seen no evidence that any of the members of the Grateful Dead ever regretted their use of this drug. This was not due simply to a general laissez-faire attitude within the band: band members and associates were known to criticize the use of heroin or cocaine, for instance, which even Garcia, the band member most partial to their use, referred to as "dead-enders."[112] It is clear that the band members valued very highly the musical approach that LSD helped them create, and the access (as they saw it) to transcendent realms that it allowed. As Lesh writes, LSD and other psychedelics were "tools to enhance awareness, to access other levels of mind, to manifest the numinous and sacred."[113]

Readers can decide for themselves whether this thoroughgoing assimilation of the LSD experience into an artistic practice and a lifestyle is a good or bad thing. But whatever one's evaluation of the experiment might be, it is certainly an *interesting* thing, an impressively realized and unique experiment, out of which emerged some truly innovative and powerful music.

Conclusion

Over a period of four years, from 1963 to 1967, rock music underwent enormous changes and almost unbelievably rapid development in every aspect of its being, whether we speak of timbral possibilities, compositional strategies, instrumental virtuosity, ensemble playing styles, social context, or other elements. This period and these changes have become so much a part of our cultural history that we can be tempted to take them for granted; however, to do so is to lose sight of their magnitude.

One of the most significant developments of this period was the possibility for rock bands to incorporate extensive amounts of improvisation into their performance practice. As we saw, this period sees the birth of a distinctively rock improvising tradition that, if lacking the subtlety and musical finesse associated with such traditions in other musical forms such as raga, qawwali, or jazz, nevertheless is noteworthy for its vigor, physicality, and adventurousness—and also, now, for its longevity, as it has passed the half-century mark. The Grateful Dead are one of a very small group of innovators who devised ways to incorporate improvisation into a rock context, with all that such a context requires, and thereby expanded the possibilities of rock performance; for this reason, it is important that we know what they did and how they did it, and that we understand the mechanisms that they invented to make it possible.

In addition to *how* they did what they did, it is also important to know *why*. The Grateful Dead's choices with regard to their music were hardly traditional. The question of originating impulses of improvising musicians is all too rarely asked, and yet it is a crucial one. What leads a musician to play in this way? Rather than leave this important question unaddressed or vaguely answered, I have argued that their motivation was at heart a religious one, and thus that their career cannot be understood without taking this aspect into consideration.

The significance of their musical work extends beyond the Grateful Dead and goes outside the confines of the musical scene. It is hardly unusual to speak of religious experience in the context of the 1960s, or LSD; both the period and the drug are strongly associated with experimentation of all kinds, including religious experimentation. Yet all too often the discussion of experimental religiosity in the 1960s and subsequently presents that experimentation either as something transitory or not entirely serious, and, hence, with little impact on other aspects of the subjects' lives, or as something leading to institutional affiliation. The presentation that I have made of the religious aspects of the Grateful Dead's musical inspiration is therefore valuable because it reminds us that religious experience can be taken seriously and acted upon—indeed, can serve as the basis for a thirty-year career—without ever being formally organized: it can be inspirational without being institutional, manifesting through the practices that it underlies.

In short, the religious experiences that members of the Grateful Dead underwent in the mid-1960s, and the musical practices that those experiences inspired, are significant for our understanding of rock's development; for our understanding of the development of improvised music more generally; and for the reminder that they give us of the range of ways in which religious experience can manifest.

So it is my hope that what you have read will increase our knowledge of the modern development of open improvisation and specifically expand the discussion to include improvising rock bands. It also puts an accent on the religious motivations of improvisation and improvisers, which have not been adequately appreciated in the literature thus far and thereby furthers a properly ethnomusicological understanding of how music relates to and works with culture—or, in this case, how music integrates into culture elements that are perceived as coming from outside of culture. Sociologist Peter Berger has argued that religion forms a "sacred canopy," outlining the boundaries of human cultural systems and valuations by showing how those systems are surrounded and supported by the divine levels of existence.[114] What this means is that, by tracing the outline of the sacred canopy, we don't just identify where the boundaries of culture are established; we also identify the region in which the interactions between culture and perceived transcendence take place.

Our long strange trip has further ramifications for the modern study of religion, in two particular ways. First of all, there is a tendency in modern studies of religion to downplay the significance of religious experience, and to undercut its importance for the founding or joining of religious movements—in other words, origins and conversion accounts and the like are often reinterpreted so as to lessen the significance of whatever religious experience may be claimed to have inspired them. Such claims to experience are often seen as legitimators, used to justify the religious infrastructure that grows up in the movement or the socially motivated decision to convert. Religious experience, from this point of view, excuses or explains religious affiliation, rather than provoking it. My discussion of the Grateful Dead problematizes this devaluation of religious experience. I have shown, instead, the pivotal importance of religious experience—and efforts to ensure access to it—for a group that was not concerned to create a religious infrastructure and thus did not need the legitimation.

Second, in broader discussions of modern developments in North American spirituality, there is the tendency to see things as going in one of two ways: as the traditional religious forms decline, people move either into diffuse, unchurched spirituality, which is presented as being fairly vague and exploratory (e.g., the idea of the cultic community, the rise of New Age thought), or into tight and explicitly organized religious structures—as we see, for example, in the example of "Jesus People," religious seekers with countercultural backgrounds who embraced fundamentalist Christianity in large numbers in the 1970s. In short, we are often presented with the contrast between diffuse "spirituality" and hardline "religion" as characteristic responses to North American religious crises in the latter half of the twentieth century.

However, our examination of the Grateful Dead problematizes this distinction as well. In the Grateful Dead's career, we see an example of a situation in which the religious experience was used as the motivating force for the creation of a defined musical and business entity. The band's religious vision was coherent enough and focused enough not to fall on the fuzzy spirituality side of things, but it was also unstructured by design, with no attempt made to turn it into a religious group or to affiliate it with such a group. Indeed, as we have seen, this was considered to be a threatening possibility and consciously avoided. A comparable case with interesting overlaps to the Grateful Dead can be found in the case of Werner Erhard, founder of est, whose experiences of transcendence gave him the conceptual framework for his seminar business.[115] Erhard's experience, like that of the Grateful Dead, shows how religious insights or experiences can be coherently and consistently put to work in the world without first being reified into an organized religion. We might call this an example of "(deliberately) unchurched religiosity," and it is what motivated the Grateful Dead's pioneering efforts in rock improvisation.

If I was to be asked which scholarly box this book fits into, I would probably answer "ethnomusicology"—admittedly, after scratching my head a little bit. This is because ethnomusicology can be most succinctly defined as the study of music in culture. Now, all cultures have limits, the most clearly visible of which are the natural limits, such as birth and death and illness. As Peter Berger argued many years ago, one essential role of religion is to safeguard these limits by creating a protective canopy or wall. But religion does something else as well: it suggests that inside these protective, enveloping walls are what we might call wormholes, or escape routes, which promise the escape from transitory culture into something eternally valid. Religion encloses culture, but it also holds out hopes for transcendence of cultural limitations. These hopes may be illusory, even deliberately deceptive, but that does not mean that they are insignificant. A full map of culture ought to show not only the walls that surround it but also the holes in those walls; for this reason, a real study of music in culture can potentially include the places where people see wormholes, or escapes from culture.

These wormholes may or may not lead to areas beyond culture. But, whether or not they do, the part of them that is within culture is affected by its culture. While the place to which people want to escape might or might not be derived from the surrounding culture, the materials used to build the wormhole are. In the 1950s and 1960s, a number of groups and people took up improvisation as a strategy for creating these wormholes, for touching on something deeper and more valid. In this regard, we have looked, for example, at the work of the Grateful Dead, John Coltrane, Sun Ra, and Albert Ayler. Their work focused around holes in the sacred canopy, holes that held out the promise that one could escape into something ultimately valid, and also that there was a gap through which revivifying energy could flow into the cultural realm. In this book, I have discussed the way in which the Grateful Dead created their wormhole, and what they thought lay beyond it.

Appendix

PERSONNEL

1 Jerry Garcia (vocals/guitar), Phil Lesh (bass/vocals), Bob Weir (vocals/guitar), and Bill Kreutzmann (drums) played at all the performances listed below.

2 Pigpen (vocals/keyboards) played at the performances up to and including April 26, 1972.

3 Keith Godchaux (keyboards) played at the performance on October 22, 1971, and at the subsequent performances.

4 Mickey Hart (drums/percussion) played at the performances from October 22, 1967, to September 20, 1970.

5 Tom Constanten (keyboards) was a member of the Grateful Dead from 1968 to 1970; however, he did not appear at any of the shows discussed in this book.

6 Donna Godchaux (vocals) played at the last four performances listed.

PERFORMANCES

February 25, 1966, Ivar Theater, Los Angeles
Available at https://archive.org/details/gd1966-02-25.sbd.unknown.20346. sbeok.shnf.

March 19, 1966, Carthay Studios, Los Angeles
Available at http://archive.org/details/gd66-03-19.sbd.scotton.81951.sbeok.flac.

May 19, 1966, Avalon Ballroom, San Francisco
Available at http://archive.org/details/gd1966-05-19.sbd.miller.106828.flac16.

September 16, 1966, Avalon Ballroom, San Francisco
Available at http://archive.org/details/gd1966-09-16.117435.vinyl.sbd.indidark-star.flac24.

October 7, 1966, Winterland Arena, San Francisco
Available at https://archive.org/details/gd66-10-07.sbd.unknown.14102.sbeok.shnf.

November 29, 1966, The Matrix, San Francisco
Available at http://archive.org/details/gd1966-11-29.sbd.thecore.4940.shnf.

March 18, 1967, Winterland Arena, San Francisco
Available at http://archive.org/details/gd1967-03-18.sbd.sacks.1594.shnf.

May 5, 1967, Fillmore Auditorium, San Francisco
Available at http://archive.org/details/gd67-05-05.sbs.yerys.1595.sbeok.shnf.

August 4, 1967, O'Keefe Centre, Toronto
Available at http://archive.org/details/gd1967-08-04.09110.sbd.vernon.shnf.

September 3, 1967, The Dance Hall, Rido Nido, California
Available at http://archive.org/details/gd1967-09-03.sbd.miller.43.sbeok.shnf.

October 22, 1967, Winterland Arena, San Francisco
Available at http://archive.org/details/gd1967-10-22.sbd.miller.116257.flac16.

November 10, 1967, Shrine Auditorium, Los Angeles
Available at http://archive.org/details/gd1967-11-10.116171.sbd.motb-0172.flac16.

January 20, 1968, Eureka Municipal Ballroom, Eureka, California
Available at https://archive.org/details/gd1968-01-20.sbd.miller.97340.sbeok.flac16.

January 22, 1968, Eagles Auditorium, Seattle
Available at http://archive.org/details/gd1968-01-22.sbd.miller.97342.sbeok.
flac16.

January 27, 1968, Eureka Municipal Auditorium, Eureka,
California
Available at http://archive.org/details/gd1968-01-20.sbd.miller.97340.sbeok
.flac16.

February 14, 1968, Carousel Ballroom, San Francisco
Available at https://archive.org/details/gd68-02-14.sbd.kaplan.15640.sbeok.
shnf.

August 23, 1968, Shrine Auditorium, Los Angeles
Available at http://archive.org/details/gd1968-08-23.sbd.sniper777.
tomP.116193.flac16.

September 20, 1970, Fillmore East, New York
Available at http://archive.org/details/gd1970-09-20.aud.weinberg.bunjes.81728.
flac16.

April 28, 1971, Fillmore East, New York
Available at https://archive.org/details/gd71-04-28.sbd.murphy.2248.
sbeok.shnf.

October 22, 1971, Auditorium Theatre, Chicago
Available at http://archive.org/details/gd1971-10-22.set2.sbd.miller.86728.
sbeok.flac16.

April 26, 1972, Jahrhunderthalle, Frankfurt, Germany
Available at http://archive.org/details/gd1972-04-26.sbd.vernon.9197.sbeok.
shnf.

August 27, 1972, Old Renaissance Fair Grounds, Veneta, Oregon
Available at http://archive.org/details/gd1972-08-27.sbd.hollister.2199.
sbeok.shnf.

September 21, 1972, The Spectrum, Philadelphia
Available at https://archive.org/details/gd72-09-21.sbd.masse.7296.sbeok.shnf.

November 21, 1973, Denver Coliseum, Denver
Available at http://archive.org/details/gd73-11-21.finley.warner.22096.sbeok.shnf.

December 2, 1973, Boston Music Hall, Boston
Available at http://archive.org/details/gd73-12-02.aud.vernon.17278.sbeok.shnf.

March 23, 1974, Cow Palace, Daly City, California
Available at http://archive.org/details/gd1974-03 23.aud.connors.hughey.gems.78599.flac16.

May 14, 1974, Adams Field House, University of Montana,
Missoula
Available at http://archive.org/details/gd1974-05-14.sbd.miller.114462.flac16.

Notes

CHAPTER 1. THE GRATEFUL DEAD

Epigraph: Bromell, *Tomorrow Never Knows*, 118–19.

1 Partridge, *Occulture*, vol. 1 and vol. 2. For a somewhat dated but still useful overview of the ways that this has manifested in popular culture, see also Christopher Partridge's *The Re-Enchantment of the West*.

2 Rave: Sylvan, *Trance Formation*; hardcore: Dines, "Sacralization of Straight-edge Punk"; drone metal Coggins, *Mysticism, Ritual and Religion*; dub: Partridge, *Dub in Babylon*.

3 Garcia, Reich, and Wenner, *Garcia*, 12.

4 Garcia, Reich, and Wenner, *Garcia*, 24.

5 You can check the song out here: Grateful Dead, "The Golden Road (To Unlimited Devotion," YouTube Video, 2:13, September 2, 2009, https://www .youtube.com/watch?v=QqDjA3DqbcM.

6 Haight-Ashbury: McNally, *Long Strange Trip*, 175. Of the original five members of the Grateful Dead, only Bill Kreutzmann (drums) and Pigpen (keyboards) were really accustomed to their instruments when the band formed. Jerry Garcia was extremely competent on both banjo and acoustic guitar, but electric guitar was relatively new to him; Phil Lesh was an accomplished trumpet player and composer, but new to electric bass; and Bob Weir, the youngest member of the band, was a relative novice on electric guitar.

7 Jackson, *Going Down the Road*, 10.

8 Nettl, "Thoughts on Improvisation," 2.

9 Nettl, "Improvisation," in *Harvard Dictionary of Music*, 406.

10 Nettl, "Thoughts on Improvisation," 19.

11 Nettl, "Thoughts on Improvisation."

12 Nettl, "Improvisation," in Grove Music Online.

13 Qureshi, *Sufi Music of India and Pakistan*; Berliner, *Thinking in Jazz*; Jost, *Free Jazz*; Bailey, *Improvisation*; Porter, *John Coltrane*; Heffley, *Northern Sun and Southern Moon*; Borgo, *Sync or Swarm*; Malvinni, *Grateful Dead*.

14 "Drone" has been defined as "a long, sustained tone in a piece of music . . . usually pitched below the melody" (Randel, *Harvard Dictionary*, 254). I use the term to refer to single tones that are employed extensively and prominently in a given piece of music. Whether or not such tones are literally sounding without change at every second of the piece in question, they do provide a more or less unchanging background to the piece.

15 Mason, *Inside Out*, 30.

16 The Brill Building, which was located in New York, on 49th Street, devoted many of its offices and studios to the music industry. During the 1950s and 1960s, such songwriters as Burt Bacharach and Hal David, Gerry Goffin and Carole King, and Tommy Boyce and Bobby Hart worked there, and the term "Brill Building" became associated with the sort of sophisticated and professional pop/rock compositions produced by these and other songwriters. In an insightful essay on the development of British progressive rock music, Chris Cutler points out the importance of such groups as the Shadows and says, "Listen for example to the guitar in 'Astronomy Domine' [an early Pink Floyd song]—it could be Hank Marvin [lead guitarist for the Shadows]." Cutler, *File under Popular*, 17.

17 Hicks, *Sixties Rock*, 31.

18 The Yardbirds, *Five Live Yardbirds*, Columbia Records, 1964.

19 Cutler, *File under Popular*, 18; Clayson, *Yardbirds*, 62.

20 Weiss, *Steve Lacy*, 79–80; Berkman, *Monument Eternal*.

21 Hayes, *Tripping*.

22 Taylor, *My Stroke of Insight*.

23 Charles Manson had hopes along those lines as well, but his music reached few people—at least until the mid-1980s infatuation with him sparked by musicians or bands such as Sonic Youth, Lydia Lunch, and the Lemonheads.

24 Adams and Sardiello, *Deadhead Social Science*.

25 See "Confessions of a Deadhead: 40 Years with the Grateful Dead," CNBC, July 1, 2015, https://www.cnbc.com/2015/07/01/confessions-of-a-deadhead -40-years-with-the-grateful-dead.html.

26 Gans, *Conversations*, 11.

27 Gans, *Conversations*, 190.

28 Dodd, *Complete Annotated Grateful Dead Lyrics*, 229.

CHAPTER 2. SETTING THE SCENE

Epigraph: "The Golden Road (To Unlimited Devotion)" was written by Jerry Garcia, Bill Kreutzmann, Phil Lesh, Ron McKernan, and Bob Weir and released in 1967.

1 Miles Davis's *Kind of Blue* was released in 1959 by Columbia Records.

2   See, for example, MacDonald and Wilson, "Musical Improvisation and Health, 9.

3   See, for example, Heble and Laver, *Improvisation and Music Education.*

4   Belgrad, *Culture of Spontaneity.*

5   Solis and Nettle, *Musical Improvisation*, xi.

6   Belgrad, *Culture of Spontaneity*, 11; see pages 9–12 for an overview.

7   Bivins, *Spirits Rejoice!*

8   Kerouac, "Essentials of Spontaneous Prose"; Ginsberg, "First Thought, Best Thought."

9   Lennie Tristano Quintet, "Digression," YouTube video, 3:06, December 17, 2011, https://www.youtube.com/watch?v=Dshu9nPhWi4; Lennie Tristano, "Intuition," YouTube video, August 2, 2011, https://www.youtube.com/watch?v=NlrfIA8ADJ8.

10   See, for instance, from a variety of viewpoints, Berendt, *World Is Sound*, 223–25; Bley, *Stopping Time*, 86–90; Kofsky, *Black Nationalism and the Revolution*, 207–43; Lewis, *Power Stronger Than Itself*, 29–43; Litweiler, *Freedom Principle*; Nisenson, *Ascension*; Szwed, *So What*, 169–73; and Wilmer, *As Serious as Your Life.*

11   Universalism could, for instance, be expressed through references to non-Western cultures, whether African (John Coltrane's *Africa/Brass* album or Sun Ra's song "Ancient Aethiopia"); Indian (with, again, Coltrane's album *India* as a notable and influential example, as well as Pharoah Sanders's *Karma*); Japanese (Pharoah Sanders's song "Japan"); or, indeed, extraterrestrial (as with many of Sun Ra's album titles, such as *Other Planes of There* or *Interstellar Low Ways*).

12   Gleason, *Jefferson Airplane*, 249; Lavezzoli, *Dawn of Indian Music*, 163–64; Gans, *Conversations with The Dead*, 66; Lesh, *Searching for the Sound*, 27.

13   Kofsky, *Black Nationalism*, 189.

14   These three Coltrane albums were brought out by Impulse! in 1966, 1968, and 1973 respectively.

15   Lesh, *Searching for the Sound*, 59. A detailed discussion of the influence of the Coltrane Quartet on the Grateful Dead's music and their approach to music may be found at http://deadessays.blogspot.com/2011/07/dead-quote-coltrane.html.

16   Allbright, *Art in the San Francisco Bay Area*, 166.

17   Lavezzoli, *Dawn of Indian Music*, 59–61.

18   Lavezzoli, *Dawn of Indian Music*, 65.

19   Ireland and Gemie, "Raga Rock," 70.

20   Hart, quoted in Lavezzoli, *Dawn of Indian Music*, 94. I want to strongly underscore the point that Hart makes about raga being a truly virtuosic form: I do not mean to suggest that what the first wave of improvising rock musicians heard in raga in any way captured the authentic intricacies, subtleties, and beauty of the form.

21   Perry, *Haight-Ashbury*, 68.

22 Pearlman, "Patterns and Sounds"; see also Bellman,"Indian Resonances in the British Invasion."

23 Ireland and Gemie, "Raga Rock," 59.

24 Lundborg, *Psychedelia*, 121, italics in original.

25 Lavezzoli, *Dawn of Indian Music*, 90.

26 Levaux, *We Have Always Been Minimalist*; Schwarz, *Minimalists*, 8–13; note his emphasis on the influence of non-Western music.

27 Lesh, *Searching for the Sound*, 21–22.

28 Schwarz, *Minimalists*, 43–44.

29 Riley writes that "Phil Lesh was always around the Tape Music Center. . . . There was a lot of crossover," but he does not specifically state that Lesh was at the premiere, and Lesh himself does not mention it in his autobiography, leading me to assume that he was not—although, of course, he would have been aware of it (in Bernstein, *Tape Music*, 221). Lesh does say that Reich was a classmate of his. *Searching for the Sound*, 42.

30 Lesh, *Searching for the Sound*, 37.

31 Lesh, *Searching for the Sound*, 38.

32 Bernstein, *Tape Music*, 247.

33 Bernstein, *Tape Music*, 243–44 (italics mine).

34 Fink, *Repeating Ourselves*, 43 (italics mine).

35 Fink, *Repeating Ourselves*, 46.

36 Fink, *Repeating Ourselves*, 46.

37 Fink, *Repeating Ourselves*, 47.

38 Groundwork for improvisation: McNally, *Long Strange Trip*, 258–59; Selvin, *Summer of Love*, 156. Which can be heard as a somewhat smoother, but still odd, 14/4. Gans and Simon, *Playing in the Band*, 56.

39 Gann, "Thankless Attempts," 302–3.

40 Nyman, *Experimental Music*, 4.

41 Elvis Presley, "Baby I Don't Care," YouTube video, 1:54, May 28, 2010, https://www.youtube.com/watch?v=gOc8-crqhog.

42 Hear, e.g., Troggs, "I Can't Control Myself," YouTube video, 3:06, October 20, 2006, https://www.youtube.com/watch?v=rzHpGjvRgTc.

43 Roberts, *Fender Bass*, 85–86.

44 Roberts, *Fender Bass*, 40, 42, 51. Due to its early prominence in the market, Fender became identified with electric bass generally (similar to what happened with, for example, Kleenex or Xerox in their respective markets). Up until the 1970s, the phrase "Fender bass" is often used, especially by non-rock players or writers, to refer to any sort of electric bass.

45 Roberts, *Fender Bass*, 58.

46 See Crowley, *Surf Beat*, especially chap. 7.

47 Gracyk, *Rhythm and Noise*, 193.

48 For discussion, see Jackson, *Grateful Dead Gear*.

49 Gendron, *Between the Mudd Club and Montmartre*, 158–224.

50 Heffley, *Northern Sun and Southern Moon*, 281.

51 Sun Ra and His Intergalactic Research Arkestra, "It's After the End of the World," YouTube video, 3:25, accessed April 19, 2023, https://www.youtube.com/watch?v=JMmyFrQ79ZA.

52 Gans, *Conversations with The Dead*, 202.

53 Perry, *Haight-Ashbury*, 54.

54 *Hippie*, like *beatnik* before it, was originally a mildly pejorative term, meaning "junior grade hipsters." Perry, *Haight-Ashbury*, 5. New world: Jerry Garcia, speaking of his brother, in Garcia, Reich, and Wenner, *Garcia*, 5.

55 Bromell, *Tomorrow*, 79, 69.

56 Bromell, *Tomorrow*, 119.

57 Knabb, *Situationist International Anthology*.

58 Debord, *Society of the Spectacle*, 13.

59 Jackson, *Garcia*, 78.

60 Sculatti and Seay, *San Francisco Nights*, 27.

61 Sculatti and Seay, *San Francisco Nights*, 23.

62 Sculatti and Seay, *San Francisco Nights*, 24.

63 Grateful Dead, "That's It for the Other One," YouTube video, 7:31, September 24, 2012, https://www.youtube.com/watch?v=7ojrruaMYYg.

64 Gleason, *Jefferson Airplane*, 72.

65 See, for example, the chapter on "Concept Art" (153–212) in Branden Joseph's *Beyond the Dream Syndicate*.

66 Gleason, *Jefferson Airplane*, 36.

67 Perry, *Haight-Ashbury*, 5.

68 Garcia, Reich, and Wenner, *Garcia*, 14.

69 Quoted in Wolfe, *Voices of the Love Generation*, 88.

70 McNally, *Long Strange Trip*, 175.

71 Perry, *Haight-Ashbury*, 52–53.

72 Garcia, Reich, and Wenner, *Garcia*, 19.

73 Gleason, *Jefferson Airplane*, 8.

74 Garcia, Reich, and Wenner, *Garcia*, 49.

75 Perry, *Haight-Ashbury*, 104–12; for manifestos, broadsides, and history of the movement, see the Digger Archives, http://www.diggers.org (accessed February 4, 2023).

76 Perry, *Haight-Ashbury*, 53.

77 For a much more detailed examination, see Perry, *Haight-Ashbury*; see also McNally, *Long Strange Trip*; Gleason, *Jefferson Airplane*.

78 Gleason, *Jefferson Airplane*, 26; Sculatti and Seay, *San Francisco Nights*, 19.

79 Gleason, *Jefferson Airplane*, 33; Tamarkin, *Got a Revolution*, 24–32.

80 Wolfe, *Electric Kool-Aid Acid Test*, 210–13.

81 Sculatti and Seay, *San Francisco Nights*, 59.

82 Jackson, *Garcia*, 28–85; McNally, *Long Strange Trip*, 22–106.

83 Garcia, Reich, and Wenner, *Garcia*, 34.

84 Sculatti and Seay, *San Francisco Nights*, 73–5.

85 Seay and Neely, "Prophets on the Burning Shore," 198–99.

86 Sculatti and Seay, *San Francisco Nights*, 73.
87 Jackson, *Going Down the Road*, 115.
88 Gleason, *Jefferson Airplane*, 315.
89 As was the case as well for Jerry Garcia.
90 Kelly, *Hippie Commie Beatnik Witches*, 9.
91 Backstrom, "Grateful Dead and Their World," 74.
92 Blush, *American Hardcore*, 42.

CHAPTER 3. HOW THE DEAD LEARNED TO JAM

Earlier versions of material presented in this chapter were published in *Grateful Dead Studies* 1 (2013/14) and Nicholas G. Meriwether, ed., *Reading the Grateful Dead: A Critical Survey* (Lanham, MD: Scarecrow), 2012, as well as "Jamming the Blues: The Grateful Dead's Development of Models for Rock Improvisation," *Critical Studies in Improvisation* 9, no. 1 (2013): https://doi.org/10.21083/csieci.v9i1.2145.

Epigraphs: Jerry Garcia is quoted in Hall and Clark, *Rock*, 164 (italics mine). Bob Weir, according to the Grateful Dead Guide blog, described the Dead's jams in a September 1972 *Crawdaddy* interview; see http://deadessays.blogspot.com/2014/03/1972-melodic-jams.html (accessed February 5, 2023). John Kokot is quoted in Backstrom, "Grateful Dead and Their World," 205. Jerry Garcia is quoted in Gans and Simon, *Playing in the Band*, 69.

1 McNally, *Long Strange Trip*, 219–36.
2 Winfree, "Searching for the Sound," 152–53.
3 Meriwether, *Deadhead's Taping Compendium*, 90.
4 See chapter 4 for discussion of approaches to improvisation that the Grateful Dead did *not* make use of, and my suggestions as to why these approaches might not have seemed useful to them, given their concerns.
5 A pulse indicates a rough rate of motion underlying musical events: a rhythm establishes a hierarchy of emphases based around that pulse. "One two three four five six etc." is a pulse, while, for example ,"ONE and a two and a THREE and a four and a five and a SIX" is a rhythm.
6 For discussion of the performance practices typical of free improv shows, see Corbett, *Listener's Guide to Free Improvisation*.
7 *Virgin Beauty*, released by Sony in 1988.
8 Lesh, *Searching for the Sound*, 58.
9 Gans, *Conversations with The Dead*, 182.
10 Jerry Garcia, quoted in Gleason, *Jefferson Airplane*, 314.
11 Willie Woods, "Cleo's Back," Motown TMG 529 (B), 1965.
12 McNally, *Long Strange Trip*, 92.
13 Willie Woods, "Cleo's Back," YouTube video, 2:37, May 4, 2022, https://www.youtube.com/wa.
14 For improvisation within musical scenes or regions, see Lewis, *Power Stronger Than Itself*; Heffley, *Northern Sun and Southern Moon*; Bailey,

Improvisation; Wilmer, *As Serious as Your Life*; Borgo, *Sync or Swarm*. For improvisation by individuals, see Watson, *Derek Bailey and the Story of Free Improvisation*; Berkman, *Monument*; Jost, *Free Jazz*; Litweiler, *Freedom*.

15 Books on Miles Davis's career: see, for example, Szwed, *So What*. For Davis's "jazz rock phase," in which he touched most closely on rock norms and approaches, see Tingen, *Miles Beyond*; Freeman, *Running the Voodoo Down*.

16 Crook, *Ready, Aim, Improvise*, 17.

17 Berliner, *Thinking in Jazz*, 95.

18 Nisenson, *Ascension*, 129, 141.

19 Cole, *John Coltrane*, 134, 139.

20 If I may be permitted a personal digression: if it doesn't include Bruce Thomas, it's not the Attractions.

21 "Chief I. K. Dairo's New York Live Show, Part 1 of 4," YouTube video, 13:18, December 28, 2017, https://www.youtube.com/watch?v=qjUyP2jHNA4.

22 Lesh, *Searching for the Sound*, 56.

23 Lesh, *Searching for the Sound*, 56.

24 Stevens, *Storming Heaven*, 238–39.

25 Comic books and Kesey: Wolfe, *Electric Kool-Aid Acid Test*, 27, 33–35; see also Stevens, *Storming Heaven*, 97; and Tanner, *Ken Kesey*, 93–94. Comic books and trips: Gaskin, *Haight Ashbury Flashbacks*, 16.

26 Merkur, "Formation of Hippie Spirituality."

27 This is theoretically true. Practically speaking, however, Pigpen very rarely takes the lead in improvisational developments.

28 Brightman, *Sweet Chaos*, 8; see also Lesh, *Searching for the Sound*, 68–76.

29 Lesh, *Searching for the Sound*, 333.

30 For example, in their first set on Nov. 29, 1966, the band played the instrumental groove of "Viola Lee Blues" for 14 bars; in the second set, 20. The second set's performance also featured an extension of the jamming between the first and second verses.

31 Meriwether, *Deadhead's Taping Compendium*, 90.

32 Maybe the best of the jug bands—YouTube them and prepare to be charmed.

33 McNally, *Long Strange Trip*, 91.

34 The closest parallel to this approach that I have heard in jazz contexts is Ornette Coleman's work with the electric version of Prime Time, e.g., on the album *Opening the Caravan of Dreams* (Caravan of Dreams Productions, 1985).

35 A chiastic structure is one that could be diagrammed as a V, or a U—it's organized in A-B-B-A form.

CHAPTER 4. IMPROVISATIONAL TACTICS

Some of the material in the "Dance Tunes" section of this chapter has been adapted from an earlier article, "Jamming the Blues: The Grateful Dead's Development of Models for Rock Improvisation," *Critical Studies in Improvisation* 9, no. 1 (2013).

1   Gans, *Conversations with The Dead*, 182.
2   Released in 2005 as part of *Fillmore West, 1969: The Complete Recordings*, disc 10.
3   They also sometimes perform acoustic opening sets in this period, emphasizing their connection to folk and roots music.
4   See Getz and Dwork, *Deadhead's Taping Companion*, for details.
5   Garcia, Reich, and Wenner, *Garcia*, 70.
6   For the rise of country-rock, see Unterberger, *Eight Miles High*, 171–202; Doggett, *Are You Ready*.
7   Miles Davis, *Bitches Brew* (Columbia Records, 1970). See Lesh, *Searching for the Sound*, 177–78.
8   See Jackson, *Grateful Dead Gear*, 131–50.
9   Gleason, *Jefferson Airplane*, 128.
10 McNally, *Long Strange Trip*, 78–79.
11 As Garcia noted, "When we first started the Warlocks [the original name for the Grateful Dead], I thought, 'wow, Pigpen is this guy who can play some keyboards, some harmonica, and he's a powerhouse singer.'" Quoted in Jackson and Gans, *This Is All a Dream*, 12.
12 McNally, *Long Strange Trip*, 69–73.
13 Lesh, *Searching for the Sound*, 8–27.
14 Jackson, *Going Down the Road*, 180.
15 The Grateful Dead performed this song many times; a representative example is the performance on September 21, 1972: YouTube video, 5:56, https://www.youtube.com/watch?v=xZ5yIc6U2Y4 (accessed May 17, 2023).
16 Gleason, "The Bands," 69.
17 Gleason, "Jerry Garcia," 315.
18 Kofsky, "Thread to the Collective Unconscious," 64.
19 Sculatti and Seay, *San Francisco Nights*, 73–75.
20 Kofsky, "Thread to the Collective Unconscious," 64.
21 Stewart, *African American Music*, Ripani, *New Blue Music*; Le Gendre, *Soul Unsung*.
22 Stewart, *African American Music*, 11.
23 Stewart, *African American Music*, 11.
24 Ripani, *New Blue Music*, 49.
25 Stewart, *African American Music*, 25–26.
26 For a discussion of the evolution of this developing interest, see John Covach, "The Hippie Aesthetic."
27 Shenk and Silberman, *Skeleton Key*, 220.
28 See, for instance, Boone, "Mirror Shatters."
29 After Pigpen's death in 1972, many of his songs left the band's active repertoire for several years, although over time many of them would re-emerge, usually sung by rhythm guitarist Bob Weir. Based on my experience and my discussions with Deadheads, I would argue that even when revived, the Pigpen songs were so-to-speak canonized as Pigpen's own, and thus were

understood in large part as evocations of and homages to Pigpen's work: David Malvinni writes that, for example, the song "In the Midnight Hour" "for the later Dead seems to have functioned as a nostalgic glance back at the 1960s" (Malvinni, *Grateful Dead*, 47). Be that as it may, the Grateful Dead's improvising practice, on the Pigpen songs as on their other material, changed greatly over time; here, I will be discussing the material in the Pigpen era only.

30 This is a general rule, and, as such, subject to exceptions, such as the version of "In the Midnight Hour" performed on September 3, 1967, at the Dance Hall in Rio Nido and later released on the two-disc compilation *Fallout from the Phil Zone* (1997, Grateful Dead Records). This version of "In the Midnight Hour" is one of the longest that the band ever performed, and its jamming goes very far "out" indeed. But this was an exceptional performance—Pigpen songs from shows preceding or following it (e.g., versions of "Turn On Your Lovelight" from the O'Keefe Centre the month before (August 4, 1967) or the Winterland Arena the month after this show (October 22, 1967) are much more controlled and conform more to the structure that I am discussing in this book.

31 Released in 2009 as *Road Trips Volume 2.2* on the Grateful Dead label.

32 Lesh, *Searching for the Sound*, 122.

33 Getz, *Deadhead's Taping Compendium*, 151.

34 Dahl, *All Music Guide to the Blues*, 283.

35 Junior Wells's *Hoodoo Man Blues* is available here: https://archive.org/details/cd_hoodoo-man-blues_junior-wells-chicago-blues-band-buddy-guy/disc1/03.+Junior+Wells'+Chicago+Blues+Band%3B+Buddy+Guy+-+Good+Morning+Schoolgirl.flac.

36 Ripani, *New Blue Music*, 53.

37 Wilson Pickett, *The Exciting Wilson Pickett* (Atlantic, 1966); Bowman, *Soulsville USA*, 61–62.

38 Malvinni, *Grateful Dead*, 47.

39 Available on *Turn On Your Love Light: The Duke Recordings, Vol. 2* (MCA, 1994).

40 Albert Ayler, *Spiritual Unity* (ESP-Disk, 1965).

41 "Dark Star," "The Other One," "Playing in the Band."

42 Jackson, *Going Down the Road*, 157.

43 "Watch: Bob Weir Talks His Musical Role in the Grateful Dead," *Relix*, August 10, 2015, https://relix.com/blogs/detail/watch_bob_weir_talks_his _musical_role_in_the_grateful_dead/.

44 Lesh, *Searching for the Sound*, 46.

45 "Scarlet Begonias," Hunter/Garcia, Ice Nine.

46 John Cale: Bockris and Malanga, *Up-Tight*, 30. Pink Floyd: Palacios, *Lost in the Woods*, 101–2.

47 George-Warren, *Garcia*, 87. See especially Lesh, *Searching for the Sound*, 63–76, for his discussion, and interpretation, of the Acid Tests.

48 The Beatles, *The White Album* (Apple Records, 1968).

49 Gleason, *Jefferson Airplane*, 318.

50 Pink Floyd, *Tonite Let's All Make Love in London . . . Plus* (For Miles Records, 1990).

51 John Coltrane, *A Love Supreme* (Impulse!, 1965).

52 John Coltrane, *Giant Steps* (Atlantic, 1960). I admit to a preference for the *Olé* album, but I am aware that I am in the minority here.

53 Jackson, *Garcia*, 142.

54 Jost, *Free Jazz*, 133–62.

55 McStravick and Roos, *Blues-Rock Explosion*, 23.

56 Hjort, *Strange Brew*, 37; Kaukonen quoted in Gleason, *Jefferson Airplane*, 111.

57 Jackson, *Garcia*, 107.

58 Brackett, "Improvisation and Value in Rock," 207.

59 Prown and Newquist, *Legends of Rock Guitar*, 38; for testimonies to the impact that Bloomfield had on the San Francisco scene, see also Wolkin and Keenom, *Michael Bloomfield*, 119–31.

60 Wolkin and Keenom, *Michael Bloomfield*, 116.

61 Wolkin and Keenom, *Michael Bloomfield*, 116.

62 Lesh, *Searching for the Sound*, 142.

63 Malvinni, *Grateful Dead*, 55.

64 Even though complete versions of "That's It for the Other One" and "Weather Report Suite" were rarely performed, it is still possible to establish what the complete versions consisted of. "Terrapin Station," by contrast, exists in a variety of forms, and it seems as though no complete version exists. The version found on the Grateful Dead's *Terrapin Station* album has seven sections, but to the best of my knowledge the Grateful Dead never performed all of these sections live. Robert Hunter, the band's lyricist, continued composing sections even after the recording, and himself recorded a version of the song with several extra sections on his *Jack O' Roses* album (Dark Star Records, 1980).

65 Garcia, Reich, and Wenner, *Garcia*, 100.

66 The best sources for overviews and discussion of these modules, often referred to as jams, are found in Polits, "Grateful Jams"; and Kennedy, "Early Thematic Jams."

67 Constanten, *Between Rock and Hard Places*, 79.

68 Jackson, *Going Down the Road*, 182.

69 Polits, "Grateful Jams," 60.

70 By 1972, "Playing in the Band" was emerging as another vehicle for the group's most far-ranging explorations, and it took over this role fully by the mid-1970s, when "Dark Star" was dropped from the repertoire. "The Other One" was also often used for this purpose, as was "Caution (Do Not Stop on Tracks)."

71 For the most thorough example of this, see Malvinni, *Grateful Dead*. See also Boone, "Mirror Shatters."

72 Dodd, *Complete Annotated Grateful Dead Lyrics*, 51.

73 For an in-depth discussion of "Dark Star" with transcription, see Boone, "Mirror Shatters."

74 The band's use of newer and more powerful gear is important in this context as well; see Jackson, *Grateful Dead Gear*, 54–66.

75 Terry Riley, quoted in Bernstein, *Tape Music*, 221.

76 Bernstein, *Tape Music*, 246; Lesh, *Searching for the Sound*, 33–38.

77 See discussion and extensive interview with Hart on the subject in Lavezzoli, *Dawn of Indian Music*, chapter 5.

78 See Kennedy, "Velvets and the Dead."

79 Fink, *Repeating Ourselves*, 20.

80 Backstrom, "Grateful Dead and Their World," 46.

81 Gans, *Conversations with The Dead*, 313.

82 Lundborg, *Psychedelia*, 121.

CHAPTER 5. WRITING ABOUT IMPROVISATION

Epigraph: Ekkehard Jost, *Free Jazz* (New York: Da Capo, 1994), 13.

1 Nettl, "Thoughts on Improvisation," 4.

2 Nettl, "Thoughts on Improvisation," 11.

3 Widdess, "Schemas and Improvisation in Indian Music," 200.

4 Bailey, *Improvisation*, x.

5 Tilley, *Making It Up Together*, 50.

6 Nettl, "Thoughts on Improvisation," 13.

7 Tilley, *Making It Up Together*, 143.

8 Slawek, "Keeping It Going," 336.

9 Blum, "Recognizing Improvisation," 27.

10 Racy, "Why Do They Improvise?," 316; Titon, *Worlds of Music*, 11.

11 Heffley, *Northern Sun and Southern Moon*, 284–85.

12 Bailey, *Improvisation*, xi–ii. It seems to me that Heffley's middle category could apply to either of Bailey's bipartite division, depending on what the performer intends by their invocation of one genre in the context of another.

13 See discussion at "The Dead's First Songs," Grateful Dead Guide, November 27, 2020, http://deadessays.blogspot.com/2020/11/the-deads-first-songs.html.

14 Nettl, "Thoughts on Improvisation."

15 Qureshi, *Sufi Music of India and Pakistan*, xiii.

16 Qureshi, *Sufi Music India and Pakistan*, 164.

17 Borgo, *Sync, or Swarm*, 191.

18 Tilley, *Making It Up Together*, 3–4.

19 Paul Berliner, *Thinking in Jazz*, 15.

20 Crook, *Ready, Aim, Improvise*, 17.

21 Jost, *Free Jazz*, 10.

22 Jost, *Free Jazz*, 154, 158.

23 Jost, *Free Jazz*, 120.

24 Boone, "Mirror Shatters."

25 Boone, "Mirror Shatters," 202–3.

26 Freeman, "Other People Play the Music."

27 Freeman, "Other People Play the Music," 105.

28 Tuedio and Spector, *Grateful Dead in Concert*, 11.

29 Tuedio and Spector, *Grateful Dead in Concert*, 13.

30 Gans, *Conversations with the Dead*, 17.

31 See the full and fascinating discussion in "The Dead's Early Thematic Jams," Grateful Dead Guide, January 8, 2010, http://deadessays.blogspot.com/2010 /01/deads-early-thematic-jams.html.

32 Malvinni, *Grateful Dead*, 13.

33 *Modal* can mean a lot of different things, but generally speaking it refers to compositional or improvisational approaches that do not emphasize harmony or chord changes; rather, they focus on the exploration of a particular set of notes (a mode) and whatever typical melodies or cadences might be associated with it. Malvinni, *Grateful Dead*, 202.

34 Malvinni, *Grateful Dead*, 138.

35 Malvinni, *Grateful Dead*, 137, 142.

36 Malvinni, *Grateful Dead*, 15.

37 Malvinni, *Grateful Dead*, 139.

CHAPTER 6. OTHER IMPROVISING ROCK BANDS

Epigraph: Bruno Nettl, "Preface." In Gabriel Solis and Bruno Nettl, eds., *Musical Improvisation: Art, Education, and Society.* (Urbana: University of Illinois Press, 2009), xii.

1 Cream, too, were based in London, but they were not so clearly identified with that scene, and particularly the UFO Club, its heart, as were Pink Floyd. From their beginnings, Cream were presented and understood as a "supergroup," an entity unto itself, not a representative of a local scene. Dave Thompson notes that "Cream (or their management) not only distanced themselves from the nuts and bolts of the psychedelic movement, they did so with a deliberation that bordered upon arrogance. It wasn't only the Happenings that they steered clear of. Almost alone of the major bands of the day [in London], Cream never played UFO or the now-swinging Middle Earth, the pulsing heart of British psychedelia" (Thompson, *Cream*, 173). Furthermore, their real development as an improvising band seems to have taken place during their stay in San Francisco in late August and September of 1967. Thompson, *Cream*, 188–92; Welch, *Legendary British Supergroup*, 114–18.

2 Tamarkin, *Got a Revolution*, 24–25.

3 Such a relationship between bands working in the same scene is not at all uncommon; we see it, for example ,with the Sex Pistols and the Clash in England in 1976–77, with the Replacements and Soul Asylum in Minneapolis

in the early to mid-1980s, or with the Lowest of the Low and Dig Circus in Toronto in the early 1990s.

4   Gans, *Conversations with the Dead*, 12; McNally, *Long Strange Trip*, 160, 500; Lesh, *Searching for the Sound*, 22–26.

5   Tamarkin, *Got a Revolution*, 20.

6   Gleason, *Jefferson Airplane*, 203.

7   Lesh, *Searching for the Sound*, 51.

8   Jefferson Airplane, *Bless Its Pointed Little Head* (RCA, 1968). You can hear the full album, here: YouTube video, 1:05:23, March 13, 2021, https://www .youtube.com/watch?v=lgX8kaX1s5c.

9   *1966 Jefferson Airplane Early and Late Shows* (Collector's Choice, 2010).

10   Gleason, *Jefferson Airplane*, 205.

11   Brightman, *Sweet Chaos*, 137.

12   You can hear a live recording of the Grateful Dead from October 1968 here: https://archive.org/details/gd1968-10-30.116833.sbd.moore-berger.flac2496.

13   Jefferson Airplane, *After Bathing at Baxters* (RCA, 1967).

14   The first fifteen minutes can be heard, however: see "Jefferson Airplane— *Spare Chaynge* (Baxter's Rehearsals 1967)," YouTube video, 24:20, June 19, 2013, https://www.youtube.com/watch?v=dQBfP5VLGTE.

15   McNally, *Long Strange Trip*, 578.

16   "Jefferson Airplane—We Can Be Together," YouTube video, 5:50, April 17, 2008, https://www.youtube.com/watch?v=cxA3Q96a8XE.

17   For a detailed discussion of the interactions between the two bands, see Caleb Kennedy, Grateful Dead Guide, September 7, 2020, http://deadessays .blogspot.com/search?q=velvets+and+dead.

18   Bockris and Malanga, *Up-Tight*, 66.

19   Or, more precisely, liminoid. As Turner put it in his "Variations on a Theme of Liminality," "Liminal phenomena are centrally integrated into the total social process, forming with all its other aspects a complete whole. . . . On the other hand, liminoid phenomena develop most characteristically outside the central economic and political process, along their margins, on their interfaces, in their 'tacit dimensions' (though, later, liminoid ideas and images may seep from these peripheries and cornices into the centre)." Turner, "Variations on a Theme," 44.

20   See Cale and Bockris, *What's Welsh for Zen*, 81–87, for details of their integration into the ongoing artistic life of Warhol's Factory.

21   Bockris and Malanga, *Up-Tight*, 148.

22   Bockris and Malanga, *Up-Tight*, 81.

23   Cale and Bockris, *What's Welsh for Zen*, 50–58; Witts, *Velvet Underground*, 28.

24   Zak, *Velvet Underground Companion*, 139.

25   Velvet Underground, *Velvet Underground and Nico* (Verve, 1967); *White Light/White Heat* (Verve, 1968); *Bootleg Series, Vol. 1: The Quine Tapes*, recorded 1969 (Polydor/Universal 314 589 067–2, 2001, compact disc).

26   Brackett, "Improvisation and Value in Rock," 212 (italics mine).

27 For a contemporary description of the band's early performances, see the article "Andy Warhol's EXPLODING PLASTIC INEVITABLE with the Velvet Underground at Poor Richard's" by Larry McCombs from the *Boston Broadside* of July 1966, reprinted in Heylin, *All Yesterday's Parties*, 24–27.

28 See, for instance, Torgoff, *Can't Find My Way Home*, chapter 5.

29 Torgoff, *Can't Find My Way Home*, 166.

30 Bockris and Malanga, *Up-Tight*, 24–25.

31 Zak, *Velvet Underground Companion*, 165.

32 Velvet Underground, *Bootleg Series*, disc 2.

33 Zak, *Velvet Underground Companion*, 154.

34 Zak, *Velvet Underground Companion*, 169.

35 Heylin, *All Yesterday's Parties*, 71.

36 Adelt, *Krautrock*, 50.

37 Morris, quoted in Heylin, *All Yesterday's Parties*, 169.

38 McGuire, quoted in Heylin, *All Yesterday's Parties*, 72.

39 M. C. Kostek in *What Goes On* (zine) 1, recounting a performance from March 1969; quoted in Bockris and Malanga, *Up-Tight*, 178.

40 Heylin, *All Yesterday's Parties*, 71.

41 "The Nothing Song": This can be heard on the bootleg *If It's Too Loud for You, Move Back!*, released by Nothing Songs Limited, recorded in Columbus, Ohio, November 4 1966. "The Ocean": as heard on *1969 Live* (Polygram, 1988, compact disc). Witts identifies the nonresolving chord progressions that the Velvet Underground used as adaptations for a rock context of La Monte Young's use of static harmonic fields to stop the perceived passage of time. Witts, *Velvet Underground*, 80.

42 Johann Jon Savage, quoted in Kugelberg, *Velvet Underground*, 168.

43 Welch, *Legendary British Supergroup*, 24.

44 Headlam, "Blues Transformations," 69; Headlam's article is highly recommended as a discussion of the way that Cream adapted blues structures to rock contexts.

45 Cream, *Live at the Grande Ballroom 1967* (bootleg).

46 Bruce's style in this period, in fact, has been aptly described as involving "relentless forward motion and creative use of the blues scale." Welch, *Legendary British Supergroup*, 52.

47 A good description of the scene can be found in Norman, *Stones*, 49–84.

48 Norman, *Stones*, 63.

49 Clayson, *Yardbirds*, 76.

50 Mason, *Inside Out*, 31.

51 Mason, *Inside Out*, 31.

52 Mason, *Inside Out*, 40.

53 Palacios, *Lost in the Woods*, 47, 68, 71–72.

54 Palacios, *Lost in the Woods*, 45.

55 Palacios, *Lost in the Woods*, 78.

56 Pink Floyd, *Tonite Let's All Make Love in London* (Instant, 1968). You can listen here: "Pink Floyd *Tonite Let's All Make Love in London* FULL ALBUM

[HD]," YouTube Video, 29:00, June 26, 2012, https://www.youtube.com/watch?v=-NN7qJ7xUgU.

57 The full history of space rock has yet to be written, but see Thompson, *Space Daze.*

58 Mason, *Inside Out*, 40.

59 Schaffner, *Saucerful of Secrets*, 49–50.

60 Thompson, *Cream*, 175

61 Clayson, *Beat Merchants*, 257.

62 Although, to be fair, by 1967 even the Monkees were incorporating some degree of improvised jamming into their live performances. Baker writes that "throughout the two month jaunt the Monkees immersed themselves in a feast of real live musicianship, both on and off stage. Extended jams were a regular occurrence, featuring all four Monkees [and] the Jimi Hendrix Experience (whilst on the tour)." Baker, *Monkeemania*, 73.

63 Palacios, *Lost in the Woods*, 103.

64 Cale and Bockris, *What's Welsh for Zen*, 113.

65 Gans, *Conversations with the Dead*, 312.

66 Troy, *One More Saturday Night*, 116.

67 Hill, *San Francisco and the Long 60s*, 326.

68 There are some extremely radical approaches to improvised music in which by definition there is no such thing as a mistake: the music is what happens, full stop. But, for most improvisers, it is quite possible to play wrong notes or to play notes wrongly. The fact that there is an unpredictable variety of acceptable musical choices at any given moment does not mean that any musical choices are acceptable, and neither does it rule out the possibility of technical errors in execution. As we have discussed, improvisational traditions grow out of musical contexts that have built-in rules and understandings.

69 Torgoff, *Can't Find My Way Home*, 140.

CHAPTER 7. MUSIC AND TRANSCENDENT EXPERIENCE

Epigraph: "Brokedown Palace," lyrics by Robert Hunter and musical arrangement by Jerry Garcia, from *American Beauty* (Universal Music Publishing Group, 1970).

1 Eric Dolphy, *Last Date* (Fontana, 1965).

2 Plato, *Republic*, 24c; Bonds, *Absolute Music*, 8.

3 See Stephens, *Devil's Music.*

4 "But even more problematic for rock 'n' roll's many white religious despisers ... was the intermingling of black and white performers. ... Often lurking behind the rock 'n' roll panic were deep fears of racial contamination and religious impurity" (Stephens, *Devil's Music*, 16).

5 Bonds, *Absolute Music*; Berendt, *World Is Sound*; Godwin, *Music, Mysticism, and Magic*; Turino, *Music as Social Life*; Kapchan, *Traveling Spirit Masters*; Mathieu, *Bridge of Waves*.

6   Speaking specifically of popular music, see, e.g., Partridge and Moberg, *Bloomsbury Handbook of Religion and Popular Music*; or the overview in Coggins, *Mysticism, Ritual, and Religion,* chapter 2.

7   See discussion of the quote's origins at Quote Investigator: https://quoteinvestigator.com/2010/11/08/writing-about-music/ (accessed February 10, 2023).

8   David Fideler notes that music was "of paramount importance" for the Pythagoreans because it represented the sensory manifestation of the fundamental numeric principles that underlie existence—"Introduction," 28.

9   See, for example, Khan, *Mysticism of Sound and Music.*

10 In *Absolute Music*, Bonds discusses this in terms of nineteenth-century battles over the nature and importance of music; such a viewpoint could, I believe, be extended to such later movements as serialism, in which a separate and abstract aesthetic sphere is created for music, one intended to be beyond the reach of history and personality.

11 Coggins, *Mysticism, Ritual, and Religion,* 50.

12 Rouget, *Music and Trance.*

13 Getz and Dwork, *Deadhead's Taping Compendium,* 409.

14 Shenk and Silberman, *Skeleton Key,* 336–37.

15 Racy, *Making Music,* 124.

16 Racy, *Making Music,* 126, 128.

17 Jarnow, *Heads.*

18 See Weiner, *Perspectives on the Grateful Dead*; Adams and Sardiello, *Deadhead Social Science*; Belleville, "Taoist Perspective in Weather Report"; Sylvan, *Traces of the Spirit*; and Seay and Neely, "Prophets on the Burning Shore" (which references a line from a Grateful Dead song).

19 For instance, Spector, "Who Is Dionysus."

20 For instance, Sardiello, "Studying Deadhead Subculture."

21 Hartley, "'We Were Given This Dance,'" 131.

22 Gans, *Conversations with The Dead,* 196.

23 Gans, *Conversations with The Dead,* 251.

24 Hibbert, "Last Great American Adventurer."

25 Gans, *Conversations with the Dead,* 242.

26 Quoted in Gans and Simon, *Playing in the Band,* 47.

27 Jackson, *Garcia,* 191.

28 Hart, *Drumming on the Edge,* 228–30.

29 Gans, *Conversations with the Dead,* 52.

30 McNally, *Long Strange Trip,* 619.

31 Dodd and Spaulding, *Grateful Dead Reader,* 133.

32 Gans, *Conversations with the Dead,* 251.

33 Gans and Simon, *Playing in the Band,* 61.

34 Lesh, *Searching for the Sound,* 69.

35 Garcia, Reich, and Wenner, *Garcia,* 100.

36 Dodd and Spaulding, *Grateful Dead Reader,* 73.

37 Brightman, *Sweet Chaos*, 133.

38 Lesh, *Searching for the Sound*, 333.

39 Gans, *Conversations with the Dead*, 164.

40 Brightman, *Sweet Chaos*, 157.

41 Gans and Simon, *Playing in the Band*, p. 18.

42 Gans, *Conversations with the Dead*, 214, italics in original.

43 Brightman, *Sweet Chaos*, 8.

44 Garcia, Reich and Wenner, *Garcia*, 98–99.

45 Gans, *Conversations with the Dead*, 215.

46 Kripal, *Comparing Religions*, 94.

47 Berger, *Sacred Canopy*.

48 Hence the modern popularity of referring to oneself as "spiritual but not religious."

49 Schmidt, *Restless Souls*.

50 Spirituality and baby boomers: see Roof, *Spiritual Marketplace*; Wuthnow, *After Heaven*; and, particularly, Wilke and Moebus, *Sound and Communication*, 820–1041. Rise of spirituality: see Roof, *Spiritual Marketplace*, 46–76; Fuller, *Spiritual but Not Religious*.

51 Roof, *Generation of Seekers*, 79.

52 Roof, *Spiritual Marketplace*, 81–82.

53 King, "Spirituality," 345.

54 Roof, *Generation of Seekers*, 31.

55 Roof's point here is generally valid, but needs to be nuanced, as there are social organizations—such as Sufi lodges—whose raison d'être is the production of mystical experiences. However, such organizations often do subordinate (at least in theory) the organization to the experience whose production is the organization's goal.

56 Roof, *Generation of Seekers*, 39.

57 Wuthnow speaks of space and dwelling as images: dwelling-style spirituality need not be associated with a specific place, and when it is, that place need not be a dwelling.

58 Wuthnow, *After Heaven*, 5.

59 See Bryan, "Grateful Dead Religious Experience."

60 See the papers gathered in Meriwether, "Experiencing Community through Grateful Dead Improvisation," in *Reading the Grateful Dead*, section 3.

61 As described in Stark and Bainbridge, *Future of Religion*, 48–49; and as brought out with regard to the Grateful Dead in Adams and Sardiello, *Deadhead Social Science*.

62 See Shenk and Silberman, *Skeleton Key*, 336–37.

63 See Gimbel, "Other One and the Other."

64 For an exhaustive discussion of these events in the first decade of the band's career, see Getz and Dwork, *Deadhead's Taping Compendium*; and Tuedio and Spector, *Grateful Dead in Concert*.

65 Barlow, "Foreword," xxv.

66 See, especially, Harrison, *Dead*, 248–54. Note that the use of *gnostic* here is nontechnical, and not intended as a specific reference to early Christian gnosticism.

67 Campbell, "Cultic Milieu and Secularization."

68 Campbell, "Cultic Milieu and Secularization," 122.

69 Balch and Taylor, "Seekers and Saucers," 849–51.

70 See "The Parking Lot Scene" in Shenk and Silberman, *Skeleton Key*, 215–16. See also see Adams and Sardiello, *Deadhead Social Science*; and the essays gathered in Meriwether, *Reading the Grateful Dead*, part 3. Jesse Jarnow's book *Heads* explores in great detail the cultic milieu that grew up around the Grateful Dead.

71 Taves, *Religious Experience Reconsidered*, 10.

72 Taves, "Explanation: Attributing Causality," in *Religious Experience Reconsidered*, chap. 3.

73 Lundborg, *Psychedelia*, 359; see also his discussion of a phenomenological approach to the study of psychedelia, 16–28.

74 Segal, "Religious Experience."

75 Beal, *Roadside Religion*.

76 Beal, *Roadside Religion*, 7–10.

77 Sylvan, *Traces of the Spirit*, 97.

78 Hartley, "We Were Given This Dance."

79 Sylvan, *Traces of the Spirit*, 99.

80 Katz, *Mysticism and Philosophical Analysis*. See also Proudfoot, *Religious Experience*; Barnard, *Exploring Unseen Worlds*; Yamane, "Narrative and Religious Experience."

81 See Newberg, *Principles of Neurotheology*.

82 For a fascinating and very readable example, see Taylor, *My Stroke of Insight*.

83 Waugh, "Dispatches from Memory," 251–52.

84 Blum, "Retrieving Phenomenology of Religion," 1027.

85 An early, sustained argument to this effect can be found in Zaehner, *Mysticism Sacred and Profane*; for a rebuttal, see Walsh, "Chemical and Contemplative Ecstasy."

86 See, for example, Devereux, *Long Trip*; Smith, *Cleansing the Doors of Perception*.

87 Smith, *Cleansing the Doors of Perception*, 31.

88 See Horowitz and Palmer, *Moksha*; Merkur, "Visionary Practices of the Jewish Apocalypticists."

89 Kripal, "Traumatic Secret," 155.

90 Hayes, *Tripping*.

91 Laski, *Ecstasy in Secular and Religious Experiences*, 41 ff.

92 Hartogsohn, *American Trip*, 7.

93 Hartogsohn, *American Trip*, 11.

94 Hartogsohn, *American Trip*, 12.

Epigraph: Jerry Garcia, quoted in Garcia, Reich, and Wenner, *Garcia: A Signpost*, 20–21.

Some of the material in "The Acid Tests" section of this chapter has been adapted from my earlier article, "Music and the Divine: The Acid Tests as Foundation Stories," *Studies in Religion/Sciences Religieuses* 45 (2014): 3–15.

1 See Kelly, "Why We Left the Farm."

2 See the discussion in Stephens, *Devil's Music*, chapter 4.

3 For a good summary of Stephen Gaskin's life and practices, see Morley, "Tripping with Stephen Gaskin."

4 In what follows, to present Gaskin's point of view, I draw from *The Caravan*, a collection of his speeches and discussions while on this journey, which have the advantage in our present context of having been delivered to outsiders to justify and explain Gaskin's views.

5 Gaskin, *Caravan*, 166 (interview with author in Washington, DC, Dec. 27, 1970).

6 Gaskin, *Caravan*, 99 (interview with author in Dayton, Ohio, Nov. 17, 1970).

7 Gaskin, *Caravan*, 128 (interview with author in Long Island, New York, Dec. 8, 1970).

8 Gaskin, *Caravan*, 208 (interview with author in Nashville, Tennessee, Jan. 7, 1971).

9 Gaskin, *Caravan*, 179 (interview with author in Washington, DC, Dec. 27, 1970).

10 Merkur, "Formation of Hippie Spirituality 1," 214.

11 Merkur, "Formation of Hippie Spirituality 2," 285–86.

12 *Blesh*, a neologism combining "blend" and "mesh," was created by science fiction author Theodore Sturgeon to describe the workings of a group mind. Sturgeon, *More Than Human*.

13 Merkur, "Formation of Hippie Spirituality 2," 240.

14 From an interview with Ken Kesey by Frank Fey, January 8, 1966, on *Grateful Dead and the Merry Pranksters: The Acid Tests Reel* (bootleg CD).

15 Gaskin, *Caravan*, 26–27.

16 Gans, *Conversations with the Dead*, 202, 206.

17 Gans, *Conversations with the Dead*, 212.

18 Garcia, Reich, and Wenner, *Garcia*, 94.

19 Hill, *San Francisco and the Long 60s*, 35.

20 Paden, *Religious Worlds*.

21 See, for example, Denzey Lewis, *Introduction to "Gnosticism,"* chap. 17.

22 Lewis and Olav, *Invention of Sacred Tradition*, 4.

23 Paden, *Religious Worlds*, 76–78.

24 Barthes, "Grain of the Voice," 142.

25 Rothstein, "Scripture and Sacred Tradition," 29.

26 Although Tom Constanten, who joined the group later, was a Scientologist at the time, he notes that this made his involvement with the Grateful Dead

challenging: "My involvement with Scientology didn't help any." Constanten, quoted in Gans and Simon, *Playing in the Band*, 135.

27   Turner, *Hungry for Heaven*, 49.

28   Benson, *Why the Grateful Dead Matter*, 66.

29   Gans, *Conversations with the Dead*, 307.

30   Gans, *Conversations with the Dead*, 311.

31   For details, see Meriwether's excellent description of the Acid Test on October 2, 1966, in "1/8/66: The Fillmore Acid Test."

32   Perry and Babbs, *On the Bus*, 148–49.

33   Greenfield, *Dark Star*, 73.

34   Turner, *Ritual Process*; Farber, "Intoxicated State/Illegal Nation," 26.

35   Jackson, *Garcia*, 92.

36   Gans, *Conversations with the Dead*, 78–79; Lesh, *Searching for the Sound*, 66–70, 69.

37   Lesh, *Searching for the Sound*, 63–76, 76.

38   Wolfe, *Electric Kool-Aid Acid Test*, 113.

39   Plummer, *Holy Goof*, 124, 126–27.

40   Whitmer, *Aquarius Revisited*, 204.

41   Rocco, *Dead Reckonings*, 126.

42   Wach, *Sociology of Religion*.

43   Plummer, *Holy Goof*, 140, 141.

44   Getz and Dwork, *Deadhead's Taping Compendium*, 90.

45   Bromley and Cowan, "Invention of a Counter-Tradition," 97.

46   MacFarlane, *Hippie Narrative*, 108.

47   Stevens, *Storming Heaven*, 325.

48   The benefit for the Springfield Creamery in Springfield, Oregon, took place on August 17, 1972. The show was filmed and made into a movie, *Sunshine Daydream*, that remained unreleased until 2013.

49   Olsson, *Listening for the Secret*, 131.

50   Lewis and Hammer, *Invention of Sacred Tradition*, 56–57.

51   Matthew 3:13–4:17; Mark 1:1–1:11; Luke 3:1–3:22; the point is made especially clearly in John 3:25–30.

52   Hjelm, "Tradition as Legitimation," 116.

53   Hjelm, "Tradition as Legitimation," 117.

54   Hjelm, "Tradition as Legitimation," 118, 117.

55   McNally, *Long Strange Trip*, 112.

56   Garcia, Reich, and Wenner, *Garcia*, 17–20.

57   Garcia, Reich, and Wenner, *Garcia*, 21.

58   Jackson, *Garcia*, 86 (emphasis mine).

59   Gans, *Conversations with the Dead*, 78.

60   McNally, *Long Strange Trip*, 168.

61   Gans, *Conversations with the Dead*, 307, 312.

62   Gans, *Conversations with the Dead*, 206.

63   Selvin, *Summer of Love*, 40.

Some of the material in this chapter has been adapted from an earlier article, "Searching for the (Sacred) Sound: Phil Lesh, the Grateful Dead, and Religion," *Journal of Religion and Popular Culture* 23 (2011): 139–54.

Epigraph: Christopher Hill, *Into the Mystic* (Rochester, NY: Park Street, 2017), 136.

1   Hart, *Drumming on the Edge*, 229.
2   Brightman, *Sweet Chaos*, 133.
3   Hart, *Drumming on the Edge*, 230.
4   See, for instance, Hutton, *Shamans*, 85–98.
5   Hutton, *Shamans*, 114–49.
6   Gans, *Conversations with the Dead*, 66.
7   Gans, *Conversations with the Dead*, 66.
8   Gans, *Conversations with The Dead*, 214.
9   McNally, *Long Strange Trip*, 174.
10 Gans, *Conversations with the Dead*, 214.
11 Barlow, quoted in Gimbel, "Other One," 192–93.
12 Barlow would later go on to describe dogma as "the most toxic aspect of religion." Barlow, "Foreword," xxv.
13 McNally, *Long Strange Trip*, 200.
14 Brightman, *Sweet Chaos*, 8.
15 See Lavezzoli, *Dawn of Indian Music*, chapter 5; or Hart's account of his introduction to Indian music in Hart, *Drumming on the Edge*, 141–43.
16 Lesh, *Searching for the Sound*, 15, 16.
17 Lesh, *Searching for the Sound*, 36.
18 Perhaps an inspiration for the title of the song "Unbroken Chain"?
19 Lesh, *Searching for the Sound*, 68.
20 Lesh, *Searching for the Sound*, 69.
21 Cioco, "Dead Beats Became Dead Heads."
22 Lesh, *Searching for the Sound*, 79.
23 Lesh, *Searching for the Sound*, 74.
24 Lesh, *Searching for the Sound*, 59.
25 George-Warren, *Garcia*, 61.
26 Hart, *Drumming on the Edge*, 230.
27 Dodd, *Complete Annotated Grateful Dead Lyrics*, 131.
28 Olsson, *Listening for the Secret*, 68.
29 Garcia, Reich, and Wenner, *Garcia*, 65.
30 George-Warren, *Garcia*, 127.
31 See Turner, *Ritual Process*.
32 Glock and Stark, *Religion and Society in Tension*, chap. 3.
33 Glock and Stark, *Religion and Society in Tension*, 41.
34 Glock and Stark, *Religion and Society in Tension*, 43.
35 For example, when the 10/4 introductory riff of "Playing in the Band" comes back in the middle of the song, the jamming that followed it could

be stretched out almost infinitely, even to the point of encompassing other entire songs before returning to "Playing." The same holds true of the 7/4 Dm–based riff in "Uncle John's Band." The two songs were in fact merged through jamming on these riffs at the Cow Palace in Daly City on March 23, 1974, where the band began with "Playing in the Band," used its introductory riff as a tool to jam into "Uncle John's Band," and then used that song's Dm riff to jam into "Morning Dew," which they then played. Having finished it, they jammed back into the Dm riff and completed "Uncle John's Band," and then made their way back into the 10/4 introductory riff to "Playing in the Band," and completed that song as well.

36   Dodd, *Complete Annotated Grateful Dead Lyrics*, 249.

37   Garcia, Reich, and Wenner, *Garcia*, 101.

38   Jackson, *Garcia*, 94.

39   Troy, *One More Saturday Night*, 116.

40   Brightman, *Sweet Chaos*, 157.

41   Weber, *Theory of Social and Economic Organization*; Wach, *Sociology of Religion*.

42   Kelly, *Hippie Commie Beatnik Witches*, 123.

43   Kelly, *Hippie Commie Beatnik Witches*, 128.

44   Lewis, *Legitimating New Religions*, 31.

45   Lewis, *Legitimating New Religions*, 25.

46   Lewis, *Legitimating New Religions*, 41.

47   Weber, "The Nature of Charismatic Authority and Its Routinization," chap. 4 in *Theory of Social and Economic Organization*.

48   Garcia, Reich, and Wenner, *Garcia*, 102.

49   Gans, *Conversations with the Dead*, 214.

50   Garcia, Reich, and Wenner, *Garcia*, 100.

51   Lesh, *Searching for the Sound*, 260.

52   McNally, *Long Strange Trip*, 131–32 (italics mine).

53   Gans, *Conversations with the Dead*, 199 (italics mine).

54   Hollenback, *Mysticism*, 298–300.

55   Kripal, *Comparing Religions*, 260.

56   Robert Hunter and Jerry Garcia, "US Blues" (1974), in Dodd, *Complete Annotated Grateful Dead Lyrics*, 218.

57   Albanese, *Republic of Mind and Spirit*, 13–15.

58   Chidester, *Authentic Fakes*, 9.

59   Chidester, *Authentic Fakes*, vii.

60   Sloterdijk, *You Must Change Your Life*; Davis, *High Weirdness*, 35.

61   Hartogsohn, *American Trip*.

62   Tarab and saltanah: Racy, *Making Music*; qawwali: Qureshi, *Sufi Music*; raga: Lavezzoli, *Dawn of Indian Music*, chapter 2; gospel: See, for example, Murphy, *Working the Spirit*.

63   Murphy, *Working the Spirit*, 149.

64   Racy, *Making Music*, 93.

65 Wilke and Moebus, *Sound and Communication*, 873–74.

66 Wilke and Moebus, *Sound and Communication*, 878.

67 See Kaler, "Making Magic with Music."

68 Belgrad, *Culture of Spontaneity*.

69 See, for example, Bellman, "Indian Resonances"; Weinstein, *Night in Tunisia*; and Lavezzoli, *Dawn of Indian Music*.

70 Berkman, *Monument Eternal*, 53.

71 "As [the Sun Ra] Arkestra's reputation spread, they became vaguely identified somewhere between the new rock and roll and free jazz of New York." Szwed, *Space Is the Place*, 240; see also 243–46.

72 In this section, I will be discussing the effects of LSD, but not the chemistry of the drug or its precise physiological functioning, subjects on which I am not competent to speak. For details in this regard and extensive references, see Perrine, *Chemistry of Mind-Altering Drugs*; Nichols and Chemel, "LSD and the Serotonin System."

73 Hentoff, "Truth Is Marching In," 17.

74 Gans, *Conversations with the Dead*, 11.

75 Szwed, *Space Is the Place*, 5.

76 Jung, "Attempting the Impossible."

77 Fiorfori, "Sun Ra's Space Odyssey," 14.

78 Dodd, *Complete Annotated Grateful Dead Lyrics*, 66.

79 John Coltrane, *Meditations* (Impulse!, 1966).

80 DeVito, *Coltrane on Coltrane*, 277.

81 DeVito, *Coltrane on Coltrane*, 263.

82 DeVito, *Coltrane on Coltrane*, 270.

83 Gans, *Conversations with the Dead*, 190.

84 Gans, *Conversations with the Dead*, 53.

85 Gans, *Conversations with the Dead*, 58.

86 Marcus, *In the Fascist Bathroom*, 211; see also Barthes, "Grain of the Voice."

87 Frith, *Sound Effects*, 164–65.

88 Perrine, *Chemistry of Mind-Altering Drugs*, 256.

89 Hill, *Into the Mystic*, 135.

90 Lundborg, *Psychedelia*, 350.

91 See Hartogsohn, *American Trip*; Jarnow, *Heads*.

92 Bromell, *Tomorrow Never Knows*, 62.

93 Wildman and Brothers, "Neurophysiological-Semiotic Model."

94 Fuller, *Stairways to Heaven*, 48.

95 Hicks, *Sixties Rock*, 63–64.

96 Hoffmann, *LSD, My Problem Child*, 17.

97 Watts, *Does It Matter?*, 81.

98 Freedman, "On the Use and Abuse of LSD," 331.

99 Nichols and Chemell, "LSD," 129; Otto, *Idea of the Holy*.

100 Osmond, "Psychotomimetic Agents," 423.

101 Nichols and Chemell, "LSD," 139.

102 Tart, *States of Consciousness*, 123, 153–55.
103 Nichols and Chemell, "LSD," 139.
104 Stevens, *Storming Heaven*, 301; Lee and Shlain, *Acid Dreams*.
105 Lewis, "Neuroscientist Marc Lewis."
106 Perry, *Haight-Ashbury*, 244, 245.
107 Perry, *Haight-Ashbury*, 245.
108 Perry, *Haight-Ashbury*, 256.
109 Perry, *Haight-Ashbury*, 255.
110 Shenk and Silberman, *Skeleton Key*, 256.
111 John Coltrane, *Om* (Impulse!, 1968); Nisenson, *Ascension*, 166, 167.
112 George-Wallen, *Garcia*, 184.
113 Lesh, *Searching for the Sound*, 36.
114 Berger, *Sacred Canopy*.
115 Erhard, *Transformation of a Man*, 108–10, 164–70; see also Demerath, *Sacred Companies*.

Bibliography

Adams, Rebecca, and Robert Sardiello, eds. *Deadhead Social Science: "You Ain't Gonna Learn What You Don't Wanna Know."* Walnut Creek, CA: AltaMira, 2000.

Adelt, Ulrich. *Krautrock: German Music in the Seventies.* Ann Arbor: University of Michigan Press, 2016.

Albanese, Catherine. *A Republic of Mind and Spirit: A Cultural History of American Metaphysical Religion.* New Haven, CT: Yale University Press, 2007.

Allbright, Thomas. *Art in the San Francisco Bay Area, 1945–1080: An Illustrated History.* Berkeley: University of California Press, 2005.

Ayler, Albert. "Untitled." *IT: International Times*, March 13, 1967, 9.

Backstrom, Melvin. "The Grateful Dead and Their World: Popular Music and the Avant-Garde in the San Francisco Bay Area, 1965–75." PhD diss., McGill University, 2017.

Bailey, Derek. *Improvisation: Its Nature and Practice in Music.* New York: Da Capo, 1993.

Baker, Glenn. *Monkeemania: The True Story of the Monkees.* London: Plexus, 1997.

Balch, Robert, and David Taylor. "Seekers and Saucers: The Role of the Cultic Milieu in Joining a UFO Cult." *American Behavioral Scientist* 20 (1977): 839–60.

Bangs, Lester. "Of Pop and Pies and Fun." In *Psychotic Reactions and Carburetor Dung*, edited by Greil Marcus, 31–51. New York: Anchor, 1987.

Barlow, John Perry. "Foreword." In Barry Barnes, *Everything I Know about Business, I Learned from the Grateful Dead*, xvii–xxxii. New York: Hachette, 2011.

Barlow, John Perry, with Robert Greenfield. *Mother American Night: My Life in Crazy Times.* New York: Crown Archetype, 2018.

Barnard, G. William. *Exploring Unseen Worlds: William James and the Philosophy of Mysticism.* Albany: State University of New York Press, 1997.

Barthes, Roland. "The Grain of the Voice." In *Images, Music, Text*, 179–89. Glasgow: Fontana, 1977.

Beal, Timothy. *Roadside Religion: In Search of the Sacred, the Strange, and the Substance of Faith*. Boston: Beacon, 2005.

Belgrad, Daniel. *The Culture of Spontaneity: Improvisation and the Arts in Postwar America*. Chicago: University of Chicago Press, 1998.

Belleville, Melinda. "The Taoist Perspective in Weather Report Suite." *Dead Letters* 3 (2006): 27–34.

Bellman, Jonathan. "Indian Resonances in the British Invasion, 1965–1968." *Journal of Musicology* 15, no. 1 (1995): 116–36.

Bender, Courtney. *The New Metaphysicals: Spirituality and the American Religious Imagination*. Chicago: University of Chicago Press, 2010.

Benson, Michael. *Why the Grateful Dead Matter*. Chicago: ForeEdge, 2016.

Berendt, Joachim-Ernst. *The World Is Sound: Nada Brahma*. Rochester, NY: Destiny, 1991.

Berger, Peter. *The Sacred Canopy: Elements of a Sociological Theory of Religion*. New York: Anchor, 1990.

Berkman, Franya. *Monument Eternal: The Music of Alice Coltrane*. Middletown, CT: Wesleyan University Press, 2010.

Berliner, Paul. *Thinking in Jazz: The Infinite Art of Improvisation*. Chicago: University of Chicago Press, 1999.

Bernstein, David W. *The San Francisco Tape Music Center: 1960s Counterculture and the Avant-Garde*. Berkeley: University of California Press, 2008.

Bivins, Jason. *Spirits Rejoice! Jazz and American Religion*. Oxford: Oxford University Press, 2015.

Bley, Paul. *Stopping Time: Paul Bley and the Transformation of Jazz*. Montreal: Véhicule, 1999.

Blum, Jason. "Retrieving Phenomenology of Religion as a Method for Religious Studies." *Journal of the American Academy of Religion* 80 (2012): 1025–48.

Blum, Stephen. "Recognizing Improvisation." In Nettl and Russell, eds., *In the Course of Performance*, 27–46.

Blush, Steven. *American Hardcore: A Tribal History*. Los Angeles: Feral House, 2001.

Bockris, Victor, and Gerard Malanga. *Up-Tight: The Story of the Velvet Underground*. London: Omnibus, 1983.

Bonds, Mark Evan. *Absolute Music: The History of an Idea*. Oxford: Oxford University Press, 2014.

Boone, Graeme. "Mirror Shatters: Tonal and Expressive Ambiguity in 'Dark Star.'" In Covach and Boone, *Understanding Rock*, 171–210.

Borgo, David. *Sync or Swarm: Improvising Music in a Complex Age*. New York: Continuum, 2005.

Bowman, Rob. *Soulsville USA: The Story of Stax Records*. New York: Schirmer, 1997.

Brackett, David. "Improvisation and Value in Rock, 1966." *Journal of the Society for American Music* 14, no. 2 (2020): 197–232.

Braunstein, Peter. "Forever Young: Insurgent Youth and the Sixties Culture of Rejuvenation." In Braunstein and Doyle, eds., *Imagine Nation*, 1–16.

Braunstein, Peter, and Michael Doyle. *Imagine Nation: American Cultural Radicalism in the 1960s*. New York: Routledge, 2001.

Brightman, Carol. *Sweet Chaos: The Grateful Dead's American Adventure*. New York: Simon and Schuster, 1998.

Bromell, Nick. *Tomorrow Never Knows: Rock and Psychedelics in the 1960s*. Chicago: University of Chicago Press, 2000.

Bromley, David, and Douglas Cowan. "The Invention of a Counter-Tradition: The Case of the North American Anti-Cult Movement." In Lewis and Hammer, *The Invention of Sacred Tradition*, 96–117.

Bryan, David. "The Grateful Dead Religious Experience." In Meriwether, *Reading the Grateful Dead*, 146–62.

Cale, John, and Victor Bockris. *What's Welsh for Zen: The Autobiography of John Cale*. London: Bloomsbury, 1999.

Campbell, Colin. "The Cultic Milieu and Secularization." *Sociological Yearbook of Religion in Britain* 5 (1972): 119–36.

Cardena, Etzel, and Michael Winkelman, eds. *Altering Consciousness: Multidisciplinary Perspectives. Vol. 1: History, Culture and the Humanities*. Santa Barbara, CA: Praeger, 2011.

Cardena, Etzel, and Michael Winkelman, eds. *Altering Consciousness: Multidisciplinary Perspectives. Vol. 2: Biological and Psychological Perspectives*. Santa Barbara, CA: Praeger, 2011.

Chernoff, John Miller. *African Music and African Sensibility: Aesthetics and Social Action in African Musical Idioms*. Chicago: University of Chicago Press, 1979.

Chidester, David. *Authentic Fakes: Religion and American Popular Culture*. Berkeley: University of California Press, 2005.

Cioco, Gary. "How Dead Beats Became Dead Heads: From Emerson and James to Kerouac and Garcia." In Gimbel, *The Grateful Dead and Philosophy*, 63–74.

Clarke, Arthur. *Childhood's End*. New York: Ballantine, 1953.

Clayson, Adam. *Beat Merchants: The Origins, History, Impact, and Rock Legacy of the 1960s British Pop Groups*. London: Blandford, 1996.

Clayson, Alan. *The Yardbirds*. San Francisco: Backbeat, 2002.

Coggins, Owen. *Mysticism, Ritual, and Religion in Drone Metal*. London: Bloomsbury, 2018.

Cole, Bill. *John Coltrane*. New York: Da Capo, 2001.

Constanten, Tom. *Between Rock and Hard Places: A Musical Autobiodyssey*. Eugene, OR: Hulogosi, 1991.

Corbett, John. *A Listener's Guide to Free Improvisation*. Chicago: University of Chicago Press, 2016.

Covach, John. "The Hippie Aesthetic: Cultural Positioning and Musical Ambition in Early Progressive Rock." In *Rock Music*, edited by Mark Spicer, 65–75. Farnham, UK: Ashgate, 2012.

Covach, John, and Graeme Boone, eds. *Understanding Rock: Essays in Musical Analysis*, New York: Oxford University Press, 1997.

Crook, Hal. *Ready, Aim, Improvise: Exploring the Basics of Jazz Improvisation*. Rottenburg, Germany: Advance Music, 1999.

Crowley, Kent. *Surf Beat: Rock's Forgotten Revolution*. New York: Backbeat, 2011.

Csikszentmihalyi, Mihaly. *Flow: The Psychology of Optimal Experience*. New York: Harper, 2008.

Cutler, Chris. *File under Popular: Theoretical and Critical Writings on Music*. New York: Autonomedia, 1993.

Dahl, Bill. *All Music Guide to the Blues*. New York: Freeman, 1996.

Daniélou, Alain. *The Ragas of Northern India*. London: Cresset, 1968.

Davis, Erik. *High Weirdness: Drugs, Esoterica, and Visionary Experiences in the Seventies*. Cambridge, MA: MIT Press, 2019.

Debord, Guy. *The Society of the Spectacle*. Translated by Donald Nicholson-Smith. New York: Zone, 1994.

Demerath, N. J. *Sacred Companies: Organizational Aspects of Religion and Religious Aspects of Organizations*. Oxford: Oxford University Press, 1998.

Denzey Lewis, Nicola. *Introduction to "Gnosticism": Ancient Voices, Christian Worlds*. Oxford: Oxford University Press, 2013.

Devereux, Paul. *The Long Trip: A Prehistory of Psychedelia*. Brisbane: Daily Grail, 1997.

DeVito, Chris. *Coltrane on Coltrane: The John Coltrane Interviews*. Chicago: A Cappella, 2010.

Dines, M. "The Sacralization of Straightedge Punk: Bhakti-yoga, Nada Brahma, and the Divine Received: Embodiment of Krishnacore." *Musicological Annual* 50, no. 2: (2015): 147–56.

Dodd, David. *The Complete Annotated Grateful Dead Lyrics*. New York: Free Press, 2005.

Dodd, David, and Diane Spaulding. *The Grateful Dead Reader*. Oxford: Oxford University Press, 2000.

Doggett, Peter. *Are You Ready for the Country? Elvis, Dylan, Parsons, and the Roots of Country Rock*. London: Penguin, 2000.

Ellens, J. Harold, ed. *Seeking the Sacred with Psychoactive Substances: Chemical Paths to Spirituality and to God*. Santa Barbara, CA: Praeger, 2014.

Ellwood, Robert. *The Sixties Spiritual Awakening*. New Brunswick, NJ: Rutgers University Press, 1994.

Erhard, Werner. *The Transformation of a Man: The Founding of EST*. New York: Crown, 1978.

Farber, David. "The Intoxicated State / Illegal Nation: Drugs in the Sixties Counterculture." In Braunstein and Doyle, eds., *Imagine Nation*, 17–40 .

Farley, Charles. *Soul of the Man: Bobby "Blue" Band*. Jackson: University Press of Mississippi, 2011.

Fideler, David. "Introduction." In *The Pythagorean Sourcebook and Library*, edited by Kenneth Sylvan Guthrie, 1–19. Grand Rapids, MI: Phanes, 1988.

Fink, Robert. *Repeating Ourselves: American Minimal Music as Cultural Practice.* Berkeley: University of California Press, 2005.

Fiorfori, Tam. "Sun Ra's Space Odyssey." *Downbeat,* May 14, 1970, 14–17.

Fox, Brian. Transcription of "Scarlet Begonias." *Bass Player,* April 2008, 81–85.

Freedman, D. X. "On the Use and Abuse of LSD." *Archives of General Psychiatry* 18 (1968): 330–47.

Freeman, Philip. *Running the Voodoo Down: The Electric Music of Miles Davis.* San Francisco: Backbeat, 2005.

Freeman, Robert. "Other People Play the Music: Improvisation as Social Interaction." In Adams and Sardiello, *Deadhead Social Science,* 75–106.

Frith, Simon. *Sound Effects: Youth, Leisure, and the Politics of Rock.* New York: Pantheon, 1981.

Fuller, Robert. *Spiritual but Not Religious.* Oxford: Oxford University Press, 2001.

Fuller, Robert. *Stairways to Heaven: Drugs in American Religious History.* Boulder, CO: Westview, 2000.

Gann, Kyle. "Thankless Attempts at a Definition of Minimalism." In *Audio Culture: Readings in Modern Music,* edited by Christoph Cox and Daniel Warner, 299–303. New York: Continuum, 2004.

Gans, David. *Conversations with The Dead: The Grateful Dead Interview Book.* New York: Citadel, 1995.

Gans, David, and Paul Simon. *Playing in the Band: An Oral and Visual History of the Grateful Dead.* Updated memorial edition. New York: St. Martin's, 1996.

Garcia, Jerry, Charles Reich, and Jann Wenner. *Garcia: A Signpost to New Space.* New York: Da Capo, 2003.

Gaskin, Stephen. *The Caravan.* Summertown, TN: Book Publishing, 2007.

Gaskin, Stephen. *Haight Ashbury Flashbacks.* Berkeley, CA: Ronin, 1990.

Gaskin, Stephen. *Monday Night Class.* Rev. ed. Summertown, TN: Book Publishing, 2005.

Gendron, Bernard. *Between the Mudd Club and Montmartre: Popular Music and the Avant Garde.* Chicago: University of Chicago Press, 2002.

George-Warren, Holly, ed. *Garcia, by the Editors of* Rolling Stone. New York: Little, Brown, 1995.

Getz, Michael M., and John R. Dwork, eds. *The Deadhead's Taping Compendium: An In-Depth Guide to the Music of the Grateful Dead on Tape.* New York: Holt, 1998.

Gimbel, Steve, ed. *The Grateful Dead and Philosophy: Getting High Minded about Love and Haight.* Chicago: Open Court, 2007.

Gimbel, Steve. "The Other One and the Other: Moral Lessons from a Reluctant Teacher." In Tuedio and Spector, *The Grateful Dead in Concert,* 191–99.

Ginsberg, Allen. "First Thought, Best Thought." In *Composed on the Tongue,* 106–17. San Francisco: Grey Fox, 2001.

Gleason, Ralph J. "The Bands—That's Where It's At." In Gleason, *The Jefferson Airplane and the San Francisco Sound,* 1–82.

Gleason, Ralph J. *The Jefferson Airplane and the San Francisco Sound.* New York: Ballantine, 1969.

Gleason, Ralph J. "Jerry Garcia: The Guru." In *The Jefferson Airplane and the San Francisco Sound*, 306–29.

Glock, Charles, and Rodney Stark. *Religion and Society in Tension*. Chicago: Rand McNally, 1965.

Godwin, Joscelyn. *Harmonies of Heaven and Earth: The Spiritual Dimensions of Music from Antiquity to the Avant Garde*. Rochester, NY: Inner Traditions, 1987.

Godwin, Joscelyn. *Music, Mysticism, and Magic: A Sourcebook*. London: Arkana, 1987.

Godwin, Joscelyn, ed. *Cosmic Music: Musical Keys to the Interpretation of Reality*. Rochester, NY: Inner Traditions, 1989.

Gracyk, Theodore. *Rhythm and Noise: An Aesthetics of Rock*. Durham, NC: Duke University Press, 1996.

Greenfield, Robert. *Dark Star: An Oral Biography of Jerry Garcia*. New York: HarperCollins, 2009.

Grimshaw, Jeremy. *Draw a Straight Line and Follow It: The Music and Mysticism of La Monte Young*. Oxford: Oxford University Press, 2011.

Hall, Douglas Kent, and Sue C. Clark. *Rock: A World Bold as Love*. New York: Cowles, 1970.

Harrison, Hank. *The Dead*. Millbrae, CA: Celestial Arts, 1980.

Hart, Mickey. *Drumming on the Edge of Magic: A Journey into the Spirit of Percussion*. San Francisco: Harpers, 1990.

Hartley, Jennifer. "We Were Given This Dance: Music and Meaning in the Early Unlimited Devotion Family." In Adams and Sardiello, *Deadhead Social Science*, 129–56.

Hartogsohn, Ido. *American Trip: Set, Setting, and the Psychedelic Experience in the Twentieth Century*. Cambridge, MA: MIT Press, 2020.

Hayes, Charles. *Tripping: An Anthology of True-Life Psychedelic Adventures*. New York: Penguin, 2000.

Hazell, Ed. "Portraits: Beaver Harris." *Modern Drummer*, November 1989, 51–52.

Headlam, Dave. "Blues Transformations in the Music of Cream." In Covach and Boone, *Understanding Rock*, 59–92.

Heble, Ajay, and Mark Laver, eds. *Improvisation and Music Education: Beyond the Classroom*. London: Routledge, 2017.

Heffley, Mike. *Northern Sun and Southern Moon: Europe's Reinvention of Jazz*. Cambridge, MA: Harvard University Press, 2005.

Heinlein, Robert. "Lost Legacy." In *Assignment in Eternity*, edited by Robert Heinlein, 96–170. New York: Fantasy, 1953.

Heinlein, Robert. *Stranger in a Strange Land*. New York: Berkeley, 1961.

Hentoff, Nat. "The Truth Is Marching In." *Downbeat*, November 17, 1966, 16–18, 40.

Heylin, Clinton. *All Yesterday's Parties: The Velvet Underground in Print, 1966–71*. New York: Da Capo, 2005.

Hibbert, Tom. "The Last Great American Adventurer: Jerome John Garcia, 1942–1995." *Q*, February 1988. http://www.rocksbackpages.com/Library/Article

/the-last-great-american-adventurer-jerome-john-garcia-1942–1995 (accessed June 1, 2016).

Hicks, Michael. *Sixties Rock: Garage, Psychedelic, and Other Satisfactions.* Urbana: University of Illinois Press, 1999.

Hill, Christopher. *Into the Mystic: The Visionary and Ecstatic Roots of 1960s Rock and Roll.* Rochester, NY: Park Street, 2017.

Hill, Sarah. *San Francisco and the Long 60s.* London: Bloomsbury, 2016.

Hjelm, Titus. "Tradition as Legitimation in New Religious Movements." In *Historicizing "Tradition" in the Study of Religion,* edited by Steven Engler and Gregory P. Grieve, 109–23. Berlin: De Gruyter, 2005.

Hjort, Christopher. *Strange Brew: Eric Clapton and the British Blues Boom.* London: Jawbone, 2007.

Hoffmann, Albert. *LSD, My Problem Child.* Translated by Jonathan Ott. New York: McGraw-Hill, 1980.

Hollenback, Jess. *Mysticism: Experience, Response, and Empowerment.* University Park: Pennsylvania State University Press, 2000.

Horowitz, Michael, and Cynthia Palmer. *Moksha: Aldous Huxley's Classic Writings on Psychedelics and the Visionary Experience.* Rochester, NY: Park Street, 1999.

Hudnut-Beumler, James. *Looking for God in the Suburbs: The Religion of the American Dream and Its Critics, 1945–1965.* New Brunswick, NJ: Rutgers, 1994.

Hutton, Ronald. *Shamans: Siberian Spirituality and the Western Imagination.* London: Hambledon, 2001.

Ireland, Brian, and Sharif Gemie. "Raga Rock: Popular Music and the Turn to the East in the 1960s." *Journal of American Studies* 53, no. 1 (2019): 57–94.

Jackson, Blair. *Garcia: An American Life.* New York: Penguin, 1999.

Jackson, Blair, ed. *Going Down the Road: A Grateful Dead Traveling Companion.* New York: Harmony, 1992.

Jackson, Blair. *Grateful Dead Gear: The Band's Instruments, Sound Systems, and Recording Sessions from 1965 to 1995.* San Francisco: Backbeat, 2006.

Jackson, Blair, and David Gans. *This Is All a Dream We Dreamed: An Oral History of the Grateful Dead.* New York: Flatiron, 2015.

Jarnow, Jesse. *Heads: A Biography of Psychedelic America.* Boston: Da Capo, 2016.

Johnson, Anna, and Mike Stax. "From Psychotic to Psychedelic: The Garage Contribution to Psychedelia." *Popular Music and Society* 29 (2006): 411–25.

Joseph, Branden. *Beyond the Dream Syndicate: Tony Conrad and the Arts after Cage.* New York: Zone, 2011.

Jost, Ekkehard. *Free Jazz.* New York: Da Capo, 1994.

Jung, Darryl. "Attempting the Impossible." *Now Weekly,* February 6–12, 1986, 11.

Kaler, Michael. "How the Grateful Dead Learned to Jam." In Meriwether, *Reading the Grateful Dead,* 67–85.

Kaler, Michael. "Jamming the Blues: The Grateful Dead's Development of Models for Rock Improvisation." *Critical Studies in Improvisation* 9, no. 1 (2013): https://www.criticalimprov.com/index.php/csieci/article/view/2145/3202 (accessed March 14, 2023).

Kaler, Michael. "Making Magic with Music: Transcendence and Transformation in the Modern Rediscovery of Radical Improvisation." In *Religion: Super Religion*, edited by Jeffrey J. Kripal, 389–404. Farmington Hills, MI: Macmillan Reference, 2018.

Kaler, Michael. "Music and the Divine: The Acid Tests as Foundation Stories." *Studies in Religion/Sciences Religieuses* 45 (2014): 3–15.

Kaler, Michael. "Searching for the (Sacred) Sound: Phil Lesh, the Grateful Dead, and Religion." *Journal of Religion and Popular Culture* 23 (2011): 139–54.

Kapchan, Deborah. *Traveling Spirit Masters: Moroccan Gnawa Trance and Music in the Global Marketplace.* Middletown, CT: Wesleyan University Press, 2007.

Katz, Stephen. *Mysticism and Philosophical Analysis.* London: Sheldon, 1978.

Kelly, Aidan. *Hippie Commie Beatnik Witches: A Social History of the New Reformed Orthodox Order of the Golden Dawn.* Tacoma, WA: Hierophant Wordsmith, 2011.

Kelly, Kevin. "Why We Left the Farm." *Whole Earth Review* 49 (Winter 1985): 56–66.

Kennedy, Caleb. "The Dead's Early Thematic Jams." Grateful Dead Guide, January 8, 2010. http://deadessays.blogspot.com/2010/01/deads-early-thematic-jams.html.

Kennedy, Caleb. "The Velvets and the Dead." Grateful Dead Guide, September 7, 2010. http://deadessays.blogspot.com/2010/09/velvets-and-dead.html.

Kerouac, Jack. "Essentials of Spontaneous Prose." In *The Portable Beat Reader*, edited by Ann Charters, 57. New York: Viking, 1992.

Khan, Hazrat Inayat. *The Mysticism of Sound and Music.* Boston: Shambhala, 1991.

King, Anna. "Spirituality: Transformation and Metamorphosis." *Religion* 26 (1996): 343–51.

King, Karen. *What Is Gnosticism?* Cambridge, MA: Belknap Press of Harvard University Press, 2003.

Knabb, Ken. *Situationist International Anthology.* N.p.: Bureau of Public Secrets, 2006.

Kofsky, Frank. *Black Nationalism and the Revolution in Music.* New York: Pathfinder, 1970.

Kofsky, Frank. *Love Cry.* Liner notes. Impulse! AS 9165, 1968. Vinyl album.

Kofsky, Frank. "A Thread to the Collective Unconscious: Jerry Garcia and Bob Weir on Music, the Haight, and the Sixties." *Dead Studies* 1 (2011): 49–74.

Kripal, Jeffrey. *Comparing Religions.* New York: Wiley-Blackwell, 2014.

Kripal, Jeffrey. *Mutants and Mystics: Science Fiction, Superhero Comics, and the Paranormal.* 2nd ed. Chicago: University of Chicago Press, 2015.

Kripal, Jeffrey. "The Traumatic Secret: Bataille and the Comparative Erotics of Mystical Literature." In *Negative Ecstasies: Georges Bataille and the Study of Religion*, edited by Jeremy Biles and Kent Brintnall, 153–68. New York: Fordham University Press, 2015.

Krippner, Stanley, and Richard Davidson. "Religious Implications of Paranormal Events Occurring during Chemically Induced 'Psychedelic' Experiences." *Pastoral Psychology* 21 (1970): 27–34.

Kugelberg, Johann. *The Velvet Underground: New York Art*. New York: Rizzoli, 2009.

Kuttner, Henry. *Mutant*. New York: Ballantine, 1953.

Laski, Marghanita. *Ecstasy in Secular and Religious Experiences*. New York: St. Martin's, 1961.

Lavezzoli, Peter. *The Dawn of Indian Music in the West*. London: Continuum, 2007.

Lee, Martin, and Bruce Shlain. *Acid Dreams: The Complete Social History of LSD: The CIA, the Sixties, and Beyond*. New York: Grove, 1991.

Le Gendre, Kevin. *Soul Unsung: Reflections on the Band in Black Popular Music*. Sheffield: Equinox, 2012.

Lesh, Phil. "Anthem of the Tone: Phil Lesh and the Modern Electric Bass." Interview by Karl Coryat, pt. 2. *Bass Player* (July 2000): 56–64.

Lesh, Phil. "Lesh Is More: Portrait of an American Beauty." Interview by Karl Coryat, pt. 2. *Bass Player* (June 2000): 39–49.

Lesh, Phil. *Searching for the Sound: My Life with the Grateful Dead*. New York: Little, Brown, 2005.

Levaux, Christophe. *We Have Always Been Minimalist: The Construction and Triumph of a Musical Style*. Oakland: University of California Press, 2020.

Lewis, George. *A Power Stronger than Itself: The AACM and American Experimental Music*. Chicago: University of Chicago Press, 2008.

Lewis, James. *Legitimating New Religions*. New Brunswick, NJ: Rutgers, 2003.

Lewis, James, and Olav Hammer, eds. *The Invention of Sacred Tradition*. Cambridge: Cambridge University Press, 2007.

Lewis, Mark. "Neuroscientist Marc Lewis on His First Acid Trip." *Newsweek*, March 3, 2012, 19.

Litweiler, John. *The Freedom Principle: Jazz after 1958*. New York: Quill, 1984.

Luhrman, Tanya. *When God Talks Back: Understanding the American Evangelical Relationship with God*. New York: Knopf, 2012.

Lundborg, Patrick. *Psychedelia: An Ancient Culture, a Modern Way of Life*. Stockholm: Lysergia, 2012.

MacDonald, R. A., and G. B. Wilson. "Musical Improvisation and Health: A Review." *Psychology of Well-Being* 4, no. 20 (2014). https://doi.org/10.1186/s13612–014–0020–9.

MacFarlane, Scott. *The Hippie Narrative: A Literary Perspective on the Counterculture*. Jefferson, NC: McFarland, 2007.

Malvinni, David. *Grateful Dead and the Art of Rock Improvisation*. Lanham, MD: Scarecrow, 2013.

Marcus, Greil. *In the Fascist Bathroom: Writings on Punk, 1977–1982*. London: Viking, 1993.

Martin, Craig. "Psychedelic Music in San Francisco: Style, Context, and Evolution." PhD diss., Concordia University, 2000.

Mason, Nick. *Inside Out: A Personal History of Pink Floyd*. London: Weidenfeld and Nicolson, 2004.

Mathieu, W. A. *Bridge of Waves: What Music Is and How Listening to It Changes the World*. Boston: Shambhala, 2010.

McNally, Dennis. *A Long Strange Trip: The Inside Story of the Grateful Dead*. New York: Broadway, 2002.

McStravick, Summer, and John Roos. *Blues-Rock Explosion*. Mission Viejo, CA: Old Goat, 2001.

Meriwether, Nicholas. "The Acid Tests." In Getz and Dwork, eds., *The Deadhead's Taping Compendium*, 84–91.

Meriwether, Nicholas. "1/6/66: The Fillmore Acid Test." In Getz and Dwork, *The Deadhead's Taping Compendium*, 91–94.

Meriwether, Nicholas. *Reading the Grateful Dead: A Critical Survey*. Lanham, MD: Scarecrow, 2012.

Merkur, Daniel. "The Formation of Hippie Spirituality 1: Union with God." In Ellens, *Seeking the Sacred with Psychoactive Substances*, 207–38.

Merkur, Daniel. "The Formation of Hippie Spirituality 2: Further and Further." In Ellens, *Seeking the Sacred with Psychoactive Substances*, 239–90.

Merkur, Daniel. "The Visionary Practices of the Jewish Apocalypticists." In *The Psychoanalytic Study of Society. Vol. 14: Essays in Honor of Paul Parin*, edited by L. B. Boyer and S. A. Grolnick, 119–48. Hillsdale, NJ: Analytic, 1989.

Monson, Ingrid. *Saying Something: Jazz Improvisation and Interaction*. Chicago: University of Chicago Press, 1997.

Morley, Gabriel Patrick. "Tripping with Stephen Gaskin: An Exploration of a Hippy Adult Educator." PhD diss., University of Southern Mississippi, 2012.

Murphy, Joseph. *Working the Spirit: Ceremonies of the African Diaspora*. Boston: Beacon, 1994.

Murray, Charles Shaar. *Boogie Man: The Adventures of John Lee Hooker in the American Twentieth Century*. New York: St. Martin's, 2000.

Napier, John. "Novelty That Must Be Subtle: Continuity, Innovation, and 'Improvisation' in North Indian Music." *Critical Studies in Improvisation* 1 (2006): 1–17.

Nettl, Bruno. "Improvisation." In *Harvard Dictionary of Music*, edited by Don Michael Randel, 406–8. Cambridge, MA: Belknap Press of Harvard University Press, 2003.

Nettl, Bruno. "Improvisation." In Grove Music Online. Accessed March 8, 2014. http://www.oxfordmusiconline.com.ezproxy.library.yorku.ca/subscriber/article/grove/music/13738#S13738.

Nettl, Bruno. "Preface." In Solis and Nettl, *Musical Improvisation*, ix–xv.

Nettl, Bruno. *The Study of Ethnomusicology: Thirty-one Issues and Concepts*. Champaign: University of Illinois Press, 2005.

Nettl, Bruno. "Thoughts on Improvisation: A Comparative Approach." *Musical Quarterly* 40 (1974): 1–19.

Nettl, Bruno, and Melinda Russell, eds. *In the Course of Performance: Studies in the World of Musical Improvisation*. Chicago: University of Chicago Press, 1998.

Newberg, Andrew. *Principles of Neurotheology*. London: Ashgate, 2010.

Nichols, David, and Benjamin Chemel. "LSD and the Serotonin System's Effects on Human Consciousness." In Cardena and Winkelman, *Altering Consciousness*, vol. 1: 121–46.

Nisenson, Eric. *Ascension: John Coltrane and his Quest*. New York: Da Capo, 1993.

Norman, Philip. *The Stones*. London: Sidgwick and Jackson, 2001.

Nyman, Michael. *Experimental Music: Cage and Beyond*. 2nd ed. Cambridge: Cambridge University Press, 1999.

O'Dea, Thomas. "Sociological Dilemmas: Five Paradoxes of Institutionalization." In *Sociological Theory, Values, and Sociocultural Change: Essays in Honour of Pitrim A. Sorokin*, edited by Edward Tiryakian, 71–89. London: Free Press of Glencoe, 1963.

Olsson, Ulf. *Listening for the Secret: The Grateful Dead and the Politics of Improvisation*. Berkeley: University of California Press, 2017.

Osmond, Humphry. "A Review of the Clinical Effects of Psychotomimetic Agents." *Annals of the New York Academy of Science* 66 (1957): 417–35.

Osto, Douglas. *Altered States: Buddhism and Psychedelic Spirituality in America*. New York: Columbia University Press, 2016.

Otto, Rudolph. *The Idea of the Holy*. Translated by John Harvey. Oxford: Oxford University Press, 1979.

Paden, William. *Religious Worlds: The Comparative Study of Religion*. 2nd ed. Boston: Beacon, 1994.

Palacios, Julian. *Lost in the Woods: Syd Barrett and the Pink Floyd*. London: Macmillan, 1998.

Partridge, Christopher. *Dub in Babylon: Understanding the Evolution and Significance of Dub Reggae in Jamaica and Britain from King Tubby to Post-Punk*. London: Equinox, 2010.

Partridge, Christopher. *The Lyre of Orpheus: Popular Music, the Sacred, and the Profane*. Oxford: Oxford University Press, 2013.

Partridge, Christopher. *Occulture: The Re-Enchantment of the West*. 2 vols. London: Bloomsbury, 2005–2006.

Partridge, Christopher, and Marcus Moberg, eds. *The Bloomsbury Handbook of Religion and Popular Music*. London: Bloomsbury, 2017.

Pearlman, Sandy. "Patterns and Sounds: The Uses of Raga in Rock." *Paste* magazine, December 1, 1966. https://www.pastemagazine.com/crawdaddy/patterns-and-sounds-the-uses-of-raga-in-rock.

Perrine, Daniel. *The Chemistry of Mind-Altering Drugs: History, Pharmacology, and Cultural Context*. Washington, DC: American Chemical Society, 1996.

Perry, Charles. *The Haight-Ashbury: A History*. New York: Wenner, 2005.

Perry, Paul, and Ken Babbs. *On the Bus: The Complete Guide to the Legendary Trip of Ken Kesey and the Merry Pranksters and the Birth of the Counterculture*. New York: Thunder's Mouth, 1997.

Pisani, Bob. "Confessions of a Deadhead: 40 Years with the Grateful Dead." CNBC, July 1, 2015. https://www.cnbc.com/2015/07/01/confessions-of-a-deadhead-40-years-with-the-grateful-dead.html.

Plummer, William. *The Holy Goof: A Biography of Neal Cassady*. New York: Thunder's Mouth, 1997.

Poggioli, Renato. *The Theory of the Avant Garde*. Cambridge, MA: Belknap Press of Harvard University Press, 1968.

Pohl, Frederick, and Cyril M. Kornbluth. *Wolfbane*. New York: Ballantine, 1969.

Polits, William. "Grateful Jams." In Getz and Dwork, *The Deadhead's Taping Compendium*, 59–61.

Porter, Lewis. *John Coltrane: His Life and Music*. Ann Arbor: University of Michigan Press, 1999.

Prevost, Edwin. *No Sound Is Innocent*. Berkeley: Small Press Distribution, 1997.

Proudfoot, Wayne. *Religious Experience*. Berkeley: University of California Press, 1985.

Prown, Peter, and H. P. Newquist. *Legends of Rock Guitar*. Milwaukee, WI: Hal Leonard, 1997.

Qureshi, Regula. *Sufi Music of India and Pakistan: Sound, Context, and Meaning in Qawwali*. Chicago: University of Chicago Press, 1986.

Racy, A. J. *Making Music in the Arab World: The Culture and Artistry of Tarab*. Cambridge: Cambridge University Press, 2003.

Racy, A. J. "Why Do They Improvise? Reflections on Meaning and Experience." In Solis and Nettl, *Musical Improvisation*, 313–22.

Randel, Dom Michael, ed. *The Harvard Dictionary of Music*. 4th ed. Cambridge: Belknap Press of Harvard University Press, 2003.

Ratliff, Ben. *Coltrane: The Story of a Sound*. New York: Picador, 2007.

Reising, Russell. "Melting Clocks and the Hallways of Always: Time in Psychedelic Music." *Popular Music and Society* 32 (2009): 523–47.

Ripani, Richard. *The New Blue Music: Changes in Rhythm and Blues, 1950–1999*. Jackson: University Press of Mississippi, 2006.

Roberts, Jim. *How the Fender Bass Changed the World*. San Francisco: Backbeat, 2001.

Rocco, John, ed. *Dead Reckonings: The Life and Times of the Grateful Dead*. New York: Schirmer, 1999.

Roof, Wade Clark. *A Generation of Seekers: The Spiritual Journeys of the Baby Boom Generation*. San Francisco: Harper, 1993.

Roof, Wade Clark. *Spiritual Marketplace: Baby Boomers and the Remaking of American Religion*. Princeton, NJ: Princeton University Press, 2001.

Rothstein, Mikael. "Scientology, Scripture, and Sacred Tradition." In Lewis and Hammer, *The Invention of Sacred Tradition*, 18–37.

Rouget, Gilbert. *Music and Trance: A Theory of the Relations between Music and Possession*. Translated by Rouget and Brunhilde Biebuyck. Chicago: University of Chicago Press, 1985.

Sardiello, Robert. "Studying Deadhead Subculture." In Adams and Sardiello, *Deadhead Social Science*, 267–80.

Sawyer, Keith. *Group Genius: The Creative Power of Collaboration*. 2nd ed. New York: Basic Books, 2017.

Schaffner, Nicholas. *Saucerful of Secrets: The Pink Floyd Odyssey*. London: Sidgwick and Jackson, 1991.

Schmidt, Leigh Eric. *Restless Souls: The Making of American Spirituality*. San Francisco: Harper, 2005.

Schwartz, Jeff. "Albert Ayler." Accessed April 15, 2012. http://www.geocities.com /jeff_l_schwartz/ayler.html.

Schwarz, K. Robert. *Minimalists*. London: Phaidon, 1996.

Sculatti, Gene, and Davin Seay. *San Francisco Nights: The Psychedelic Music Trip, 1965–1968*. New York: St. Martin's, 1985.

Seay, Davin, and Mary Neely. "Prophets on the Burning Shore." In *Stairway to Heaven: The Spiritual Roots of Rock and Roll*, edited by Davin Seay and Mary Neely, 187–217. New York: Ballantine, 1986.

Segal, Alan. "Religious Experience and the Construction of the Transcendent Self." In *Paradise Now: Essays on Early Jewish and Christian Mysticism*, edited by April DeConick, 27–40. Atlanta, GA: Society for Biblical Literature, 2006.

Segal, Alan. "Transcribing Experience." In *With Letters of Light: Studies in the Dead Sea Scrolls, Early Jewish Apocalypticism, Magic, and Mysticism in Honor of Rachel Elior*, edited by Daphna Arbel and Andrei Orlov, 365–82. Berlin: De Gruyter, 2011.

Selvin, Joel. *Summer of Love*. New York: Cooper Square, 1994.

Shenk, David, and Steve Silberman. *Skeleton Key: A Dictionary for Deadheads*. New York: Doubleday, 1994.

Slawek, Stephen. "Keeping It Going: Terms, Practices, and Processes of Improvisation in Hindustani Instrumental Music." In Nettl and Russell, *In the Course of Performance*, 335–68.

Slesinger, Ryan. "'And Closed My Eyes to See': Buddhist Resonances in the Lyrics of the Grateful Dead." In Meriwether, *Reading the Grateful Dead*, 109–21.

Sloterdijk, Peter. *You Must Change Your Life: On Anthropotechnics*. Translated by Wieland Haban. Cambridge: Polity, 2018.

Smith, Huston. *Cleansing the Doors of Perception: The Religious Significance of Entheogenic Plants and Chemicals*. New York: Putnam, 2000.

Solis, Gabriel, and Bruno Nettl. *Musical Improvisation: Art, Education, and Society*. Urbana: University of Illinois Press, 2009.

Spector, Stan. "Who Is Dionysus and Why Does He Keep Following Me Everywhere?" *Dead Letters* 2 (2003): 19–28.

Stapledon, Olaf. *Odd John*. New York: Berkeley, 1965.

Stark, Rodney, and William Bainbridge. *The Future of Religion*. Berkeley: University of California Press, 1985.

Steinbeck, Paul. *Message to Our Folks: The Art Ensemble of Chicago*. Chicago: University of Chicago Press, 2017.

Stephens, Randall. *The Devil's Music: How Christians Inspired, Condemned, and Embraced Rock and Roll*. Cambridge, MA: Harvard University Press, 2018.

Stevens, Jay. *Storming Heaven: LSD and the American Dream*. New York: Grove, 1987.

Stewart, Earl. *African American Music: An Introduction*. New York: Schirmer, 1998.

Sturgeon, Theodore. *More than Human*. New York: Ballantine, 1952.

Sylvan, Robin. *Traces of the Spirit: The Religious Dimensions of Popular Music*. New York: New York University Press, 2002.

Sylvan, Robin. *Trance Formation: The Spiritual and Religious Dimensions of Global Rave Culture*. London: Routledge, 2005.

Szwed, John. *So What: The Life of Miles Davis*. New York: Simon and Schuster, 2002.

Szwed, John. *Space Is the Place: The Lives and Times of Sun Ra*. New York: Da Capo, 1998.

Tamarkin, Jeff. *Got a Revolution: The Turbulent Flight of the Jefferson Airplane*. New York: Atria, 2003.

Tanner, Stephen. *Ken Kesey*. Boston: Twayne, 1983.

Tart, Charles. *States of Consciousness*. New York: Dutton, 2000.

Taves, Ann. *Religious Experience Reconsidered*. Princeton, NJ: Princeton University Press, 2009.

Taylor, Jill Bolte. *My Stroke of Insight*. New York: Penguin, 2009.

Thomas, J. C. *Chasin' the Trane: The Music and Mystique of John Coltrane*. Garden City, NY: Doubleday, 1975.

Thompson, Dave. *Cream: How Eric Clapton Took the World by Storm*. London: Virgin, 2006.

Thompson, Dave. *Space Daze: The History and Mystery of Electronic Ambient Space Rock*. Los Angeles: Cleopatra, 1994.

Tilley, Leslie. *Making It Up Together: The Art of Collective Improvisation in Balinese Music and Beyond*. Chicago: University of Chicago Press, 2019.

Tingen, Paul. *Miles Beyond: The Electric Explorations of Miles Davis, 1967–1991*. New York: Billboard, 2001.

Titon, Jeff. *Worlds of Music: An Introduction to the Music of the World's Peoples*. 2nd ed. New York: McGraw-Hill, 1992.

Torgoff, Martin. *Can't Find My Way Home: America in the Great Stoned Age*. New York: Simon and Schuster, 2004.

Troy, Sandy. *One More Saturday Night: Reflections with the Grateful Dead, Dead Family, and Dead Heads*. New York: St. Martin's, 1991.

Tuedio, Jim, and Stan Spector, eds. *The Grateful Dead in Concert: Essays on Live Improvisation*. Jefferson, NC: McFarland, 2010.

Turino, Thomas. *Music as Social Life: The Politics of Participation*. Chicago: University of Chicago Press, 2008.

Turner, Steve. *Hungry for Heaven*. London: Hodder and Stoughton, 1995.

Turner, Victor. *The Ritual Process: Structure and Anti-Structure*. New Brunswick, NJ: Transaction, 2007.

Turner, Victor. "Variations on a Theme of Liminality." In *Secular Ritual*, edited by Sally Moore and Barbara Myerhoff, 35–52. Assen, Netherlands: Van Gorcum, 1977.

Unterberger, Richie. *Eight Miles High: Folk Rock's Flight from Haight-Ashbury to Woodstock*. Berkeley, CA: Backbeat, 2003.

Wach, Joachim. *Sociology of Religion*. Chicago: University of Chicago Press, 1944.

Walsh, Roger. "Chemical and Contemplative Ecstasy: Similarities and Differences." In *Hallucinogens: A Reader*, edited by Charles Grob, 72–82. New York: Putnam, 2002.

Watson, Ben. *Derek Bailey and the Story of Free Improvisation*. New York: Verso, 2004.

Watts, Alan. *Does It Matter? Essays on Man's Relation to Materiality*. New York: Pantheon, 1968.

Waugh, Earl. "Dispatches from Memory: Genealogies of Tradition." In *Historicizing "Tradition" in the Study of Religion*, edited by Steven Engler and Gregory Grieve, 245–65. Berlin: De Gruyter, 2005.

Weber, Max. *Theory of Social and Economic Organization*. Translated by A. M. Henderson and Talcott Parsons. New York: Free Press, 1947.

Weiner, Robert, ed. *Perspectives on the Grateful Dead*. Westport, CT: Greenwood, 1999.

Weinstein, Norman. *A Night in Tunisia: Imaginings of Africa in Jazz*. Metuchen, NJ: Scarecrow, 1992.

Weiss, Jason. *Steve Lacy: Conversations*. Durham, NC: Duke University Press, 2006.

Welch, Chris. *Cream: The Legendary British Supergroup*. London: Balafon, 2000.

White, Christopher. *Other Worlds: Spirituality and the Search for Invisible Dimensions*. Cambridge, MA: Harvard University Press, 2018.

Whitmer, Peter. *Aquarius Revisited: Seven Who Created the Sixties Counterculture That Changed America*. New York: Macmillan, 1987.

Widdess, Richard. "Schemas and Improvisation in Indian Music." In *Language, Music, and Interactions*, edited by Ruth Kempson, Christine Howes, and Martin Orwin, 197–209. London: College Press, 2013.

Wildman, Wesley, and Leslie Brothers. "Neurophysiological-Semiotic Model of Religious Experience." In *Neuroscience and the Person*, edited by Robert Russell, Nancy Murphy, and Michael Artib, 347–413. Vatican City: Vatican Observatory, 2002.

Wilke, Annette, and Oliver Moebus. *Sound and Communication: An Aesthetic Cultural History of Sanskrit Hinduism*. Berlin: de Gruyter, 2010.

Williams, Michael. *Rethinking "Gnosticism": An Argument for Dismantling a Dubious Category*. Princeton, NJ: Princeton University Press, 1996.

Wilmer, Valerie. *As Serious as Your Life: John Coltrane and Beyond*. London: Serpent's Tail, 1992.

Winfree, Jason. "'Searching for the Sound': Grateful Dead Music and Interpretive Transformation." In Tuedio and Spector, *The Grateful Dead in Concert*, 152–63.

Witts, Richard. *The Velvet Underground*. London: Equinox, 2006.

Wolfe, Leonard. *Voices of the Love Generation*. Boston: Little, Brown, 1968.

Wolfe, Tom. *The Electric Kool-Aid Acid Test*. New York: Farrar, Straus and Giroux, 1982.

Wolkin, Jan Mark, and Bill Keenom. *Michael Bloomfield: If You Love These Blues.* San Francisco: Miller Freeman, 2000.

Wood, Brent. "The Eccentric Revolutions of Phil Lesh." In Tuedio and Spector, *The Grateful Dead in Concert,* 43–57.

Woods, Willie. "Cleo's Back." Performed by Junior Walker. Motown TMG 529 (B), 1965.

Wright, Jack. *The Free Musics.* N.p.: Spring Garden Music Editions, 2017.

Wuthnow, Robert. *After Heaven: Spirituality in America since the 1950s.* Berkeley: University of California Press, 1998.

Yamane, David. "Narrative and Religious Experience." *Sociology of Religion* 61 (2000): 171–89.

Young, Charles M. "The Awakening of the Dead." In *Garcia,* edited by the Editors of *Rolling Stone,* 124–29. Boston: Little, Brown, 1995.

Zaehner, R. C. *Mysticism Sacred and Profane.* 1957. Oxford: Oxford University Press, 1969.

Zaehner, R. C. *Zen, Drugs, and Mysticism.* New York: Pantheon, 1972.

Zak, Albin. *The Velvet Underground Companion.* New York: Schirmer, 1997.

Index

Page numbers in *italics* refer to tables.

and culture, 128–29; deemphasising, 78; defined, 14; as dense in acid rock phase, 77; and disorientation, 147; easing into, 63; as end of tunes, 63; and enjoyment, 127 (*see also* joy); as exhausting, 72; expansion/contraction, 67; vs. expectations, 83; as experiment, 45; flowing nature, 105–6; as format out of chaos, 45–46; ghettoizing, 11; history of, 23; history of Grateful Dead, 5–6, 11, 18; as homogeneous, 52; Indian classical music, 27–28; jazz, 16, 24–25, 49, 50, 51–53, 130–31, 226; jazz and Grateful Dead, 65, 108, 136; Jost on, 125 (*see also individual songs*); and live performance, 13; in mainstream, 23; as making statement, 23; markers, 68–69; and minimalism's audible structures, 32; paralleling LSD, 103; pointers, 68–69; as praying, 58, 205; qawwali, 18, 129; as rehearsed, 11; and return to chorus, 103; and rhythm section liberation, 101; rock overview, 6, 15–17; and social relations, 139; and spirituality, 18; starting (*see* trap doors); as structured, 46, 48–49, 59; tactics not used, 119–23; teaching about, 130; as transitions, 108; treatment of covers (overview), 97, 99; turning points, 118–19; and two drummers, 98. *See also* Framework

improvisation, approaches to understanding: Bailey, 126, 128, 251n12; Blum, 127; Boone, 133; Borgo, 129–30; Deadness, 136; eight approaches to improvisation, 74–76, 79–88, 118; freedom, 127–28; Freeman, 133–34; idiomatic/non-idiomatic, 128; improvisation as unresolvable contradictions, 136; improvisation as conceptual space, 126; Jost, 125; Malvinni, 136–37; models, 126–32; Nettl, 125–26; Qureshi, 129; Racy, 127; Slawek, 127; Spector, 135–36; Tilley, 126, 130–31; Titon, 127; Tuedio, 135–36; Widdess, 126

improvisation, other rock bands, 139–40; conceptual boundaries, 160; Cream, 155, 252n1, 254n46; Jefferson Airplane, 140–44, 155, 160; Monkees, 255n62; Pink Floyd, 155–56, 160; Velvet Underground, 156–57, 160, 254n41

improvisation and religion, 18, 222–24, 226, 227

improvisation and transcendence, 164–65, 167, 169, 170–71, 205, 226. *See also* altered reality

In C (composition), 29

Indian classical music, 26–29, 32, 109–10, 120, 148–49, 205–6, 223

interactive spontaneity, 80

interludes, 96–97

"Interstellar Overdrive" (song), 154

"In the Midnight Hour," (song), 42, *61*, 87, 91–93, 96, 249nn29–30

Into the Mystic (Hill), 201

introduction of songs, 61

"Intuition" (song), 24

Ireland, Brian, 28

Jack O' Roses (album), 250n64

Jackson, Al, 91

Jackson, Blair, 108

James, William, 124

jams. *See* improvisation

jazz, 24; and bands/groups, 52, 53–54; and competence, 86; and Cream, 151; and dancing, 82; and Grateful Dead's improvisation, 65, 108, 139; improvisation, 16, 24–25, 49, 50, 51–53, 130–31, 226; as influencing Lesh's playing, 100; and religion, 224; as rock influenced, 49–50; and sections, 108; and space, 52–53; and tradition, 53; tropes, 25–26. *See also* free jazz; modal jazz

jazz rock phase (1972–74), 10, 70, 78, 105. *See also* jazz rock phase

Jefferson Airplane, 16, 79–80, 140–44, 145, 155, 160

Jenner, Peter, 153, 154

Jesus People, 186

Jimi Hendrix Experience, 255n62

"Johnny B. Goode" (song), 80

John Wesley Harding (Dylan), 78

Jones, Elvin, 53–54

Jost, Ekkehard, 46, 108, 125, 132

journeys and environments, 123–24

joy, 9–10, 38–39, 127

Jung, Carl, 23

Junior Walker and the All-Stars, 51

88–96; as important, 13; jazz rock phase, 79; and musical development, 78–79; quality of, 35; recording, 10, 102; vs. rehearsal, 104; Wall of Sound setup, 10, 35. *See also* improvisation

Long Strange Trip (McNally), 46

"Lost Legacy" (Heinlein), 57

Love (band), 86, 113

Love Supreme, A (album), 108

LSD, 229–31, 233–34; and brain, 230–31; and Coltrane, 232; and culture, 183–84; dechronicization, 229; depersonalization, 229; experiences as legitimate, 19–20, 182–83; fundamental effects of, 229; Grateful Dead usage, 209; and Grateful Dead associated with, 141, 142, 158, 229; and group consciousness, 30; Hill on, 201; Kantner on, 141; and Lesh, 30; and music, 231–32; paralleling improvisation, 103; and Pigpen, 209; and religious context, 183–84, 228–29; as "the sacrament," 209; and transcendence, 232; users as confident, 39. *See also* Acid Tests; drugs; psychedelia/psychedelic music

Lucas, Peter, 33

Luhrman, Tanya, 222

Lunch, Lydia, 23

Lundborg, Patrick, 124, 177–78, 229

lyrics, 101

MacLise, Angus, 147–48

magic, 18; of Acid Tests, 191–92, 207; and the Framework, 48; Garcia on, 170, 215; of rock bands, 55; setting place for, 210

"Main Ten, The" (module), 114, 135

Malone, Deadric, 93

Malvinni, David, 46, 87, 93, 111, 136–37, 249n29

"Mama Tried" (song), 99

Manfred Mann, 150

Manson, Charles, 20, 242n23

Marcus, Greil, 1, 228

marijuana, 158

markers, 68–69

Marley, Bob, 20

Marquee (London venue), 153

Marvin, Hank, 242n16

Marx, Karl, 217

Maslow, Abraham, 229

Mason, Nick, 153–54

Mathieu, W. A., 162

Matrix Club, 41, 141

Mayall, John, 150

MC5, 17, 145–46

McGuire, Wayne, 148–49

McKernan, Ron "Pigpen": as blues performer, 80; bringing soulfulness, 86; death of, 75, 248–49n29; Grateful Dead history, 12; on "Good Morning Little Schoolgirl," 90; improvisation in action, 64–65; improvisation on "Alligator," 69; improvisation on "Cream Puff War," 62; improvisation on "The Same Thing," 67; instrument knowledge, 241n6; as leader, 90, 96, 247n27; David Malvinni on, 87; on "In the Midnight Hour," 92; musicologists avoiding songs of, 87; and psychedelics, 209; riffing, 66; singing, 87, 90, 92–93, 94–95, 248–49n29; songs as dance tunes, 75, 85, 87–96, 157; and spirituality, 20; on "Turn On Your Love Light," 94–95

McNally, Dennis, 39, 46, 219

Menuhin, Yehudi, 26

Meriwether, Nicholas, 47, 59, 157

Merkur, Daniel, 57, 187–88

Merry Pranksters, 188; as anarchistic, 212; end of, 195; Grateful Dead as members, 191; and hippie spirituality, 188; and Mime Troupe, 40; as religious movement, 192–93; and science fiction, 57; as stealing show, 30. *See also* Acid Tests; Kesey, Ken

Message to Our Folks (Steinbeck), 52

Mickey and the Hartbeats (band), 142, 143

Middle Earth, 252n1

Mime Troupe (artist collective), 30, 40

"Mind Left Body" (song), 114

"Mind Left Body Jam" (module), 114

minimalism, 29, 31–32, 120

mistakes, 157–59, 226, 255n68

modal, defined, 252n33

modal analysis, 135–36, 252n33

modal jazz, 24, 25–26, 49–50

modules, 74, 76, 113–15

Moebus, Oliver, 223

play, 38
"Playing in the Band" (song), 75, 79, 106, 112, 114, 135, 250n70, 261–62n35
playing the main groove, 96–97
Plummer, William, 193
Pohl, Frederick, 57
pointers, 68–69
popularity, 155
praying, 58
precomposed patterns, 74. *See also* modules
Presley, Elvis, 33
"primitive" myths, 23, 146
Primitives, 147
Pritchard, Mike, 37–38
professionalism, 79–80, 86, 117–18, 155, 157–59
Prown, Peter, 109
psychedelia/psychedelic music: as alternative reality, 28; and Cream, 252n1; extremes of, 10; and identity of scene, 39; influence of Young, 17; and intoxication, 39; and religion, 178, 229; songs about drugs, 40; and telepathy, 187; transitions, 124. *See also* LSD
psychedelic direction. *See* acid rock phase
pulse, 31, 49, 58–59, 246n5
punk rock, 17, 44
Pythagoreans, 162, 163, 226, 256n8

qawwali performances, 18, 129
Qureshi, Regula, 128–9

R&B, 85–6, 150, 153, 155. *See also* blues; Cream
racism, 255n4
Racy, Ali Jihad, 127, 164–65, 223
ragas, 7, 14, 27, 32, 109–10, 243n20
rave culture, 9
rave-ups, 15–16
Ready, Aim, Improvise (Crook), 53
reality, 28
recombinant teleology, 31–32
Red Krayola, 17
reductionism, 187
Reed, Lou, 145, 147
reenchantment, 7
Reich, Steve, 30, 244n29

religion, defined, 171–72
religion/spirituality, 233–36; and altered reality, 133; American Metaphysical Religion, 221; authentic fakes, 222; Church of Unlimited Devotion, 166; constructivism, 180, 181; dogma, 204, 261n12; and drugs, 182–84, 228 (*see also* transcendence/religious experiences); entrainment, 201–2; experimentation, 185–86; Garcia as spokesperson, 203; and Gaskin, 186–87; Grateful Dead as not masters, 227; Grateful Dead as religion, 20–21, 174–77, 205; Grateful Dead associated with, 165–67; Grateful Dead stages of, 167–71; Grateful Dead testimonies, 167–71, 179–80; gnosticism, 1–2; golden ages, 194–95, 218 (*see also* myth of origins); and improvisation, 18, 222–24, 226, 227 (*see also* improvisation and transcendence); influencing music, 18 (*see also* improvisation and religion); and jazz, 224; and Jefferson Airplane, 141; and LSD, 228; and Merry Pranksters, 192–93; and music (general), 162–64; and musical phenomenon, 216–19; myth of origins, 175, 189–95, 197–200, 229; religion defined, 171–72; religious model of Grateful Dead, 212–16; and rigidity, 203–4; space and dwelling, 257n58; spirituality vs. religion, 171–74; and telepathy, 186–87; as undefinable, 203. *See also* improvisation and transcendence; outsider religion; transcendence/religious experiences
religious ecstasy, 129
religious imagination, 220–21
religious model of Grateful Dead, 212–16
religious studies, 180
responsibility, 122
"Revelation" (song), 86
revolution, 144, 145–46
"Revolution 9" (song), 106
rhythmic congruence, 83–85
rhythm sections, 24, 25, 101
riffs, 26, 66, 121, 123, 262n35
Riley, Terry, 29, 120, 224, 244n29
Ripani, Richard, 83
Road Trips (album series), 13

Roberts, Jim, 33–34

rock music, 233; and "art," 154–55, 224 (*see also* Pink Floyd; Velvet Underground); as bands, 54–55; and bass playing, 33–34; and Christians, 162, 190, 255n4; and collective expression, 26; and Coltrane, 25; cultural capital, 35; funding/support, 154; guitars, 34; and improvisation, 6, 15–17, 86 (*see also* improvisation, other rock bands); and jazz standards, 86; as juvenilia, 33; maturity of, 35; and meaning, 5; roots, 35; and sloppy rhythm sections, 79–80; and tradition, 78, 80–81; as "yes," 2, 3

Rodia, Simon, 219

Rolling Stones, 40–41, 86

Roof, Wade Clark, 173, 174, 257n56

Rothstein, Mikael, 190

Rouget, Gilbert, 163

Rowe, Keith, 153

saltanah, 164–65

"Same Thing, The" (song), *61*, 63, 67

Samwell-Smith, Paul, 152

Sanders, Pharoah, 224

San Francisco rock music scene, 36–43

Sawyer, Keith, 130–31

Saying Something (Monson), 53

"Scarlet Begonias" (song), 75, 85

Schwartz, Delmore, 145

science fiction, 56–57, 154

Scott, Joseph, 93

Sculatti, Gene, 41

Scully, Rock, 142–43, 157, 215

Searching for the Sound (Lesh), 206, 207–8

Seay, David, 41

sections, 136. *See also* movement through sections

Seeking the Sacred with Psychoactive Substances (Merkur), 187–88

Segal, Alan, 178

selling out, 152

Selvin, Joel, 199

Shadows (band), 242n16

shamanism, 201–2, 206, 209

Shankar, Ravi, 14, 26–27

shared ritual experiences, 175

Shenk, David, 164, 175, 179

Shepp, Archie, 132

significance, 228

Silberman, Steve, 164, 175, 179

Simon and Garfunkel, 114

"Sister Ray" (song), 146

sitar, 27

Situationist International (movement), 37

situations, 33

Skeleton Key (Shenk and Silberman), 164, 175

Skull and Roses (album), 10, 78

Slawek, Stephen, 127

Slick, Grace, 143, 158

Society of the Spectacle, The (Debord), 37

soloing over changes, 74, 79–81

solos: blues-derived, 42, 86; Clapton on, 155; in "Cream Puff War," 62; and Garcia, 50–51, 70, 74, 79; Lesh on, 80; Lesh and Weir, 57; modal jazz, 24; in Pink Floyd, 153; and sloppy rhythm sections, 79–80; Tudeio and Spector on, 135–36; in "Viola Lee Blues," 62

"Somebody to Love" (song), 142

song fusions, 71

Sonic Youth, 17, 23

soteriological speculations, 175

soul, 85–86

Sounds of India, The (album), 26

sounds/sound collages, 103–7, 119, 122

sound systems, 10, 34–35

space. *See* sounds/sound collages

space rock, 17, 154

"Spare Chaynge" (song), 143

spectacles, 37

Spector, Stan, 135–36

speculative fiction, 56–57

Spinners, 166

Spirits Rejoice! (Bivins), 24

spirituality, defined, 172–74, 257n56

spirituality vs. religion, 171–74, 178

spiritual masters, 227

Spiritual Unity (album), 99

spokespeople, 35

spontaneity, 80, 208, 210–11, 214. *See also* openness

spontaneous prose, 24

"Spoonful" (song), 151–52

Springsteen, Bruce, 54

Two from the Vault (album), 98

Tyner, McCoy, 53–54, 99

UFO, 154, 252n1

"Uncle John's Band" (song), 71, 72, 112, 114, 262n35

universalism, 25, 163, 243n11

universal structures, 209–10

Unlimited Devotion Family, 179

upright bass, 34

"Variations on a Theme of Liminality" (Turner), 253n19

From the Vault (album series), 13

Velvet Underground (band), 15, 16, 38, 104, 120, 144–50, 156, 160, 254n41

"Velvet Underground, The" (Morris), 149

verses, 61–62

"Viola Lee Blues" (song), 59, *61*, 62, 70, 119, 146–47, 247n30

Virgin Beauty (album), 48–49

virtuality, 133

Volunteers (song), 144

Wach, Joachim, 193

Wake of the Flood (album), 10

Wall of Sound setup, 10, 35

Warhol, Andy, 38, 145, 147

Warren, Billy, 89

Watts, Alan, 229

Watts Tower, 219

Waugh, Earl, 181

"Weather Report Suite" (song), 111, 250n64

"We Can Be Together" (song), 144

Weir, Bob: changes in improvisation feel, 67; on "Estimated Prophet," 226; and Garcia, 99; Grateful Dead history, 12; and "Good Lovin'," 85; on "Good Morning Little Schoolgirl," 90; on improvisation, 45–46, 63, 135; improvisation in action, 64–65; improvisation on "Alligator," 69; improvisation on "Cream Puff War,"

62; improvisation on "Dancing in the Streets," 66; improvisation on "Playing in the Band," 106; innovation of resources, 80, 99; instrument knowledge, 241n6; on jazz, 50; on lack of spiritual mastery, 227; singing Pigpen songs, 248–49n29; solos, 57; and spirituality, 20–21; and steady gigging, 119; on style of music, 75; on "Turn On Your Love Light," 94, 95

Welch, Chris, 150

Wells, Junior, 88–89, 121

Western art music (general), 31

When God Talks Back (Luhrman), 222

White Album (album), 106

Who (band), 104, 153

Wiccans, 197

Widdess, Richard, 126

"Wild Thing" (song), 33

Wilke, Annette, 223

Williamson, Sonny Boy, 88

Wilson, Wynne, 154

Winfree, Jason, 46–47

Winterland 1973 (album), 13

within songs model, 74, 75, 97–101, 119

Wizard of Oz, The (Baum), 221–22

Wolfbane (Pohl and Kornbluth), 57

Wolfe, Thomas, 57, 188, 191, 192, 193, 195

Wooden Shjips (band), 17

Woodstock, 143

Workingman's Dead (album), 10

Wright, Rick, 153

Wuthnow, Robert, 174, 257n58

Yardbirds (band), 15–16, 150, 152

"You Don't Have to Ask" (song), 59, 60

Young, La Monte, 29, 147, 149, 254n41

Young, Neil, 17, 54

"You're So Square" (song), 33

Zen, 188

Zone, the, 164